CONFIDENTIALITY

AUSTRALIA
LBC Information Services
Sydney

CANADA and USA
Carswell
Toronto – Ontario

NEW ZEALAND
Brooker's
Auckland

SINGAPORE and MALAYSIA
Thomson Information (S.E. Asia)
Singapore

CONFIDENTIALITY

by

R. G. TOULSON, M.A., LL.B.
A Justice of the High Court and Master of the Bench of the Inner Temple

&

C. M. PHIPPS, M.A.
A Barrister of the Middle Temple

LONDON
SWEET & MAXWELL
1996

Published in 1996 by
Sweet & Maxwell Limited of
100 Avenue Road
London, NW3 3PF

Computerset by Mendip Communications Ltd, Frome, Somerset
Printed in Great Britain by Hartnolls Ltd, Bodmin

No natural forests were destroyed to make this product:
only farmed timber was used and re-planted

ISBN 0 421 52590 8

ACKNOWLEDGMENTS

We would both like to thank Joyce Lester for her speed, efficiency, patience and unfailing good humour in typing and re-typing endless drafts of this book.

R.G.T.
C.M.P.

My parents used to have a puritan tract which intrigued me by its title "The fighf and the groanf of the long fuffering and forely diftreffed". Writing this book, while trying to maintain a practice, has caused many heartfelt "fighf and groanf", but the most "long fuffering and forely diftreffed" have been my wife and family. Words cannot adequately express the debt which I owe to them all, but especially to Elizabeth, for her continued support, interest and unselfishness, but for which life would have been impossible.

R.G.T.

I too would like to thank my family and, in particular, my parents for all their unstinting support and encouragement.

C.M.P.

PREFACE

Nearly a hundred and fifty years ago, on October 20, 1848, the Prince Consort applied, *ex parte*, for an injunction against Mr William Strange, a printer and publisher carrying on business at 21 Paternoster Row, to restrain him from exhibiting or reproducing a collection of etchings made by Queen Victoria and the Prince for private use. The matter eventually came before the Lord Chancellor, Lord Cottenham, who began his judgment[1] with the statement that the importance which had been attached to the case arose entirely from the exalted station of the plaintiff and not from the facts, which fell so clearly within established principles as to present no difficulty. He went on to declare that "a breach of trust, confidence or contract would of itself entitle the plaintiff to an injunction", and with those words he ushered in a jurisdiction broader than had ever previously been recognised.

Development of the jurisdiction was slow over the next hundred years. In 1948 *Saltman's* case[2] gave it a new injection of life. In the last half century it has grown much faster. It is no accident that this period of growth has coincided with a time of unprecedented change in methods of information storage and copying, communication and surveillance, which have brought with them the computer hacker, the electronic eavesdropper and the peeping Tom with a telephoto lens.

Unlike patent and copyright law, which are governed by statute (and are outside the scope of this book), the law of confidentiality is almost entirely judge made. In 1981 the Law Commission proposed the abolition of the action for breach of confidence and its replacement by a new statutory tort, but the proposal was not adopted.

Much water has flowed under the bridge since the Law Commission's recommendations. The absence of a statutory framework has allowed flexibility in the development of the law. But it has to be recognised that such development has not always been coherent or consistent, and that it has left fundamental issues unresolved. The jurisprudential foundation and essential ingredients of the law of confidentiality still involve matters of debate. On them depend questions who may sue whom and what remedies are available. There are also major uncertainties regarding defences or possible defences, including bona fide purchase, change of position and "public interest".

Roscoe Pound,[3] writing more than half a century ago, distinguished between text books containing doctrinal writing and those which were a mere key to the cases. He observed that there was as great a need for doctrinal writing in modern times as in the formative period of the law, because whereas in its formative period the courts had little to go on and much to bring about, in

---

[1] (1849) 1 Mac. & G. 25 at 40.
[2] (1948) 65 R.P.C. 203.
[3] Dean of Harvard Law School, 1916 to 1936.

modern times judges have too much to go on to permit working over the vast mass of available material:

> "The labours of counsel, with the aid of the modern apparatus of digests and cyclopaedias, put before them an enormous mass of authoritative matter in which they must find starting points for reasoning or analogies or rules."[4]

The law of confidentiality is in many ways still in its formative period, despite a large mass of material.

The objects of this book are to examine the historical origins of the action for breach of confidence and its development through the more important cases; to attempt an analysis of the present state of the law, its foundations and principles (although to try to rationalise all the authorities would be an impossible task); and to discuss particular areas of difficulty and possible answers. We also consider certain relationships involving duties of confidence and confidentiality in the legal process.

Confidentiality is a fascinating and absorbing, as well as an important, branch of the law. The cases are varied and full of interest, and it would be an ideal subject for law students. Unfortunately it is not widely taught at universities. Perhaps if it were taught more, some of the present doctrinal confusion would have been dispelled.

April 1, 1996

R.G.T.
C.M.P.

---

[4] Roscoe Pound, *The Formative Era of American Law* (1938), p. 165.

CONTENTS

PART 1—ORIGIN AND PRINCIPLES OF CONFIDENTIALITY

ix

PART 2—PARTICULAR RELATIONSHIPS

PART 3—**CONFIDENTIALITY AND THE LEGAL
     PROCESS**

TABLE OF CASES

TABLE OF STATUTES

TABLE OF STATUTORY INSTRUMENTS

ORIGIN AND PRINCIPLES OF CONFIDENTIALITY

This part of the book is concerned with general principles. Chapters I to X consider the origins and development of the law of confidentiality, its essential elements, who may sue and be sued, and the remedies available for breach of confidence. Chapters XI and XII consider respectively the impact of the European Convention on Human Rights and questions of conflict of laws.

CHAPTER I

HISTORICAL INTRODUCTION

EARLY ORIGINS

In *Coco v. A.N. Clark (Engineers) Ltd* Megarry J. said[1]:   **1–01**

> "The equitable jurisdiction in cases of breach of confidence is ancient;
> confidence is the cousin of trust. The Statute of Uses, 1535, is framed in
> terms of 'use, confidence or trust'; and a couplet, attributable to Sir
> Thomas More, Lord Chancellor avers that
>> 'Three things are to be ... in Conscience: Fraud, Accident and things
>> of Confidence.'
> (See 1 Rolle's Abridgement 374). In the middle of the last century, the
> great case of *Prince Albert v. Strange* (1849) 1 Mac. & G. 25 reasserted the
> doctrine."

It is doubtful, however, whether "confidence" in the time of Sir Thomas
More bore any resemblance to its present day meaning. Bacon in his Essay on
the Statute of Uses explained the meaning of confidence as follows:

> "The special trust lawful is, as when I infeoff some of my friends, because I
> am to go beyond the seas, or because I would free the land from some
> statute, or bond, which I am to enter into, or upon intent to be reinfeoffed,
> or intent to be vouched, and so to suffer a common recovery, or upon
> intent that the feoffees shall infeoff over a stranger, and infinite the like
> intents and purposes, which fall out in men's dealings and occasions; and
> this we call confidence, ..."

Moreover, for more than a century before *Prince Albert v. Strange* courts of
equity were decidedly cautious in their approach to cases which would now be
regarded as involving confidence and did not proceed on any broad or general
jurisdiction.

The early reported cases concerned letters, literary works and recipes for   **1–02**
medicines. In *Pope v. Curl*[2] Alexander Pope obtained an injunction against the
bookseller Curl restraining him from selling a book entitled "Letters from
Swift, Pope and others". The Lord Chancellor, Lord Hardwicke, continued the

---

[1] [1969] R.P.C. 41 at 46.
[2] (1741) 2 Atk. 342.

injunction in relation to the letters from Pope to Swift but not vice versa. The basis of the distinction was that property in such letters belonged to the author; that the sending of a letter did not constitute a gift to the receiver; that the receiver had only a "special property", possibly property in the paper and at most joint property with the writer; and that such limited property did not give to the receiver licence to publish to the world.

In *Duke of Queensberry v. Shebbeare*[3] the personal representatives of Lord Clarendon obtained an injunction restraining the defendant from publishing a previously unpublished history by Lord Clarendon. Dr Shebbeare's case was that he had acquired the manuscript from his co-defendant Mr Gwynne, whose father had been given it by Lord Clarendon. The injunction was continued on the ground that it was not to be presumed that Lord Clarendon had thereby intended Mr Gwynne to "have the profit of multiplying it in print".

1–03   These and other cases of unauthorised publication of writings were analysed in *Millar v. Taylor*.[4] The importance of this copyright case lies in its discussion of common law rights of property and in the reliance placed on it in *Prince Albert v. Strange*.[5] The facts were simple. Millar claimed ownership of a book of poems by James Thompson, entitled "The Seasons", copies of which he printed and sold. Taylor also printed and sold copies of the work, acting without Millar's permission. Millar sued for damages for trespass on the case. He brought the action in the Court of King's Bench, presided over by Lord Mansfield.

The case was argued first in June 1767, but the judges were unable to agree and it was ordered to be re-argued. It was argued for the second time in 1768. Judgment was finally delivered in April 1769, the plaintiff having, in the meantime, died. Lord Mansfield recorded that it was the first occasion since his appointment on which the court had been unable to reach unanimity despite repeated attempts to do so. Lords Mansfield, Willes and Aston JJ. found for the plaintiff. Yates J. dissented.

There were three issues:

(1) whether copyright existed at common law;
(2) if it did, whether it was lost on first publication;
(3) whether any such common law right was removed by the Statute of Anne 1709, under which authors of unpublished works could obtain a copyright for a term of 14 years, renewable for a further 14 years.

On the common law questions, the defendant's argument was that there was no common law right of property detached from a physical object, and therefore no right of literary property. The owner of a document had the right to its use, but once he transferred to another the ownership of the physical document, or a copy of it, that person acquired at common law an equal right to make such use of it as he pleased.

This argument was rejected by the majority. Lord Mansfield who had great experience of the subject, having (as he said) appeared as counsel in most of the cases cited in Chancery, said[6]:

"I use the word 'copy' in the technical sense in which that name or term has

---

[3] (1758) 2 Eden 329.
[4] (1769) 4 Bur. 2303.
[5] (1849) 1 De G. & Sm. 652; (1849) 1 Mac. & G. 25.
[6] *Millar v. Taylor* (1769) 4 Bur. 2303 at 2396.

been used for ages, to signify an incorporeal right to the sole printing and publishing of somewhat intellectual, communicated by letters. It has all along been expressly admitted 'that, by the common law, an author is intitled to the copy of his own work until it has been once printed and published by his authority;' and 'that the four cases in Chancery,[7] cited for that purpose, are agreeable to the common law; and the relief was properly given, in consequence of the legal right.'

The property in the copy, thus abridged, is equally an incorporeal right to print a set of intellectual ideas or modes of thinking, communicated in a set of words and sentences and modes of expression. It is equally detached from the manuscript, or any other physical existence whatsoever. ...

From what source, then, is the common law drawn, which is admitted to be so clear, in respect of the copy before publication? From this argument—because it is just, that an author should reap the pecuniary profits of his own ingenuity and labour. It is just, that another should not use his name, without his consent. It is fit that he should judge when to publish, or whether he ever will publish. It is fit he should not only choose the time, but the manner of publication; how many; what volume; what print. It is fit, he should choose to whose care he will trust the accuracy and correctness of the impression; in whose honesty he will confide, not to foist in additions: with other reasonings of the same effect. ...

But the same reasons hold, after the author has published. He can reap no pecuniary profit, if, the next moment after his work comes out, it may be pirated upon worse paper and in worse print, and in a cheaper volume."

Yates J., dissenting, observed that no logical distinction could be drawn between literary compositions and any other production of the brain, such as mechanical inventions.

The matter was considered by the House of Lords in *Donaldson v. Beckett*,[8] on appeal from a decree of the Court of Chancery founded on the decision in *Millar v. Taylor*.[9] The opinions of the judges were taken. A majority agreed with *Millar v. Taylor* on the common law questions, but not on the effect of the Statute of Anne 1709. The House of Lords voted to reverse the decree. On the common law questions, the views of the majority of the judges in *Millar v. Taylor* were ultimately to be reversed by the House of Lords, but not until 80 years later in *Jefferys v. Boosey*.[10]

In *Thompson v. Stanhope*[11] Lord Apsley L.C. granted an injunction to restrain the publication of letters, following the precedents of *Forrester v. Waller*, *Webb v. Rose*, *Pope v. Curl* and *Duke of Queensberry v. Shebbeare*. No reference is made in the report to *Donaldson v. Beckett*, decided by the House of Lords four weeks earlier, nor to *Millar v. Taylor*.

Those cases and the principles on which they rested were considered in a trio **1–04** of cases in equity between 1813 and 1818—*Percival v. Phipps*, *Southey v. Sherwood* and *Gee v. Pritchard*.

In *Percival v. Phipps*[12] the defendant Phipps had published in a newspaper a

---

[7] *Webb v. Rose* May 24, 1732, cited 4 Bur. 2330; *Pope v. Curl* (1741) 2 Atk. 342; *Forrester v. Waller* June 13, 1741, cited 4 Burr. 2331 and *Duke of Queensberry v. Shebbeare* (1758) 2 Eden 329.
[8] (1774) 4 Bur. 2408.
[9] (1769) 4 Bur. 2303.
[10] (1854) 4 H.L.C. 815.
[11] (1774) Amb. 737.
[12] (1813) 35 E.R. 225.

letter purportedly written by the plaintiff to the defendant Mitford. The plaintiff had subsequently stated publicly that it was a forgery. Mitford asserted that it was genuine and that he had passed it to Phipps with the plaintiff's consent. To corroborate his version Mitford passed to Phipps a number of other letters from the plaintiff, which Phipps wished to publish in order to rebut the allegation that he had published false information on spurious authority. The plaintiff sought an injunction to restrain him from doing so. The application was based on grounds both of literary property and that the publication would amount to a breach of confidence. The application failed.

The Vice-Chancellor expressed doubt whether a court of equity could restrain publication of private correspondence on grounds of breach of confidence, independent of contract or a right of property in the correspondence. He also took a restricted view of the class of correspondence in which there could be a right of property based on the concept of a literary work, and he held that the defendants' reasons for publication were sufficient for a court of equity not to intervene.

In *Southey v. Sherwood*[13] Lord Eldon L.C. refused the poet Southey an injunction to restrain the publication of a poem which he had placed with a publisher 23 years earlier, holding that such injunctions were only granted to prevent the use of that which was the exclusive property of another.

Gee v. Pritchard[14] was another case of an injunction to restrain the publication of letters. The plaintiff claimed both that the letters were her property and that their proposed publication would be a breach of private confidence. Lord Eldon granted the injunction, following the precedents of his predecessors Lord Hardwicke and Lord Apsley, but he did so expressly and only on the ground of the plaintiffs' right of property.

1–05   Lord Eldon also took a cautious approach to claims for injunctions to restrain misuse of secret medical recipes for which either there was no patent or the patent had expired. He refused injunctions in *Newbery v. James*[15] and *Williams v. Williams*,[16] observing in the latter that he did not think that on general principles the court ought to struggle to protect such secrets. In *Yovatt v. Winyard*[17] Lord Eldon granted an injunction restraining the defendant from using or communicating certain recipes for veterinary medicines, but on the ground (according to the headnote) that he had obtained knowledge of them by a breach of trust. The defendant had been employed by the plaintiff and during his employment surreptitiously obtained access to the plaintiffs' books of recipes, which he copied. The report does not give Lord Eldon's reasons beyond stating that he granted the injunction upon the ground of there having been a breach of trust and confidence.

Green v. Folgham[18] also involved a breach of trust in relation to a medical recipe, but in that case the recipe was the subject of an express trust.

In *Abernethy v. Hutchinson*[19] the plaintiff was a distinguished surgeon and lecturer at St Bartholomew's Hospital. The defendants were publishers and sellers of *The Lancet*. The action was brought for an injunction to restrain them from reproducing the plaintiff's lectures, the text of which must have been

[13] (1817) 2 Mep. 435.
[14] (1818) 2 Swans. 402.
[15] (1817) 2 Mer. 446.
[16] (1817) 3 Mer. 157.
[17] (1820) 1 Jac. & W. 394.
[18] (1823) 1 Sim. & St. 398.
[19] (1824) 3 L.J.Ch. 209.

taken down in shorthand by a student and supplied to the defendants for publication contrary to the plaintiff's express wishes.

After days of argument, during which various possible grounds of relief were canvassed, Lord Eldon finally granted an injunction on the ground that there was an implied contract between the plaintiff and his students that they would not publish his lectures for profit; and that, although there was no implied contract between the plaintiff and the defendants, they must have procured the text of the lectures in an undue manner from those who were under a contract not to publish, and that this was a form of fraud in a third party sufficient to enable the court to grant an injunction against them.[20]

In summary, the cases before *Prince Albert v. Strange*[21] did not establish any general right of relief in respect of misuse or threatened misuse of confidential information. The cases in which the courts intervened may be classified as cases of actual or threatened:

(1) infringement by the defendant of a right of property recognised at common law;
(2) breach of contract by the defendant;
(3) breach of trust by the defendant; or
(4) use by the defendant of information knowingly obtained from a party who was himself acting in breach of contract or trust in supplying it.

Prince Albert v. Strange

In *Prince Albert v. Strange*[22] the plaintiff obtained an injunction against the **1–06** defendant restraining him from publishing a catalogue of private etchings made by Queen Victoria and Prince Albert. As well as describing the etchings, the catalogue announced a proposed exhibition of them and implied falsely that the publication had royal consent. The catalogue was compiled from copies surreptitiously made by an employee of a printer in Windsor, to whom plates of the etchings had been sent for the purpose of making copies for the Queen and Prince.

The plaintiff's principal argument was that publication of the catalogue infringed their right of property in the etchings on the basis of *Millar v. Taylor*[23] and similar authorities. Secondly, it was argued that the information in the catalogue was derived from a breach of trust, and therefore the plaintiff was entitled to an injunction against a knowing recipient by analogy with *Abernethy v. Hutchinson*.[24] The defendant's argument was that mere description of the etchings did not infringe any property right of the Queen and Prince at common law and that he was not party to any breach of trust.

The Vice-Chancellor, Sir Knight Bruce, held in favour of the plaintiff on both **1–07** grounds and his judgment was upheld on appeal by Lord Cottenham L.C. On

---

[20] See also *Tipping v. Clarke* (1843) 2 Hare 383. A person who surreptitiously obtained information which he could only have obtained from a person in breach of contract in communicating it could not be permitted to avail himself of that breach of contract.
[21] (1849) 1 De G. & Sm. 652; (1849) 1 Mac. & G. 25.
[22] (1849) 1 De G. & Sm. 652; (1849) 1 Mac. & G. 25.
[23] (1769) 4 Bur. 2303.
[24] (1824) 3 L.J.Ch. 209.

the issue of property, the Vice-Chancellor adopted Yates J.'s argument in *Millar v. Taylor* that there was no difference between literary works and other products of the brain, such as mechanical or artistic creations. He held also that the owner's common law right of property was infringed as much by description without consent as by copying without consent. On the second issue the Vice-Chancellor regarded the circumstances as so obviously redolent of the etchings having been obtained by a breach of trust as to warrant an injunction on that ground.

Lord Cottenham L.C. said at the outset of his judgment that the importance attached to the case arose entirely from the exalted station of the plaintiff, and not from the facts, which so clearly fell within established principles as not to cause any difficulty. After summarising the facts, he said[25]:

> "It was said by one of the learned counsel for the Defendant, that the injunction must rest upon the ground of property or breach of trust; both appear to me to exist. The property of an author or composer of any work, whether of literature, art or science, in such work unpublished and kept for his private use or pleasure, cannot be disputed, after the many decisions in which that proposition has been affirmed or assumed."

He continued[26]:

> "Upon the first question, therefore, that of property, I am clearly of opinion that the exclusive right and interest of the Plaintiff in the composition or work in question being established, and there being no right or interest whatever in the Defendant, the Plaintiff is entitled to the injunction of this Court to protect him against the invasion of such right and interest by the Defendant, which the publication of any catalogue would undoubtedly be; but this case by no means depends solely upon the question of property, for a breach of trust, confidence, or contract, would of itself entitle the Plaintiff to an injunction ... .
>
> If, then, these compositions were kept private, except as to some given to private friends and some sent to Mr Brown for the purpose of having certain impressions taken, the possession of the Defendant, or of his intended partner Judge, must have originated in a breach of trust, confidence or contract, in Brown or some person in his employ taking more impressions than were ordered, and retaining the extra number, or in some person to whom copies were given, which is not to be supposed, but which, if the origin of the possession of the Defendant or Judge, would be equally a breach of trust, confidence or contract, *Duke of Queensberry v. Shebbeare* (2 Eden 329); and upon the evidence on behalf of the Plaintiff, and in the absence of any explanation on the part of the Defendant, I am bound to assume that the possession of the etchings by the Defendant or Judge has its foundations in a breach of trust, confidence or contract, as Lord Eldon did in the case of Mr Abernethy's lectures (3 Law J. Chanc. 209); and upon this ground also I think the Plaintiff's title to the injunction sought to be discharged, fully established."

Lord Cottenham's observation that the case fell clearly within established

---

[25] *Prince Albert v. Strange* (1848) 1 Mac. & G. 25 at 42.
[26] *ibid.* at 44.

principles did less than justice to the defendant's arguments. On the question of property, there was substantial force in the argument that the case went significantly beyond *Millar v. Taylor*[27] or any other precedent and that mere description of the etchings did not involve any usurpation of the plaintiff's ownership. On the question of equity, the case fell within the principle of *Abernethy v. Hutchinson*[28] if the circumstances were such that the defendant must have known of the unlawful conduct of the person showing him the etchings, for in that case (as in *Abernethy v. Hutchinson*) his own conduct would be regarded in equity as a form of fraud by a third party. The circumstances were suspicious, but the defendant denied on affidavit any knowledge or suspicion of unlawfulness.

The decision has been treated as authority for the grant of an injunction   **1–08**
against someone who has acquired information to which he was not entitled, without notice of any breach of duty on the part of the person who imparted it to him, but who cannot claim to be a purchaser for value.[29] In this respect also the case did not fall within any previously settled principles.

More generally it has been seen as a landmark case because of the broad statement that "a breach of trust, confidence or contract would of itself entitle the plaintiff to an injunction", although it is questionable whether Lord Cottenham was there intending to lay down three independent categories in which an injunction would be granted, or merely using a compendious phrase wide enough to cover the facts of the case without intending or attempting any precise definition of the legal requirements. The trust or confidence owed by Brown to the plaintiff arose from his contract, and Lord Cottenham's judgment does not suggest that he was intending to consider them in isolation.

The century after *Prince Albert v. Strange*

During the 100 years between *Prince Albert v. Strange* and *Saltman*   **1–09**
Engineering Co. Ltd v. Campbell Engineering Co. Ltd,[30] the main cases on confidentiality are significant for their lack of any uniform jurisprudential basis. The confidences were mostly commercial and arose generally in the context of contracts, such as contracts of partnership, employment, agency or sale.

In *Morison v. Moat*[31] the action arose from a partnership to manufacture and sell "Morison's Universal Medicine". The medicine was not the subject of any patent. The original partners were the plaintiffs' father, who was the inventor of the medicine, and the defendant's father. The plaintiffs' father disclosed the secret of the recipe to the defendant's father on terms that he was not to tell anyone else. Shortly before his death, the defendant's father gave the recipe to the defendant. After the expiry of the partnership the defendant manufactured and sold the medicine for his own account. The plaintiffs, to whom the recipe had been bequeathed under their father's will, obtained an injunction to restrain the defendant. Turner, V.-C. said[32]:

"That the Court has exercised jurisdiction in cases of this nature does not, I

[27] (1769) 4 Bur. 2303.
[28] (1824) 3 L.J.Ch. 209.
[29] *Printers & Finishers Ltd v. Holloway* [1965] R.P.C. 239 at 253 and 257, *per* Cross J.
[30] (1948) 65 R.P.C. 203.
[31] (1851) 9 Hare 241, affirmed (1852) 21 L.J.Ch. (N.S.) 248.
[32] (1851) 9 Hare 241 at 255.

think, admit of any question. Different grounds have indeed been assigned for the exercise of that jurisdiction. In some cases it has been referred to property, in others to contract, and in others, again, it has been treated as founded upon trust or confidence, meaning, as I conceive, that the Court fastens the obligation on the conscience of the party, and enforces it against him in the same manner as it enforces against a party to whom a benefit is given the obligation of performing a promise on the faith of which the benefit has been conferred; but, upon whatever grounds the jurisdiction is founded, the authorities leave no doubt as to the exercise of it."

1–10   The approach of taking the jurisdiction as established, without futher inquiry into its jurisprudential basis, has been followed in many subsequent cases with the consequence that the uncertainty to which the Vice-Chancellor referred has continued. The Vice-Chancellor did, however, provide the earliest judicial definition of what was meant by "trust or confidence" for the purposes of this jurisdiction.

The Vice-Chancellor dealt with the defendant's argument that the effect of an injunction would be to give the plaintiffs a better right than that of a patentee by saying that[33]:

> " ... what we have to deal with here is, not the right of the Plaintiffs against the world, but their right against the Defendant. It may well be that the Plaintiffs have no title against the world in general, and may yet have a good title against this Defendant ... ."

Despite the language of title, it would seem that the injunction must have been based on a personal obligation of the defendant towards the plaintiffs, rather than a property right in the plaintiffs; for if they had a right of property, it is difficult to see why it would not be good against the world.

The Vice-Chancellor also commented, without having to decide the point, that it might have been different if the defendant were a purchaser for value of the secret without notice of any obligation affecting it. This too remains an unsettled question.

1–11   *Gartside v. Outram*[34] is best known as the origin of the "defence of iniquity", but it also involved consideration of the basis of the jurisdiction. The plaintiff brokers filed a bill for an injunction to restrain a former clerk from disclosing any of their dealings. The defendant in his answer stated that the plaintiffs were in the habit of defrauding their principals, and in support of his answer he filed interrogatories, to which the plaintiffs objected. It was held that there was no privilege to prevent them from answering, the discovery being relevant to the defendant's answer which, if proved, would be a defence to the bill.

Wood V.-C. said[35]:

> "The equity upon which the bill is founded is a perfectly plain and simple one, recognized by a number of authorities and most salutary to be

---

[33] *Prince Albert v. Strange* (1851) 9 Hare 241 at 258.
[34] (1857) 26 L.J.Ch. (NS) 113.
[35] *ibid.* at 114.

enforced, by which any person standing in the confidential relation of a clerk or servant is prohibited, subject to certain exceptions, from disclosing any part of the transactions of which he thus acquires knowledge. But there are exceptions to this confidence, or perhaps, rather only nominally, and not really exceptions. The true doctrine is, that there is no confidence as to the disclosure of iniquity. You cannot make me the confidant of a crime or a fraud, and be entitled to close up my lips upon any secret which you have the audacity to disclose to me relating to any fraudulent intention on your part: such a confidence cannot exist."

This places the jurisdiction on the relationship between the parties, although at the end of his judgment Wood V.-C. said[36]:

"The real ground of the jurisdiction, as it is properly put, is founded first upon property, because the Court attempts not to interfere with morals, except in administering civil rights connected with rights of property. There is the property of the employer in those secrets of his business which he is obliged to communicate to others, and which are not to be trifled with. It is a sacred and solemn deposit, but there is no property in these transactions with this gentlemen which were of the character I have been describing, and in his answer he has made no disclosures except as to these fraudulent transactions."

Although Wood V.-C. said that the court was concerned with the administration of civil rights connected with rights of property and not morals, he was clearly influenced by considerations of public interest in holding that there could be no property in secrets of an iniquitous character.

In *Pollard v. Photographic Company*[37] North J. took a different approach. **1–12** The plaintiff had photographs of herself taken by the defendant. Without her consent, the defendant used one of the negatives to make a form of Christmas card and displayed a copy of it in his shop window for sale. The plaintiff obtained an injunction to restrain the defendant from selling copies of the photograph. North J. dismissed as irrelevant the defendant's argument that his conduct did not injure any property right of the plaintiff. He said[38]:

"The right to grant an injunction does not depend in any way on the existence of property as alleged; nor is it worth while to consider carefully the grounds upon which the old Court of Chancery used to inferfere by injunction. But it is quite clear that, independently of any question as to the right at law, the Court of Chancery always had an original and independent jurisdiction to prevent what that Court considered and treated as as a wrong, whether arising from a violation of an unquestionable right or from breach of contract or confidence, as was pointed out by Lord *Cottenham* in *Prince Albert v. Strange*."

North J. compared the photographer to a person who obtained confidential

---

[36] *Gartside v. Outran* (1857) 26 L.J.Ch. (N.S.) 113.
[37] (1888) 40 Ch.D. 345.
[38] *ibid.* at 354.

information in the course of his employment and who would not be permitted to make improper use of it; and he held that it was an implied term of the defendant's contract that prints from the negative would be appropriated only to the plaintiff's use.

1–13   In *Merryweather v. Moore*[39] Kekewich J. cited part of the passage from North J.'s judgment in *Pollard v. Photographic Company* set out above and went on to say[40]:

> "... it is sometimes difficult to say whether the Court has proceeded on the implied contract or the confidence, for I will put aside once for all any cases arising on express contract. Perhaps the real solution is that the confidence postulates an implied contract: that, where the Court is satisfied of the existence of the confidential relation, then it at once infers or implies the contract arising from that confidential relation—a contract which thus calls into exercise the jurisdiction to which I have referred."

Implied contract can be a useful device, as in *Abernethy v. Hutchinson*,[41] but it is not apparent why a relationship intended to be confidential need involve the postulation of a fictitious contract in order for equity to intervene. On the other hand the terms (whether express or, more usually, implied) on which any confidential relationship came into existence should rightly be regarded as fundamental whether in contract or in equity.

1–14   This approach was taken by the Court of Appeal in *Lamb v. Evans*.[42] The plaintiff engaged the defendants on a commission basis to obtain advertisements for publication in a trade directory. The advertisers provided the defendants with blocks for printing their advertisements. The defendants subsequently went to work for a rival publication and used the same blocks for identical advertisements. The plaintiff obtained an injunction to prevent them from doing so.

The Court of Appeal decided the case on the basis of principles of agency. Lindley L.J. said[43]:

> "What right has any agent to use materials obtained by him in the course of his employment and for his employer against the interest of that employer? I am not aware that he has any such right. Such a use is contrary to the relation which exists between principal and agent. It is contrary to the good faith of the employment, and good faith underlies the whole of an agent's obligations to his principal."

Bowan L.J. went back to the source of the relationship. He said that the plaintiff's entitlement to an injunction[44]:

> "... depends entirely, I think, upon the terms upon which the employment was constituted through which the fiduciary relation of principal and agent came into existence. I think my Brothers have already during the course of the argument expressed what I fully believe, that there is no distinction

[39] [1892] 2 Ch. 518.
[40] *ibid.* at 522.
[41] (1824) 3 L.J.Ch. 209.
[42] [1893] 1 Ch. 218.
[43] *ibid.* at 226.
[44] *ibid.* at 229.

between law and equity as regards the law of principal and agent. The common law, it is true, treats the matter from the point of view of an implied contract, and assumes that there is a promise to do that which is part of the bargain, or which can be fairly implied as part of the good faith which is necessary to make the bargain effectual. What is an implied contract or an implied promise in law? It is that promise which the law implies and authorises us to infer in order to give the transaction that effect which the parties must have intended it to have and without which it would be futile ... . It seems to me that in this case the proper inference to be drawn would be that it was part of the understanding that these materials were not to be used otherwise than for the purposes of the employment in the course of which they were obtained."

Lindley and Bowen L.JJ. both referred to the misuse of "materials", a point further emphasised by Kay L.J. After considering *Morison v. Moat*,[45] *Abernethy v. Hutchinson*[46] and *Prince Albert v. Strange*,[47] he said[48]:

So that I think the doctrine ... does extend to every case in which a man has obtained materials (I use the word advisedly, because it would be very difficult indeed to grant an injunction to prevent a man using his knowledge)—where a man has obtained materials while he was in the position of agent for another—materials which were obtained by him in the course of that agency and were to be used for the purposes for which his principal had employed him."

Subsequent development of the law has not been so confined. In *Reid and Sigrist Ltd v. Moss and Mechanism Ltd*,[49] for example, Luxmoore J. said: **1–15**

"Undoubtedly there is a well recognised rule in the law relating to Master and Servant that a servant cannot use to the detriment of his master information of a confidential or secret nature entrusted to the servant or learnt by him in the course of his employment. There are many cases in the books on the subject. In some of them it has been debated what is the precise ground to be assigned for the exercise of the jurisdiction of the Court. Is it to be referred to property or contract, or is it to be founded upon trust or confidence? But whatever may be the true ground on which the jurisdiction is founded there is no doubt as to its existence."

"Information of a confidential or secret nature" is potentially much wider than "materials". In *Printers & Finishers Ltd v. Holloway*,[50] Cross J. said: **1–16**

"The mere fact that the confidential information is not embodied in a document but is carried away by the employee in his head is not, of course,

---

[45] (1851) 9 Hare 241.
[46] (1824) 3 L.J.Ch. 209.
[47] (1849) 1De G. & Sm. 652; (1849) 1 Mac. & G. 25.
[48] [1893] 1 Ch. 218 at 236.
[49] (1932) 49 R.P.C. 461 at 480.
[50] [1965] R.P.C. 239 at 255.

of itself a reason against the granting of an injunction to prevent its use or disclosure by him."

Nevertheless, Kay L.J. touched on a major problem when he referred in *Lamb v. Evans* to the difficulty of extending the doctrine to the use of knowledge. There is not only the difficulty of enforcement, but also a potential clash between legitimate competing interests: on the one hand that secrets should be respected, and on the other hand that a skilled person should not be restricted from making use of his skills. The boundary between knowledge of particular secrets derived from confidential sources and more general knowledge may be elusive, particularly since the latter may be derived to a greater or lesser extent from the former. This topic has been considered in many subsequent cases, including notably *Herbert Morris Ltd v. Saxelby*,[51] *Printers & Finishers Ltd v. Holloway*[52] and *Faccenda Chicken Ltd v. Fowler*.[53]

No such problem arose in *Robb v. Green*,[54] in which Kay L.J. was again a member of the Court of Appeal. An employee surreptitiously copied his employer's customer list for the purpose of soliciting orders from them after setting up in business on his own account. The claim was for damages, delivery up of the list and an injunction to restrain him from making use of the information so obtained.

The court followed the analysis of Bowen L.J. in *Lamb v. Evans*, but, whilst he had said in that case that there was no distinction between the law and equity as regards the law of principal and agent, the court in *Robb v. Green* did distinguish between the remedies available. Kay L.J. said that an injunction ought to be granted "either on the ground of breach of trust or breach of contract", and that "a document surreptitiously made in breach of the trust imposed in the servant clearly ought to be given up to be destroyed." He continued[55]:

> "As to the damages, I think there is more difficulty. The right to them depends on whether the conduct of the defendant can be regarded as a breach of an implied contract. According to the view taken by Bowen L.J. in *Lamb v. Evans*, it can; and in the result I come to the conclusion that the judgment in that respect must be upheld."

This is in accordance with classical doctrine that damages cannot be awarded for breach of an equitable obligation except under the jurisdiction derived from Lord Cairns's Act.[56]

The crucial fact in *Robb v. Green* was that the defendant copied the customer list while still in the plaintiff's employment. This point was emphasised in *Wessex Dairies Ltd v. Smith*[57] by Maugham L.J. who noted that in *Robb v. Green* the defendant was not restrained from sending out circulars to customers whose names he could remember.

1–17 The availability of equitable relief to restrain misuse of confidential information, not only by the confidant but also by a third party recipient, was

---

[51] [1916] A.C. 688.
[52] [1965] R.P.C. 239.
[53] [1987] 1 Ch. 117.
[54] [1895] 2 Q.B. 315.
[55] *ibid.* at 320.
[56] Chancery Amendment Act 1858 (now section 50 of the Supreme Court Act 1981).
[57] [1935] 2 K.B. 80 at 89.

reaffirmed by the Court of Appeal in *Ashburton v Pape*.[58] Copies of privileged letters written by Lord Ashburton to his solicitor had been obtained by the defendant from a clerk employed by the solicitor. Swinfen Eady L.J. said[59]:

> "The principle upon which the Court of Chancery has acted for many years has been to restrain the publication of confidential information improperly or surreptitiously obtained or of information imparted in confidence which ought not to be divulged. Injunctions have been granted to give effectual relief, that is not only to restrain the disclosure of confidential information, but to prevent copies being made of any record of that information, and, if copies have already been made, to restrain them from being further copied, and to restrain persons into whose possession that confidential information has come from themselves in turn divulging or propagating it."

In *Herbert Morris Ltd v. Saxelby*[60] there was no misconduct by the defendant **1–18** during his employment, but the plaintiffs, who were manufacturers of lifting machinery, sought to enforce against him a covenant against being involved as principal, agent or employee, in the sale or manufacture of lifting machinery of various types within the United Kingdom for a term of seven years after the end of his employment. The plaintiffs had a leading position in the market. The defendant was an engineer. The covenant was held to be unenforceable.

The employers' argument was that the covenant was a reasonable provision for the protection of their property, namely trade secrets and customer connection. The argument of counsel for the employee conceded that it was permissible for a clause to protect "the filching of the employer's property such as trade secrets or customers' connection" but objected to the covenant on the ground that its real object was to protect against mere competition. This argument was essentially adopted by the various members of the Judicial Committee.

Lord Atkinson contrasted, on the one hand, "trade secrets ..., such as secret processes of manufacture, which may be of great value" and documents containing commercially sensitive information, such as lists of customers and their requirements, all of which were to be regarded as "private and confidential documents, the property of the [plaintiffs]" from, on the other hand, more general employee know-how, saying[61]:

> "The respondent cannot, however, get rid of the impressions left upon his mind by his experience of the appellants' works; they are part of himself; and in my view he violates no obligation express or implied arising from the relation in which he stood to the appellants by using in the service of some persons other than them the general knowledge he has acquired of their scheme of organisation and methods of business."

Lord Parker said that[62]:

> "... the reason, and the only reason, for upholding such a restraint on the

---

[58] [1913] 2 Ch. 469.
[59] *ibid.* at 475.
[60] [1916] A.C. 688.
[61] *ibid.* at 703.
[62] *ibid.* at 710.

part of an employee is that the employer has some proprietary right, whether in the nature of trade connection or in the nature of trade secrets, for the protection of which such a restraint is—having regard to the duties of the employee—reasonably necessary. Such a restraint has, so far as I know, never been upheld if directed only to the prevention of competition or against the use of personal skill and knowledge acquired by the employee in his employer's business."

Lord Shaw also used the language of property[63]:

"Trade secrets, the names of customers, all such things which in sound philosophical language are denominated objective knowledge—these may not be given away by a servant; they are his master's property, and there is no rule of public interest which prevents a transfer of them against the master's will being restrained. On the other hand, a man's aptitudes, his skill, his dexterity, his manual or mental ability—all those things which in sound philosophical language are not objective, but subjective—they may and they ought not to be relinquished by a servant; they are not his master's property; they are his own property; they are himself."

1–19   In *Mechancial and General Inventions Co. v. Austin*[64] the plaintiffs were patentees of a system for installing sun roofs in cars. They provided details to the defendants with a view to entering into a licence agreement, which did not materialise. The House of Lords upheld a finding by the jury that there was a contract whereby the information disclosed to the defendants was to be used only under a licence agreement and also its award of £35,000 damages.

From the note of the defendants' argument,[65] it appears that the contract alleged was an implied contract. It was argued on their behalf that no such contract should be inferred and that,

"The appellants are really complaining of something in the nature of a breach of trust or confidence, for which relief, if there be any, must be sought in a Court of equity, and not by way of damages at common law."

Lord Atkin said[66]:

"It is quite sufficient to support the contract averred that the terms upon which the information was disclosed were that it was to be used for a particular purpose only. The giving of the information is ample consideration, and use for any other purpose would be a breach. The analogy of a contract of bailment I think supports this view."

Saltman's case

1–20   *Saltman Engineering Co. Ltd v. Campbell Engineering Co. Ltd*[67] is a landmark case, both because of its re-affirmation of the equitable doctrine of

[63] *Herbert Morris Ltd v. Saxelby* [1916] A.C. 688 at 714.
[64] [1935] A.C. 346.
[65] *ibid.* at 350–351.
[66] *ibid.* at 370.
[67] (1948) 65 R.P.C. 203.

confidence independent of contract, and because of its attempt to define the quality of confidence necessary for the doctrine to apply. The plaintiffs supplied the defendants with drawings of tools for the manufacture of leather punches. After supplying punches to the plaintiffs, the defendants retained the drawings, which they used for manufacturing and selling other punches to other purchasers. The plaintiffs alleged breach of contract and breach of confidence, and claimed relief including an order for delivery up of the drawings and all tools made from them, an injunction and an inquiry as to damages.

The Court of Appeal held that it was unnecessary to decide the question of breach of contract, because there was a plain breach of confidence in that the drawings had been supplied for the limited purpose of manufacturing punches for the plaintiffs, and (*per* Somervell L.J.[68]) that the plaintiffs' relief under that head was as great as it could be under any other.

Lord Greene M.R. said[69]:

> "The information, to be confidential, must, I apprehend, apart from contract, have the necessary quality of confidence about it, namely it must not be something which is public property and public knowledge. On the other hand, it is perfectly possible to have a confidential document, be it a formula, a plan, a sketch, or something of that kind, which is the result of work done by the maker upon materials which may be available for the use of anybody; but what makes it confidential is the fact that the maker of the document has used his brain and thus produced a result which can only be produced by somebody who goes through the same process."

The court declined to order the destruction of the tools made by the defendants but ordered an inquiry as to damages, to cover both past and future acts, under Lord Cairns Act.

Since *Saltman* there has been vigorous growth in the use of the action for **1–21** breach of confidence to the extent that the modern development of the law may fairly be regarded as dating from that case. The decision provided a great impetus for the use of the action to prevent industrial piracy,[70] from which its use spread to the protection of personal confidences (*Argyll*[71]) and government secrets (*Attorney-General v Jonathan Cape Ltd*[72]).

In 1981 the Law Commission produced a report on Breach of Confidence[73] in which it commented on the many uncertainties concerning the ultimate legal foundation of the jurisdiction, its ambit and the remedies available, and recommended that the law be placed on a statutory basis. It drafted a Breach of Confidence Bill, which would have created a statutory tort of breach of confidence and abrogated all principles of equity and common law relating to breach of confidence, except in cases of proceedings for breach of contract or contempt of court. The recommendations were not accepted and the law has continued to develop on a case by case basis.

The development of the modern law of confidentiality may be considered **1–22** under the following headings:

---

[68] *Saltman* (1948) 65 R.P.C. 203 at 217.
[69] *ibid.* at 215.
[70] See Lord Oliver's summary of the history of the breach of confidence action in "Spycatcher: Confidence, Copyright and Contempt" *Israel Law Review* (1989), Vol. 23, No. 4, at 407.
[71] [1967] Ch. 302.
[72] [1976] 1 Q.B. 752.
[73] Cmnd. 8388 (1981).

(1) Foundation;
(2) Essential features of confidentiality;
(3) Duration of confidentiality;
(4) Public sector confidentiality;
(5) Detriment, public interest and "clean hands";
(6) Confidentiality and third parties;
(7) Involuntary or mistaken disclosure;
(8) Confidentiality and privacy;
(9) Remedies;
(10) European Convention on Human Rights;
(11) Confidentiality and foreign law.

These subjects are dealt with in the Chapters which follow.

CHAPTER II

FOUNDATION

Possible bases

The Law Commission in its 1981 Report[1] observed that there was uncertainty **2–01** as to the nature and scope of the action for breach of confidence owing to its somewhat obscure legal basis, and quoted the words of Professor Gareth Jones[2]:

> "A cursory study of the cases, where the plaintiff's confidence has been breached, reveals great conceptual confusion. Property, contract, bailment, trust, fiduciary relationship, good faith, unjust enrichment, have all been claimed, at one time or another, as the basis of judicial intervention. Indeed some judges have indiscriminately intermingled all these concepts. The result is that the answer to many fundamental questions remains speculative."

Since then tort has entered the list of possible candidates, but fundamental questions remain.

Determining the legal basis of confidentiality is important to any coherent development of the law. On it depends who may sue and be sued, what defences are available and what remedies may be granted. The lack of clear and satisfactory answers to many of these questions stems from uncertainty as to the legal basis of the jurisdiction.

In the *Spycatcher* case Lord Goff said[3]:

> "I have ... deliberately avoided the fundamental question whether, contract apart, the duty lies simply 'in the notion of an obligation of conscience arising from the circumstances in or through which the information was communicated or obtained' (see *Moorgate Tobacco Co. Ltd v. Philip Morris Ltd (No. 2)* (1984) 156 C.L.R. 414, 438, *per* Deane J., and see also *Seager v. Copydex Ltd* [1967] 1 W.L.R. 923, 931, *per* Lord Denning M.R.), or whether confidential information may also be regarded as property (as to which see Dr Francis Gurry's valuable monograph on *Breach of Confidence* (1984), pp. 46–56 and Professor Birks' *An Introduction to the Law of Restitution* (1985), pp. 343–344)."

---

[1] Cmnd. 8388 (1981), para. 3.1.
[2] Jones, "Restitution of benefits obtained in breach of another's confidence" (1970) 86 L.Q.R. 463.
[3] [1990] 1 A.C. 109 at 281.

2–02 There is no doubt that an obligation of confidence may arise under an express or implied term of a contract. It is also clearly established that courts of equity have recognised a duty of confidence arising independently of contract. If that duty arises from an equitable obligation of conscience *simpliciter*, according to traditional authority the remedies would not include damages (except under the jurisdiction derived from Lord Cairns' Act and now contained in section 50 of the Supreme Court Act 1981). So, for example, in *Robb v. Green*[4] the Court of Appeal held that the plaintiff's entitlement to damages depended on whether he could establish a breach of an implied contract or only a breach of an equitable duty of confidence.

If, however, there is a proprietary right in confidential information, or certain forms of confidential information, a plaintiff may have proprietary remedies. Furthermore, if wrongful interference with a proprietary right in confidential information is a tort, a plaintiff would have a right to common law damages against the tortfeasor.

Conflicting views on information as property

2–03 The question whether (statute apart) there can be property in ideas or information goes back to the issues debated in *Millar v. Taylor*[5] (in which the judgments repay reading). Now, as then, opinions are divided.

The question depends on what is meant by property, a matter of complexity upon which much has been written. As Professor Cornish has commented:

> "The root difficulty of such a question is the flexibility of the property notion in English law and the many ends to which it is applied.[6]"

It is therefore not surprising that different views have been expressed.

2–04 In *Phipps v. Boardman*[7] a solicitor to the trustees of a will and a beneficiary under the will trust bought shares in a company in which the trust had a substantial holding. At the time of the negotiations the purchasers were in the position of agents of the trustees and, as such, learned information relevant to the company, which they did not fully report to the trustees. From their special position they gained the opportunity to make a profit from the purchase of the shares and the knowledge that it was there to be made. The House of Lords held by a majority that the purchasers were liable to account for their profits from the purchase as constructive trustees, having used their position to make a personal profit without the full knowledge and consent of their principals.

The judges were divided on the question whether the information obtained by the purchasers was to be regarded as trust property in the strict sense. Lords Dilhorne,[8] Cohen[9] and Upjohn[10] considered that it was not; Lords Hodson[11] and Guest[12] that it was. Lord Upjohn said[13]:

---

[4] [1895] 2 Q.B. 315.
[5] (1769) 4 Bur. 2303. See para. 1
[6] Cornish, *Intellectual Property: Patents, Copyright, Trade Marks and Allied Rights* (2nd ed., 1989, Sweet & Maxwell) p. 240.
[7] [1967] 2 A.C. 46.
[8] *ibid.* at 89–90.
[9] *ibid.* at 102.
[10] *ibid.* at 127–128.
[11] *ibid.* at 107 and 110.
[12] *ibid.* at 115.
[13] *ibid.* at 127.

"In general, information is not property at all. It is normally open to all who have eyes to read and ears to hear. The true test is to determine in what circumstances the information has been acquired. If it has been acquired in such circumstances that it would be a breach of confidence to disclose it to another then courts of equity will restrain the recipient from communicating it to another. In such cases such confidential information is often and for many years has been described as the property of the donor, the books of authority are full of such references; knowledge of secret processes, 'know-how', confidential information as to the prospects of a company or of someone's intention or the expected results of some horse race based on stable or other confidential information. But in the end the real truth is that it is not property in any normal sense but equity will restrain its transmission to another if in breach of some confidential relationship."

Lord Hodson disagreed. He said[14]:

"... I dissent from the view that information is of its nature something which is not properly to be described as property. We are aware that what is called 'know-how' in the commercial sense is property which may be very valuable as an asset."

Lord Hodson also cited[15] a passage from the judgment of Bowen L.J. in *Aas v. Benham*,[16] in which he commented on an observation of Cotton L.J. in *Dean v. MacDowell*[17] that:

"Again if he" (that is, a partner) "makes any profit by the use of any property of the partnership, including, I may say, information which the partnership is entitled to, there the profit is made out of the partnership property."

Bowen L.J. commented:

"He is speaking of information which a partnership is entitled to in such a sense that it is information which is the property, or is to be included in the property of the partnership—that it to say, information the use of which is valuable to them as a partnership, and to the use of which they have a vested interest."

The arguments and authorities are discussed in further detail below,[18] but it is **2–05** suggested that Lord Upjohn's analysis is to be preferred. The passages cited by Lord Hodson from *Dean v. MacDowell* state the sense in which information has sometimes been referred to as "belonging to" a partnership (*i.e.* information valuable to the partnership and which the partnership has a right to use), but the basis of such right lies in the relationship between the partners.

The information in *Phipps v. Boardman* was of the same character in that its use was of potential value to the trustees and it was obtained by the purchasers in the capacity of agents for the trustees.

[14] *Phipps v. Boardman* [1967] 2 A.C. 46 at 107.
[15] *ibid.* at 109–110.
[16] [1891] 2 Ch. 244 at 258.
[17] (1878) 8 Ch.D. 345 at 354.
[18] See paras. 2–12—2–16, below.

Similarly in *Bell v. Lever Bros*[19] Lord Blanesbury said, in relation to private cocoa speculations by directors of a company engaged in the cocoa market, that:

> "... the company has no concern in his profit and cannot make him accountable for it unless it appears—this is the essential qualification—that in earning that profit he has made use *either* of the property of the company *or* of some confidential information which has come to him as a director of the company." (Emphasis added.)

The director's liability in the latter case would arise not from the confidential information constituting property, but from use of his fiduciary position to make a personal profit without his principal's knowledge.

Conflicting views on damages

2–06 In *Nichrotherm Electrical Ltd v Percy*,[20] Harman J. ordered an inquiry as to damages for breach of confidence and breach of copyright. In the Court of Appeal the matter proceeded, by agreement, on the basis that the breach of confidence relied upon by the plaintiff involved breach of an implied contract, and on that ground the court did not have to consider further the basis of the enquiry as to damages. But the court was clearly troubled by the form of order at first instance, and Lord Evershed, M.R. observed[21]:

> "If the confidence, breach of which is alleged or proved, is imposed by or arises out of contract, express or implied, then the remedy would, I assume, be by way of damages at law as upon a breach of contract. If, on the other hand, the confidence infringed is one imposed by the rules of equity, then the remedy would be, prima facie, by way of injunction or damages in lieu of an injunction under Lord Cairns' Act."

In *Ackroyds (London) Ltd v. Islington Plastics Ltd*[22] Havers J. granted an injunction and inquiry into damages for breach of contract and breach of confidence, but the basis of the award of damages for breach of confidence does not appear to have been considered, probably because there was no distinction on the facts between the breach of contract and breach of confidence and, therefore, the question was immaterial to the outcome.

2–07 In *Seager v. Copydex Ltd*[23] the plaintiff entered into negotiations with the defendants with a view to their marketing a carpet grip invented by him and for which he had a patent. During the negotiations the plaintiff suggested to the defendants an alternative form of grip. After the negotiations fell through, the defendants marketed a grip closely similar to the plaintiff's suggested alternative. The plaintiff claimed an injunction and damages. The defendants were found to have made use unconsciously of information supplied to them in confidence. The Court of Appeal declined to grant an injunction or an account of profits but ordered an inquiry as to damages.

[19] [1932] A.C. 161 at 194.
[20] [1956] R.P.C. 272.
[21] [1957] R.P.C. 207 at 213.
[22] [1962] R.P.C. 97.
[23] [1967] 1 W.L.R. 923.

Following the precedent of *Mechanical and General Inventions Co. v. Austin*[24] the plaintiff would appear to have had a good case for relying on breach of an implied contract, but there is no reference to that authority being cited; and the decision of the Court of Appeal was expressly based not on any theory of implied contract, but on the principle of equity that a person who receives information in confidence shall not take unfair advantage of it.

In *Seager v. Copydex Ltd (No. 2)*[25] the Court of Appeal directed that the damages be assessed, by analogy with damages for conversion, on the basis of the market value of the information misused by the defendants. Lord Denning M.R. said that just as a satisfied judgment in trover transferred the property in the goods, so the confidential information would belong to the defendants once the damages were paid.

This has prompted the comment:

> "The Court of Appeal had already held ... that the confidence was purely equitable. What it was now doing was to hold that equity would condone, nay facilitate, the compulsory acquisition by the defendant of the plaintiff's property; a state of affairs that would have exceeded the comprehension of the masters of equity who spoke in England before darkness enveloped all."[26]

The analogy of conversion has also been criticised by others including Professor Cornish[27]:

> "Altogether, the analogy to damages for misappropriation of a single tangible article is inept, given in particular the more obvious comparison to patents and copyright and the more flexible approach to damages which applies to their infringement."

While it seems entirely just that the plaintiff should have been compensated for the fact that information supplied by him to the defendants in confidence was used by them without his permission to their commercial advantage, the *Seager v. Copydex* decisions present difficulties of analysis.

The finding that the defendants were in breach of an obligation in equity has **2–08** been criticised on the basis that the equitable duty is founded on a duty to be of good faith, and that breach of such duty is inconsistent with the finding that there was no conscious plagiarism by the defendants; nor was there any finding that their honest belief that they were entitled to act as they did was unreasonable.[28]

If an ex-employee unconsciously plagiarised an idea obtained in a previous employment, it seems unlikely that a court would hold him liable in absence of a breach of an express covenant, but that would be on the basis that his duty of confidentiality did not extend to such information.[29]

---

[24] [1935] A.C. 346.

[25] [1969] 1 W.L.R. 809.

[26] *Meagher, Gummow and Lehane on Equity: Doctrines and Remedies* (3rd ed., 1992 Butterworths), para. 4118. Contrast also *Franklin v. Giddins* [1978] Qd.R. 72 (see para. 8–017, below).

[27] Cornish, *Intellectual Property: Patents, Copyright, Trade Marks and Allied Rights* (2nd ed., 1989, Sweet & Maxwell) p. 239.

[28] Professor Gareth Jones, "Restitution of benefits obtained in breach of another's confidence" (1970) 86 L.Q.R. 463.

[29] *Printers & Finishers Ltd v. Holloway* [1965] R.P.C. 239 at 256–257. (See paras. 3–04 and 3–13, below.)

A greater difficulty arises from the combination of the finding that the defendants were in breach of an equitable obligation and an award of damages on a tortious basis. A possible interpretation of *Seager v. Copydex* is that it established a new head of tortious liability for breach of confidence, analogous to conversion and based on the plaintiff's proprietary right in the information.[30] There is force in the comments of Goff and Jones[31]:

> "In our view it would have been happier if the court had rejected the analogy of the law of conversion and had instead made a *quantum meruit* award. If the basis of the confider's right is not property but the confidant's equitable duty of good faith, it is not evident that the confidant must make restitution if he uses confidential information innocently, having no reason to believe that, in doing so, he is betraying another's confidence; and we have suggested that he should not be so liable. Moreover, it may not be just in every case to conclude that information *belongs* to the confidant once damages are assessed and paid. For there may be circumstances where it is proper both to grant an injunction as to the future and a *quantum meruit* claim for the value of the benefits conferred during the time when the confidant was not enjoined."

Alternatively, there would have been no problem with an award of damages at common law if the case had been presented and decided on the basis of breach of implied contract. The question would then have been what damage the plaintiff suffered by reason of the breach; and, on the basis that he lost the ability to exploit the information for himself, it would be permissible to assess that loss by reference to its market value.

2–09 In the telephone tapping case of *Malone v. Metropolitan Police Commissioner*[32] one of the grounds on which the plaintiff sought, unsuccessfully, a declaration that it was unlawful for the defendant to tap his telephone line was based on a claimed right of confidentiality. Sir Robert Megarry V.-C. said[33]:

> "This is an equitable right which is still in the course of development, and is usually protected by the grant of an injunction to prevent disclosure of the confidence. Under Lord Cairns' Act 1858 damages may be granted in substitution for an injunction; yet if there is no case for the grant of an injunction, as when the disclosure has already been made, the unsatisfactory result seems to be that no damages can be awarded under this head: see *Proctor v. Bayley* (1889) 42 Ch.D. 390. In such a case, where there is no breach of contract or other orthodox foundation for damages at common law, it seems doubtful whether there is any right to damages, as distinct from an account of profits. It may be, however, that a new tort is emerging (see *Goff and Jones, The Law of Restitution* (2nd ed. 1978), pp. 518, 519 and Gareth Jones (1970) 86 L.Q.R. 463, 491), though this has been doubted: see *Street, The Law of Torts* 6th ed. (1976), p. 377. Certainly the subject raises many questions that are so far unresolved ... "

---

[30] For a critique of this interpretation and its problems see Prof. P. M. North, "Breach of Confidence: Is there a New Tort?" 12 J.S.P.T.L. 149. The theory is discussed further at paras. 2–12—2–16, below.

[31] Goff and Jones, *The Law of Restitution* (4th ed., 1993), p. 692.

[32] [1979] 1 Ch. 344.

[33] *ibid.* at 360.

In its Report on Breach of Confidence in 1981[34] the Law Commission expressed the different view, in paragraph 4.76, that:

"It is a reasonable inference from the decision in *Seager v. Copydex Ltd* that damages are awardable for a past breach of confidence."

But it qualified that view by adding:

"On the other hand it can be argued that it is not clear from that case whether the damages which were ordered to be assessed were intended to include loss suffered in respect of the past breach of confidence or only to provide compensation in lieu of an injunction. The subsequent decision in *Seager v. Copydex Ltd (No. 2)*, in which the Court of Appeal had to determine the basis of assessment for the damages ordered in the earlier case, has not clarified the position in this respect."

In *English v. Dedham Vale Properties*[35] Slade J. said that he read *Seager v. Copydex Ltd* as a case in which the court granted damages in lieu of an injunction.

In *Dowson & Mason Ltd v. Potter*[36] an employee of the plaintiffs in breach of **2–10** duty divulged confidential information to another company, who used it to compete with his employers. The plaintiffs sued the employee and the company. Both submitted to an order for an inquiry as to damages. Subsequently an issue arose as to the basis on which damages were to be assessed. The company contended that damages should be assessed by reference to the value of the information, following *Seager v. Copydex Ltd*. The plaintiffs contended successfully for assessment by reference to their loss of profits. The Court of Appeal held that *Seager v. Copydex Ltd* laid down no general rule as to the appropriate basis of assessment in such a case, and applied the principle stated by Lord Wilberforce in *General Tire and Rubber Co. v. Firestone Tyre & Rubber Co. Ltd*[37]:

"As in the case of any other tort (leaving aside cases where exemplary damages can be given) the object of damages is to compensate for loss or injury. The general rule at any rate in relation to 'economic' torts is that the measure of damages is to be, so far as possible, that sum of money which will put the injured party in the same position as he would have been in if he had not sustained the wrong."

However, there was no analysis of the underlying basis of the order for damages, which had not been articulated in any judgment, since the order was made by consent.

In the *Spycatcher* case Lord Goff said[38]:

"An important section of the law of restitution is concerned with cases in which a defendant is required to make restitution in respect of benefits acquired through his own wrongful act— notably cases of waiver of tort; of benefits acquired by certain criminal acts; of benefits acquired in breach

[34] Cmnd. 8388 (1981).
[35] [1978] 1 W.L.R. 93 at 111.
[36] [1986] 1 W.L.R. 1419.
[37] [1975] 1 W.L.R. 819 at 824.
[38] [1990] 1 A.C. 109 at 286.

of a fiduciary relationship; and, of course, of benefits acquired in breach of confidence. The plaintiff's claim to restitution is usually enforced by an account of profits made by the defendant through his wrong at the plaintiff's expense. This remedy of an account is alternative to the remedy of damages, which in cases of breach of confidence is now available, despite the equitable nature of the wrong, through a beneficent interpretation of the Chancery Amendment Act 1858 (Lord Cairns' Act) ... ."

In *Universal Thermosensors Ltd v. Hibben*[39] Sir Donald Nicholls V.-C. referred to *Seager v. Copydex Ltd* and, in particular, the passage in Lord Denning's judgment to the effect that a recipient of confidential information should not get a start over others by using it, at any rate without paying for it, even if the case was not one for an injunction. The Vice-Chancellor added:

> "An award of damages in such circumstances would not be a novelty. There are several fields where the courts have awarded damages to a plaintiff whose property is wrongfully used by another even though the plaintiff has not suffered pecuniary loss by such user. The cases concerning this principle, sometimes called 'the "user" principle', can be found gathered together in *Stoke-on-Trent City Council v. W. & J. Wass Ltd* [1988] 1 W.L.R. 1406, 1416–1418."

2–11   *Stoke-on-Trent City Council v. W. & J. Wass Ltd* is authority for the proposition that in tort (including torts involving interference with property or proprietary rights) as a general rule damages are to be assessed by reference to the loss sustained by the plaintiff; but that, exceptionally, in certain cases (such as trespass to land, patent infringement and certain cases of nuisance or detinue) the user principle may apply to enable the plaintiff to recover a reasonable sum for the use made of his property.

The principle was approved in *Inverugie Investments Ltd v. Hackett*,[40] where Lord Lloyd said:

> "The principle need not be characterised as exclusively compensatory, or exclusively restitutionary; it combines elements of both."

The property/tort theory considered

2–12   There are formidable difficulties in the way of any treatment of the action for breach of confidence as an action in tort based on infringement of a proprietary interest. The objections may be grouped under the headings of precedent, conceptual analysis and logical consequence.

As a matter of precedent, the view held by Lord Mansfield and the majority of the judges in *Miller v. Taylor*[41] that the common law recognised an incorporeal right to a set of ideas was ultimately rejected by the House of Lords in *Jefferys v. Boosey*.[42] Lord Brougham said[43]:

---

[39] [1992] 1 W.L.R. 840 at 856.
[40] [1995] 1 W.L.R. 713 at 718, P.C.
[41] (1769) 4 Bur. 2303.
[42] (1854) 4 H.L.C. 814. For a valuable description of Lord Mansfield's contribution to the development of the law of intellectual property, see Professor James Oldham, *The Mansfield Manuscripts* (1992, University of North Carolina Press) Vol. 1, Chap. 12.
[43] (1854) 4 H.L.C. 814 at 966.

"Whatever can be urged for property in a composition, must be applicable to property in an invention or discovery. It is the subject matter of the composition, not the mere writing, the mere collection of words, that constitutes the work. It may describe an invention, as well as contain a narrative or poem, and the right to the exclusive property in the invention, the title to prevent anyone from describing it to others, or using it himself (before it is reduced to writing) without the inventor's leave, is precisely the same with the right of the author to exclude all men from the multiplication of his work. But in what manner has this ever been done or attempted to be done by inventors? Never by asserting a property at common law in the inventor, but by obtaining a grant from the Crown."

He added[44]:

"I also consider the statute of Anne itself as plainly indicating the opinion of the legislature that there was no copyright at common law."

Lord Brougham recognised that the author of an unpublished manuscript had a right to the manuscript, and was entitled to publish the composition, or not, as he saw fit.[45] In later authorities it was held that the "so-called copyright that remains in an author in respect of an unpublished work" at common law could be passed to another independently of the manuscript.[46] But the right so recognised was in the *form* of the composition, not the ideas or information which it contained, as was explained by Lord Oliver in a lecture given to the Hebrew University of Jerusalem in 1989[47]:

"Now the action of confidence is entirely an equitable invention ... . The common law recognised the right of property of an author in his unpublished work, but what it protected was the mode of expression not the information expressed. The idea that information imparted or acquired in confidence or as a result of a confidential relationship, such as a doctor and a patient, could be legally protected by the courts seems to have arisen only in the early nineteenth century."

He also referred to the basis of the action being[48]:

"... that equity intervenes to preserve the confidentiality of information not because information is susceptible of a *proprietary* claim but because its use in the hands of the defendant is unconscionable."

In *Nichrotherm Electrical Co. Ltd v. Percy*[49] Lord Evershed M.R. also **2–13** rejected the suggestion of property in ideas, saying:

"... a man who thinks of a mechanical conception and then communicates it to others for the purpose of their working out means of carrying it into effect does not, because the idea was his (assuming that it was), get

---

[44] *Jefferys v. Boosey* (1854) 4 H.L.C. 814.
[45] *ibid.* at 962.
[46] *Re Dickens* [1935] 1 Ch. 267 at 286.
[47] "Spycatcher: Confidence, Copyright and Contempt" *Israel Law Review*, (1989) Vol. 23, No. 4, 407 at 413.
[48] *ibid.* at 421.
[49] [1957] R.P.C. 207 at 209.

proprietary rights equivalent to those of a patentee. Apart from such rights as may flow from the fact, for example, of the idea being of a secret process communicated in confidence or from some contract of partnership or agency or the like which he may enter into with his collaborator, the originator of the idea gets no proprietary rights out of the mere circumstance that he first thought of it."[50]

It may be argued that this is hard to reconcile with the concept of a secret recipe as capable of being the subject of a trust (See *Green v. Folgham*.[51]) But it is perfectly possible to recognise a fiduciary relationship (*e.g.* between trustee and beneficiary or between partners) involving obligations in relation to confidential information, without regarding such information as property in the strict sense of the word.[52]

In *Seager v. Copydex Ltd* itself the judgment of the Court of Appeal on liability was expressly founded on "the broad principle of equity that he who has received information in confidence shall not take unfair advantage of it".[53] That principle does not require any underlying proprietary right.

Lord Denning, M.R. expressed the same view in *Fraser v. Evans*[54]:

"The jurisdiction is based not so much on property or on contract as on the duty to be of good faith. No person is permitted to divulge to the world information which he has received in confidence, unless he has just cause or excuse for doing so."

A similar view was expressed in the High Court of Australia in *Moorgate Tobacco Co. Ltd v. Philip Morris Ltd (No. 2)*[55] by Deane J. (with the concurrence of Gibbs C.J. and Mason, Wilson and Dawson JJ.):

"It is unnecessary, for the purposes of the present appeal, to attempt to define the precise scope of the equitable jurisdiction to grant relief against an actual or threatened abuse of confidential information not involving any tort or any breach of some express or implied contractual provision, some wider fiduciary duty or some copyright or trade mark right. A general equitable jurisdiction to grant such relief has long been asserted and should, in my view, now be accepted: see *The Commonwealth v. John Fairfax & Sons Ltd*.[56] Like most heads of exclusive equitable jurisdiction its rational basis does not lie in proprietary right. It lies in the notion of an obligation of conscience arising from the circumstances in or through which the information was communicated or obtained."

It has also been held that the information in an examination paper does not constitute "intangible property" capable of falling within section 4 of the Theft Act 1968.[57]

---

[50] See also *Federal Commissioner of Taxation v. United Aircraft Corporation* (1943–1944) 68 C.L.R. 525 at 534 (High Court of Australia), *per* Latham C.J., referred to at para. 7–09, below.
[51] (1823) 1 Sim. & Stu. 398.
[52] *Phipps v. Boardman* [1967] 2 A.C. 46 at 102, *per* Lord Cohen, and at 127–128, *per* Lord Upjohn.
[53] [1967] 1 W.L.R. 923 at 931, *per* Lord Denning M.R. Lord Goff in the *Spycatcher* case treated *Seager v. Copydex Ltd* as founded on obligation of conscience rather than proprietary rights. See [1990] 1 A.C. 109 at 281.
[54] [1969] 1 Q.B. 349 at 361.
[55] (1984) 156 C.L.R. 414 at 437–438.
[56] (1980) 147 C.L.R. 39 at 50–52.
[57] *Oxford v. Moss* (1979) 68 Cr.App.R. 183.

Conceptually, if there is no such thing as property in a secret idea or **2–14** invention,[58] it would be a strange form of property which comes into existence on the transmission of information about that idea on a confidential basis and ceases to exist on its wider publication. This would be unlike any normal form of property.

In truth, as Professor Gareth Jones has commented[59]:

> "Confidential information is conceptually very much *sui generis*. It is an intangible; and, consequently, it would be 'wrong to confuse the physical records with [the information] itself...; for if you put them on a duplicator and produce one hundred copies you have certainly not multiplied your asset in proportion'.[60] It has, too, the quality that it may be transmitted to a limited class without destroying its value; so, know-how 'can be communicated to or shared with others outside the manufacturer's own business,' for example, under licence.[61] Conversely the nature of confidential information is such that no one, save the person who imparted it, may realise for some time that it has been communicated in breach of confidence. For similar reasons it is not always easy to protect a purchaser of confidential information from his seller who subsequently sells the same information to another innocent third party.
>
> Information is not like other choses in action, such as debt or copyright, which lend themselves more easily to a classical analysis in terms of property."

There is also a danger of circularity of reasoning in concluding, because **2–15** equity intervenes by injunction or other remedy, that the reason for the intervention lies in the protection of a proprietary interest. This point was recognised by Gummow J. in *Smith Kline & French Laboratories (Australia) Ltd v. Department of Community Services*,[62] citing *Colbeam Palmer Ltd v. Stock Affiliates Pty Ltd*[63] and *E.I. Du Pont de Nemours Powder Company v. Masland*,[64] where Holmes J. said:

> "The word property as applied to trade-marks and trade secrets is an unanalysed expression of certain secondary consequences of the primary fact that the law makes some rudimentary requirements of good faith."

These objections, powerful though they are, would be no compelling reason for the courts not to recognise confidential information as a form of property, if to do so would resolve problems and assist the development of the law on a principled and rational basis. But, if anything, the opposite would be the case. Professor Finn has observed[65]:

> "Certain types of information and particularly trade secrets doubtless can

---

[58] *Jefferys v. Boosey* (1854) 4 H.L.C. 814; *Nichrotherm Electrical Co. Ltd v. Percy* [1957] R.P.C. 207. *Federal Commissioner of Taxation v. United Aircraft Corporation* (1943) 68 C.L.R. 525 at 534.

[59] "Restitution of benefits obtained in breach of another's confidence" (1970) 86 L.Q.R. 463 at 464.

[60] *Rolls-Royce Ltd v. Jeffrey (Inspector of Taxes)* [1962] 1 All E.R. 801 at 805, *per* Lord Radcliffe.

[61] *ibid.*

[62] [1990] F.S.R. 617 at 673–674; (affirmed (1991) 28 F.C.R. 291).

[63] (1968) 122 C.L.R. 25 at 34, *per* Windeyer J.

[64] (1917) 244 U.S. 100 at 102.

[65] Finn, *Fiduciary Obligations* (1977) paras. 295–296. Note also his comment at paragraph 293, "Perhaps the most sterile of debates which have arisen around the subject of information received in confidence is whether or not such information should be classified as property."

have certain of the attributes of property. Information can for example be intrinsically valuable; it can be the subject matter of a trust; it can be communicated for a consideration; it can be included in the 'property' which passes to a trustee in bankruptcy.

But even if from such similarities one wishes to create a form of abstract property, difficulties immediately arise. If all information is described as property, it is nonetheless meaningless to give a property basis to the jurisdiction relieving against misuse of information. All such 'property' is not protected by the courts. The information, and the circumstances of its communication must, as will be seen, possess certain characteristics before protection will be given. If only some information is described as property, *i.e.* information protected by the courts, to call that information property is merely to add yet another consequence to a decision taken for reasons quite unrelated to property considerations."

2–16   Nowhere are the difficulties of adopting property as a basis of the jurisdiction more acute than in relation to the "innocent" third party. The concept of an action for breach of confidence based on a broad principle that one should not break, or co-operate with another in breaking, a personal duty of confidence is fundamentally different from the concept of an action based on tortious infringement of a property right analogous to trespass to goods.

If the concept is based on equitable principles, no liability would be expected to attach to a third party recipient of confidential information for acts done by him in ignorance that there had been any breach of confidence. So, it has been held that, in order to be fixed with an obligation of confidence, a third party must know that the information was confidential.[66] On discovering that there had been such breach the third party would ordinarily then come under a duty of confidence, at least if he were a volunteer.[67] On the other hand, it might be unfair to impose such a duty on him if he had paid in good faith for the information, or had subsequently incurred effort or expense in putting it to use, or had otherwise undergone a change of circumstances, except possibly on terms compensating him for the loss or prejudice which he would otherwise suffer.[68]

However, if the concept is based on a tort of infringement of property analogous to conversion, the mental innocence of the third party would be no defence and he would be liable in damages for his past innocent misuse of the plaintiff's confidential information,[69] a liability analogous to the statutory liability to damages of an infringer of copyright.[70]

The only way of avoiding strict liability for innocent misuse of confidential information would be for the courts to create a special defence not ordinarily available in cases of tortious infringement of property rights.

In short, as Professor Gareth Jones has said[71]:

"No property theory can satisfactorily determine, even with the aid of equity, the question of the liability of the person who innocently exploits a

---

[66] *Fraser v. Thames Television* [1984] 1 Q.B. 44 at 65. *Valeo Vision S.A. v. Flexible Lamps Ltd* [1995] R.P.C. 205 at 226–228. See also the Report of the Law Commission Cmnd. 8388 (1981), para. 4.12.

[67] *Printers & Finishers Ltd v. Holloway* [1965] R.P.C. 239 at 253 and 257, *per* Cross J. and *Fraser v. Thames Television* [1984] 1 Q.B. 44.

[68] See para. 7–06, below.

[69] Compare *Marfani & Co. Ltd v. Midland Bank Ltd* [1968] 1 W.L.R. 956.

[70] *Paterson Zochonis & Co. Ltd v. Merfarken Packaging Ltd* [1986] 3 All E.R. 522.

[71] "Restitution of benefits obtained in breach of another's confidence" (1970) 86 L.Q.R. 463 at 465.

secret. For example, there may be circumstances where it is just that a volunteer should be free of any liability to account for profits made through the use of confidential information. Conversely, it may not be difficult to imagine a case where even a bona fide purchaser ought to be enjoined, albeit on terms, from using information which he later learns was given him in breach of another's confidence."

Other possible explanations for damages

If the property solution is rejected as a basis of the jurisdiction (as it is **2–17** suggested that it should be), it would be equally unsatisfactory that monetary compensation should be capable of being awarded for past misuse of confidential information only where there was a case for the grant of an injunction, as Sir Robert Megarry V.-C. observed in *Malone v. Metropolitan Police Commissioner*.[72] The surprise is that the courts should still be grappling for a satisfactory explanation on what basis (other than breach of contract) this may be done.

Lord Goff's suggestion in the *Spycatcher* case[73] that damages are now available for breach of confidence, despite the equitable nature of the wrong, through a "beneficent interpretation" of Lord Cairns' Act, is not entirely satisfactory.

In neither *Seager v. Copydex Ltd* nor *Seager v. Copydex Ltd (No. 2)*[74] did the Court of Appeal make any reference to Lord Cairns's Act providing the basis for damages. Further, it is not difficult to imagine cases in which there could be no grounds for the grant of an injunction, for example, because there was no threat to repeat a past breach, or because the information had ceased to be confidential for reasons which might be quite independent of the defendant's breach (as in *Mustad & Son v. Dosen*[75]). In such a case, to describe an award of damages for a past breach as being in lieu of an injunction would involve more than a beneficent interpretation of Lord Cairns's Act. It would be a fiction.

An alternative partial solution might be advanced under the rubric of **2–18** restitution, under which a wrongdoer may be required to restore benefits obtained through his own wrongful act. In *Spycatcher*[76] Lord Goff recognised this principle as applying to benefits obtained in breach of confidence. This would justify the wrongdoer being ordered to pay over the value of the benefit received, regardless of the availability of an injunction; and so, on the facts of *Seager v. Copydex Ltd*, would afford a legitimate basis for the defendants being required to pay the "market value" of the information misused.

That would have the same effect as a *quantum meruit* award, which Goff and Jones[77] suggest would have been a happier basis of the award in *Seager v. Copydex Ltd*. However, the authors recognise that it is difficult to square that approach with an award of damages. It would be still more difficult to justify expectation damages (*i.e.* damages for loss of anticipated profits), as in *Dowson & Mason Ltd v. Potter*,[78] on a restitutionary basis.

[72] [1979] 1 Ch. 344 at 360.
[73] [1990] 1 A.C. 109 at 286.
[74] [1967] 1 W.L.R. 923; [1969] 1 W.L.R. 809.
[75] [1964] 1 W.L.R. 109.
[76] [1990] 1 A.C. 109 at 286.
[77] Goff and Jones, *The Law of Restitution* (4th ed., 1993), p. 692.
[78] [1986] 1 W.L.R. 1419.

Equitable compensation

2–19   A more satisfactory solution (not dependent on Lord Cairns's Act or on the developing principles of restitution) would be to recognise that equitable compensation may be awarded for breach of an equitable duty of confidence, just as it may be awarded for breach of duty by a fiduciary (*Nocton v. Ashburton*[79]). This accords with the view expressed by Professor Finn that[80]:

> " ... no great violence to principle is wrought if they [*i.e.* awards of damages for breach of an equitable obligation of confidence] are regarded as modern developments in the compensatory jurisdiction of Equity which was so forcefully reaffirmed by Viscount Haldane L.C. in *Nocton v. Ashburton*."

The law relating to fiduciary relationships is one of the least clearly defined areas of the law,[81] but there is a close parallel between a person owing an equitable obligation of confidence and a person owing a fiduciary obligation, and there seems no good reason in principle why a person should not be required to provide compensation in equity (sometimes called equitable damages) for breach of an equitable obligation of confidence as in a case of breach of a fiduciary obligation.

Seager v. Copydex Ltd was explained in this way in *U.S. Surgical Corporation v. Hospital Products International Pty Ltd* by McLelland J., who said[82]:

> "Apart from the limited power to award damages in addition to or in substitution for equitable relief, conferred by the Supreme Court Act, 1970, S.68 (following Lord Cairns' Act), which is of no present relevance, the court has an inherent power to grant relief by way of monetary compensation for breach of a fiduciary or other equitable obligation: see *Nocton v. Lord Ashburton* [1914] A.C. 932 at pp. 946, 956, 957; *McKenzie v. McDonald* [1927] V.L.R. 134 at p. 146; *Holmes v. Walton* [1961] W.A.R. 96; *cf. Seager v. Copydex Ltd* [1967] 1 W.L.R. 923; [1967] 2 All E.R. 415; [1969] 1 W.L.R. 809; [1969] 2 All E.R. 718."

2–20   Just as the doctrine of fiduciary duty is not limited to direct relationships[83] but extends to a person who dishonestly assists in a breach of trust by another (*Royal Brunei Airlines v. Tan*[84]), or who receives (by accident or misconduct) assets emanating from another in the knowledge that he was not intended to do so (*Chase Manhattan Bank N.A. v. Israel-British Bank (London) Ltd*[85]), there seems no reason in principle why equitable compensation for breach of a duty of confidence should not equally be awarded against a person who knowingly

---

[79] [1914] A.C. 932.
[80] Finn, *Fiduciary Obligations* (1977), para. 388.
[81] See *Henderson v. Merrett Syndicates Ltd* [1995] 2 A.C. 145 at 206, *per* Lord Browne-Wilkinson.
[82] [1982] 2 N.S.W.L.R. 766, 816. (Reversed on other grounds (1984) 156 C.L.R. 41). See also Davidson, "The Equitable Remedy of Compensation", 13 *Melbourne University Law Review* 349.
[83] *White v. Jones* [1995] 2 A.C. 207 at 271, *per* Lord Browne-Wilkinson,
"... the special relationship (*i.e.* a fiduciary relationship) giving rise to the assumption of responsibility held to exist in Nocton's case does not depend on any mutual dealing between A and B, let alone on any relationship akin to contract. Although such factors may be present, equity imposes the obligation because A has assumed to act in B's affairs."
[84] [1995] 2 A.C. 378.
[85] [1981] Ch. 105.

assists in a breach of confidence by another,[86] or who knowingly receives confidential information by mistake or misconduct and misuses it.[87]

Although there is considerable historical authority on the difference between compensation in equity and damages at common law,[88] the House of Lords held in *Target Holdings Limited v. Redferns*[89] that the principles underlying both are the same, the fundamental object being to compensate the innocent party for the loss caused by the wrong.

New Zealand, Canada and Australia

It is instructive to compare the development of the law in New Zealand, Canada and Australia. **2–21**

In *Aquaculture Corporation v. New Zealand Green Mussel Co. Ltd*[90] the defendants misused confidential information, supplied by the plaintiff, in manufacturing and marketing a product. The plaintiff claimed that its own business prospects had been injured by the defendants' irresponsible marketing campaign. Damages for the plaintiff's loss were assessed at $1.5 million, but the trial judge held that he had no power to award compensatory damages. This ruling was reversed on appeal. Delivering the judgment of the Court of Appeal of New Zealand, Cooke P. said[91]:

> "There is now a line of judgments in this Court accepting that monetary compensation (which can be labelled damages) may be awarded for breach of a duty of confidence or other duty deriving historically from equity ... . In some of these cases the relevant observations were arguably obiter, but we think that the point should now be taken as settled in New Zealand. Whether the obligation of confidence in a case of the present kind should be classified as purely an equitable one is debatable, but we do not think that the question matters for any purpose material to this appeal. For all purposes now material, equity and common law are mingled or merged. The practicality of the matter is that in the circumstances of the dealings between the parties the law imposes a duty of confidence. For its breach a full range of remedies should be available as appropriate, no matter whether they originated in common law, equity or statute."

Cooke P. drew support from this approach not only from New Zealand authorities but also from the decisions of the Supreme Court of Canada in *LAC Minerals Ltd v. International Corona Resources Ltd*[92] and of Rogers J. in the Supreme Court of New South Wales in *Catt v. Marac Australia Ltd*.[93]

In *Lac Minerals* the plaintiff owned mining rights on land on which it was **2–22** drilling exploratory holes. In the course of negotiations with a view to a possible partnership or joint venture (which never materialised), the plaintiff revealed to the defendant information about the drilling results, from which it was clear

---

[86] See Chap. VII, below.
[87] See Chap. VIII, below.
[88] See Meagher, Gummow and Lehane, *Equity: Doctrines and Remedies* (3rd ed., 1992) paras. 2301 *et seq.*
[89] [1995] 3 W.L.R. 352.
[90] [1990] 3 N.Z.L.R. 299.
[91] *ibid.* at 301.
[92] [1990] F.S.R. 441.
[93] (1986) 9 N.S.W.L.R. 639.

that an adjacent property was likely to have valuable deposits. The plaintiff attempted to acquire the mining rights in the adjacent property but was out bid by the defendant, which developed the mine on its own account. The plaintiff sought a declaration that the defendant held the mining rights on constructive trust for the plaintiff on the grounds either of breach of fiduciary duty or of breach of confidence. It was found that, but for the defendant's use of the relevant information, the plaintiff would have obtained the mining rights and developed the mine for itself.

Three issues therefore arose: first, whether the defendant acquired the mining rights in breach of fiduciary duty (in which case there could be no dispute about the defendant holding the rights on trust for the plaintiff); secondly, whether the defendant acted in breach of confidence; and thirdly, if so, what remedy was available.

The Supreme Court held (by a majority) that the parties were not in a fiduciary relationship, but (unanimously) that the defendant acted in breach of confidence. On the question of remedy, the majority (La Forest, Lamer and Wilson JJ.) upheld the plaintiff's argument in favour of the imposition of a constructive trust. The minority (Sopinka and McIntyre JJ.) considered damages a more appropriate remedy. There was, however, no difference between the judges as to the range of remedies which it lay within the court's power to award. On this the most detailed analysis was that of Sopinka J. He said[94]:

> "The foundation of action for breach of confidence does not rest solely on one of the traditional jurisdictional bases for action of contract, equity or property. The action is *sui generis* relying on all three to enforce the policy of the law that confidences be respected: see Gurry, *Breach of Confidence* (Clarendon Press, Oxford, 1984) at pp. 25–26, and Goff & Jones, *The Law of Restitution*, (3rd ed., Sweet & Maxwell, 1986) at pp. 664–667.
>
> This multi-faceted jurisdictional basis for the action provides the court with considerable flexibility in fashioning a remedy. The jurisdictional basis supporting the particular claim is relevant in determining the appropriate remedy ... . A constructive trust is ordinarily reserved for those situations where a right of property is recognised ... .
>
> Although confidential information has some of the characteristics of property, its foothold as such is tenuous ... .
>
> As a result, there is virtually no support in the cases for the imposition of a constructive trust over property acquired as a result of the use of confidential information ... .
>
> Although unjust enrichment has been recognised as having an existence apart from contract or tort under a heading referred to as the law of restitution, a constructive trust is not the appropriate remedy in most cases ... .
>
> While the remedy of the constructive trust may continue to be employed in situations where other remedies would be inappropriate or injustice would result, there is no reason to extend it to this case.
>
> The conventional remedies for breach of confidence are an accounting of profits or damages. An injunction may be coupled with either of these remedies in appropriate circumstances. A restitutionary remedy is appropriate in cases involving fiduciaries because they are required to disgorge

[94] [1990] F.S.R. 441 at 495–497.

any benefits derived from the breach of trust. In a breach of confidence case, the focus is on the loss to the plaintiff and, as in tort actions, the particular position of the plaintiff must be examined. The object is to restore the plaintiff monetarily to the position he would have been in if no wrong had been committed: see *Dowson & Mason Ltd v. Potter* [1986] 2 All E.R. 418, (C.A.) and *Talbot v. General Television Corp. Pty Ltd* [1980] V.R. 224. Accordingly, this object is generally achieved by an award of damages, and a restitutionary remedy is inappropriate."

The majority considered that the imposition of a constructive trust was the appropriate remedy as the surest way of putting the plaintiff in the position that it would have been in but for the defendant's breach of confidence; and that the restitutionary principle, which enables a court to give to a plaintiff something which has been wrongly taken from him (a restitutionary proprietary award), or its monetary value (a personal restitutionary award), should by analogy apply equally in the situation in which the wrongdoer has acquired a benefit which would otherwise have accrued for the benefit of the plaintiff.

In Australia there has been searching analysis, particularly by Meagher, **2–23** Gummow and Lehane[95] and (in his judicial capacity) by Gummow J. in *Corrs Pavey v. Collector of Customs*[96] and *Smith, Kline & French Laboratories (Australia) Ltd v. Secretary to the Department of Community Services and Health*.[97] Meagher, Gummow and Lehane have observed that[98]:

"... the equitable duty of confidence has now sufficiently developed (as has the law of trusts to a much greater degree) to be regarded as occupying a specific field of its own, but subject always to the caveat that where there are questions as to the direction of further development (for example, in dealing with third parties who receive information) these can best be answered by looking to the source whence the stream has sprung. Thus, it will be contended that the third party who participates in breach of a duty of confidence is accountable under the second limb of *Barnes v. Addy* (1874) 9 Ch.App. 244 at 251, no less than is a participant in a breach by a delinquent fiduciary within the strict modern acceptance of that term."

In *Smith, Kline & French* Gummow J. said[99]:

"It seems clear enough that knowledge *per se* is not proprietary in character; see *Moorgate Tobacco Co. Ltd v. Philip Morris Ltd* (1982) 64 F.L.R. 387 at 404–405, affirmed (1984) 156 C.L.R. 414; *Boardman v. Phipps* [1967] 2 A.C. 46 at 89–92, 102–103, 127–129, but compare 106–107, 115. Further, it is clear in Australia that the equitable jurisdiction to grant relief against an actual or threatened abuse of confidential information, not involving any tort or breach of contract, fiduciary duty, copyright or trade mark, is based not in pre-existing proprietary right, but in an obligation of conscience arising in the circumstances of the case: *Moorgate Tobacco Co. Ltd v. Philip Morris Ltd (No. 2)*."[1]

[95] Meagher, Gummow and Lehane, *Equity: Doctrines and Remedies* (3rd ed., 1992).
[96] (1987) 74 A.L.R. 428.
[97] [1990] F.S.R. 617, affirmed [1991] 28 F.C.R. 291.
[98] Meagher, Gummow and Lehane, *op. cit.*, para. 4107.
[99] [1990] F.S.R. 617 at 673.
[1] (1984) 156 C.L.R. 414.

Gummow J. also held it to be established law in Australia that the court had an inherent jurisdiction to award monetary compensation, independent of its statutory powers under any derivative of Lord Cairns's Act, for breach of an equitable duty of confidence, as appears from the following part of his judgment[2]:

"I should have hoped that any controversy as to the applicability of Lord Cairns's Act and its derivatives to claims in respect of purely equitable rights (rather than tortious or contractual rights) had been quelled by the recent analysis by Mr Dean in his work, *The Law of Trade Secrets* (1990), pp. 317–320, 329. I have indicated my views in *Concept Television Productions Pty Ltd v. Australian Broadcasting Corporation* (1988) 12 I.P.R. 129 at 136. This Court is, by statute, a court of equity as regards matters otherwise within its jurisdiction ... . This brings with it, in a case such as the present, the inherent jurisdiction to grant relief by way of monetary compensation for breach of an equitable obligation, whether of trust or confidence. After all, long before the birth of Lord Cairns, delinquent trustees were brought to book in Chancery and, independently of any tracing remedy *in rem*, were obliged to make up from their own pockets the value of trust funds which had been lost: *Re Dawson dec'd* [1966] 2 N.S.W.R. 211. And as to the personal liability of fiduciaries other than trustees, see *Catt v. Marac Australia Ltd* (1986) 9 N.S.W.L.R. 639. If it transpires that the applicants are entitled to an inquiry [as to pecuniary loss], it would, in my view, be on this basis in the inherent equitable jurisdiction ... ."

Conclusion

2–24   Common to the approach adopted in New Zealand, Canada and Australia is the recognition that the essential foundation of the law of confidentiality lies in an obligation arising from the circumstances under which the information was obtained. This is consistent with the historical development of the action for breach of confidence in England.

In cases of contract, such obligation may arise from an express or implied term of the contract. Such obligation may also arise by imposition of law. Just as a duty of care or a fiduciary duty may arise both under the terms of a contract and by imposition of law,[3] similarly a duty of confidence may arise both under a contract and by imposition of law.[4]

It may not appear to make a practical difference whether, contract apart, the action for breach of confidence:

(1) is founded on an equitable obligation, for breach of which the court may now award monetary compensation in addition to or instead of other equitable remedies, or

---

[2] [1990] F.S.R. 617 at 634.

[3] *Henderson v. Merrett Syndicates Ltd* [1995] 2 A.C. 145 at 206, *per* Lord Browne-Wilkinson: "The existence of a contract does not exclude the co-existence of concurrent fiduciary duties (indeed, the contract may well be their source); but the contract can and does modify the extent and nature of the general duty that would otherwise arise."

[4] *e.g. Lamb v. Evans* [1893] 1 Ch. 218; *Robb v. Green* [1895] 2 Q.B. 315.

(2) is founded on a multi-faceted jurisdiction under which the court may award a full range of equitable and common law remedies.

It is suggested that the first is the preferable analysis, both historically and conceptually. The action for breach of confidence has come to occupy its own area within the law, and it may in that sense be described as *sui generis*, but it is desirable for its coherent development that its underlying foundation should be clear.

The circumstances in which a person may obtain confidential information **2–25** vary widely. Broadly they may be divided into the following classes:

(1) *Direct receipt.* A discloses confidential information to X. This is the simplest case.

(2) *Indirect receipt.* A discloses confidential information to B, who passes it to X. X may know that it is confidential at the time or he may not discover that until later, by which time he may have incurred expense or otherwise altered his position in the belief that he was entitled to use the information or he may himself have passed on the information.

(3) *Accidental receipt.* X obtains information regarded by A as confidential as a result, directly or indirectly, of accident, carelessness or mistake on the part of A or some person to whom A has passed the information.

(4) *Surreptitious receipt.* X obtains information regarded by A as confidential as a result, directly or indirectly, of reprehensible conduct, to which X may or may not be a party.

It can be seen that in some instances there will be an obvious, direct relationship of confidentiality between A and X; in some instances, there may be said to be an indirect relationship of confidentiality between A and X; in some instances the information has not reached X under or by reason of any relationship of confidentiality.

Other distinctions can also be drawn. For example, information may be disclosed voluntarily or under compulsion of law.

The essential questions common to all these cases are what obligation, if any, should be imposed on X, and what is the appropriate remedy for breach. If the law of confidentiality, contract apart, is regarded as having a multi-faceted and undefined jurisdictional basis, a court looking for principles on which to fashion its continued development in such varied cases will have to proceed either with no distinct understanding of its underlying basis beyond a vague amalgam of ideas drawn from different sources, or else by seeking in some way to choose between the different facets and to identify the principles underlying the facet judged to be relevant. Just such conceptual uncertainty has led to confusion in the case law. If, as is suggested, the true foundation of the jurisdiction, contract apart, is an obligation of conscience (for breach of which compensation can be awarded on the principles discussed above), it is to that underlying source that the courts should look when seeking to develop the law in a coherent and principled fashion.

CHAPTER III

ESSENTIAL FEATURES OF CONFIDENTIALITY

General principle

3–01   In the *Spycatcher* case Lord Goff[1] took as his starting point the following statement of general principle,

> "I start with the broad principle (which I do not intend in any way to be definitive) that a duty of confidence arises when confidential information comes to the knowledge of a person (the confidant) in circumstances where he has notice, or is held to have agreed, that the information is confidential, with the effect that it would be just in all the circumstances that he should be precluded from disclosing the information to others. I have used the word 'notice' advisedly, in order to avoid the (here unnecessary) question of the extent to which actual knowledge is necessary; though I of course understand knowledge to include circumstances where the confidant has deliberately closed his eyes to the obvious."

To that general principle, Lord Goff recognised three limiting principles:

(1) the general principle is premised upon information being confidential and can therefore generally have no application once the information has entered the "public domain";
(2) the duty of confidentiality does not apply to useless information nor to trivia;
(3) confidentiality may in certain circumstances be negated by public interest.

Attempts at definition

3–02   Lord Goff's statement of general principle is, as he stated, not intended to be definitive in that it does not seek to define confidential information or to determine when a person is to be taken as having notice that information is confidential. Nor do the cases provide any single, comprehensive formula.

In some cases the courts have deliberately avoided any such attempt, preferring the approach that confidential communications can be recognised without further definition.

[1] [1990] 1 A.C. 109 at 281.

38

A notable example is the decision of Ungoed-Thomas J. in *Argyll v. Argyll*,[2] which established the protectability of marital confidences. The parties had been through a highly publicised divorce. The ex-husband sold his story to a Sunday newspaper. The plaintiff obtained an injunction to restrain publication. The defendants unsuccessfully argued that the relationships which could give rise to a duty of confidentiality were confined to those which were contractual or professional, or where public security was involved.

Ungoed-Thomas J. said[3]:

"If this were a well-developed jurisdiction doubtless there would be guides and tests to aid in exercising it. But if there are communications which should be protected and which the policy of the law recognises should be protected ... then the court is not to be deterred merely because it is not already provided with fully developed principles, guides, tests, definitions and the full armament for judicial decision. It is sufficient that the court recognises that the communications are confidential, and their publication within the mischief which the law as its policy seeks to avoid, without further defining the scope and limits of the jurisdiction."

In other cases, attempts have been made to identify and analyse the essential features.

In *Coco v. A. N. Clark (Engineers) Ltd*[4] Megarry J. identified three features **3–03** if, apart from contract, a case of breach of confidence is to succeed:

(1) the information must be of a confidential nature;
(2) the information must have been communicated in circumstances importing an obligation of confidence;
(3) there must be unauthorised use[5] of the information.

This threefold classification has been adopted in many subsequent cases, although Lord Denning M.R. said in *Durnford & Elliott v. Johnson & Firth Brown*[6] that there was a fourth requirement, that enforcement of confidentiality should not be unreasonable.

Information must be objectively confidential and its confidentiality must affect the recipient

The importance of the distinction between the first and second features is the **3–04** recognition that information must be objectively confidential, and not merely treated as such, in order to attract protection; but it does not follow that because the features are separable they are necessarily unlinked.

In relation to the requirement that the information should be of a confidential nature, Sir Robert Megarry V.-C. referred to the difficulties of definition, in a commercial setting, in *Thomas Marshall Ltd v. Guinle*[7]:

---

[2] [1967] 1 Ch. 302.
[3] *ibid.* at 330.
[4] [1969] R.P.C. 41 at 47.
[5] "Unauthorised use" might be taken to mean unauthorised by the confider or unauthorised by law. We therefore prefer the word "misuse". This requirement is discussed at para. 3–13, below.
[6] [1978] F.S.R. 143 at 148.
[7] [1979] 1 Ch. 227 at 248.

"It is far from easy to state in general terms what is confidential information or a trade secret. Certain authorities were cited, but they did not carry matters very far. Plainly 'something which is public property and public knowledge' is not confidential: see *Saltman Engineering Co. Ltd v. Campbell Engineering Co. Ltd* (1948) 65 R.P.C. 203, 215, *per* Lord Greene M.R. On the other hand, 'something that has been constructed solely from materials in the public domain may possess the necessary quality of confidentiality: for something new and confidential may have been brought into being by the application of the skill and ingenuity of the human brain. Novelty depends on the thing itself, and not upon the quality of its constitutent parts': *Coco v. A. N. Clark (Engineers) Ltd* [1969] R.P.C. 41, 47, a case that was not cited, but in part draws on the *Saltman* case, which was. Costs and prices which are not generally known may well constitute trade secrets or confidential information: see *Herbert Morris Ltd v. Saxelby* [1916] 1 A.C. 688, 705, referring to prices."

He went on to suggest, as a matter of principle, four elements which might assist in identifying confidential information in an industrial or trade setting:

(1) the party claiming confidentiality must believe that release of the information would be injurious to him or of advantage to his rivals or others;
(2) the party claiming confidentiality must believe that the information is confidential, *i.e.* not already in the public domain;
(3) his belief under the two previous heads must be reasonable;
(4) the information must be judged in the light of the usage and practices of the particular industry or trade concerned.

Sir Robert Megarry was there viewing the matter primarily in terms of the confider's belief, but it must be equally pertinent, when considering whether the information has the necessary element of confidentiality, to consider the matter through the eyes of the reasonable person in the position of the alleged confidant. This point was made by Cross J. in *Printers & Finishers Ltd v. Holloway*,[8] in the case of an ex-employee, in the following example:

"Suppose such a man to be told by his new employers that at this or that stage in the process they encounter this or that difficulty. He may say to himself: 'Well, I remember that on the corresponding piece of machinery in the other factory such-and-such a part was set at a different angle or shaped in a different way': or again, 'When that happened we used to do this and it seemed to work,' 'this' being perhaps something which he had been taught when he first went to the other factory, or possibly an expedient which he had found out for himself by trial and error during his previous employment.

Recalling matters of this sort is, to my mind, quite unlike memorising a formula or list of customers or what was said (obviously in confidence) at a particular meeting. The employee might well not realise that the feature or expedient in question was in fact peculiar to his late employer's process and factory; but even if he did, such knowledge is not readily separable from his general knowledge of the flock printing process and his acquired

---

[8] [1965] R.P.C. 239 at 256.

skill in manipulating a flock printing plant, and I do not think that any man of average intelligence and honesty would think that there was anything improper in his putting his memory of particular features of his late employer's plant at the disposal of his new employer. The law will defeat its own object if it seeks to enforce in this field standards which would be rejected by the ordinary man."

The same concept is echoed in the judgment of Megarry J. in *Coco v. Clark*,[9]   **3–05** when dealing with the second requirement, that the information must have been communicated in circumstances importing an obligation of confidence:

"From the authorities cited to me, I have not been able to derive any very precise idea of what test is to be applied in determining whether the circumstances import an obligation of confidence. ... It may be that that hard-worked creature, the reasonable man, may be pressed into service once more; for I do not see why he should not labour in equity as well as at law. It seems to me that if the circumstances are such that any reasonable man standing in the shoes of the recipient of the information would have realised that upon reasonable grounds the information was being given to him in confidence, then this should suffice to impose upon him the equitable obligation of confidence. In particular, where information of commercial or industrial value is given on a business-like basis and with some avowed common object in mind, such as a joint venture or the manufacture of articles by one party for the other, I would regard the recipient as carrying a heavy burden if he seeks to repel a contention that he was bound by an obligation of confidence: see the *Saltman*[10] case at 216."

The Law Commission[11] considered whether different principles should govern confidentiality of information of a commercial or industrial nature from other categories of information, but concluded that such a distinction was impracticable and unnecessary.

FACTORS NEGATING CONFIDENTIALITY

Information required to be made public

The courts will refuse to attach the quality of confidence to information   **3–06** which the law itself requires to be made public. In *Initial Services Ltd v. Putterill*[12] the plaintiffs sought to restrain a former employee from publishing information about an alleged price fixing agreement between the plaintiffs and other companies. The defendant pleaded in his defence that the plaintiffs were party to an agreement which ought to have been registered under the Restrictive Practices Act 1956. The plaintiffs applied unsuccessfully to strike out the allegation. Lord Denning M.R. said[13]:

"If the allegations of the defence are correct, there was an agreement or arrangement between these laundry firms which should have been registered. If it had been registered, particulars of it would have been entered in the register. Once on the register, any individual on paying the

[9] [1969] R.P.C. 41 at 48.
[10] (1948) 65 R.P.C. 203.
[11] Report Cmnd 8388 (1981), para. 2.11.
[12] [1968] 1 Q.B. 396. See para. 6–07, below.
[13] *ibid.* at 406.

requisite amount, I think one shilling, could have obtained full particulars of that agreement or arrangement. Now I ask myself: Is this laundry company entitled to say that that information is confidential, seeing that they ought to have supplied it themselves to the registrar, and it would then have been made public? There is an argument at least that such information was not within the realm of confidence to which the master could hold his servant."

Intention to publish

In *Times Newspapers Ltd v. MGN Ltd*[14] Sir Thomas Bingham M.R. expressed considerable doubt whether the necessary quality of confidence could attach to Lady Thatcher's memoirs in circumstances in which the book was shortly due to be published, although he expressed no final view and regretted that because of the timescale the decision whether to grant an interlocutory injunction had had to be made after brief argument and without full time for reflection.

There was a separate problem in that for other reasons it was impossible to define, sufficiently at least for the purposes of granting an injunction, which parts of the book were confidential.

It is suggested that the fact that the plaintiffs intended to publish the material did not prevent it from having the quality of confidence prior to its intended publication.

Many examples could be given. A company may intend to apply for a patent. That involves publication of the secret. It would be surprising if an employee or other person to whom the details were imparted in confidence, or a third party who obtained them from such a person, could contend that the information lacked the quality of confidence because the company intended to publish it.

It would be surprising if the Chancellor of the Exchequer's budget proposals were held not to have the quality of confidence on the day before the budget, because he was intending to publish them.[15]

The same would apply to a company's yearly or half-yearly results in advance of publication.

In *Shelley Films Ltd v. Rex Features Ltd*[16] an injunction was granted to restrain disclosure of details of a film costume prior to the film's release.

Trivial or useless information

3–07   The rule that confidentiality does not attach to trivial or useless information reflects the underlying rationale of the jurisdiction. The reasoning was expressed by Deane J. in *Moorgate Tobacco Co. Ltd v. Philip Morris Ltd (No. 2)*[17] as follows:

"Like most heads of exclusive equitable jurisdiction, its rational basis does not lie in proprietary right. It lies in the notion of an obligation of conscience arising from the circumstances in or through which the

---

[14] [1993] E.M.L.R. 443.
[15] Or take the D-day landing plans referred to by Bingham L.J. in *Spycatcher* in the Court of Appeal [1990] 1 A.C. 109 at 215. See para. 3–08, below.
[16] [1994] E.M.L.R. 134.
[17] (1984) 156 C.L.R. 414 at 438.

information was communicated or obtained. Relief under the jurisdiction is not available, however, unless it appears that the information in question has 'the necessary quality of confidence about it' (*per* Lord Greene M.R., *Saltman*[18]) and that it is significant, not necessarily in the sense of commercially valuable (see *Argyll v. Argyll*[19]) but in the sense that the preservation of its confidentiality or secrecy is of substantial concern to the plaintiff."

In *Spycatcher*[20] Scott J. referred as an example to *McNicol v. Sportsman's Book Stores*,[21] where the plaintiff was the originator of a betting system based on the age of the moon. Maugham J. refused an injunction to protect its alleged confidentiality. Scott J. said that:

"The ground for the refusal was that the information was 'perfectly useless'."[22]

In *Stephens v. Avery*[23] the plaintiff revealed to a friend details of a lesbian relationship with a woman who was murdered. The friend passed the information to a newspaper, which published it. Sir Nicolas Browne-Wilkinson V.-C. refused to strike out a claim against the confidant and the newspaper for damages for breach of confidence. One of the grounds unsuccessfully relied upon by the newspaper was that the information was mere gossip or "trivial tittle-tattle" outside the protection of the law.[24] Rejecting this argument, Sir Nicolas Browne-Wilkinson said[25]:

"As to the submission that there is no confidentiality in tittle-tattle and gossip, Mr. Wilson relied on a passage in the *Coco* case [1969] R.P.C. 41, 48, where Megarry, J. said:
> ' ... I doubt whether equity would intervene unless the circumstances are of sufficient gravity; equity ought not to be invoked merely to protect trivial tittle-tattle, however confidential.'

Since the *Coco* case was exclusively concerned with information which was of industrial value, those remarks were plainly obiter dicta. Moreover, I have the greatest doubt whether wholesale revelation of the sexual conduct of an individual can properly be described as 'trivial' tittle-tattle. Again, although it is true that the passage I have quoted occurs in that part of the judgment which deals with the nature of information which can be protected, it is to be noted that the judge appeared to be considering when equity would give a remedy, not dealing with the fundamental nature of the legal right. If, as I think he was, Megarry J. was saying that the discretion to grant an injunction or to award damages would not be exercised in a case which was merely trivial, I agree. But the exercise of

[18] [1948] 65 R.P.C. 203 at 215.
[19] [1967] Ch. 302 at 329.
[20] [1990] 1 A.C. 109 at 149.
[21] (1930) McG.C.C. 116.
[22] *McNicol* may also be seen as a case in which the plaintiff did not come to court with "clean hands". See para. 6–25, below.
[23] [1988] 1 Ch. 449.
[24] *ibid.* at 452.
[25] *ibid.* at 454.

such a discretion can only be decided in the light of all the circumstances. Those cannot be known until there has been a trial."

Although Sir Nicolas Brown-Wilkinson V.-C. saw the question of triviality as a factor going to the exercise of the court's discretion, rather than to the principle whether a duty of confidence was owed, in *Spycatcher* Lord Goff recognised it as a "limiting principle ... that the duty of confidence applies neither to useless information, nor to trivia."[26]

If a matter is not such that the preservation of its confidentiality would be thought by a person of ordinary honesty and intelligence to be of any substantial concern to the plaintiff, there is sense in not attaching to it any duty of confidence.

Public domain

3–08   In the *Spycatcher* case Lord Goff described the expression "public domain" as meaning:

> "no more than that the information in question is so generally accessible that, in all the circumstances, it cannot be regarded as confidential."[27]

The essence of a secret is that it is not publicly known. The essence of the law of confidentiality is that it is designed to protect secrecy. If information is known to the public at large, the law of confidentiality cannot apply to it.

Bingham L.J. gave a vivid illustration in the *Spycatcher*[28] case in the Court of Appeal:

> "Forty-four years ago there can have been few, if any, national secrets more confidential than the date of the planned invasion of France. Any Crown servant who divulged such information to an unauthorised recipient would plainly have been in flagrant breach of his duty. But it would be absurd to hold such a servant bound to treat the date of the invasion as confidential on or after (say) 9 June 1944 when the date had become known to the world. A purist might say that the Allies, as confiders and owners of the information, had by their own act destroyed its confidentiality and so disabled themselves from enforcing the duty, but the common sense view is that the date, being public knowledge, could no longer be regarded as the subject of confidence."

That example is at one end of the spectrum, but the authorities show that the expression "public domain" is not limited to that type of case. Information may be said to be in the public domain which, although not in fact known to the public at large, is accessible by means not involving use of information imparted on a confidential basis. There the problem is more complex.

3–09   In deciding whether or not in such a case the information should be regarded as confidential, the degree of accessability is obviously an important factor. Cross J. said in *Franchi v. Franchi*[29]:

[26] [1990] 1 A.C. 109 at 282.
[27] *ibid.* at 282.
[28] *ibid.* at 215.
[29] [1967] R.P.C. 149 at 152–153.

"Clearly a claim that the disclosure of some information would be a breach of confidence is not defeated simply by proving that there are other people in the world who know the facts in question besides the man as to whom it is said that his disclosure would be a breach of confidence and those to whom he has disclosed them.

There appear to be no English cases on this branch of the law of trade secrets, but the plaintiffs referred me to the United States case of *Vulcan Detinning Co. v. Assam* (1918) 185 N.Y. App. Div. 399 . . . where it was held that the fact that a German and a Dutch firm had complete knowledge of the process in question which one of the defendants (an employee of the plaintiffs) had disclosed to the other defendant was no bar to the plaintiff's success. If it is not impertinent for me to say so, that seems to me sound sense. It must be a question of degree depending on the particular case, but if relative secrecy remains, the plaintiff can still succeed.[30]"

What amounts to "relative secrecy" can be a difficult matter. Information may be public within one circle, but not another, as it may be public in Mauritius but not in Manchester.

Accessability may also depend on the skills and knowledge of the particular defendant, which may therefore also be a relevant factor. Suppose, for example, that a company, C, consulted a solicitor, S, with a view to litigation on its behalf against an ex-employee, E, to restrain him from using certain technical know-how in his employment by another company. Suppose that another company in the industry, hearing of the dispute, approached S or an employee of S and offered him money to provide it with details of the same know-how. Suppose further that the technical know-how was not exclusive to C, and was capable of being acquired from other legitimate sources by a person with E's skills, but only by someone with his skills. E might well be entitled to regard as being within the "public domain" know-how which he knows that he could acquire by his own skills and knowledge from another public source, whereas S (or his employee) could say no such thing.

If E were obliged to continue to treat the information as confidential that could inhibit his proper ability to develop and use his own skills, and might place him under a disadvantage compared with others in his sphere of employment. No such considerations would apply to S (or his employee).

In each case the decision should accord with the usage and practices of the relevant industry or profession (factors which Sir Robert Megarry in *Thomas Marshall Ltd v. Guinle*[31] regarded as pertinent to the question whether the information possessed the necessary quality of confidence) and the standards of the man of average intelligence and honesty (invoked by Cross J. in *Printers & Finishers Ltd v. Holloway*[32]).

In this context it is instructive to consider the decisions of the Court of Appeal in *Woodward v. Hutchings*[33] and *Schering Chemicals Ltd v. Falkman Ltd.*[34]

In *Woodward v. Hutchins* the Court of Appeal discharged an injunction **3–10** against a former press relations agent to a group of singers who had embarked

---

[30] See also *Spycatcher* [1990] 1 A.C. 109 at 260, *per* Lord Keith; *Commonwealth of Australia v. John Fairfax & Sons Ltd* (1980) 147 C.L.R. 39 at 54, *per* Mason J.
[31] [1979] 1 Ch. 227 at 248.
[32] [1965] R.P.C. 239 at 256.
[33] [1977] 1 W.L.R. 760.
[34] [1982] 1 Q.B. 1.

on the publication in the media of details of the group's private lives, including what was described by Lord Denning M.R. as "a very unsavoury episode in a Jumbo Jet". The plaintiffs failed on two grounds.

First, it was held that since the group had retained the press agent "to have themselves presented to the public in a favourable light", they could not complain afterwards if he revealed unfavourable details, it being in the public interest that the truth should be known.

Secondly, it was held that the information was not confidential because it was in the public domain. Lord Denning said[35]:

> "But what is confidential? As Bridge L.J. pointed out in the course of the argument, Mr Hutchins, as a press agent, might attend a dance which many others attended. Any incident which took place at the dance would be known to all present. The information would be in the public domain. There could be no objection to the incidents being made known generally. It would not be confidential information. So in this case the incident on the Jumbo Jet was in the public domain. It was known to all passengers on the flight. Likewise with several other incidents in the series."

3–11   But suppose instead that the defendant had been a solicitor, instructed by one or more of the group in connection with the incident in the aircraft. It is hard to conceive that the court would in that case have refused an injunction restraining him from selling the story to the media.

In *Schering Chemicals Ltd v. Falkman Ltd*[36] the plaintiffs manufactured a pregnancy testing drug marketed as "Primodos". An issue arose as to its safety and it was withdrawn from the market. The plaintiffs retained the first defendants to give the plaintiffs' executives media and public relations training in order to counteract bad publicity, and for this purpose they supplied to the first defendants a large amount of information about the drug. The first defendants' team included the second defendant, Elstein, a professional broadcaster. He subsequently, without the plaintiffs' permission, approached a television company and gave them information from which they made a documentary on the drug. It was contended on their behalf that the information on which the film was based was all available to the public. The Court of Appeal by a majority (Lord Denning M.R. dissenting) upheld an injunction against the broadcaster and the television company restraining the broadcasting of the film.

Templeman L.J. said[37]:

> "In my judgment, when Mr Elstein agreed for reward to take part in the training course and received and absorbed information from Schering, he became under a duty not to use that information and impliedly promised Schering that he would not use that information for the very purpose which Schering sought to avoid, namely, bad publicity in the future, including publicity which Schering reasonably regarded as bad publicity. Schering reasonably regard the film 'The Primodos Affair' as bad publicity based on information which they supplied to Mr Elstein to enable him to

---

[35] [1977] 1 W.L.R. 760 at 764.
[36] [1982] 1 Q.B. 1.
[37] *ibid.* at 37.

advise Schering. Mr Elstein could have made a film based on Primodos if he had not taken part in the training programme, but 'The Primodos Affair' film only came into existence because Mr Elstein received from Schering information for one purpose and used that information for another purpose, for his own gain and to the detriment, as they reasonably believe, of Schering."

In both *Woodward v. Hutchins* and *Schering Chemicals Ltd v. Falkman Ltd* **3–12** the defendants' professional skills were engaged to produce good publicity for the plaintiffs and were used by them to produce bad publicity. This was regarded as a reason for refusing an injunction in the former case; but for granting it in the latter case (where paradoxically, the public interest in knowing the truth about Primodos was far greater than any public interest in the private lives of a group of singers). Unless the engagement was in some way disreputable, it is suggested that the approach in *Schering Chemicals Ltd v. Falkman Ltd* is to be preferred. But the more important difference is in their approach to the question of confidentiality and the public domain.

The simplest and most satisfactory explanation of *Woodward v. Hutchins* is that there was nothing in the defendant's engagement which required him to regard as confidential the behaviour of the plaintiffs in a public place. If, on the other hand, the plaintiffs had consulted a solicitor about the incident in the aircraft, he would have been under a duty to use the information given to him for the purpose for which it was given and not otherwise.

In *Schering Chemicals Ltd v. Falkman Ltd* information was given to the defendants in confidence, and although such information might be obtained from other sources, it was nevertheless perceived by the plaintiffs (reasonably in the eyes of the court) that the defendants would do harm to the plaintiffs if the programme, compiled from information supplied in confidence, were broadcast on a major television network, using information supplied in confidence as a springboard.[38] If the decision is still good law it can only be on that limited basis; but doubt has been expressed[39] whether it can stand with the decision in the *Spycatcher* case.[40]

Misuse

It is an essential ingredient of the action for breach of confidence that **3–13** confidential information has been or is threatened to be, misused.[41] The principle is self-evident, but determining what is misuse can present difficult questions.

Where a duty of confidence exists, misuse need not be intentional in order to found liability.[42] This is not to be confused with the situation where the nature of the information and position of the parties are such that someone of ordinary intelligence and honesty in the shoes of the recipient would be likely to use the

---

[38] The springboard doctrine is discussed further in Chap. IV, below.
[39] Lord Oliver, "Spycatcher: Confidence, Copyright and Contempt" (1989) *Israel Law Review*, Vol. 23, No. 4, at 422.
[40] [1990] 1 A.C. 109.
[41] The debatable question whether the misuse must also cause detriment is discussed in Chap. VI.
[42] *Seager v. Copydex Ltd* [1967] 1 W.L.R. 923.

information, consciously or unconsciously, without any apprehension of being under restraint; in such a case the recipient's defence to an allegation of breach of confidence would not be that the alleged breach was unintentional, but that he owed no duty.[43]

There is no definitive formulation of what constitutes misuse. Misuse will typically take the form of disclosure to another, but it need not do so. An ex-employee may misuse his former employer's customer list without disclosing it to anyone else. Conversely, not every disclosure of information imparted in confidence will amount to misuse. What constitutes misuse must in each case depend on the scope of the duty owed.

Factors justifying disclosure

In *Tournier v. National Provincial and Union Bank*[44] the Court of Appeal held that the duty of confidence owed by a banker to his customer is impliedly subject to qualifications, which Bankes L.J. said could not be exhaustively defined, but could be classified under four headings:

(1) where disclosure was made with the express or implied consent of the customer;
(2) where disclosure was made under compulsion of law;
(3) where there was a duty to the public to disclose;
(4) where the interests of the bank required disclosure.

Such factors are not unique to the relationship of banker and customer, but involve considerations of wider application. Although Bankes L.J. referred to the qualifications as implied qualifications of an implied contractual duty of secrecy, the underlying considerations are equally relevant to the parallel jurisdiction in equity.

Express or implied consent

3–14   A person cannot be in breach of a duty of confidence to another by disclosure of information or material to which the other consents. Consent to disclosure may be express or implied, and general or limited. A person seeking life insurance, who gives information about his health to his insurance broker, impliedly consents to the broker passing on the information to the underwriter, but not to the press.

Disclosure required by law

3–15   The law cannot at the same time require a person to treat information as confidential and compel him to disclose it, and therefore disclosure required by law cannot be misuse.[45] Such requirement may arise in a variety of ways.

A number of statutory provisions require the disclosure of information otherwise confidential.[46] In litigation, a duty of confidence to another is no bar

---

[43] *Printers & Finishers Ltd v. Holloway* [1965] R.P.C. 239 at 256–257.
[44] [1924] 1 K.B. 461 at 473.
[45] The subject of confidentiality and foreign law raises separate problems as to which see Chap. XII, below.
[46] In *Tournier v. National Provincial & Union Bank* [1924] 1 K.B. 461 at 473 Bankes L.J. gave the example of the Bankers Books Evidence Act 1879.

to discovery, although the court in its discretion will only compel the production of otherwise confidential documents if it considers it necessary to do so.[47] Nor is duty of confidence to another a ground for refusal by a witness to answer questions or produce documents if ordered to do so by a court or tribunal of competent jurisdiction, although again a court will require a witness to disclose otherwise confidential information only if disclosure is necessary for attainment of justice in the particular case.[48]

Duty to the public

The courts have recognised that a person may lawfully disclose a confidence **3–16** to the extent that its disclosure is required to prevent serious harm. Sometimes the matter is approached in terms of any duty being qualified or negated, and sometimes in terms of public interest affording a defence to a breach of duty. It is suggested that the first is more accurate, although it may be pedantic to complain of the use of the phrase "public interest defence" since it has become so common. This subject is discussed in further detail below.[49]

Disclosure required in the interests of the confidant

The important word here is "required". Disclosure or use of confidential **3–17** information will often be motivated by self-interest, without being in any sense necessary. But there may be circumstances in which the confidant has a real need to be permitted to disclose or use such information and where the courts will not imply or impose an obligation preventing him from doing so. Brennan J. captured the flavour when he referred in *Esso Australia Resources Ltd. v. Plowman*[50] to cases "where disclosure of the material is fairly required for the protection of the party's legitimate interests". What is "fairly required" and what are "legitimate interests" will necessarily depend on the circumstances and the nature of the relationship between the confider and confidant.

One type of case which may be seen as falling within this category is that of the ex-employee who has learned confidential information during his employment, which has become inseparable from the general skill and knowledge that he needs to use for earning his living.

Another purpose for which it may be necessary for a party to refer to information otherwise confidential is in order to establish or protect his legal rights against other parties or to defend himself.

In *Hassneh Insurance v. Mew*[51] Colman J. held that the implied contractual duty of confidence which arises between the parties to an arbitration agreement is subject to the qualification that it does not prevent disclosure of the award "if it is reasonably necessary for the establishment or protection of an arbitrating

---

[47] *D. v. N.S.P.C.C.* [1978] A.C. 171; *Science Research Council v. Nasse* [1980] A.C. 1028; *British Steel Corporation v. Granada Television Ltd* [1981] A.C. 1096.

[48] *Duchess of Kingston's Case* (1776) 20 St.Tr. 355 at 386–391; *Garner v. Garner* (1920) 36 T.L.R. 196; *Attorney-General v. Mulholland and Foster* [1963] 2 Q.B. 477; *Attorney-General v. Clough* [1963] 1 Q.B. 773; *D. v. N.S.P.C.C.* [1978] A.C. 171 at 238 and 243; *British Steel Corporation v. Granada Television Ltd* [1981] A.C. 1096; *Macmillan Inc. v. Bishopsgate Investment Trust plc* [1993] 1 W.L.R. 1372. See also Contempt of Court Act 1981, s.10.

[49] See Chap. VI, below.

[50] [1994–1995] 183 C.L.R. 10 at 36.

[51] [1993] 2 Ll.Rep. 243 at 249.

party's legal rights *vis-à-vis* a third party". In so holding Colman J. drew on the judgments of the Court of Appeal in *Tournier*.[52]

3–18   In *Lillicrap v. Nalder*[53] property developers sued their solicitors for negligently failing to advise them on rights of way affecting their title to property which they bought when the defendants were acting for them. Negligence was admitted, but the solicitors disputed the plaintiffs' claim that, if properly advised, they would not have entered into the transaction. They sought to allege that on previous occasions they had advised the plaintiffs on similar matters affecting other properties and that their advice had been ignored. On an interlocutory application the judge refused to allow the solicitors to refer in their pleadings to previous retainers, and ordered that they deliver up to the plaintiffs all confidential documents relating to those retainers and refrain from publishing them. He said:

> "The bringing of a claim for negligence in relation to a particular retainer will normally be a waiver of privilege and confidence for facts and documents relating to that retainer, but not without more for those relating to other discrete retainers."

The Court of Appeal agreed with that statement of principle, saying that the waiver could only extend to matters relevant to an issue in the proceedings. But, said Dillon L.J.[54]:

> "the waiver must go far enough, not merely to entitle the plaintiff to establish his cause of action, but to enable the defendant to establish a defence to the cause of action if he has one."

The Court of Appeal accordingly reversed the judge's decision. A confider cannot therefore rely on confidence to prevent the confidant from defending himself against subsequent attack by the confider.

3–19   Suppose, however, that the attack had come from someone other than the confider. Supppose, for example, that criticism of a hospital consultant's treatment of a case (*e.g.* involving alleged euthanasia) by other members of staff led to his prosecution, or to professional disciplinary proceedings,[55] or to the health authority taking steps under his contract to suspend or dismiss him. Grave injustice might be done to the doctor if he were not free to disclose matters concerning the patient which he would otherwise be required to treat as confidential.

Another example would be that of a solicitor who (not uncommonly) acted for a person buying a property with a mortgage loan and for the mortgagee. Suppose that the borrower defaulted and the mortgagee sued the solicitor, alleging that the affair had been a mortgage fraud and that the solicitor was a party to it. It might be important to the solicitor's defence to refer to otherwise

---

[52] [1924] 1 K.B. 461.
[53] [1993] 1 W.L.R. 94.
[54] *ibid.* at 99.
[55] In *Duncan v. Medical Practitioners Disciplinary Committee* [1986] 1 N.Z.L.R. 513 (N.Z. High Court) and *R. v. Institute of Chartered Accountants of England and Wales, ex p. Brindle* [1994] B.C.C. 297 at 312, *per* Hirst L.J., it was recognised that a professional person was entitled to use confidential information to defend himself against disciplinary charges.

confidential information concerning the transaction or other aspects of the purchaser's affairs or previous transactions.[56]

It is suggested that the legitimate interests of the confidant may in appropriate cases include disclosure to another party who has a legitimate interest in the matter, for example, disclosure by a wholly owned subsidiary to its holding company.

A possible approach is to say that it is all a matter for the court's discretion. In **3–20** *Webster v. James Chapman & Co.* Scott J. said[57]:

"The court must, in each case where protection of confidential information is sought, balance on the one hand the legitimate interests of the plaintiff in seeking to keep the confidential information suppressed and on the other hand the legitimate interests of the defendant in seeking to make use of the information. There is never any question of an absolute right to have confidential information protected. The protection is the consequence of the balance to which I have referred coming down in favour of the plaintiff."

Equitable relief is always discretionary. But an essential ingredient of the action for breach of confidence, before reaching any question of discretion, is that there must be actual or threatened misuse of confidential information. What constitutes misuse depends on the scope of the duty, which is not a matter of discretion but a matter of law, requiring analysis of the facts and application of principle.

In so far as a contractual duty is relied upon, determining its scope is a matter of contractual analysis. In so far as an equitable duty is relied upon, there is force in the observation that:

"equitable principles are best developed by reference to what conscionable behaviour demands of the defendant not by 'balancing' and then overriding those demands by reference to matters of social or political opinion."[58]

Preservation of confidentiality may affect the interests of the confider, the confidant and other people (including the public at large). There has been more discussion of the extent to which duties of confidence should be qualified so as to permit disclosure in cases of potential harm to others than in cases of potential harm to the confidant. But the judgment of Bankes L.J. in *Tournier v. National Provincial and Union Bank*[59] illustrates that there is scope for the courts to recognise a qualification of a duty of confidence, not only where disclosure is necessary to prevent harm to others, but also where disclosure is necessary for the protection of the confidant.

---

[56] The position is not, however, entirely clear, for it has been stated by the Court of Appeal that solicitors and barristers are not entitled, without their client's consent, to refer to privileged communications in order to defend themselves against an application for a wasted costs order: *Ridehalgh v. Horsefield* [1994] Ch. 205. See para. 18–02 below.

[57] [1989] 3 All E.R. 939 at 945.

[58] *Smith v. Kline & French Ltd v. Department of Community Services* [1990] F.S.R. 617 at 663, *per* Gummow J.

[59] [1924] 1 K.B. 461.

Reasonableness

3–21   In *Dunford & Elliott v. Johnson & Firth Brown*[60] Lord Denning M.R. held that the three requisites of Megarry J. in *Coco v. Clark*[61] did not cover the full ground and that there was a further principle, that the courts would recognise and enforce confidentiality only to the extent that it was reasonable to do so.

This principle has not been explicitly followed in later cases, but there is no doubt that the concept of the reasonable man has influenced the development of the law of confidentiality. It has found expression in various forms.

First, in *Coco v. Clark*[62] itself Megarry J. pressed into service "that hard-worked creature, the reasonable man" in determining whether information should be regarded as confidential.

Secondly, in many cases the difficult question has been not whether there is any duty of confidence but what is its scope.

3–22   In *Smith Kline & French v. Community Services*[63] a question arose as to the extent of the duty owed by a government department to a pharmaceutical company in relation to confidential information supplied for the purpose of obtaining approval of a drug. On appeal the court, after referring to Megarry J.'s judgment in *Coco v. Clark*, said[64]:

> "However, this test does not give guidance as to the scope of an obligation of confidence, where one exists. Sometimes the obligation imposes no restriction on use of the information, as long as the confidee does not reveal it to third parties. In other circumstances, the confidee may not be entitled to use it except for some limited purpose. In considering these problems, and indeed the whole question, it is necessary not to lose sight of the basis of the obligation to respect confidences:
> > 'It lies in the notion of an obligation of conscience arising from the circumstances in and through which the information was communicated or obtained.'
> This is quoted from *Moorgate Tobacco Co. Ltd. v. Philip Morris Ltd. (No. 2)* (1984) 156 C.L.R. 414 at 438, *per* Deane J., with whom the other members of the court agreed ... . Similar expressions recur in other cases: see *Seager v. Copydex Ltd* [1967] R.P.C. 349 at 368:
> > 'The law on this subject ... depends on the broad principle of equity that he who has received information in confidence shall not take unfair advantage of it.'
> To avoid taking unfair advantage of it does not necessarily mean that the confidee must not use it except for the confider's limited purpose. Whether one adopts the 'reasonable man' test suggested by Megarry J. or some other, there can be no breach of the equitable obligation unless the court concludes that a confidence reposed has been abused, that unconscientious use has been made of the information."

3–23   In determining the scope of any obligation (or what would be "unconscientious use" of the information) the court is bound to be influenced by

---

[60] [1978] F.S.R. 143 at 148.
[61] [1969] R.P.C. 41 at 47.
[62] *ibid.* at 48.
[63] (1991) 28 F.C.R. 291.
[64] *ibid.* at 303–304.

consideration of what is reasonable, and there are plenty of examples among English cases: *Tournier v. National Provincial and Union Bank*[65] (banker); *Printers & Finishers Ltd v. Holloway*[66] (employee); *Hellewell v. Chief Constable of Derbyshire*[67] (police).

Thirdly, in relation to the so-called public interest defence,[68] consideration of the reasonableness of the confidant's behaviour features in the courts' judgments. See, for example, the judgment of Bingham L.J. in *W v. Egdell*,[69]

> "Where a man has committed multiple killings under the disability of serious mental illness, decisions which may lead directly or indirectly to his release from hospital should not be made unless a reasonable authority is properly able to make an informed judgment that the risk of repetition is so small as to be acceptable. A consultant psychiatrist who becomes aware, even in the course of a confidential relationship, of information which leads him, in the exercise of what the court considers a sound professional judgment, to fear that such decisions may be made on the basis of inadequate information and with a real risk of consequent danger to the public is entitled to take such steps as are reasonable in all the circumstances to communicate the grounds of his concern to the responsible authorities."

Necessity of identification of information claimed to be confidential

Information alleged to be confidential must be specific in the sense that it is **3–24** clear and identifiable as confidential.[70] The problem arises especially with alleged trade secrets, where elements of the information for which protection is sought may be in the public domain or within a former employee's general expertise. In some cases there may be confidentiality about a system even if it is made up of parts which are familiar. In *Under Water Welders & Repairers Ltd v. Street and Longthorne* Buckley J. said[71]:

> "The fact that all the individual units of equipment that are employed in a particular operation may be articles that can be obtained in the general market and the fact that systems are well known to those concerned in whatever sort of activity is involved, does not mean that there cannot be *some degree of confidentiality* about the way in which they are used to achieve a particular result." (Emphasis added.)

It is, however, for the plaintiff to establish with particularity what is alleged to be confidential.

Further, it is a cardinal rule that an injunction must be framed in such a way that the party affected can know with certainty what he is or is not allowed to

---

[65] [1924] 1 K.B. 461.
[66] [1965] R.P.C. 239 at 256.
[67] [1995] 1 W.L.R. 804.
[68] See Chap. VI, below.
[69] [1990] 1 Ch. 359 at 424. See also *Hellewell v. Chief Constable of Derbyshire* [1995] 1 W.L.R. 804 at 810, *per* Laws J.
[70] *Amway Corporation v. Eurway International Ltd* [1974] R.P.C. 82 at 86–87; *Potters-Ballotini Ltd v. Weston-Baker* [1977] R.P.C. 202 at 205–206; *O'Brien v. Komesaroff* (1982) 150 C.L.R. 310 at 324–328; and *Fraser v. Thames Television Ltd* [1984] 1 Q.B. 44 at 63.
[71] [1968] R.P.C. 498 at 506–507.

do. In *Potters-Ballotini Ltd v. Weston-Baker*[72] and *Lawrence David Ltd v. Ashton*[73] applications for interlocutory injunctions to restrain alleged misuse of confidential information, which was insufficiently defined, were refused for that reason.

Those cases concerned alleged trade secrets, but the problem also arose in *Times Newspapers Ltd v. MGN Ltd*,[74] in which an unsuccessful attempt was made to restrain the unauthorised, advance publication of extracts from Lady Thatcher's memoirs. Leggatt L.J. said:

> "It is a matter of regret that because the plaintiffs are constrained to concede that vital parts of the book should be excepted from the scope of any injunction, and because the drafting of such an exception could not, in my judgment, be satisfactorily achieved, as the plaintiffs' draft demonstrates, the continued pirating of passages from the book cannot be effectually restrained by the plaintiffs, whatever prospects they may enjoy of eventually recovering damages."

Who may sue?

3–25   The person suing must be someone to whom the relevant duty of confidence is owed. In *Fraser v. Evans*[75] the plaintiff prepared a confidential report for the Greek Government. A copy of the report was leaked to a newspaper and the plaintiff sought an injunction to prevent publication or use of its contents. It was held that the plaintiff had no standing to complain. Lord Denning M.R. said[76]:

> "The jurisdiction is based not so much on property or on contract as on the duty to be of good faith. ... But the party complaining must be the person who is entitled to the confidence and to have it respected. He must be a person to whom the duty of good faith is owed. ... There is no doubt that Mr Fraser was himself under an obligation of confidence to the Greek Government. ... The Greek Government entered into no contract with Mr Fraser to keep it secret. ... They were the people to say aye or no whether it should be communicated elsewhere, or be published generally. It follows that they alone have any standing to complain if anyone obtains the information surreptitiously or proposes to publish it."

An interesting question is what happens when the right to use confidential information, *e.g.* technical know-how, is "assigned". It has been suggested that, if confidential information is not property, the "assignor" cannot pass to the "assignee" his personal right to have the information treated as confidential, and therefore the "assignee" cannot sue to enforce a duty of confidence[77]; but has at most a right to compel the "assignor" to take action.[78]

---

[72] [1977] R.P.C. 202 at 206.
[73] [1991] 1 All E.R. 385 at 393.
[74] [1993] E.M.L.R. 443 at 448.
[75] [1969] 1 Q.B. 349.
[76] *ibid.* at 361.
[77] See the judgment of Hope J.A. in the Supreme Court of New South Wales in *Moorgate Tobacco Co. Ltd v. Philip Morris Ltd* (1982) 64 F.L.R. 387 at 404. The point was not referred to in the judgment of Deane J. in the High Court of Australia (1984) 156 C.L.R. 414.
[78] Professor Cornish, *Intellectual Property: Patents, Copyright, Trade Marks and Allied Rights* (2nd ed., 1989) para. 8–44.

In *Morison v. Moat*[79] the defendant was held to owe a duty of confidence to the plaintiff in respect of the recipe for "Morison's Universal Medicine", details of which were supplied by the plaintiff's father to the defendant's father. Turner V.-C. stressed that:

> "what we have to deal with here is, not the right of the Plaintiffs against the world, but their right against the Defendant."[80]

and he distinguished *Canham v. Jones*[81] as a case (unlike *Morison v. Moat*[82]) based on property and not confidence. The injunction against the defendant was therefore based not on an assignment of a proprietary right, but on the principle that the defendant owed a duty in conscience towards the plaintiff to respect the original confidence in which the information was supplied.

If therefore the original confider has passed confidential information to another person, with the intention that the latter shall enjoy the full benefit of it, that person may be entitled to prevent disclosure or misuse of the information by the confidant on the principle of the duty of good faith referred to by Lord Denning in *Fraser v. Evans*.[83]

---

[79] (1851) 9 Hare 241; (affirmed (1852) 21 L.J. Chanc. (N.S.) 248).
[80] *ibid.* at 258.
[81] (1813) 2 V. & B. 218.
[82] (1851) 9 Hare 241; (affirmed (1852) 21 L.J. Chanc. (N.S.) 248).
[83] [1969] 1 Q.B. 349.

CHAPTER IV

DURATION OF CONFIDENTIALITY

General principle

4–01   In principle a duty of confidentiality should cease if the information loses the quality of confidence, whether through passage of time, loss of secrecy or other change of circumstances. Most of the reported cases concern loss of secrecy.

Loss of secrecy

4–02   In 1928 the House of Lords held in *O. Mustad & Son v. Dosen*[1] that an injunction could not be granted to restrain misuse of confidential information about a "secret" process after the plaintiffs had applied for a patent for it, since by that publication, in the words of Lord Buckmaster, "The secret, as a secret, had ceased to exist."[2]

   In later cases the courts have considered whether the same principle applies where the publication has been made not by the plaintiff, but by a third party or by the defendant.

Terrapin and the springboard theory

4–03   Because *Mustad* was not reported until 1964, it was not cited in *Terrapin Ltd v. Builders' Supply Company (Hayes) Ltd*, decided by Roxburgh J. in 1959.[3] *Terrapin* is significant for the introduction of the so-called "springboard doctrine".

   The defendants manufactured portable buildings to the plaintiffs' design. The plaintiffs disclosed to the defendants in confidence details of proposed modifications. Subsequently the defendants sold in competition with the plaintiffs a form of portable building containing many of the plaintiffs' revised features. It was argued for the defendants that the plaintiffs' conduct in selling buildings and publishing brochures which disclosed all their features discharged any obligation of confidentiality by the defendants, since the information could no longer be regarded as secret. Roxburgh J. rejected this argument. Founding on Lord Greene's judgment in *Saltman's* case, he said[4]:

---

[1] [1964] 1 W.L.R. 109.
[2] *ibid.* at 111.
[3] But not fully reported at first instance until [1967] R.P.C. 375, although the decision of the Court of Appeal was reported at [1960] R.P.C. 128.
[4] [1967] R.P.C. 375 at 391–392.

"As I understand it, the essence of this branch of the law, whatever the origin of it may be, is that a person who has obtained information in confidence is not allowed to use it as a spring-board for activities detrimental to the person who made the confidential communication, and spring-board it remains even when all the features have been published or can be ascertained by actual inspection by any member of the public. The brochures are certainly not equivalent to the publication of the plans, specifications, other technical information and know-how. The dismantling of a unit might enable a person to proceed without plans or specifications, or other technical information, but not, I think, without some of the know-how, and certainly not without taking the trouble to dismantle. I think it is broadly true to say that a member of the public to whom the confidential information had not been imparted would still have to prepare plans and specifications. He would probably have to construct a prototype, and he would certainly have to conduct tests. Therefore, the possessor of the confidential information still has a long start over any member of the public ... . It is, in my view, inherent in the principle upon which the *Saltman* case rests that the possessor of such information must be placed under a special disability in the field of competition in order to ensure that he does not get an unfair start ... ."

The *Mustad* and *Terrapin* debate

In *Peter Pan Manufacturing Corporation v. Corsets Silhouette Ltd*[5] the **4-04** relationship between the reasoning of Roxburgh J. in the *Terrapin* case and of Lord Buckmaster in *Mustad's* case arose for consideration, but Pennycuick J. did not find it necessary to decide the issue, which he referred to as one of considerable general importance and difficulty.

The point arose again in *Cranleigh Precision Engineering Ltd v. Bryant.*[6] The defendant, as managing director of the plaintiffs, invented an above-ground swimming pool with two unique features. While still in the plaintiffs' employment, he learned of a Swiss patent for a similar pool but lacking the two special features. After leaving the plaintiffs' employment the defendant obtained an assignment of the Swiss patent. The plaintiffs brought two actions against him. In the first action, they obtained an injunction to restrain him from using the knowledge he had gained in confidence about the plaintiffs' product, in particular the two unique features. In the second action they claimed an injunction to prevent the defendant from using the information obtained by him about the Swiss patent and sought damages.

The defendant argued that confidentiality ceased when information entered the public domain; that all confidentiality concerning the Swiss patent ended on its publication; and that in so far as *Terrapin* provided a precedent for injunctive relief after the supposed secret had ceased to be secret as a result of publication, it was inconsistent with *Mustad's* case.

Roskill J. found that the defendant acted in breach of his duty to the plaintiffs in concealing from them the information which he had learned about the Swiss

---

[5] [1963] R.P.C. 45; [1964] 1 W.L.R. 96. *Peter Pan* is interesting on a separate point for its recognition of an account of profits as a remedy available for breach of confidence.
[6] [1966] R.P.C. 81.

patent and in taking no steps to protect the plaintiffs against its possible consequences; and that he acted in breach of confidence in using, after he left the plaintiffs, the information which he had acquired about the Swiss patent and its possible effect on the plaintiffs' business for his own advantage. He distinguished *Mustad's* case on the ground that in that case the plaintiffs had themselves been the publishers of the specification, whereas in the present case the publishers were the Swiss applicants. He accordingly followed *Terrapin* and granted an injunction and damages.

4–05   The reasoning of Roskill J. was criticised by the Law Commission in its Report on Breach of Confidence[7]:

> "Notwithstanding the view of *Mustad* taken by Roskill J., however, it is doubtful whether an obligation of confidence, as distinguished from any express or implied contractual obligation which may exist between the parties, can persist after the information in question has reached the public domain, irrespective of the way in which it has come into the public domain. Suppose an inventor has given particulars of a certain device to a draughtsman who accepts an obligation in respect of that information. The draughtsman passes on that information to a third party, who knows that he is obtaining the information in breach of the draughtsman's obligation of confidence. Subsequently all the details of the device are independently published in a trade journal. Is the third party thereafter subject to indefinite restraint in making and marketing the device at a time when any of his trade rivals are free to exploit the information in the article?"

The Law Commission also referred to divergent opinions in the American courts between those which followed *"the Rule in Shellmar"*,[8] according to which a defendant could be enjoined in perpetuity from using what he had once misused, and those which followed *"the Rule in Conmar"*,[9] under which a defendant who had misused information might nevertheless legitimately use it once it had passed into the public domain. The Law Commission preferred the latter.

It is suggested that this is the better view. The ratio of *Mustad* was that "The secret, as a secret, had ceased to exist"[10] on its publication to the world at large. That would have been equally so, whether it had been published by a third party or by a person to whom it was entrusted. It is difficult to see how there can be a duty to preserve the existence of something which has ceased to exist.[11]

However, in *Speed Seal Products Ltd v. Paddington*[12] the Court of Appeal, founding on the reasoning of Roskill J. in *Cranleigh Precision Engineering*,[13] held that a duty of confidentiality does not cease upon publication of confidential information to the public at large by the person himself owing the duty.

[7] Cmnd. 8388 (1981), at para. 4.29.
[8] *Shellmar Products Co. v. Allen-Qualley Co.* (1936) 87 F.2d 104.
[9] *Conmar Products Corporation v. Universal Slide Fastener Co. Inc.* (1949) 172 F.2d 150.
[10] [1964] 1 W.L.R. 109 at 111.
[11] *X AG v. A Bank* [1983] 2 All E.R. 464 at 475, *per* Leggatt J.:
"[Counsel] ... raised the curious concept of confidentiality which no longer was ... . The reality of the matter is that once confidence escapes, like air from a punctured tyre, the confidence is no more."
[12] [1985] 1 W.L.R. 1327.
[13] [1966] R.P.C. 81.

Spycatcher[14]

Peter Wright, a former intelligence officer, in breach of his contract of service **4-06** with the Crown and of the provisions of the Official Secrets Act 1911, contracted with Australian publishers for the publication of his memoirs of his service in MI5. The book was distributed world wide. The *Sunday Times* bought the serialisation rights and published the first instalment shortly before the book went on sale in the USA. The Attorney-General sought an injunction to restrain the *Sunday Times* from serialising further extracts. The House of Lords held unanimously that the *Sunday Times* had acted in breach of duty of confidence in publishing the first extract, but refused by a majority to grant an injunction to prevent further serialisation because the entire book was now in the public domain.

In considering the position of the *Sunday Times*, the House also considered the position of Peter Wright, although he was not a party to the proceedings. It was necessary to do so, because the argument on behalf of the Crown was that an English court would grant an injunction against Peter Wright, on the ground that an obligation of confidence still attached to him, and that such duty continued to attach in conscience to third parties. This was described by Lord Goff as a "formidable argument"[15] and caused him to consider the premise on which it was based, *viz.* the continuing duty of confidence said to be owed by Peter Wright.

Lord Goff approached the issue from the starting point that a duty of **4-07** confidence can only apply in respect of information which is confidential; from which the logical consequence should be that, if confidential information ceases to be confidential, the duty of confidence should end (as held in *Mustad*). Referring to *Cranleigh Precision Engineering* Lord Goff said[16]:

> "... it seems to me that the true basis of the decision was that, in reliance on the well known judgment of Roxburgh J. in the 'springboard' case, *Terrapin Ltd v. Builders' Supply Co. (Hayes) Ltd* [1967] R.P.C. 375, the defendant was in breach of confidence in taking advantage of his own confidential relationship with the plaintiff company to discover what a third party had published and in making use, as soon as he left the employment of the plaintiff company, of information regarding the third party's patent which he had acquired in confidence."

Lord Goff did not consider that *Cranleigh Precision Engineering*[17] supported any general principle that, if it is a third party who puts the confidential information into the public domain, the confidant would not be released from his duty of confidence. He therefore disapproved the reasoning in *Speed Seal*.[18] Lord Goff reserved the question (since it had not been fully argued) whether some more limited obligation (analogous to the springboard doctrine) might nevertheless continue to rest on a confidant who, in breach of confidence, destroyed the confidential nature of the information entrusted to him, whilst he rejected the broader argument of the Crown that a confidant who publishes

---

[14] *Attorney-General v. Guardian Newspapers Ltd (No. 2)* [1990] 1 A.C. 109.
[15] *ibid.* at 285.
[16] *ibid.* at 285.
[17] [1966] R.P.C. 81.
[18] [1985] 1 W.L.R. 1327.

confidential information to the world can remain under a further obligation not to disclose it, simply because it was he who wrongly destroyed its confidentiality. This rejection of the Crown's main argument forms an essential part of the *ratio* of Lord Goff's speech, because, in Lord Goff's words, it enabled him to "consider the specific issues in the case unfettered by its otherwise considerable force".[19]

4–08 Lord Keith and Lord Brightman dealt with the matter more concisely. Lord Keith cited Lord Widgery's judgment in *Attorney-General v. Jonathan Cape Ltd*,[20] in which he held that the confidential character of public confidences lapsed when publication would no longer do public harm. Lord Keith said that the question whether Mr Wright would be at liberty to publish *Spycatcher* in England did not arise for immediate consideration, but, since such publication would cause no further harm:

> "... the case for an injunction now against publication by or on behalf of Mr Wright would in my opinion rest upon the principle that he should not be permitted to take advantage of his own wrongdoing."[21]

Lord Brightman said[22]:

> "In my opinion the reason why the court would, or might, grant an injunction against Wright if he now brought himself within the jurisdiction and sought to publish *Spycatcher* here, is not that such an order would recognise a subsisting duty of confidence, but that it would impede the unjust enrichment of Wright, or preclude him from benefiting, tangibly or intangibly, from his own wrongdoing; or perhaps that the copyright of the work would in equity be vested in the Crown, as suggested by three of Your Lordships."

4–09 A majority of the House therefore rejected the concept of a duty of confidentiality subsisting after the information had lost the quality of confidence while leaving open the possibility of an injunction against repetition of wrongful disclosure by the wrongdoer, based not on a continuing duty but on the desirability of preventing him from profiting from his past breach.

Lord Griffiths, dissenting, considered that an injunction would have been granted against Mr Wright on the basis of a continuing duty of confidence and ought to have been granted against the *Sunday Times*.

Lord Jauncey considered that an injunction would have been granted against Peter Wright, and should have been granted also against the *Sunday Times* if to do so would have been effective to prevent further serialisation, but that the grant of such an injunction would be a vain act in circumstances in which that any other newspaper could publish whatever extracts it wished.

Injunction to prevent profit from past misconduct?

4–10 The concept of granting injunctive relief, not for the purpose of preventing a threatened breach of duty, but for the purpose of preventing a wrongdoer from

---

[19] *Attorney-General v. Guardian Newspapers Ltd (No. 2)* [1990] 1 A.C. 109 at 289.
[20] [1976] 1 Q.B. 752 at 771.
[21] *ibid.* at 259.
[22] *ibid.* at 266.

profiting from past misconduct, presents problems. Since it is not based on any continuing duty of confidence, but on the broader principle that wrongdoers should not be allowed to take advantage of their wrongdoing, there would be no justification for limiting it to cases of breach of confidence; but it is unclear whether it would apply to all forms of civil liability, or only to deliberate acts, or to acts involving some form of moral obliquity (and, if so, how they are to be defined).

If an injunction could be granted on the broad principle that a wrongdoer should not be permitted to profit from his wrongdoing, an exceptionally strong case on the facts arose in *Kaye v. Robertson*.[23] In that case a journalist entered without permission a hospital room where the plaintiff was recovering from brain injuries and took photographs of him without his fully informed consent. The defendants not only obtained the photographs by trespass, but their conduct towards the plaintiff was a "monstrous invasion of his privacy" (*per* Bingham L.J.[24]) committed for commercial gain. However, the Court of Appeal (Glidewell, Bingham and Leggatt, L.JJ.) held that it had no power in law to grant an injunction prohibiting the defendants from publishing the photographs so as to prevent them from profiting from the taking of the photographs, *i.e.* from their own trespass, attractive though the argument might appear to be.[25]

In the *Spycatcher* case Lord Goff gave the example of convicted criminals being invited to sell their stories on release from prison.[26] He observed that this is highly offensive to many people; but doubted whether that fact provided an appropriate basis for defining the scope of a confidant's civil obligations at common law.

Further, if the object is to prevent commercial profiteering from past misconduct, why should injunctive relief be limited to the wrongdoer and not extend to those co-operating with him for commercial profit? If the *Sunday Times* was guilty of breach of confidence in publishing Peter Wright's first instalment, why should it not itself have been prohibited from publishing further extracts in order to prevent it too from continuing to exploit a prior wrong to which it had been party? Only one of their Lordships, Lord Griffiths, would have gone that far.[27]

Conclusions on springboard

It is noteworthy that the House of Lords expressed no disapproval of the **4–11** decision in the *Cranleigh Precision Engineering*[28] case, nor of the springboard doctrine stated in *Terrapin*.[29] On the contrary, Lord Goff impliedly considered

---

[23] [1991] F.S.R. 62.

[24] *ibid.* at 70.

[25] *ibid.* at 69.

[26] [1990] 1 A.C. 109 at 289. It is not a novel practice. In 1874 the imposter in the *Titchborne* case, Arthur Orton (otherwise Thomas Castro, otherwise Sir Roger Titchborne, Bart.) was finally sent to prison for 14 years. On his release, encouraged by a newspaper, he published his story.

[27] See also the judgment of the European Court of Human Rights in *Observer and Guardian v. United Kingdom* (1991) 14 E.H.R.R. 153 at 195–196 and *Sunday Times v. United Kingdom (No. 2)* (1991) 14 E.H.R.R. 229 at 243–244, echoing Lord Oliver's objections in his dissenting speech in *Spycatcher (No. 1)* [1987] 1 W.L.R. 1248 at 1318. The matter is discussed further in Chap. XI, below.

[28] [1966] R.P.C. 81.

[29] [1967] R.P.C. 375.

both to be right, although in relation to the former only as he interpreted it, *i.e.* as a springboard case (and not as applied by the Court of Appeal in the *Speed Seal*[30] case).

As the Law Commission argued in its report on Breach of Confidence,[31] the springboard doctrine is not in total conflict with the principle that information cannot enjoy the protection of the action for breach of confidence once it has entered the public domain, but rather is a limited qualification of it. The object of the springboard doctrine is merely to ensure that the recipient of confidential information does not obtain an unfair start by misuse of information received in confidence. Subsequent decisions have confirmed that the protection given should be related to the unfair advantage which the defendant would otherwise obtain, and, accordingly, that an injunction should not normally extend beyond the period for which the unfair advantage is likely to continue.[32]

4–12   Lord Goff's analysis of the of the *Cranleigh Precision Engineering* case, in the passage cited above, may at first sight be thought somewhat elliptical. For, as Lord Goff stated, the principle of confidentiality can only apply to information to the extent that it is confidential and it can therefore ordinarily have no application to information which has entered the public domain.

The defendant's argument in the *Cranleigh Precision Engineering* case was that the third party's patent application put knowledge of the subject matter in the public domain, just as in the *Mustad* case. At first sight the argument appears cogent.

There were, however, two important features in *Cranleigh Precision Engineering* case. The first was that not only did the defendant's knowledge of the third party's patent come to him in his capacity as the company's managing director from its patent agents, but he immediately realised its significance for the company from facts which were not in the public domain. The second is that, although he was under a duty to the company to bring his knowledge of the patent to the board's attention, he deliberately concealed it in order to make use of it to his advantage and against the interests of the company. Roskill J. emphasised these matters in his judgment. Accordingly, as between himself and the plaintiffs, it did *not* lie in the defendant's mouth to rely on the "public domain" defence to justify his use of information which he had deliberately and wrongfully concealed from his employers.

Typically cases of breach of confidence involve the passing by A to B of confidential information, which B wrongly divulges to C. *Cranleigh Precision Engineering* does not fall into that pattern, but is rather a case of an agent using his position as agent to acquire information which is pertinent to his principal's affairs and which is not known to his principal, and then using that information for his personal benefit without the principal's fully informed consent. This is a classic example of breach of fiduciary duty by an agent, for which the courts will grant an injunction, damages or an account of profits. It is analogous in its essential elements to *Phipps v. Boardman*.[33]

---

[30] [1985] 1 W.L.R. 1327.

[31] Cmnd. 8388 (1981), para. 4.31.

[32] *Potters-Ballotini Ltd v. Weston-Baker* [1977] R.P.C. 202 at 206, *per* Lord Denning M.R. ("Although a man must not use such information as a springboard to get a start over others, nevertheless that springboard does not last for ever.") *Roger Bullivant Ltd v. Ellis* [1987] F.S.R. 172 at 184, *per* Nourse L.J. ("All these observations support the view that the injunction should not normally extend beyond the period for which the unfair advantage may reasonably be expected to continue. That is in my judgment the period for which an injunction should normally be granted in springboard cases.")

[33] [1967] 2 A.C. 46. See para. 2–04, above.

Passage of time and change of circumstances

In *Attorney-General v. Jonathan Cape Ltd*[34] Lord Widgery C.J. recognised in **4–13** the case of public confidences that:

> "There must, however, be a limit in time after which the confidential character of the information, and the duty of the court to restrain publication, will lapse."

He added that:

> "It may, of course, be intensely difficult in a particular case, to say at what point the material loses its confidential character, on the ground that publication will no longer undermine the doctrine of Cabinet responsibility."

The principle that, on information losing its confidential character, the duty of confidence ceases must apply equally in the case of private confidences. In applying that principle, due attention must be paid in each case to the original purpose of the duty of confidence. In the case of private confidence, the duty exists "to protect the personal, private and proprietary interests of the citizen".[35] The duration of such duty will vary according to the nature of the information and the nature of the relationship.

It may be difficult, as in the case of public confidences, to identify the point at which such information loses its confidential character, and any statement of principle can only be expressed in general terms. The remarks which follow are intended merely to be illustrative.

The General Medical Council states in its advice to doctors on standards of professional conduct and medical ethics[36]:

> The fact of a patient's death does not of itself release a doctor from the obligation to maintain confidentiality. In cases where consent has not previously been given, the extent to which confidential information may properly be disclosed by a doctor after someone's death cannot be specified in absolute terms and will depend on the circumstances. These include the nature of the information disclosed, the extent to which it has already appeared in published material and the period which elapsed since the person's death."

The implication of the G.M.C.'s advice is that it regards the duty to a living patient as life long (subject to other qualifications, which are discussed in the chapter on medical confidence).

In the case of employees it is well recognised that termination of the employment will bring to an end the duty of confidence in relation to some forms of confidential information (that is, information which has become part of the employee's general skill and knowledge), but not in relation to the narrower band of information which may qualify for continued protection under the head of trade secrets.[37]

---

[34] [1976] 1 Q.B. 752 at 771.
[35] *Commonwealth of Australia v. John Fairfax & Sons Ltd* (1980) 147 C.L.R. 39 at 51, *per* Mason J.
[36] "Professional Conduct and Discipline: Fitness to Practice" (December 1993), para. 91.
[37] See Chap. XVI, below.

Trade secrets, too, may lose their confidentiality by other means than by entering the public domain. In *Thomas Marshall Ltd v. Guinle*[38] Sir Robert Megarry V.-C. suggested, *inter alia*, that, for information to constitute a trade secret, the party claiming confidentiality must reasonably believe that the release of the information would be injurious to him or of advantage to his rivals or others. A trade secret may cease to have that quality, for example, through changes in the confider's business or through technological advances rendering the trade secret obsolescent.

---

[38] [1979] 1 Ch. 227 at 248.

CHAPTER V

PUBLIC SECTOR CONFIDENTIALITY

The application of the doctrine of confidence to government secrets should **5–01**
not be confused with the doctrine of public interest immunity, which is part of
the law of evidence.[1] Public interest immunity (or Crown privilege as it used to
be known) has a long history. Under this doctrine, documents which would
otherwise be disclosable in litigation may be immune from production if wider
public interest so requires.

In *Conway v. Rimmer*[2] the House of Lords adopted the principle expressed **5–02**
by Lord Reid:

"I would therefore propose that the House ought now to decide that
Courts have and are entitled to exercise a power and duty to hold a balance
between the public interest, as expressed by a Minister, to withhold certain
documents or other evidence, and the public interest in ensuring the
proper administration of justice."

Lord Reid also observed that:

"Virtually everyone agrees that Cabinet minutes and the like ought not to
be disclosed until such time as they are only of historical interest."

Fortuitously, the first case in which the courts were asked to apply the
equitable doctrine of confidentiality to the workings of government in fact
concerned the publication of details of cabinet discussions. In *Attorney-General
v. Jonathan Cape Ltd*[3] the Attorney-General sought an injunction restraining
publication of Richard Crossman's *Diaries of a Cabinet Minister*. It was argued,
unsuccessfully, by the defendants that the principle underlying such cases as
Prince Albert v. Strange,[4] *Saltman*[5] and *Argyll*[6] should be restricted to private
relationships and not extend to Government secrets.

Lord Widgery C.J. said[7]:

---

[1] *D. v. N.S.P.C.C.* [1978] A.C. 171 at 241, *per* Lord Simon. Public interest immunity is discussed in
Chap. XXI, below.
[2] [1968] A.C. 910 at 952.
[3] [1976] 1 Q.B. 752.
[4] (1848) 1 Mac. & G. 25.
[5] (1948) 65 R.P.C. 203.
[6] [1967] Ch. 302.
[7] [1976] 1 Q.B. 752 at 769–770.

"I cannot see why the courts should be powerless to restrain the publication of public secrets, while enjoying the *Argyll* powers in regard to domestic secrets. Indeed, as already pointed out, the court must have power to deal with publication which threatens national security, and the difference between such a case and the present case is one of degree rather than kind. I conclude, therefore, that when a Cabinet Minister receives information in confidence the improper publication of such information can be restrained by the court, and his obligation is not merely to observe a gentleman's agreement to refrain from publication."

Lord Widgery went on to hold as a matter of principle that:

"The Attorney-General must show
    (a) that ... publication would be a breach of confidence;
    (b) that the public interest requires that the publication be restrained; and
    (c) that there are no other facts of the public interest contradictory of and more compelling than that relied upon."

This required a balancing exercise. Lord Widgery refused an injunction because 10 years and three general elections had passed since the events described in the diaries, and he concluded after reading the book that:

"I cannot believe that the publication at this interval of anything in volume one would inhibit free discussion in the Cabinet of today, even though the individuals involved are the same, and the national problems have a distressing similarity with those of a decade ago.[8]"

5–03   Lord Widgery's approach was followed by Mason J. in *Commonwealth of Australia v. John Fairfax & Sons Ltd.*[9] He said:

"However, the plaintiff must show, not only that the information is confidential in quality and that it was imparted so as to import an obligation of confidence, but also that there will be 'an unauthorised use of that information to the detriment of the party communicating it' (*Coco v. A. N. Clark (Engineers) Ltd*).[10] The question then, when the executive government seeks the protection given by equity, is: What detriment does it need to show?

The equitable principle has been fashioned to protect the personal, private and proprietary interests of the citizen, not to protect the very different interests of the executive government. It acts, or is supposed to act, not according to standards of private interest, but in the public interest. This is not to say that equity will not protect information in the hands of the government, but it is to say that when equity protects government information it will look at the matter through different spectacles.

---

[8] *Attorney-General v. Jonathan Cape Ltd* [1976] 1 Q.B. 752 at 771.
[9] [1969] R.P.C. 41 at 47.
[10] (1980) 147 C.L.R. 39 at 51–52.

It may be a sufficient detriment to the citizen that disclosure of information relating to his affairs will expose his actions to public discussion and criticism. But it can scarcely be a relevant detriment to the government that publication of material concerning its actions will merely expose it to public discussion and criticism. It is unacceptable in our democratic society that there should be a restraint on the publication of information relating to government when the only vice of that information is that it enables the public to discuss, review and criticise government action.

Accordingly, the court will determine the government's claim to confidentiality by reference to the public interest. Unless disclosure is likely to injure the public interest, it will not be protected."

This principle was approved and applied in the *Spycatcher* case.[11] In that case Peter Wright's book had been disseminated world wide to the extent of over a million copies and was freely available in the United Kingdom. There was therefore no longer a secret to protect, and any damage which might be caused had already been caused.

While the *Spycatcher* case was working its way through the English courts, **5–04** *Lord Advocate v. The Scotsman Publications Ltd*[12] was proceeding through the Scottish courts, reaching the House of Lords after the *Spycatcher* decision. The case concerned the memoirs of another former member of the security service, Anthony Cavendish. After permission to publish had been requested, and refused, he had 500 copies printed at his own expense. He provided 279 copies to private individuals, before giving an undertaking to the Crown not to distribute any further copies without advance notice. A copy came into the hands of *The Scotsman* newspaper, which published an article including some of the material.

The Government brought proceedings for an injunction to restrain further publication. They sought to distinguish *Spycatcher* on the grounds that Anthony Cavendish's memoirs, unlike Peter Wright's, were not in general circulation. It was conceded by the Government that the contents of the book did not include any material damaging to national security. But it was argued that publication was damaging, irrespective of the innocuous nature of the contents, because it would lower morale, encourage copy cats, and cause foreign security powers to lose confidence in the ability of the British security and intelligence services to protect their own secrets.

The House of Lords held that the combination of circumstances (that the book did not contain any material damaging to national security and that publication on a limited scale had already taken place) meant that the Government had no arguable case that further publication would do any material damage to the public interest. The contents were not going to be harmful, and in so far as the fact of publication might be harmful, it had already happened.

Lord Keith (with whose speech Lord Griffiths and Lord Goff agreed)[13] added:

"It was argued for the appellant that the dismissal of this appeal would

---

[11] [1990] 1 A.C. 109 at 258, *per* Lord Keith; 270, *per* Lord Griffiths and 283, *per* Lord Goff. See also Chap. IV, above.
[12] [1990] 1 A.C. 812.
[13] *ibid.* at 822–823.

have the effect that any newspaper which received an unsolicited book of memoirs by a present or former member of the Security or Intelligence Service would be free to publish it. That is not so. If there had been no previous publication at all and no concession that the contents of the book were innocuous the newspaper would undoubtedly itself come under an obligation of confidence and be subject to restraint. If there had been a minor degree of prior publication, and no such concession it would be a matter for further investigation whether further publication would be prejudicial to the public interest, and interim interdict would normally be appropriate."

It is implicit that it would be for the Government to have to establish that further publication would be detrimental to the public interest, following the judgments of Mason J. in *Commonwealth of Australia v. John Fairfax & Sons Ltd*[14] and of the House of Lords in the *Spycatcher* case.[15] Those judgments also addressed "detriment" and "public interest" not only in relation to government secrets, but in relation to the law of confidentiality more generally. There is room for debate about the principles applicable in relation to each: and about whether there are differences of principle in private and public cases, or merely differences of application reflecting differences in the subject matter. These are discussed in the next Chapter.

5–05   There seems no reason to suppose that the principles relating to public sector confidentiality are limited to central government. They may equally apply, it is suggested, to local government. Many activities formerly carried out by central or local government are now carried out by bodies variously described as NGOs (Non-Governmental Organisations), NDPBs (Non-Departmental Public Bodies), EGOs (Extra-Governmental Organisations) or QUANGOS (Quasi-Autonomous Non-Governmental Organisations). According to a government report, there were 1,345 NDPBs in 1994. According to a different survey, there were 5,521 non-elected bodies carrying out executive functions on behalf of the Government, of which 4,723 operated at local level.[16] Insofar as such bodies are carrying out functions comparable to those of government, comparable principles should apply to them.

In *Esso Australia Resources Ltd v. Plowman*[17] Mason C.J. (with whom Dawson and McHugh JJ. agreed) went further. The case arose from contracts for the supply of natural gas by oil companies to two public utilities. Disputes under the contracts were referred to arbitration. The oil companies wished to prevent commercially sensitive information from being disclosed outside the arbitration. Mason C.J. rejected the oil companies' argument that a duty of confidence was owed to them by virtue of the fact that information was provided in, and for the purposes of, the arbitration. He went on to suggest, *obiter*, that if such a duty were owed, the case should be viewed as one involving governmental secrets, rather than personal or commercial secrets, and therefore it would have to be established that the public interest demanded non-disclosure. He explained his reasoning as follows[18]:

[14] (1980) 147 C.L.R. 39.
[15] [1990] 1 A.C. 109.
[16] Andrew Marr, "Ruling Britannia" (1995) p. 78, citing from Public Bodies 1994, published by the Cabinet Office, and Democratic Audit of the UK, Paper 2, "Ego-Trip", Human Rights Centre, University of Essex/Charter 88 Trust, 1994.
[17] [1994–1995] 183 C.L.R. 10.
[18] *ibid.* at 32.

"The approach outlined in John Fairfax[19] should be adopted when the information relates to statutory authorities or public utilities because, as Professor Finn notes,[20] in the public sector '[t]he need is for compelled openness, not for burgeoning secrecy.' The present case is a striking illustration of this principle. Why should the consumers and the public of Victoria be denied knowledge of what happens in these arbitrations, the outcome of which will affect, in all probability, the prices chargeable to consumers by the public utilities?"

Mason C.J.'s approach differed from that adopted by the majority of the House of Lords in *British Steel Corporation v. Granada Television Ltd*,[21] as he recognised. Moreover, whether or not the principles relating to public sector confidentiality should apply to a public utility seeking to enforce an obligation of confidentiality, it is difficult to see why such principles should apply where a commercial organisation seeks to enforce an obligation of confidentiality against a public utility in order to protect its commercial secrets. There is, it is suggested, a fallacy in viewing the information which the oil companies were seeking to protect as government secrets.

---

[19] *Commonwealth of Australia v. John Fairfax & Sons Ltd* (1980) 147 C.L.R. 39.
[20] Finn, "Confidentiality and the 'Public Interest'" (1984) 58 *Australian Law Journal* 497 at 505.
[21] [1981] A.C. 1096.

CHAPTER VI

DETRIMENT, PUBLIC INTEREST AND "CLEAN HANDS"

DETRIMENT

6–01   In *Coco v. A. N. Clark (Engineering) Ltd*[1] Megarry J. observed:

"Some of the statements of principle in the cases omit any mention of detriment; others include it. At first sight, it seems that detriment ought to be present if equity is to be induced to intervene; but I can conceive of cases where a plaintiff might have substantial motives for seeking the aid of equity and yet suffer nothing which could fairly be called detriment to him, as when the confidential information shows him in a favourable light but gravely injures some relation or friend of his whom he wishes to protect. The point does not arise for decision in this case, for detriment to the plaintiff plainly exists."

6–02   In the *Spycatcher* case[2] opinions were divided. Lord Keith[3] said:

"It is worthy of some examination whether or not detriment to the confider of confidential information is an essential ingredient of his cause of action in seeking to restrain by injunction a breach of confidence. Presumably that may be so as regards an action for damages in respect of a past breach of confidence. If the confider has suffered no detriment thereby he can hardly be in a position to recover compensatory damages. However, the true view may be that he would be entitled to nominal damages. ... Further, as a general rule, it is in the public interest that confidences should be respected, and the encouragement of such respect may in itself constitute a sufficient ground for recognising and enforcing the obligation of confidence even where the confider can point to no specific detriment to himself. Information about a person's private and personal affairs may be of a nature which shows him up in a favourable light and would by no means expose him to criticism. The anonymous donor of a very large sum to a very worthy cause has his own reasons for wishing to remain anonymous, which are unlikely to be discreditable. He should surely be in a position to restrain disclosure in breach of confidence of his identity in

[1] [1969] R.P.C. 41 at 48.
[2] [1990] 1 A.C. 109.
[3] *ibid.* at 255–256.

connection with the donation. So I would think it a sufficient detriment to the confider that information given in confidence is to be disclosed to persons whom he would prefer not to know of it, even though the disclosure to him would not be harmful to him in any positive way. The position of the Crown, as representing the continuing government of the country may, however, be regarded as being special ... . The Crown ... as representing the nation as a whole, has no private life or personal feelings capable of being hurt by the disclosure of confidential information. In so far as the Crown acts to prevent such disclosure or to seek redress for it on confidentiality grounds, it must necessarily, in my opinion, be in a position to show that the disclosure is likely to damage or has damaged the public interest."

Lord Griffiths[4] considered that detriment, or potential detriment, to the confider must be established before a private individual was entitled to a remedy for breach of confidence, since the remedy was fashioned to protect the confider and not to punish the confidant, and therefore there was little point in extending it to a confider who did not need protection.

Lord Goff[5] wished to keep the point open, but observed that it might depend on how wide a meaning could be given to the word "detriment".

In *Smith Kline & French Laboratories (Australia) Ltd v. Department of Community Services*[6] Gummow J., after reviewing the authorities, noted that the issue remains open in Australia but expressed his view that: **6–03**

"The basis of the equitable jurisdiction to protect obligations of confidence lies ... in an obligation of conscience arising from the circumstances in or through which the information, the subject of the obligation, was communicated or obtained: *Moorgate Tobacco Co. Ltd v. Philip Morris Ltd (No. 2)*[7] ... . The obligation of conscience is to respect the confidence, not merely to refrain from causing detriment to the plaintiff. The plaintiff comes to equity to vindicate his right to observance of the obligation, not necessarily to recover loss or to restrain infliction of apprehended loss. To look into a related field, when has equity said that the only breaches of trust to be restrained are those that would prove detrimental to the beneficiaries?"

This shows a difference of approach in principle from that of Megarry J. in *Coco v. A. N. Clark (Engineering) Ltd*[8] who, although reserving his opinion, considered that at first sight detriment ought to be present if equity is to be induced to intervene. Moreover, if in principle the touchstone is the obligation of conscience to respect confidence, rather than to refrain from causing detriment, it may be questioned why the same should not apply equally in relation to public confidences (subject to any public interest defence).

There are, however, pragmatic considerations. The Law Commission[9] considered the effect of death on the action for breach of confidence. By section 1(1) of the Law Reform (Miscellaneous Provisions) Act 1934 all causes of **6–04**

---

[4] *Attorney-General v. Guardian Newspapers Ltd (No. 2)* [1990] 1 A.C. 109 at 270.
[5] *ibid.* at 281–282.
[6] [1990] F.S.R. 617 at 664.
[7] (1984) 156 C.L.R. 414 at 438.
[8] [1969] R.P.C. 41 at 48.
[9] *Breach of Confidence*, Cmnd. 8388 (1981), paras. 4.105–4.107.

action, except for defamation, subsisting against or vested in any person on his death survive against or, as the case may be, for the benefit of the estate. But there may be situations falling outside the scope of that section, as illustrated by the following example from the Law Commission's Report[10]:

"... there is the situation in which a person who has imparted information in confidence to another dies before any breach of confidence has taken place. His personal representatives will have a right of action for any subsequent breach only if the information is of a 'quasi proprietorial' character—such as information relating to 'know-how'—which can be regarded as an asset of the deceased person's estate. The personal representatives of a deceased patient cannot employ the action for breach of confidence to protect the relations or friends of the deceased from distress resulting from the doctor's disclosure of his deceased patient's confidences."

It is doubtful whether that would be a correct statement of law today. If a doctor who treated a celebrity suffering from AIDS during his final illness were subsequently to sell to a newspaper intimate details which had been revealed to him by his former patient in confidence, and in the expectation that the doctor would continue to respect that confidence after the patient's death, it is more probable that a court would regard the obligation of confidence as subsisting after his death[11]; and would grant to the personal representatives (depending on the circumstances) an injunction and/or an account of profits as the only effective means of enforcing the obligation.[12] In such a case it could not be said that the deceased would suffer detriment from the publication, but it would seem contrary to justice that the doctor should make a windfall from his breach of his obligation. Privilege may survive in favour of a deceased's estate[13] and it is hard to see why a court should not recognise the survival of an obligation of confidentiality.

It is suggested that the key, whether the case is approached in equity or in contract, lies in correctly identifying in each set of circumstances the nature of the obligation and the interest which it is intended to protect. This was the approach taken by Scott J. at first instance in the *Spycatcher* case. After citing *Moorgate Tobacco Co. Ltd v. Philip Morris Ltd (No. 2)*[14] and *Commonwealth of Australia v. John Fairfax & Sons Ltd*,[15] he said[16]:

"The dicta in these two cases place the origin of the duty of confidence not in contract, express or implied, but in equity. But the ambit of the duty of confidence imposed by equity will depend, in my view, on the same type of judicial approach to the surrounding circumstances of the case as that

[10] *Breach of Confidence*, Cmnd. 8388 (1981), para. 4.107.
[11] See para. 13–17, below.
[12] Compare *White v. Jones* [1995] 2 A.C. 207 at 268 where the House of Lords held that a solicitor whose negligence in drawing a will led to the inability of an intended beneficiary to inherit as the testator had intended, was liable to the intended beneficiary, because otherwise there would be no effective means of enforcing the obligation owed by the solicitor to the deceased.
[13] *Bullivant v. Attorney General for Victoria* [1901] A.C. 196.
[14] (1984) 156 C.L.R. 414.
[15] (1980) 147 C.L.R. 39.
[16] [1990] 1 A.C. 109 at 147–148.

adopted where an implicit term is treated as the basis of the duty. As long ago as 1893 the Court of Appeal concluded that there was no distinction between the duty of confidence placed on an agent by implied contract and that imposed on him by equity; see *Lamb v. Evans* [1893] 1 Ch. 218."

In the case of private confidences, the confider may have an interest in the information being kept confidential, regardless of whether disclosure would be positively harmful to him, for reasons which may be perfectly understandable (and which would be understood by any reasonable person in the position of the confidant). If so, for the reasons suggested by Lord Keith in the *Spycatcher* case, that should be sufficient to found a cause of action; and the question whether unauthorised disclosure in such circumstances is considered to involve "detriment" is an exercise in semantics. If on the other hand the confider has no substantial interest in the information being kept confidential, it would follow that the information would not possess the necessary quality of confidence to found an obligation of confidentiality.[17]

In the case of public confidences, the interest intended to be protected is the public interest, and it is therefore logical that the jurisdiction should only come into play in circumstances where disclosure would be injurious to the public interest. It is for that reason that cases of public confidence involve what Lord Goff referred to in the *Spycatcher* case as the additional requirement of establishing that the public interest would be harmed by publication.[18] Conversely, it is misleading in such cases to speak of a public interest defence, since the injurious effect of publication on the public interest is an ingredient required to be established in order for the jurisdiction to arise.

PUBLIC INTEREST

The defence of iniquity

The earliest manifestation of what has come to be referred to as the public **6–05** interest defence was the so-called defence of iniquity, which owed its origin to the judgment of Sir William Page-Wood V.-C. in *Gartside v. Outram.*[19]

Gartside v. Outram was reinterpreted, and the beginnings of a broader principle recognised, in *Weld-Blundell v. Stephens.*[20] The plaintiff sent a letter to the defendant, an accountant, instructing him to investigate the affairs of a company, with which he had dealings, and making libellous statements about those responsible for running the company. The defendant's partner carelessly left the letter at the company's office. Libel actions were successfully brought against the plaintiff by persons defamed in the letter (one of whom he described as "an ingenious thief"). The plaintiff sued the accountant for negligence.

The defendant argued that there was no duty of confidence in relation to the letter, since the libels amounted to a malicious wrong. The argument failed. Warrington and Scrutton L.JJ. interpreted *Gartside v. Outram* (questionably, perhaps) as a case in which the court had declined to exercise its equitable

---

[17] *Moorgate Tobacco Co. Ltd v. Philip Morris Limited (No. 2)* (1984) 156 C.L.R. 414 at 438. See Chap. III, above.
[18] [1990] 1 A.C. 109 at 283.
[19] (1857) 26 L.J.Ch. (N.S.) 113. See para. 1–11 above.
[20] [1919] 1 K.B. 520, affirmed [1920] A.C. 956.

jurisdiction in favour of the plaintiffs and left them to their remedy at law. Bankes and Warrington L.JJ. considered that there could be circumstances in which the duty of confidence would be overridden by a duty to the public, and they drew a distinction between a document concerning a past crime and a crime in contemplation.

Scrutton L.J. said[21]:

> "Under the decision in *Reg. v. Cox and Railton*[22], when the accused has consulted his solicitor after the commission of a crime for the legitimate purpose of being defended the communication is privileged, the privilege being that of the client. If then the solicitor in breach of this confidence and privilege announced his intention of informing the prosecution of the contents of his client's communication, I cannot believe that the Court would not restrain him before communication or give damages against him for breach of his contract of employment after communication, even though those damages were based on his having provided evidence to prove the client guilty of a crime he had in fact committed. The reason would be that the public policy that crime should be punished would be outweighed by the public policy that accused persons should be properly defended, and contracts necessary for their defence observed. There is a public policy in not lightly interfering with freedom of contract: *per* Jessel M.R. in *Printing and Numerical Registering Co. v. Sampson*."[23]

Scrutton L.J., however, was in a minority on the plaintiff's entitlement to damages, the majority (both in the Court of Appeal and in the House of Lords) holding that he was entitled to nominal damages only, since the damages which he had been ordered to pay in the libel actions were to be regarded as caused by his own wrongful acts.

In the House of Lords,[24] the defendant limited his argument to the latter issue of causation, but Viscount Finlay commented:

> "It would be startling if it were the law that an agent who is negligent in the custody of a letter handed to him in confidence by his principal might plead in defence that the letter was libellous. There may, of course, be cases in which some higher duty is involved. Danger to the State or public duty may supersede the duty of the agent to his principal. But nothing of that nature arises in this case."

6–06   In *Tournier v. National Provincial and Union Bank of England*[25] the Court of Appeal had to consider what duty of confidentiality was owed by a bank to its customer. The Court (Bankes, Scrutton and Atkin L.JJ.) held that there was necessarily implied into the contract between them a duty of confidentiality, but subject to qualifications.

Bankes L.J. said[26]:

> "On principle I think that the qualifications can be classified under four

[21] [1919] 1 K.B. 520 at 544.
[22] (1884) 14 Q.B.D. 153 at 175.
[23] (1875) L.R. 19 Eq. 462, 465.
[24] [1920] A.C. 956 at 965.
[25] [1924] 1 K.B. 461.
[26] *ibid.* at 473.

heads: (a) Where disclosure is under compulsion by law; (b) where there is a duty to the public to disclose; (c) where the interests of the bank require disclosure; (d) where the disclosure is made by the express or implied consent of the customer."

In relation to the second qualification Bankes L.J. said:

"Many instances of the second class might be given. They may be summed up in the language of Lord Finlay in *Weld-Blundell v. Stephens*,[27] where he speaks of cases where a higher duty than the private duty is involved, as where 'danger to the State or public duty' may supersede the duty of the agent to his principal."

Scrutton and Atkin L.JJ.,[28] agreed that the term necessarily to be implied into the contract between a bank and its customer must be subject to qualifications, entitling the bank to make disclosure in certain circumstances, including for prevention of or protection against frauds or crimes.

The contractual analysis

The contractual analysis begun in *Weld-Blundell* and *Tournier* was further **6–07** developed in *Initial Services Ltd v. Putterill.*[29] The plaintiffs ran a laundry. The defendant, who had been their sales manager, resigned and took with him various documents which, according to him, were part of or related to a price fixing agreement entered into between the plaintiffs and other launderers, but not registered, contrary to the Restrictive Practices Act 1956. The defendant passed the documents to a newspaper, which published two articles on the subject. The plaintiffs sued the defendant for breach of an implied term of his contract of employment not to disclose to third parties confidential information relating to the plaintiffs obtained during his employment. The defendant alleged in his defence that the plaintiffs were part of a cartel conducting business in breach of statute, and he denied that his disclosure of their activities was in breach of the implied term of the contract relied on by the plaintiffs. The plaintiffs applied, unsuccessfully, to strike out the paragraphs of the defence containing the defendant's allegations as disclosing no defence.

Breach of the provisions of the Restrictive Practices Act was not a criminal offence, and it was argued by the plaintiffs that the relevant qualification to the implied duty of confidentiality owed by an employee was limited to crime or fraud. This argument was rejected.

Lord Denning M.R. accepted that every contract of employment contained an implied obligation that the employee would not, during or after his employment, disclose information or documents received in confidence; but the obligation was subject to exceptions. As to the scope of the relevant exception, he said[30]:

"In *Weld-Blundell v. Stephens*,[31] Bankes L.J. rather suggested that the

[27] [1920] A.C. 956 at 965.
[28] [1924] 1 K.B. 46 at 480–481, 483–484 and 486.
[29] [1968] 1 Q.B. 396.
[30] *ibid.* at 405–406.
[31] [1919] 1 K.B. 520 at 527.

exception is limited to the proposed or contemplated commission of a crime or a civil wrong. But I should have thought that was too limited. The exception should extend to crimes, frauds and misdeeds, both those actually committed as well as those in contemplation, provided always —and this is essential—that the disclosure is justified in the public interest. ...

The disclosure must, I should think, be to one who has a proper interest to receive the information. Thus it would be proper to disclose a crime to the police; or a breach of the Restrictive Trade Practices Act to the registrar. There may be cases where the misdeed is of such a character that the public interest may demand, or at least excuse, publication on a broader field, even to the press."

Salmon L.J. said[32]:

"Suppose the servant had entered into a contract with the master not to disclose certain information, would that contract be enforceable or would it be illegal? To my mind that must depend on the circumstances of the particular case. Consider this case: the Restrictive Trade Practices Act, 1956, is an Act which certainly was very much concerned with the public interest. It imposed an obligation upon these plaintiffs to disclose to the registrar the agreements into which they had entered with their fellow launderers in relation to the supply of goods. That obligation was imposed in the public interest. ...

Suppose the master had said to the servant,
'We, of course, appreciate that these agreements into which we have entered ought in the public interest to be disclosed to the registrar, but we hope that the registrar will never find out about them. We propose to ignore our statutory obligation to disclose these agreements. You must agree with us that you will never make any disclosure about them to anyone.'
Suppose that the servant had agreed. I am by no means convinced that any court would do other than regard such an agreement as illegal on the ground that it was clearly contrary to the public interest. I do not think that the law would lend assistance to anyone who is proposing to commit and to continue to commit a clear breach of a statutory duty imposed upon him in the public interest."

Winn L.J. adopted the same approach, saying[33]:

"I agree with both of the judgments delivered by my Lords. I desire to say that for my own part my approach to this problem has been in substance identical with that of Salmon L.J. It seems to me that the proper function of an implied term of a contract is either to dot the i's and cross the t's of the express terms or to fill in some lacuna left by the contracting parties which must properly be filled by the implied term in order to give business efficacy, and produce the true intent of those contracting parties. As my

[32] [1968] 1 Q.B. 396 at 409–410.
[33] ibid. at 410–411.

Lord has said, the question whether or not a term properly to be implied in a contract is enforceable in law must be decided by asking whether it would have been enforced had it been an express term. I entirely agree, if I may respectfully say so, with that approach, which has been my own approach also to this problem."

To pose the question whether a term "properly to be implied" is enforceable may be said to be tortuous in that there cannot be "properly implied" into a contract a term which would be unenforceable; but the sense is clear, namely that the court should not imply a term requiring secrecy in circumstances where, if there were an express term to that effect, the court would refuse to enforce it as contrary to public policy.

The same analysis was advanced by Gummow J. in the Federal Court of Australia in *Corrs Pavey Whiting & Byrne v. Collector of Customs*.[34] Referring to *Gartside v. Outram*, he said that: **6–08**

"... any court of law or equity would have been extremely unlikely to imply in a contract between master and servant an obligation that the servant's good faith to his master required him to keep secret details of his master's gross bad faith to his customers. Likewise, before any express contractual obligation of confidence is enforced at law or in equity the term relied on must be valid at law."

He added[35] that where the plaintiff asserted a contractual right of confidence, the law of contract (supplemented by equitable defences where equitable relief was sought) sufficiently dealt with the matter. Where the plaintiff asserted an equitable duty of confidence, the principle applicable was no wider than that:

"... information will lack the necessary attribute of confidence if the subject matter is the existence or real likelihood of the existence of an iniquity in the sense of a crime, civil wrong or serious misdeed of public importance, and the confidence is relied upon to prevent disclosure to a third party with a real and direct interest in redressing such crime, wrong or misdeed."

In other words equity, following the law, would not impose an equitable obligation to do that which in contract would be unenforceable.

Misdeeds may include "anti-social" conduct in the sense of "activities which, whilst not in breach of the law, are seriously contrary to the public interest".[36] But that has to be judged according to generally accepted standards, as was emphasised by Sir Nicolas Browne-Wilkinson V.-C. in *Stephens v. Avery*[37] in relation to alleged sexual "wrongdoing":

"If it is right that there is now no generally accepted code of sexual morality applying to this case, it would be quite wrong in my judgment for any judge to apply his own personal moral views, however strongly held, in deciding the legal rights of the parties. The court's function is to apply the law, not personal prejudice. Only in a case where there is a generally

---

[34] (1987) 74 A.L.R. 428 at 449.
[35] *ibid.* at 450.
[36] *Francome v. Mirror Group Newspapers Ltd* [1984] 1 W.L.R. 892 at 895–896.
[37] [1988] 1 Ch. 449 at 454.

accepted moral code can the court refuse to enforce rights in such a way as to offend that generally accepted code."

Serious harm to the public

6–09 The reasoning which applies in cases of serious misdeeds has been extended to cases where there is serious danger of harm, without misconduct necessarily being the cause, but differing views have been expressed about the scope of the principle involved.

In *Beloff v. Pressdram Ltd*[38] Ungoed-Thomas J. said:

> "The defence of public interest clearly covers and, in the authorities does not extend beyond, disclosure, which ... must be disclosure justified in the public interest, of matters carried out or contemplated, in breach of the country's security, or in breach of law, including statutory duty, fraud, or otherwise destructive of the country or its people, including matters medically dangerous to the public; and doubtless other misdeeds of similar gravity."

By contrast, in *Woodward v. Hutchins*[39] Lord Denning M.R. took an altogether broader approach. He said,

> "There is no doubt whatever that this pop group sought publicity. They wanted to have themselves presented to the public in a favourable light so that audiences would come to hear them and support them ... . If a group of this kind seek publicity which is to their advantage, it seems to me that they cannot complain if a servant or employee of their afterwards discloses the truth about them. If the image which they fostered was not a true image, it is in the public interest that it should be corrected. *In these cases of confidential information it is a case of balancing the public interest in maintaining the confidence against the public interest in knowing the truth.*" (Emphasis added.)

In *Lion Laboratories Ltd v. Evans*[40] Griffiths L.J. said:

> "I am quite satisfied that the defence of public interest is now well established in actions for breach of confidence ... .
> I can see no sensible reason why this defence should be limited to cases in which there was been wrongdoing on the part of the plaintiffs. I believe that the so-called iniquity rule evolved because in most cases where the facts justified a publication in breach of confidence, it was because the plaintiff had behaved so disgracefully or criminally that it was judged in the public interest that his behaviour should be exposed. No doubt it is in such circumstances that the defence will usually arise, but it is not difficult

---

[38] [1973] 1 All E.R. 241 at 260.
[39] [1977] 1 W.L.R. 760 at 763–764. See Chap. III, above.
[40] [1985] Q.B. 526 at 550.

to think of instances where, although there has been no wrongdoing on the part of the plaintiff, it may be vital in the public interest to publish a part of his confidential information."

Obviously something may present a serious risk to the medical health of the public, national security, the administration of justice or a matter of comparable public importance such that it may fairly be regarded as vital in the public interest that a person possessing such information should be free to disclose it to an appropriate third party, whether or not the matter involves individual wrongdoing (by the Plaintiff or anyone else). As in the case of "iniquity", so also in the case of such information, it may be said that no court would imply a contractual obligation prohibiting such disclosure, or enforce an express contractual prohibition, and that such information would be regarded both at common law and in equity as lacking the necessary attribute of confidence to prevent such disclosure. It is perfectly possible to accommodate such an extension to *Gartside v. Outram*[41] within the framework of the analysis favoured by Gummow J. in the *Corrs Pavey* case, and there are strong grounds to do so. It would be wholly unsatisfactory if, for example, a hospital doctor were prevented by his contract of employment from notifying the Department of Health of an imminent risk to public health detected by him in the course of his hospital duties, whether misconduct was involved or not.

That is very different from the approach adopted by the Court of Appeal in *Woodward v. Hutchins*.[42] It could hardly be suggested that the group's desire to foster a good public image presented a danger to the public. Notwithstanding the absence of any such danger, the Court of Appeal considered that it was free to balance generally "the public interest in maintaining the confidence against the public interest in knowing the truth" and resolved in favour of the latter.

Spycatcher

In the *Spycatcher* case, Lord Goff said[43]:   **6–10**

" ... although the basis of the law's protection of confidence is that there is a public interest that confidences should be preserved and protected by the law, nevertheless that public interest may be outweighed by some other countervailing public interest which favours disclosure. This limitation may apply, as the learned judge pointed out, to all types of confidential information. It is this limiting principle which may require a court to carry out a balancing operation, weighing the public interest in maintaining confidence against a countervailing public interest favouring disclosure.

Embraced within this limiting principle is, of course, the so called defence of iniquity. In origin, this principle was narrowly stated, on the basis that a man cannot be made 'the confidant of a crime or a fraud': see *Gartside v. Outram* (1857) L.J.Ch. 113 at 114, *per* Sir William Page Wood V.-C. But it is now clear that *the principle extends to matters of which disclosure is required in the public interest*: see *Beloff v. Pressdram Ltd* [1973] 1 All E.R. 241 at 260, *per* Ungoed-Thomas J., and *Lion Laboratories*

---

[41] [1857] 26 L.J.Ch. (N.S.) 113.
[42] [1977] 1 W.L.R. 760.
[43] [1990] 1 A.C. 109 at 282–283.

Ltd v. Evans [1985] Q.B. 526 at 550, *per* Griffiths L.J. It does not however follow that the public interest will in such cases *require* disclosure to the media, or to the public by the media. There are cases in which a more limited disclosure is all that is *required*: see *Francome v. Mirror Group Newspapers Ltd* [1984] 1 W.L.R. 892. A classic example of a case where limited disclosure is *required* is a case of alleged iniquity in the Security Service. Here there are a number of avenues for proper complaint; these are set out in the judgment of Sir John Donaldson M.R." (Emphasis added.)

The principle recognised by Lord Goff is therefore limited to matters of which disclosure is *required* in the public interest, and then applies only to such form of disclosure as the public interest requires. In *Francome v. Mirror Group Newspapers Ltd*[44] the Court of Appeal upheld an interlocutory injunction restraining the defendants from general publication of tapped telephone conversations, which allegedly revealed breaches by a well-known jockey of the rules of racing and possibly the criminal law, but the court was willing for them to be disclosed to the Jockey Club and the police. It is difficult to see that the public interest would *require* disclosure, unless the matter concerned serious wrongdoing or some present, serious risk of the kind suggested in the extracts from *Beloff v. Pressdram Ltd* and *Lion Laboratories Ltd v. Evans*, set out above, to which Lord Goff referred. It is noteworthy that Lord Goff did not include reference to *Woodward v. Hutchins*, which was cited in argument, but the broader approach adopted in that case is by implication disapproved.

Although Lord Goff said that the application of the principle "may" (not must) "require a court to carry out a balancing operation", it is suggested that the nature of such a balancing exercise is limited to determining whether the perceived damage to the public is of such gravity as to make disclosure "vital in the public interest" (*per* Griffiths L.J. in *Lion Laboratories v. Evans Ltd*), rather than some more general inquiry whether it would be better from the public viewpoint if the confidence were breached than honoured.

The true principle underlying the "public interest defence"

6–11   On this reasoning, the true principle is not (as dicta in some cases suggest) that the court will permit a breach of confidence whenever it considers that disclosure would serve the public interest more than non-disclosure, but rather that no obligation of confidence exists in contract or in equity, in so far as the subject matter concerns a serious risk of public harm (including but not limited to cases of "iniquity") and the alleged obligation would prevent disclosure appropriate to prevent such harm.

This principle is consistent, in cases where confidence is founded on contract, with ordinary principles of contract law. Public considerations have led the courts to restrict freedom of contract by means of the doctrine that they will treat as unenforceable certain contracts whose performance would be contrary to public policy. However, in developing that doctrine the courts have exercised considerable restraint for reasons stated by Jessel M.R. in *Printing and Numerical Registering Co. v. Sampson*[45]:

[44] [1984] 1 W.L.R. 892.
[45] (1875) L.R. 19 Eq. 462 at 465.

"It must not be forgotten that you are not to extend arbitrarily those rules which say that a given contract is void as being against public policy, because if there is one thing which more than another public policy requires, it is that men of full age and competent understanding shall have the utmost liberty of contracting, and that their contracts when entered into freely and voluntarily shall be held sacred and shall be enforced by Courts of justice. Therefore, you have this paramount public policy to consider—that you are not lightly to interfere with this freedom of contract."

There is no general rule that a breach of contract may be excused if, on balance, the court considers that it would benefit the public at large for the contract to be broken, and it would be contrary to ordinary principles of contract law to introduce benefit to the public at large as a justification when a contract involves a promise of confidentiality.

The difficulties of such an approach are apparent from the judgment of Millet J. in *Price Waterhouse v. BCCI*.[46]

Price Waterhouse v. BCCI: a general discretion to dispense with confidentiality?

An inquiry into the supervision of BCCI under the Banking Act 1987 was set **6–12** up under the Chairmanship of Bingham L.J. by the Treasury and the Bank of England. The inquiry had no statutory power to enforce the attendance of witnesses or to compel the production of documents, and the judge rejected the argument that the Bank of England could have required production of documents for the purposes of the inquiry under section 39 of the Banking Act (since that section empowered the Bank of England to require the production of documents only if necessary for the performance of its supervisory function, not for the purpose of enabling the inquiry to review its performance). The inquiry requested Price Waterhouse to submit evidence and produce documents.

Price Waterhouse performed various functions in relation to BCCI, including co-ordinating the worldwide audits of the companies in the group. It was concerned that most of the information in its possession was confidential to BCCI, and that much of it was also covered by a duty of banking confidentiality owed by BCCI to its customers, of which Price Waterhouse had notice. It sought a declaration that it was not precluded from supplying information or documents to the inquiry.

The essential question was whether Price Waterhouse owed an implied contractual duty to BCCI (any equitable duty being no different from its contractual duty), or an equitable duty to any customer of BCCI, not to disclose to the inquiry information which was relevant to its purpose.

An important aim of the banking supervisory system is the prevention and detection of fraud. BCCI collapsed in circumstances which involved serious allegations of fraud and serious questions as to the adequacy of the banking

---

[46] [1992] BCLC 583. The collapse of BCCI and subsequent litigation and inquiries gave rise to various confidentiality problems. See also *El Jawhary v. BCCI* [1993] BCLC 396; *R. v. Institute of Chartered Accountants of England and Wales, ex p. Brindle* [1994] BCC 297; *Morris v. Director of Serious Fraud Office* [1993] BCLC 580.

supervisory system. The purpose of the Bingham inquiry was to investigate how the supervisory system had operated and to make recommendations. It was for this purpose that Price Waterhouse was asked to provide information to the inquiry.

6–13   If an outbreak of legionnaire's disease in a hospital led to the area health authority setting up a voluntary inquiry to investigate the causes and to make recommendations for the future, it is difficult to imagine a court holding that a doctor's relationship (contractual or otherwise) with his patient bound him not to provide the inquiry with information relevant to its task. It could be said that the Bingham inquiry was investigating a matter of similar public gravity.

It was therefore open to the court to hold that Price Waterhouse's implied contractual duty of secrecy to BCCI did not extend to precluding it from providing information to the inquiry (although this was not the reasoning that the court adopted).

6–14   There was a procedural problem in Price Waterhouse seeking a declaration that it did not owe any equitable obligation to any customer of BCCI which would preclude it from providing information to the inquiry, in that the firm was seeking a declaration in advance in an action to which the customers potentially affected were not parties. However, this point does not appear to have been raised by anyone.

After citing passages from the speeches of Lord Griffiths and Lord Goff in the *Spycatcher* case[47] and from the judgment of Bankes L.J. in *Tournier*,[48] Millett J. said[49]:

> "In all the cases cited to me in which the public interest in favour of disclosure has prevailed, it has been the public interest in the detection or prevention of wrong-doing, or in preventing a miscarriage of justice, or in the maintenance of public safety. An express contractual undertaking not to make disclosure in such circumstances would be against public policy. However, if those who set up the inquiry had thought that the public interest required that all relevant material should be made available to it, they could have set it up under the Tribunal of Inquiries and Evidence Act 1921. No doubt there were good reasons for not doing so. But they were content to rely upon the voluntary submission of evidence by those willing to co-operate with the inquiry. Where the information is confidential, the choice whether to volunteer it ought prima facie in my view to rest with the person to whom the duty of confidence is owed, rather than with the person who owes it. An express contractual undertaking not to co-operate with the inquiry would not, I apprehend, be contrary to public policy. That, however, is not the test which has been laid down by the authorities. The duty of confidentiality, whether contractual or equitable, is subject to a limiting principle. It is subject to the right, not merely the duty, to disclose information where there is a higher public interest in disclosure than in maintaining confidentiality.
>
> I have reached the conclusion that in the particular circumstances of the present case the public interest in favour of disclosure ought to prevail."

It is not clear from this passage whether the judge meant:

[47] [1990] 1 A.C. 109 at 268 and 282.
[48] [1924] 1 K.B. 461 at 472–473.
[49] [1992] BCLC 583 at 601.

(a) that although an express term that Price Waterhouse should not pass confidential information to the inquiry would have been enforceable, the court would not imply a duty of confidentiality of the same ambit; or

(b) that although an express term that Price Waterhouse should not pass confidential information to the inquiry would not have been contrary to public policy, it would not be enforced.

The first approach is contrary to that of the Court of Appeal in *Initial Services* **6–15** *Ltd v. Putterill*[50] (a decision referred to with approval by Lord Griffiths in the passage from his speech in *Spycatcher* cited by Millett J.), which has been followed in other cases. In *Spycatcher*, for example, Scott J. said[51]

"The court would obviously never, by means of an implied term, impose on an ex-employee a duty which would have been unenforceable if it had been incorporated into an express term. But in deciding upon the ambit of the implied term the same considerations will, in my view, be relevant as would be relevant to an examination of whether an express term was enforceable."

The second approach is also unsatisfactory.

It is one matter to hold that public policy would require a court to declare a term unenforceable because its enforcement would be contrary to public policy. It is another matter to declare in advance, on grounds of public interest, that a party is free not to comply with a contractual undertaking, even though public policy does not require the undertaking to be treated as unenforceable.

To do so is at best contradictory (because to say that the public interest does not require an obligation to be treated as unenforceable, but requires it not to be enforced, is self-contradicting). At worst, it is tantamount to the court assuming a general discretion, on grounds of public interest, to authorise a party not to perform a contractual obligation, even though its performance would be insufficiently harmful to be contrary to public policy.

Since the judge concluded that "an express contractual undertaking not to co-operate with the inquiry would not ... be contrary to public policy" (*i.e.* the public interest would not have required such an undertaking to be treated as unenforceable), the declaration ought on that basis to have been refused.

Public and private confidences, public interest and burden of proof

If there were a general defence in all confidentiality cases that disclosure **6–16** would on balance benefit the public at large, ultimately the difference between cases of public and private confidence would be that in the former category the onus would be on the plaintiff to show that disclosure would on balance be harmful to the public, whereas in the latter category the onus would be on the defendant to show that the disclosure would on balance be beneficial. In the *Spycatcher* case Lord Goff regarded the need in cases of public confidence[52]

---

[50] [1968] 1 Q.B. 396.
[51] [1990] 1 A.C. 109 at 146.
[52] *ibid.* at 283.

"not only to show that the information is confidential but also to show that it is in the public interest that it should not be published" as an additional requirement, which suggests more than a mere inversion of the burden of proof.

Disclosure to regulators

6–17   In *Re A Company's Application*[53] Scott J. considered the scope of an employee's duty of confidentiality in the context of disclosure to an industry regulator. A company which carried on a business regulated under the Financial Services Act 1986 dismissed its compliance officer. In discussions about compensation for alleged unfair dismissal he mentioned that he intended to report the company to the financial services regulator, FIMBRA, for breach of the regulatory scheme introduced under the Act, and to the Inland Revenue for misfeasances by the company's directors.

In response to that threat the company obtained an Anton Piller order against him, enabling it to recover various documents belonging to it from his home, and it applied for an interlocutory injunction to restrain him from making use of any confidential documents or information relating to the company's affairs pending trial. Presumably in order to forestall any "clean hands" argument, the company volunteered an undertaking itself to place before FIMBRA and the Inland Revenue any documents in its possession relating to the matters identified in the defendants' affidavits and defence as matters meriting investigation. The defendant in turn volunteered an undertaking not to disclose his placing of information with FIMBRA or the Inland Revenue to other persons apart from his legal advisers. The key issue was whether the defendant was to be restrained, pending trial, from making the threatened disclosures to FIMBRA and the Inland Revenue. The company argued that it was a case of naked blackmail. The defendant denied any blackmailing attempt.

Scott J. refused to restrain the defendant from disclosing the matters in question to FIMBRA or the Inland Revenue. He defined the issue by saying[54]:

> "I ask myself whether an employee of a company carrying on the business of giving financial advice and of financial management to members of the public under the regulatory umbrella provided by F.I.M.B.R.A. owes a duty of confidentiality that extends to barring disclosure of information to F.I.M.B.R.A."

He answered the question[55]:

> "I doubt whether an employee of a financial services company owes a duty of confidence which extends to an obligation not to disclose information to the regulatory authority F.I.M.B.R.A."

In the same way, no doubt, an employee in a firm of solicitors would not owe a duty of confidence extending to an obligation to refrain from disclosing

---

[53] [1989] Ch. 477. For a review of the case, see Lomnicka, "The Employee Whistleblower and the Duty of Confidentiality" (1990) 106 L.Q.R. 42.

[54] [1989] Ch. 477 at 481.

[55] *ibid.* at 482.

information about alleged misconduct to the Law Society, nor an employee in the health service to refrain from disclosing similar information to the General Medical Council.

Scott J. dealt in similar fashion with the Inland Revenue, saying,

> "If confidential details which did not relate to fiscal matters were disclosed to the Inland Revenue, that would, in my opinion, be as much a breach of the duty of confidentiality as the disclosure of that information to any other third party. But if what is disclosed to the Inland Revenue relates to fiscal matters that are the concern of the Inland Revenue I find it difficult to accept that the disclosure would be in breach of a duty of confidentiality."

Scott J. also held that it was not for him to conduct a preliminary investigation into the merits of the allegations where the disclosure was proposed to be made to a body which itself had responsibility for investigating such matters.

The judge accepted that the company might be right in its assertion that the proposed disclosure was a blackmailing ploy. But if the defendant owed no contractual duty not to disclose information to FIMBRA, malicious motivation could not make the proposed disclosure a breach of contract.

Informant's motives

The informant's motives were also considered irrelevant in *British Steel* **6–18** *Corporation v. Granada Television Ltd*[56] by Lord Fraser, with whom Lord Russell agreed, and, *semble*, by Viscount Dilhorne, although Lord Salmon in his dissenting speech took a different view.[57]

It does not follow that the informant's motives and beliefs are necessarily irrelevant in all cases. A doctor, for example, who discloses confidential information about a patient, without the patient's consent, will not be in breach of duty to his patient if he acts in the reasonably held belief that disclosure is necessary for the prevention of serious harm to others (*W. v. Egdell*[58]).

Medical hazard

In *W. v. Egdell*[59] the plaintiff, a paranoid schizophrenic, shot and killed five **6–19** people and injured two others. He pleaded guilty to manslaughter on the ground of diminished responsibility and was ordered to be detained in a secure hospital. For the purpose of an application to a mental health review tribunal

---

[56] [1981] A.C. 1096 at 1177, *per* Viscount Dilhorne; 1185, *per* Lord Salmon; 1202, *per* Lord Fraser and 1204, *per* Lord Russell.

[57] See also *Lion Laboratories Ltd v. Evans* [1985] 1 Q.B. 526 at 536. In *Initial Services Ltd v. Putterill* [1968] 1 Q.B. 396 at 406 Lord Denning M.R., suggested, *obiter*, that it might make a difference if the informant acted out of malice or for reward.

[58] [1990] 1 Ch. 359.

[59] *ibid.*

with a view towards his ultimate release, the plaintiff, through his solicitors, retained the defendant, a consultant psychiatrist, to report on his state of mental health. The defendant formed a more serious view of the plaintiff's condition than had been taken by the medical officer responsible for his treatment, and his report was adverse to the plaintiff's application. After considering the report, the plaintiff, through his solicitors, withdrew his application. The defendant was so concerned about the difference between his views and those formed by the medical officer that, without the plaintiff's consent, he forwarded a copy of his report to the assistant medical director at the hospital. The plaintiff brought an action against the defendant alleging breach of confidence. The claim failed before Scott J. and on appeal.

From the report the appeal appears to have proceeded on the basis that it was common ground that the defendant owed the plaintiff a duty of confidence, and that the court was required to carry out a balancing exercise to decide whether that duty was overridden by public interest sufficient to justify a breach of that confidence.[60]

Bingham L.J. observed[61] that, where the relationship between doctor and patient was contractual, the question was whether the doctor's disclosure was or was not a breach of contract. The Court of Appeal held that it was not. Bingham L.J. stated the decisive factor as follows[62]:

"Where a man has committed multiple killings under the disability of serious mental illness, decisions which may lead directly or indirectly to his release from hospital should not be made unless a responsible authority is properly able to make an informed judgment that the risk of repetition is so small as to be acceptable. A consultant psychiatrist who becomes aware, even in the course of a confidential relationship, of information which leads him, in the exercise of what the court considers a sound professional judgment, to fear that such decisions may be made on the basis of inadequate information and with a real risk of consequent danger to the public is entitled to take such steps as are reasonable in all the circumstances to communicate the grounds of his concern to the responsible authorities."

At first instance Scott J.'s approach had been to seek to identify the scope of the relevant duty owed by the defendant to the plaintiff. He said,[63] in part of his judgment which was quoted by Sir Stephen Brown P. in the Court of Appeal with apparent approval[64]:

"It is convenient for me first to ask myself what duty of confidence a court of equity ought to regard as imposed on Dr Egdell by the circumstances in which he obtained information from and about W. and prepared his report. It is in my judgment plain, and the contrary has not been suggested, that the circumstances did impose on Dr Egdell a duty of confidence. If, for instance, Dr Egdell had sold the contents of his report to a newspaper, I do not think any court of equity would hesitate for a moment before

[60] W. v. Egdell [1990] 1 Ch. 359 at 412, 415 and 422.
[61] ibid. at 422.
[62] ibid. at 424.
[63] ibid. at 389.
[64] ibid. at 411–412.

concluding that his conduct had been a breach of his duty of confidence. The question in the present case is not whether Dr Egdell was under a duty of confidence; he plainly was. The question is as to the breadth of that duty. Did the duty extend so as to bar disclosure of the report to the medical director of the hospital?"

Scott J. then referred to the speech of Lord Goff in the *Spycatcher* case in **6–20** relation to the limiting of a duty of confidence on grounds of public interest.

Dr Egdell was clearly fearful of the risk to the public from the possible premature release into the community of a dangerous schizophrenic who had, according to his report, a seriously abnormal interest in the making of home made bombs. If the plaintiff had confided that he planned to commit murder through evil intent, no court would have held that there was an implied obligation on the part of the defendant to keep that information to himself, nor would it have upheld an express agreement to do so. Should different principles apply because the perceived danger to the public arose from illness, not malice? It would be surprising if any court had thought so. The danger to the public was such that, although there was a confidential relationship between the parties, the duty of confidence impliedly undertaken by the defendant did not extend to withholding information about the plaintiff's state of health from the responsible medical authorities.

New Zealand

In New Zealand it has been held by the Court of Appeal that: **6–21**

"What has been called ever since *Gartside v. Outram* (1856) 26 L.J.Ch. 113 the defence of iniquity is an instance, and probably the prime instance, of the principle that the law will not protect confidential information if the publication complained of is shown to be in the overriding public interest: see generally *Lion Laboratories Ltd v. Evans* [1985] Q.B. 526; *Attorney-General for the United Kingdom v. Wellington Newspapers Ltd* [1988] 1 N.Z.L.R. 129, at 176–177, 178; *Attorney-General v. Observer Ltd* [1990] 1 A.C. 109, at 268–269 and at 282–283."[65]

Australia

Australian courts have generally preferred the narrower "public interest **6–22** defence" enunciated in such cases as *Beloff v. Pressdram Ltd*[66] to the broader version put forward by Lord Denning M.R. in *Woodward v. Hutchins.*[67]

In *Castrol Australia Pty Ltd v. Emtech Associates Pty Ltd*[68] Rath J. observed that the public interest "exception" could not universally be extended to all crimes committed, as Bankes L.J. pointed out in *Weld-Blundell v. Stephens*[69]; but that exclusion from protection of designs "to destroy the public welfare" expressed a concept authoritatively expressed by Viscount Finlay in the same

[65] *European Pacific Banking Corp. v. Television New Zealand Ltd* [1994] 3 N.Z.L.R. 43 at 46.
[66] [1973] 1 All E.R. 241 at 260.
[67] [1977] 1 W.L.R. 760.
[68] (1980) 33 A.L.R. 31 at 54.
[69] [1919] 1 K.B. 520 at 527 and 528.

case, when he referred to cases where some "higher duty is involved" and said that "danger to the state or public duty may supersede the duty of the agent to his principal".[70]

Rath J. also cited with agreement Ungoed-Thomas J.'s summary in *Beloff v. Pressdram Ltd*[71] (approved by Lord Goff in *Spycatcher*[72]), saying that it expressed no more than a reasonable elaboration of Viscount Finlay's "higher duty" concept and was an acceptable statement of the law as to the defence of public interest in an action for breach of confidence. He added[73]:

> "What is particularly important in Ungoed-Thomas J.'s formulation of principle is his emphasis on the gravity of the conduct that may give rise to the defence. If there is to be a defence labelled public interest, some such confinement of its vague boundaries is in my view essential."

Rath, J. declined to follow the broader test applied by Lord Denning M.R. in *Woodward v. Hutchins*,[74] saying that[75]:

> "If Lord Denning's quoted statement is taken literally the court will test the legitimacy of breach of confidence by its conception of the balance of public interest in the particular circumstances of the case."

He went on to say that the court[76]:

> "... must have regard to matters of a more weighty and precise kind than a public interest in the truth being told ... In a sense [the plaintiffs'] image was a matter of 'public interest', but not in the sense that as a matter of public policy the defendants were entitled, or required, to break confidence."

6–23   In *Corrs Pavey Whiting & Byrne v. Collector of Customs*[77] Gummow J. was also critical of *Woodward v. Hutchins* and, like Rath J., adopted a narrower analysis of the principle underlying the "public interest defence". He reiterated his views in *Smith Klein & French Laboratories (Australia) Ltd v. Department of Community Services*[78]:

> "My views upon the wisdom of adopting in Australia the English authorities in which the 'public interest' defence has been constructed in recent years from what may be thought inadequate historical and doctrinal materials, have been expressed in *Corrs Pavey Whiting & Byrne v. Collection of Customs (Vic)* ..., at 451–458. Those views are consistent with what was said by Rath J. in *Castrol Australia Pty Ltd v. EmTech Associates Pty Ltd*, ..., at 210–216 and by Hutley A.P. in *David Syme & Co. Ltd v. General Motors-Holden's Ltd* [1984] 2 N.S.W.L.R., 294 at 305–306. They are reinforced by a reading of the latest English decision on the

---

[70] [1920] A.C. 956 at 965.
[71] [1973] 1 A.E.R. 241 at 260.
[72] [1990] 1 A.C. 109 at 282.
[73] (1980) 33 A.L.R. 31 at 55.
[74] [1977] 1 W.L.R. 760.
[75] (1980) 33 A.L.R. 31 at 56.
[76] *ibid.*
[77] (1987) 74 A.L.R. 428 at 445–450. See para. 3–20, above.
[78] [1990] F.S.R. 617 at 662–663.

subject, *W., v. Egdell* [1990] 2 W.L.R. 471 at 488–489. There, concepts drawn from the law as to discovery, contempt, contract, fiduciary duty, and undue influence, as well as from the equitable obligations of confidence owed to government and between citizens, are mixed to produce a curious melange, without an indication of the significance of what was being done.

No doubt the terms 'confidence' and 'confidential' appear in authorities in all these fields, but it by no means follows that they are used in the same sense across the legal spectrum. ...

Further, I would accept the submissions by counsel for the applicants in the *SK&F* proceedings that (i) an examination of the recent English decisions shows that the so-called 'public interest' defence is not so much a rule of law as an invitation to judicial idiosyncrasy by deciding each case on an *ad hoc* basis as to whether, on the facts overall, it is better to respect or to override the obligation of confidence, and (ii) equitable principles are best developed by reference to what conscionable behaviour demands of the defendant not by 'balancing' and then overriding those demands by reference to matters of social or political opinion."

In *Esso Australia Resources Ltd v. Plowman*,[79] a case concerning arbitration proceedings, Brennan J. observed that in determining the scope of an implied obligation of confidentiality a party will not be taken to have intended that it would keep confidential documents or information when that party had an obligation, albeit not a legal obligation, to satisfy a public interest—more than mere curiosity—in knowing what was contained in the documents or information. Mason C.J. (with whom Dawson and McHugh J.J. concurred) said that the precise scope of the public interest exception to a duty of confidentiality remained unclear.

Conclusions on the public interest defence in England

In any country which professes the rule of law and places value on the rights **6–24** of individuals, it is a fundamental precept that those rights should not be lightly overridden in the name of public interest. Courts should do so only with great caution, taking care that they act on clearly identified and jurisprudentially sound principles.

Whether English law recognises a "defence of public interest" as broad as its critics have suggested is therefore a question of considerable importance. The concept of such a broad defence appears to have originated in *Woodward v. Hutchins*,[80] which does suggest that it is for the court to decide in each case on an ad hoc basis whether, on the facts, it is better to respect or override the obligation of confidence; and the result in that case may well be regarded as an instance of judicial idiosyncrasy.[81] There are also dicta in later cases which support the same general approach, but other authorities suggest that the true principle is narrower.

The preferable view is that the question is not whether disclosure would serve the public better than non-disclosure, but whether there is a real public

[79] [1994–1995] 183 C.L.R. 10.
[80] [1977] 1 W.L.R. 760.
[81] Contrast *Schering Chemicals Ltd v. Falkman Ltd* [1982] 1 Q.B. 1 and see the comments at para. 3–12, above.

need for disclosure, such that a duty of non-disclosure would be contrary to public policy and unenforceable, either generally or, more narrowly, in relation to the disclosure under consideration.

Such public need is most likely to exist where non-disclosure would demonstrably tend to the promotion of serious wrongdoing or serious public harm. Assessing the importance of the need for disclosure may involve a balancing exercise, but one to be carried out in accordance with, not in substitution for, the underlying principle.

This approach is based on a conceptually sound principle and maintains a proper respect for private rights. To say, on the other hand, that private rights may be overridden whenever it is in the public interest to do so is far too vague, and leaves quite undefined the principle on which a court is to decide whether public interest "outweighs" the right to confidentiality.

CLEAN HANDS

6–25   The so-called "public interest" defence is not to be confused with the discretion of the court to refuse equitable relief in cases where the plaintiff is not seen to come with clean hands. That discretion applies as much to confidentiality cases as to any other. A colourful illustration is provided by *McNicol v. Sportsman's Book Stores*.[82] The plaintiff sold to subscribers a supposedly successful method of predicting horse-race winners by the age of the moon, on express terms that each purchaser would treat the information as private and confidential for his own personal use. The defendant intended to publish a review of results of using the system, without divulging its precise rules. The plaintiff's application for an injunction to restrain the defendant from doing so failed before Maugham J., among other reasons because he did not consider that the assistance of the court should be given to the plaintiff in circumstances in which:

> "... the poor people all over this country who are deceived into paying two guineas for this system are getting something which is perfectly worthless."[83]

6–26   Sometimes both concepts may be invoked in the same case, as, for example, in *Hubbard v. Vosper*.[84] The defendant had been a member of the Church of Scientology for 14 years. He attended a course, for which he paid a fee, and signed an undertaking not to divulge course materials to those not entitled to receive them. He later wrote a book criticising the teaching and practise of scientology. The Church (and its founders) sued the defendant, alleging breach of a contractual duty of confidence, and sought an interlocutory injunction restraining publication of his book.

Lord Denning M.R. considered that an injunction should be refused because, on the material before the court, the courses appeared to contain such

---

[82] (1930) McG.C.C. 116.
[83] *ibid.* at 125. In *Spycatcher* [1990] 1 A.C. 109 at 149 Scott J. cited *McNicol* as a case where the information lacked the quality of confidence because it was trivial.
[84] [1972] 2 Q.B. 84.

dangerous medical quackery that no confidence could be claimed to keep them secret.[85]

Megaw L.J. agreed with Lord Denning M.R., but he also referred to evidence that the plaintiffs sought to enforce secrecy on cult members by improper methods, and he accepted the defendant's proposition[86]:

> "that there is here evidence that the plaintiffs are or have been protecting their secrets by deplorable means ... and, that being so, they do not come with clean hands to this court in asking this court to protect these secrets by the equitable remedy of an injunction."

In the subsequent case of *Church of Scientology v. Kaufman*[87] Goff J. followed both approaches.

---

[85] *Hubbard v. Vosper* [1972] 2 Q.B. 84 at 95–96.
[86] *ibid.* at 101.
[88] [1973] R.P.C. 627.

CHAPTER VII

CONFIDENTIALITY AND THIRD PARTIES

Information properly disclosed

7–01   A third party may receive confidential information or material for a proper purpose. A general practitioner might, for example, provide medical information about a patient to a consultant for the purpose of obtaining the consultant's opinion or send a specimen of the patient's blood to a laboratory for the purpose of HIV testing. (The question whether this would require the patient's express consent is discussed in Chapter XIII, but for the present it is assumed that the general practitioner is acting lawfully.) The consultant or analyst receiving the information or specimen would as a general proposition be under a duty of confidentiality to the patient not to use the information or material otherwise than for the purpose for which it was provided.

Information improperly disclosed

7–02   A third party may also receive confidential information or material in circumstances where the supplier is in breach of a duty of confidence to another (the confider). Where the third party receives information knowing that it has been disclosed by his informant in breach of confidence, he will himself owe a duty of confidence to the confider.[1] This principle is derived from the doctrine that it is equitable fraud in a third party knowingly to assist in a breach of trust, confidence or contract by another: *Abernethy v. Hutchinson*[2] and *Prince Albert v. Strange*.[3] Conversely a third party has no liability for acts done innocently (*Fraser v. Thames Television*[4]).

7–03   There has been debate over what constitutes sufficient knowledge for the conscience of a third party to be bound. The relevant equitable principle is the same as applies to accessories to a breach of trust. In *Royal Brunei Airlines v. Tan*[5] the Privy Council re-examined the principle in relation to that subject and reviewed the authorities, including the much cited judgment of Lord Selborne L.C. in *Barnes v. Addy*.[6] Lord Nicholls, delivering the judgment of the Board, held that failure to exercise reasonable diligence was insufficient to establish liability against a third party who procured or assisted in a breach of trust, and

[1] *Spycatcher* [1990] 1 A.C. 109 at 261, *per* Lord Keith; at 281, *per* Lord Goff.
[2] (1824) 3 L.J.Ch. 209.
[3] (1848) 1 Mac & G. 25.
[4] [1984] 1 Q.B. 44 at 65.
[5] [1995] 2 A.C. 378.
[6] (1874) L.R. 9 Ch.App. 244.

that it was necessary to establish that he had failed "to observe the standard which would be observed by an honest person" placed in his circumstances. He preferred that formulation to posing the test in terms of whether the third party had "knowingly" assisted in a breach of trust, because a question posed in the latter form led too often into tortuous convolutions about the sort of knowledge required.

Dishonesty is a natural word to use in relation to misappropriation of trust assets. It is an equally natural word to use in relation to misuse of confidential information of a commercially valuable kind. In the case of confidential information of a non-commercial character other expressions might more naturally be used to convey the gravity of misconduct required, such as wilful or reckless disregard of its confidentiality.[7] Unconscionable is another word which reflects the root of the jurisdiction in an equitable duty of conscience, but suffers from the disadvantage referred to by Lord Nicholls of not being in everyday use by non-lawyers and requiring its own definition. The important thing is that for a third party to be held liable in equity for a breach of confidence, more is required than merely careless, naive or stupid behaviour.[8] There must be awareness that the information was confidential or willingness to turn a proverbial blind eye.

Where the supply of confidential information to a third party involves the supplier in a breach of a contractual duty of confidence, the third party will be liable for the tort of inducement of breach of contract if he makes himself party to the receipt of the information with knowledge that the supplier is acting in breach of contract.[9] Conversely, the third party will not be liable if he lacks that knowledge, unless he deliberately shuts his eyes to suspicion.[10]

There is no comparable action in tort for inducement of a breach of trust or, by analogy, breach of an equitable duty of confidence, because the position of secondary parties to a breach of an equitable duty is adequately dealt with by the principles developed in *Barnes v. Addy*[11] and *Royal Brunei Airlines v. Tan*.[12] The Court of Appeal so held in relation to inducement of breach of trust in *Metall und Rohstoff A.G. v. Donaldson Lufkin & Jenrette Inc.*[13]

In *Valeo Vision S.A. v. Flexible Lamps Ltd*[14] the plaintiffs supplied **7–04** confidential information to M, who wrongly disclosed it to the defendants. The defendants, unaware of M's breach of confidence, used the information in competition with the plaintiffs. The plaintiffs claimed damages from the defendants, not on the basis that the defendants were party to M's misconduct, but on the simple basis that it was inequitable that they should retain the benefit

---

[7] In *Hivac Ltd v. Park Royal Scientific Instruments Ltd* [1946] 1 Ch. 169 at 172 Lord Greene M.R. said, "The defendants and the employees on the evidence appear quite clearly to have known exactly what they were doing, and they knew that, at any rate, it was morally reprehensible, if not legally wrong."

[8] *Printers & Finishers Ltd v. Holloway* [1965] R.P.C. 239. The case was pleaded under the head of inducement of breach of contract (see 247), but it is difficult to suppose that on the same facts a lesser degree of knowledge would be sufficient to establish liability under the head of assisting in breach of an equitable obligation of confidence.

[9] *Hivac Ltd v. Park Royal Scientific Instruments Ltd* [1946] 1 Ch. 169. *Ansell Rubber Co. Pty Ltd v. Allied Rubber Industries Pty Ltd* [1972] R.P.C. 811.

[10] *British Industrial Plastics Ltd v. Ferguson* [1940] 12 All E.R. 479, H.L. *Printers & Finishers Ltd v. Holloway* [1965] R.P.C. 239. Compare *Emerald Construction Co. Ltd v. Lowthian* [1966] 1 W.L.R. 691 at 700.

[11] (1874) L.R. 9 Ch.App. 244.

[12] [1995] 2 A.C. 378.

[13] [1990] 1 Q.B. 391.

[14] [1995] R.P.C. 205.

of their innocent misuse of confidential information. Aldous J. dismissed the claim, holding that the conscience of the defendants could not be bound, and therefore any claim against them in equity failed, in circumstances in which they had no knowledge of the breach of confidence.

Innocent recipient with subsequent knowledge of improper disclosure

7–05   The position of a third party who receives confidential information innocently and subsequently learns that it was supplied to him in breach of confidence is more difficult. In principle, lack of notice at the time of its receipt that the information was subject to a duty of confidence should not prevent the recipient from himself coming under such a duty as from the time of his discovering the true position, *provided* that he had not in good faith incurred detriment by paying for the information or perhaps by incurring expense of money or effort in consequence of obtaining it (for example, in further research or development).

Leaving the proviso aside, the principle accords with authority. In *Printers & Finishers Ltd v. Holloway*[15] Cross J. said:

> "If authority is needed for the grant of an injunction against someone who has acquired—or may have acquired—information to which he was not entitled without notice of any breach of duty on the part of the man who imparted it to him but who cannot claim to be a purchaser for value, I think that it can be found in the case of *Prince Albert v. Strange* (1850) 1 MacN. and G. 25. There the court granted an injunction against a defendant who was not—or at all events was assumed by the court not to have been—implicated in the breach of confidence in question. There again, however, the precise wording of any injunction will require careful consideration."

Where the proviso applies, the position is unclear.

"Bona fide purchase" and change of position

7–06   In *Morison v. Moat*[16] Turner V.-C. in granting an injunction against the defendant, observed,

> "It might indeed be different if the Defendant was a purchaser for value of the secret without notice of any obligation affecting it; and the Defendant's case was attempted to be put upon this ground ... but I do not think that this view of the case can avail him .... So far as the secret is concerned he is a mere volunteer deriving under a breach of trust or of contract."

In *Stevenson Jordan & Harrison Ltd v. MacDonald & Evans*[17] the defendant publishers resisted a claim for an injunction to prevent publication of a book allegedly containing material obtained in breach of confidence on the grounds that they were bona fide purchasers for value. At first instance Lloyd-Jacob J.

---

[15] [1965] R.P.C. 239 at 253; see also *Fraser v. Evans* [1969] 1 Q.B. 349 at 361.
[16] (1851) 9 Hare 241 at 263–264.
[17] (1951) 68 R.P.C. 190.

ruled against the existence of such a defence and granted an injunction. His decision was reversed on other grounds and the Court of Appeal declined to express an opinion on the point, although Lord Evershed M.R. observed,[18] *obiter*, that it would be "somewhat shocking" if a third party purchaser persisted in plans to implement use of confidential material after becoming aware of the breach of duty by which it had been supplied to him.

In *Wheatley v. Bell*[19] Helsham C.J. in the Supreme Court of New South Wales granted an injunction against a bona fide purchaser, holding that the defence of bona fide purchase only applied to property rights and that there were no property rights attached to equities involved in the protection of confidence.

In *Spycatcher (No. 1)* Nourse L.J. said in interlocutory proceedings: **7–07**

"As for the newspapers and any other third party into whose hands the confidential information comes, an injunction can be granted against them on the simple ground that equity gives relief against all the world, including the innocent, save only a bona fide purchaser for value without notice."[20]

This passage was cited at first instance by Sir Nicolas Browne-Wilkinson V.-C. in *Spycatcher (No. 1)*[21] and by Lord Donaldson M.R. in *Spycatcher (No. 2)*, who said[22]:

"Since the right to have confidentiality maintained is an equitable right, it will (in legal theory and practical effect if the aid of the court is invoked) 'bind the conscience' of third parties, unless they are bona fide purchasers for value without notice (*per* Nourse L.J. on 25 July, 1986 in the interlocutory proceedings: *Attorney General v. Observer Ltd* Court of Appeal (Civil Division) Transcript No. 696 of 1986)."

Professor Gareth Jones, in an article entitled "Restitution of Benefits Obtained in Breach of Another's Confidence", observed[23]:

"Judicial dicta, and the Reporters of the *Restatement of Torts*, accept that a good-faith purchaser who has no notice of any breach of confidence should be free to use and exploit confidential information even though he is subsequently told that it has been sold to him in breach of another's confidence.

Superficially this is an attractive conclusion which marks off the position of the bona fide purchaser from that of the innocent volunteer, such as the donee. Moreover, it preserves the certainty of commercial transactions. Bona fide purchase would certainly be a good defence if the plaintiff's action was based on the defendant's infringement of the plaintiff's equitable property in the particular information. But it is questionable

---

[18] (1952) 69 R.P.C. 10 at 16.
[19] [1984] F.S.R. 16; [1982] 2 N.S.W.L.R. 544.
[20] Nourse L.J. used the same words in *Goddard v. Nationwide Building Society* [1987] 1 Q.B. 671 at 685.
[21] [1987] 1 W.L.R. 1248 at 1265.
[22] [1990] 1 A.C. 109 at 177.
[23] (1970) 86 L.Q.R. 463 at 478–479.

whether the mere payment of money should, in itself, defeat a restitutionary claim whose essence is a duty of good faith, a duty not to take
unfair advantage of the plaintiff's confidence. Contrast these two cases,

(a) D, a business man, pays R for some information which, unknown
to D, R has imparted to D in breach of P's confidence. Two weeks
later P discovers the true facts and tells D, at which time D has
incurred no further expenditure.

(b) D, a business man, pays R for certain information which,
unknown to D, R has imparted to D in breach of P's confidence. D
begins to develop a grip, using this information. His expenditure
on plant, machinery and leasehold premises has been very
substantial. D is then told by P, who has just discovered R's
duplicity, the true facts. Three years have elapsed since he paid R
for the information.

If bona fide purchase is accepted as a defence, then P will fail in both
these cases. In (b) it is right that he should do so. But is there not a great
deal to be said for granting him relief in (a), on the terms that he
reimburses D his expenditure? This expenditure apart, there has been no
detrimental change of position. In such a case, certainty of transaction can
be preserved by the recognition of a strong rebuttable presumption that a
good-faith purchaser is deemed to have changed his position to his
detriment; and the financial interests of the defendant can be safeguarded
by the condition that the plaintiff reimburses him his expenditure, with
interest, before he is granted relief. The application of a flexible notion of
change of position may, it is suggested, balance more effectively than an
absolute defence of bona fide purchase the competing equities of the
honest purchaser and the deceived plaintiff."

Other writers have also argued for a flexible approach in cases where an
innocent third party has suffered detriment by expending resources in
obtaining or exploiting information supplied to him in breach of another's
confidence.[24]

7–08   In *Lipkin Gorman v. Karpnale Ltd*[25] the House of Lords held that in principle
a defence of detrimental change of position is available in restitutionary claims
to:

"a person whose position has so changed that it would be inequitable in all
the circumstances to require him to make restitution, or alternatively to
make restitution in full",[26]

the explanation being that:

"where an innocent defendant's position is so changed that he will suffer
an injustice if called upon to repay or repay in full, the injustice of requiring
him so to repay outweighs the injustice of denying the plaintiff
restitution."[27]

---

[24] Professor Cornish, *Intellectual Property: Patents, Copyright, Trade Marks and Allied Rights* (2nd
ed., 1986), para. 8–031; Meagher, Gummow and Lehane, *Equity: Doctrines and Remedies* (3rd
ed., 1992), para. 4122.
[25] [1991] 2 A.C. 548 at 577–580.
[26] *ibid.*
[27] *ibid.* at 580.

If that defence is available to one who has received money belonging to another, there is at least as strong an argument for saying that it should be available to one who has received information in breach of a duty of confidence owed to another. Indeed, the case for the latter may be stronger, because (as Lord Goff recognised in *Lipkin Gorman*) a claim to recover money at common law is made as a matter of right, whereas the obligation of the third party recipient of confidential information supplied in breach of confidence to another is founded on an obligation of conscience, which *ex hypothesi*, cannot bind him to do (or abstain from doing) that which it would in all the circumstances be inequitable to require him to do (or abstain from doing).

Although the expression "purchaser for value" of confidential information is **7-09** of respectable antiquity, going back to *Morison v. Moat*,[28] and has been used by distinguished judges, it is apt to mislead because of its implication of transfer of property. It is suggested that the true position was stated by Latham C.J. in *Federal Commissioners of Taxation v. United Aircraft Corporation*,[29] when he said:

> "I am unable to regard the communication of information as constituting a transfer of property. Upon such a communication the transferor still has everything he had before ... . Knowledge is valuable, but knowledge is neither real nor personal property. A man with a richly stored mind is not for that reason a man of property. ... It is only in a loose metaphorical sense that any knowledge as such can be said to be property."[30]

The expression "purchaser for value" of confidential information should be understood in a similarly metaphorical sense.

If, contrary to this view, confidential information is a form of equitable property, there would be logic in affording to the bona fide purchaser of such property an absolute defence to any claim based on his use of the property, regardless of the adequacy of the consideration which he paid or any other circumstances.

If not, and if "bona fide purchaser" is merely a loose description of a person who pays money for the supply of information in ignorance that it is being supplied to him in breach of another's confidence, his position on discovering the truth should be governed by considerations of conscience rather than misleading analogies with transfer of property rights.

The fact that he innocently acts to his detriment by paying for the supply of the information should not automatically afford him an absolute right in all circumstances to continue to use the information after discovering the truth, but is, and should be regarded as, a form of detrimental change of position. In any case where there has been a detrimental change of position in good faith by the recipient of information supplied in breach of another's confidence, it should be for the Court to decide in all the circumstances whether, balancing the parties' respective interests and the justice or injustice which would result to each from the grant or refusal of the relief claimed, any such relief should be granted and, if so, on what terms.[31]

[28] (1851) 9 Hare 241.
[29] (1943) 68 C.L.R. 525 at 534 (High Court of Australia).
[30] The question whether the law of confidentiality is based on a theory of property is discussed more fully in Chap. II, above.
[31] This approach is consistent with the views of Goff and Jones, *The Law of Restitution* (4th ed., 1993), pp. 695–696.

CHAPTER VIII

INVOLUNTARY OR MISTAKEN DISCLOSURE

8–01   Disclosure otherwise than through a consensual relationship or transaction may occur in a variety of ways.

Obligatory disclosure

8–02   A person may be required to disclose information which he would normally regard as confidential. Tax payers, for example, are required to disclose details of their income to the revenue. The revenue owes a duty of confidence to every tax payer in respect of such information.[1] There need not therefore be a voluntary imparting of information in order for the recipient to be under an equitable obligation of confidence arising from the nature of the information and the circumstances of its receipt.

Just as a photographer employed to take a person's photograph owes a duty of confidence to the customer in respect of the material obtained,[2] so a police authority empowered to take a "mug shot" of an arrested person owes an equitable obligation to that person under the law of confidence not to make improper use of the material obtained.[3]

The scope of the duty may vary from one case to another according to the circumstances in which, and purpose for which, the material was obtained. In *Hellewell v. Chief Constable of Derbyshire*[4] Laws J. held that the police might make reasonable use of the photograph for the purpose of the prevention and detection of crime, the investigation of alleged offences and the apprehension of suspects or persons unlawfully at large. Limited circulation of the mug shot of the plaintiff (who had 32 convictions including 19 for offences of dishonesty) to shopkeepers who were considered to have legitimate cause for apprehension if he were to visit their premises, was not improper use of it.

8–03   The general principle was stated in *Marcel v. Commissioner of Police*[5] by Sir Christopher Slade:

"In my judgment, documents seized by a public authority from a private citizen in exercise of a statutory power can properly be used only for those

---

[1] *R. v. Inland Revenue Commissioners, ex p. National Federation of Self-Employed and Small Businesses Ltd* [1982] A.C. 617 at 654, *per* Lord Scarman; *R. v. Inland Revenue Commissioners, ex p. Preston* [1985] A.C. 835 at 864, *per* Lord Templeman; *Lonrho Plc v. Fayed (No. 4)* [1994] Q.B. 775.
[2] *Pollard v. Photographic Company* (1888) 40 Ch.J. 345.
[3] *Hellewell v. Chief Constable of Derbyshire* [1995] 1 W.L.R. 804.
[4] *ibid.*
[5] [1992] Ch. 225 at 262.

purposes for which the relevant legislation contemplated that they might be used. The user for any other purpose of documents seized in a draconian power of this nature, without the consent of the person from whom they were seized, would be an improper exercise of the power. Any such person would be entitled to expect that the authority would treat the documents and their contents as confidential, save to the extent that it might use them for the purposes contemplated by the relevant legislation."

The Court of Appeal recognised that the duty in that regard lay not only in public law but also in the private law of confidentiality. But just as the recipient of information voluntarily imparted to him in confidence may be compelled to disclose it by process of law, so may the recipient of information which was itself supplied to him under compulsion.

In *Marcel's* case a development company sued a purchaser for default in contracts for the purchase of some flats. The purchaser alleged that he was induced to enter the contracts by misrepresentations made by three agents of the company. The three were arrested by the police on suspicion of conspiracy to defraud the purchaser (with which they were later charged, but the charges were dropped) and documents were seized from them. The purchaser served a *subpoena duces tecum* on the police requiring them to produce the seized documents at the trial of the action brought by the company. The police allowed the purchaser's solicitor to inspect and copy some of the documents before the *subpoena* was formally served. The three agents issued proceedings against the police, the purchaser and his solicitor, to prevent use of the documents in the civil action.

The Court of Appeal held that voluntary disclosure of the seized documents by the police to the purchaser, without a *subpoena*, would have been a breach of duty of confidence; but that the police might be compelled to produce them on *subpoena*, just as the owners of the seized documents might themselves have been compelled to produce them on *subpoena*. The Court expressed differing views about the propriety of the disclosure of the documents after issue of the *subpoena* but prior to the requirement for their formal production in court. Dillon L.J. said that he could see the practical sense of producing them prior to the trial so that they could be sifted and administrative arrangements made to facilitate the conduct of the civil proceedings, provided that it was remembered that the documents were not the property of the police. Sir Christopher Slade, while having sympathy with the course taken by the police, said that they should not have disclosed the documents without the consent of the owners or the authority of the court.

The plethora of powers given to different bodies for obtaining information **8–04** under the Companies Act 1985, the Insolvency Act 1986, the Police and Criminal Evidence Act 1984, the Criminal Justice Act 1987 and other statutes, and the potential for the powers of compulsion under one statute to be used to obtain information supplied by compulsion under another, have combined to produce almost as many possible permutations as a football pools coupon.[6] This has given rise to some complex questions of confidentiality, especially in cases where the facts are complicated, the documents are voluminous and

---

[6] For a summary, see John L. Powell Q.C. "Obtaining documents from official and regulatory sources in prosecuting civil claims" (*12th Cambridge International Symposium on Economic Crime and Money Laundering*, September 1994).

various regulatory bodies are involved.[7] In the case of *BCCI*, for example, the group carried on business through 365 branches and agencies in about 70 countries. The group's records were scattered throughout the world. In the United Kingdom alone there were 100 million documents, of which by January 1992 some 40 million documents in 26,000 boxes had been logged on computer.[8]

8–05   The principles and potential complexities are illustrated by *Re Arrows Ltd (No. 4)*.[9] N was a director and principal shareholder of Arrows Ltd. When the company collapsed he was examined by the liquidators, under section 236 of the Insolvency Act 1986, and transcripts were made. A person examined under that section may not refuse to answer questions on the ground that his answers would be self-incriminating.[10] At the time of his examination N was also under investigation by the Serious Fraud Office (SFO). The SFO subsequently served a notice on the liquidators, under section 2(3) of the Criminal Justice Act 1987 requiring the liquidators to produce the transcripts to the SFO for use as evidence in criminal proceedings against him.

It was argued on behalf of N that the *Marcel* principle applied, and that the liquidators owed a private law duty to him not to produce the transcripts to the SFO. The House of Lords rejected that argument. They recognised the validity of the *Marcel* principle within its limits, *i.e.* to prevent voluntary disclosure otherwise than for the purposes for which the information or material was obtained. But, said Lord Browne-Wilkinson[11]:

> "In my view, where information has been obtained under statutory powers the duty of confidence owed on the *Marcel* principle cannot operate so as to prevent the person obtaining the information from disclosing it to those persons to whom the statutory provisions either require or authorise him to make disclosure."

Moreover, even though the statutory provisions under which the first body (*i.e.* the liquidators) obtained information by compulsion might not require or authorise that body to pass it on to a second body (*i.e.* the SFO), the second body might be empowered to require its disclosure under its own statutory powers. This was so in *Re Arrows Ltd*, where the SFO claimed production under the Criminal Justice Act 1987, under which its powers were wide. Lord Browne-Wilkinson said[12]:

> "Subject to limited exceptions the Act of 1987 expressly overrides any duty of confidence 'imposed by or under' any statute other than the Taxes Management Act 1970: section 3(3) of the Act of 1987. Similarly, the fact that section 2(9) and (10) of the Act of 1987 expressly preserves two specific duties of confidence (legal professional privilege and banking confidence) shows that all other common law duties of confidence are overridden."

---

[7] *Re Esal (Commodities) Ltd* [1989] BCLC 59; *Re Esal (Commodities) Ltd (No. 2)* [1990] BCC 708; *Morris v. Director of Serious Fraud Office* [1993] BCLC 580; *Re Maxwell Communications Corporation plc (No. 3)* [1995] 1 BCLC 521.
[8] *Morris v. Director of Serious Fraud Office* [1993] BCLC 580.
[9] [1995] 2 A.C. 75.
[10] *Bishopsgate Investment Management Ltd v. Maxwell* [1993] Ch. 1.
[11] [1995] 2 A.C. 75 at 102.
[12] *ibid.* at 99.

N also relied on public interest immunity.[13] It was argued that although his own *private law* right in the confidentiality of information extracted from him under statutory powers was subject to the statutory powers of the SFO under the Act of 1987, there was a wider *public* interest in ensuring that information extracted was used only for the purpose for which the statutory power to obtain it was conferred (*Conway v. Rimmer*[14]; *Alfred Crompton Amusement Machines Ltd v. Customs & Excise Commissioners (No. 2)*).[15] So it was submitted that N's transcripts, having been obtained under section 236 of the Insolvency Act 1986, could be used only for the purposes of the liquidation.

This argument caused the House of Lords to examine the extent of the duty of confidentiality owed by liquidators to persons examined under section 236. They concluded that the Act of 1986 contemplated liquidators disclosing information and documents obtained by them to others, including disclosure for the purposes of criminal proceedings. Accordingly, liquidators could not give any assurance to a person examined under section 236 that his answers would not be disclosed to prosecuting authorities and the claim that the answers enjoyed public interest immunity also failed. **8–06**

In addition to those cases in which a supplier of information has no choice in the matter, there are also cases in which disclosure of otherwise confidential information is obligatory if a person wishes to pursue a particular activity (*e.g.* to carry on a business for which a licence is required). Many examples could be given. Such disclosure may be described as voluntary in one sense but obligatory in another. Whichever way it is classified, the recipient will owe to the confider a duty of confidentiality, the extent of which will depend on the purposes for which it is provided.

In *R. v. Licensing Authority Established under Medicines Act 1968, ex p. Smith Kline & French Laboratories Ltd*[16] the applicants were manufacturers of a drug used in the treatment of gastric ulcers. The Medicines Act 1968 prohibits the manufacture or sale of any medicinal product except in accordance with a product licence granted by the appropriate licensing authority. By a combination of the provisions of the Act, regulations made under it and EC directives, an application for a licence had to be supported by a large amount of information of an obviously confidential nature. The applicants sought declarations to the effect that the licensing authority was not entitled to have regard to information supplied by the applicants, when considering applications by other companies for licences to market generic versions of the drug. The application failed. Lord Templeman said[17]: **8–07**

"If the appellants choose to apply for a product licence under the Act, they choose to provide information to the licensing authority for the purposes of the Act. It is not unconscionable for the licensing authority to make use of that information in the public interest for the purposes of the Act, although it would be unconscionable for the licensing authority to disclose that information to third parties for other purposes."

Looking at the purposes of the Act, Lord Templeman concluded that,

[13] For fuller discussion of public interest immunity see Chap. XXI, below.
[14] [1968] A.C. 910 at 946.
[15] [1974] A.C. 405.
[16] [1990] 1 A.C. 64.
[17] *ibid.* at 104.

"... it is the right and duty of the licensing authority to make use of all the information supplied by any applicant for a product licence which assists the licensing authority in considering whether to grant or reject any other application, or which assists the licensing authority to perform any of its other functions under the Act of 1968."

A similar question arose under different statutory provisions in New Zealand[18] and in Australia[19] with a similar result in each case.

8–08 In Australia the court rejected "the test of confider's purpose" (argued for by the company) as governing the scope of the confidant's duty in such a case. The confider's purpose in disclosing the information was narrow (to obtain a licence). The authority's purpose was wider (to protect public health and safety). In considering whether the confidant's use of the information was unconscionable, it was necessary to consider the purpose of the regulations under which the information was provided, rather than merely the purpose of the provider.

8–09 In New Zealand, Jeffries J. approached the question whether there had been a breach of a duty of confidentiality by considering the nature of the relationship between the parties. He said[20]:

"It is not a bilateral commercial relationship. It has no contractual base whatsoever. ... The parties are forced into the relationship by statute law. The Minister and his departmental officers are responsible for consenting to the use of new medicines which if faulty can have catastrophic effects of which thalidomide is an example. The Minister and Department are acting on issues in granting consent of the foremost public importance being the health of the nation ....

In the circumstances, as disclosed by this case, I would think it wrong to impose such a strict and narrow duty of confidentiality on a Government Department so as to prevent access to its own records of prior applications, and its accumulated knowledge and experience when performing the task of approving another pharmaceutical product which is identical, or nearly so."

Unwitting disclosure

8–10 Disclosure may also occur unwittingly, whether by accident, mistake or surreptitious conduct on the part of another. In *Spycatcher* Lord Goff, after stating the general principle that a duty of confidence arises when confidential information comes to the knowledge of a person in circumstances where he has notice that the information is confidential, with the effect that it would be just in all the circumstances that he should be precluded from disclosing the information to others, added[21]:

"I realise that, in the vast majority of cases, in particular those concerned with trade secrets, the duty of confidence will arise from a transaction or

---

[18] *Smith Kline and French Laboratories Ltd v. Att.-Gen.* [1989] 1 N.Z.L.R. 385.
[19] *Smith Kline and French Laboratories (Australia) Ltd v. Community Services* [1990] F.S.R. 617, *per* Gummow J.; affirmed (1991) 28 F.C.R. 291 (Full Court of the Federal Court).
[20] [1989] 1 N.Z.L.R. 385 at 396–397.
[21] [1990] 1 A.C. 109 at 281.

relationship between the parties—often a contract, in which event the duty may arise by reason of either an express or an implied term of that contract. It is in such cases as these that the expressions 'confider' and 'confidant' are perhaps most aptly employed. But it is well settled that a duty of confidence may arise in equity independently of such cases; and I have expressed the circumstances in which the duty arises in broad terms, not merely to embrace those cases where a third party receives information from a person who is under a duty of confidence in respect of it, knowing that it has been disclosed by that person to him in breach of his duty of confidence, but also to include certain situations, beloved of law teachers—where an obviously confidential document is wafted by an electric fan out of a window into a crowded street, or where an obviously confidential document, such as a private diary, is dropped in a public place, and is then picked up by a passer-by."

A variant of the last examples would be the case where a person's private diary is removed from him by a street pickpocket, who then drops it in disappointment that it is not a purse.

Doubts have been expressed whether a duty of confidence can arise through receipt of information as a result of deliberately surreptitious behaviour. The Law Commission said in its Report on Breach of Confidence[22]:

"We conclude that under the present law it is very doubtful to what extent, if at all, information becomes impressed with an obligation of confidence by reason solely of the reprehensible means by which it has been acquired, and irrespective of some special relationship between the person alleged to owe the obligation and the person to whom it is alleged to be owed."

However, if a duty of confidence can be owed by the recipient of obviously confidential information obtained by mistake, the same must apply with added force where it has been obtained surreptitiously. It would be absurd if a duty was owed in equity by the finder of a private diary dropped in the street, but not by the pickpocket, whose conscience should be more greatly affected.

It has been held that in the case of mistaken payments the recipient may owe a fiduciary duty to the party from whom the funds originated without there having been any prior fiduciary relationship originating in a consensual transaction, the mistaken receipt being itself sufficient to found an obligation of conscience.[23]

It may be equally just that a person who receives information of a confidential nature in circumstances where he knows that it has come to him by accident, mistake or misconduct, should be restricted in his use of such information by an obligation of conscience, and this is supported by a body of authority.

Prince Albert v. Strange

In *Prince Albert v. Strange* the Solicitor General argued that:　　　　**8–11**

"The information, which has been here made use of by the Defendant was

---

[22] Cmnd. 8388 (1981), para. 4.10.
[23] *Chase Manhattan Bank N.A. v. Israel-British Bank (London) Ltd* [1981] Ch. 105. Cited with approval by Millett J. at first instance in *Agip (Africa) Ltd v. Jackson* [1990] Ch. 265 at 290.

improperly obtained; either there was a breach of contract or there was a crime committed. In neither case could the Defendant obtain a title to use the information so acquired."[24]

Lord Cottenham L.C. said[25] that on the affidavit evidence the collection of royal etchings described in the catalogue published by the defendant could only have been formed by "impressions surreptitiously and improperly obtained", and that since the defendant was unable to suggest any mode by which they could have been properly obtained, so as to entitle the possessor to use them for publication, it must be assumed that the defendant's possession had its foundation in a breach of trust, confidence or contract. The tenor of the judgment does not suggest that he would have taken a more favourable view if the etchings had been surreptitiously obtained in some other way.

The principle in *Ashburton v. Pape*

8–12   In *Ashburton v. Pape*[26] the defendant surreptitiously obtained copies of letters between the plaintiff and his solicitor from a clerk employed by the solicitor, so there was both surreptitious behaviour and breach of a confidential relationship. Swinfen Eady L.J. expressed the principle as follows:

"The principle upon which the Court of Chancery has acted for many years has been to restrain the publication of information improperly or surreptitiously obtained or of information imparted in confidence which ought not to be divulged."

These words were adopted by Mason J. (later Mason C.J.) in *Commonwealth of Australia v. John Fairfax & Sons Ltd.*[27]

In *Ashburton v. Pape*[28] the defendant relied heavily on the decision of the Court of Appeal in *Calcraft v. Guest.*[29] In that case the defendant obtained copies of documents, in respect of which the plaintiff was entitled to claim privilege, from the executors of a solicitor whose predecessor had acted for the plaintiff's predecessor in title. The Court of Appeal held that, although the plaintiff was entitled to claim privilege against having to produce the documents, the defendant was entitled to give secondary evidence of their content by producing the copies which he had in fact obtained.

Ashburton v. Pape[30] and *Calcraft v. Guest*[31] do not lie happily together, as has been recognised in subsequent cases.[32] In *Goddard v. Nationwide Building Society*[33] and *Webster v. James Chapman & Co.*[34] they were explained on the basis that they are examples of two separate principles. *Calcraft v. Guest*[35]

---

[24] (1848) 1 Mac & G. 25 at 38.
[25] *ibid.* at 41–45.
[26] [1913] 2 Ch. 469 at 475.
[27] (1980) 147 C.L.R. 39 at 50.
[28] [1913] 2 Ch. 469.
[29] [1898] 1 Q.B. 759.
[30] [1913] 2 Ch. 469.
[31] [1898] 1 Q.B. 759.
[32] See Chapter XX below.
[33] [1987] 1 Q.B. 670.
[34] [1989] 3 All E.R. 939.
[35] [1898] 1 Q.B. 759.

relates to that part of the law of evidence which concerns the scope of protection afforded by the doctrine of legal professional privilege. *Ashburton v. Pape*[36] relates to the law of confidentiality. Under the former, a litigant who has in his possession copies of documents to which legal professional privilege attaches may produce those copies as secondary evidence of the documents, with the practical result that the benefit of the privilege belonging to the opposing party is lost. Under the latter, where a confidential document falls into the hands of the opposing party (or his solicitor) by mistake or misconduct, of which he is aware, the court's equitable jurisdiction is available to compel him to deliver up the document and to prevent him from making use of the information contained in it.

The correctness of *Calcraft v. Guest*[37] has been doubted,[38] and the effect of *Ashburton v. Pape*[39] and later cases has been to diminish its significance. Whatever its status as authority for a rule of evidence, it is not an authority on the law of confidentiality. On the other hand, a series of cases have now confirmed the principle stated by Swinfen Eady L.J. in *Ashburton v. Pape*[40] and have extended it to information obtained by mistake known to the recipient.[41]

Extension of *Ashburton v. Pape* to mistake

In *English & American Insurance Ltd v. Herbert Smith* (where the defendant **8–13** solicitors' decision to read papers erroneously sent to them was taken in good faith, acting upon guidance given by the Law Society and in the belief that their paramount duty was to their clients) Sir Nicolas Browne-Wilkinson V.-C. rejected the argument[42] that the principle recognised in *Ashburton v. Pape* and *Goddard v. Nationwide Building Society* did not apply where there was "an accidental escape of information to the third party" or that the recipient need be "improperly implicated in the leakage of the information".

He also drew a distinction between innocent receipt of a document and innocent receipt of the information contained in it, saying:

> "If somebody is handed a letter addressed to another marked 'Private and Confidential', that letter having been handed to him in error, and he chooses to read it notwithstanding seeing that it is marked 'Private and Confidential', and as a result acquires the information contained in that letter, I find it difficult to say that he is not implicated in the leakage of the information contained in that letter."[43]

---

[36] [1913] 2 Ch. 469.
[37] [1898] 1 Q.B. 759.
[38] *English & American Insurance Ltd v. Herbert Smith* [1988] F.S.R. 232 at 237, *per* Sir Nicolas Browne-Wilkinson V.-C.; *R. v. Uljee* [1982] 1 N.Z.L.R. 561.
[39] [1913] 2 Ch. 469.
[40] *ibid.* at 475.
[41] *Goddard v. Nationwide Building Society* [1987] 1 Q.B. 670; *Guiness Peat Ltd v. Fitzroy Robinson* [1987] 1 W.L.R. 1027; *English & American Insurance Ltd v. Herbert Smith* [1988] F.S.R. 232; *Webster v. James Chapman & Co.* [1989] 3 All E.R. 939; *Derby & Co. Ltd v. Weldon (No. 8)* [1991] 1 W.L.R. 73.
[42] [1988] F.S.R. 232 at 237.
[43] *ibid.* at 238.

Telephone tapping

8–14   In *Malone v. Metropolitan Police Commissioner*[44] the plaintiff sought a declaration that the tapping of his telephone line by the police, on the authority of the Home Secretary, was unlawful on various grounds, including confidentiality. His claim was rejected by Sir Robert Megarry V.-C. who said[45]:

> "What was in issue in the *Coco*[46] case was a communication by an inventor or designer to a manufacturer, and the alleged misuse of that information by the manufacturer. In the present case, the alleged misuse is not by the person to whom the information was intended to be communicated, but by someone to whom the plaintiff had no intention of communicating anything: and that, of course, introduces a somewhat different element, that of the unknown overhearer.
>
> It seems to me that a person who utters confidential information must accept the risk of any unknown overhearing that is inherent in the circumstances of communication. Those who exchange confidences on a bus or a train run the risk of a nearby passenger with acute hearing or a more distant passenger who is adept at lip-reading. Those who speak over garden walls run the risk of the unseen neighbour in a tool-shed nearby. Office cleaners who discuss secrets in the office when they think everyone else has gone run the risk of speaking within earshot of an unseen member of the staff who is working late. Those who give confidential information over an office intercommunication system run the risk of some third party being connected to the conversation. I do not see why someone who has overheard some secret in such a way should be exposed to legal proceedings if he uses or divulges what he has heard. No doubt an honourable man would give some warning when he realises that what he is hearing is not intended for his ears; but I have to concern myself with the law, and not with moral standards. There are, of course, many moral precepts which are not legally enforceable.
>
> When this is applied to telephone conversations, it appears to me that the speaker is taking such risks of being overheard as are inherent in the system. . . .
>
> No doubt a person who uses a telephone to give confidential information to another may do so in such a way as to impose an obligation of confidence on that other: but I do not see how it could be said that any such obligation is imposed on those who overhear the conversation, whether by means of tapping or otherwise."

The contrast drawn in this passage between a person to whom confidential information is consciously confided and the unintended overhearer may suggest that Megarry V.-C. considered that a duty of confidentiality required some deliberate act of confiding. If so, other and subsequent authorities show that the duty is not so confined. As to his detailed reasoning, there is an obvious difference between one who overhears a conversation in a bus or other public place, and an electronic eavesdropper who taps a private telephone line. The first involves no surreptitious or improper conduct; the second does.

---

[44] [1979] 1 Ch. 344.
[45] *ibid.* at 376.
[46] *Coco v. A. N. Clark (Engineers) Ltd* [1969] R.P.C. 41.

There is an interesting reference in Meagher, Gummow and Lehane[47] to a **8–15** decision of Fullager J.,

"Thus (as Fullager J. pointed out in *Concrete Industries (Monier) Ltd v. Gardner Bros & Perrott (WA) Pty Ltd* (Vic S.C., August 18 1977, unreported) it is not a defence that the plaintiff did not impart the information to the defendant and that he got it by his own hard work as an industrious eavesdropper."

This approach is consistent with the principle laid down by Swinfen Eady L.J. in *Ashburton v. Pape*[48] and with later authority.

Megarry V.-C. also held in *Malone v. Metropolitan Police Commissioner* that, if telephone eavesdropping would otherwise be in breach of a duty of confidentiality, there was just cause for it in the circumstances of the particular case because its sole purpose was for the detection and prevention of serious crime. This was a much more satisfactory reason for the refusal of the declaration claimed.[49]

Malone was distinguished by the Court of Appeal in *Francome v. Mirror Group Newspapers.*[50] The plaintiff, a well-known jockey, sought and obtained an interlocutory injunction to restrain the defendants from publishing information derived from unauthorised tapping of his telephone. The tapping was a criminal offence under the Wireless Telegraphy Act 1949.[51] The defendants contended that there could be no right of action against them, or against the eavesdroppers who recorded the plaintiff's conversations, and relied for that proposition on *Malone*. Sir John Donaldson M.R. described it as a "rather surprising proposition". The court rejected the argument that the decision in *Malone* negatived the right to confidentiality alleged by the plaintiff, and stressed that Megarry V.-C. had been dealing only with a case of authorised tapping by the police; but because the matter was before the court on an interlocutory application, it was unnecessary for it to make a final decision whether there had been a breach of a duty of confidentiality.[52]

Data storage and computer hackers

Section 5 of the Data Protection Act 1984 prohibits a person from holding **8–16** personal data (meaning data consisting of information which relates to a living individual who can be identified from that information) without being registered as a data user. The Act also places restrictions on the disclosure of such data, and contains provisions for persons concerned to discover the data held relating to them and to have inaccuracies corrected.

The Computer Misuse Act 1990 makes computer hacking a criminal offence. The Act was based on the Law Commission's Report No. 186 on *Computer*

---

[47] Meagher, Gummow and Lehane, *Equity: Doctrines and Remedies* (1992, 3rd ed.), para. 4109.
[48] [1913] 2 Ch. 469 at 475.
[49] In *Malone v. United Kingdom* (1984) 7 E.H.R.R. 14 the European Court of Human Rights decided that there had been a violation of article 8 of the European Convention on Human Rights because the law did "not indicate with reasonable clarity the scope and manner of exercise of the relevant discretion conferred on the public authorities". This led to the Interception of Communications Act 1985.
[50] [1984] 1 W.L.R. 892.
[51] See now the Interception of Communications Act 1985.
[52] See also *R. v. Preston* [1994] 2 A.C. 130 at 150.

Misuse.[53] It is not confined to conduct aimed at personal data, but would cover, for example, a company which hacked into the computer system of a rival in order to discover details of its customers, prices and costings, business plans, technical formulae or other commercial secrets. It would also apply to a person who obtained information about another by hacking into the computer system of a third party data user, such as a hospital authority or British Telecom.[54]

Information of an obviously confidential nature so obtained, whether from the computer system of the person concerned or that of a third party, and whether of a personal character or not, would clearly fall within the category of confidential "information improperly or surreptitiously obtained" (*per* Swinfen Eady L.J. in *Ashburton v. Pape*[55]), and it would be surprising if the courts would have any hesitation in restraining the use of such information. It is also hard to see any logical reason for equity to distinguish between electronic interception of mail, physical interception of mail and electronic interception of telephone calls.

Obtaining of confidential information through trespass

8–17   In *Franklin v. Giddins*[56] the defendant trespassed on the plaintiff's orchard and stole some budwood cuttings from a new and commercially valuable strain of nectarine (called "Franklin Early White"), which the plaintiff had developed by selective cross-breeding over a considerable number of years. The plaintiff could have sued in trover, but the consequence of judgment being satisfied would have been that property in the subject-matter would then have vested in the defendant (see the observations of Lord Denning M.R. in *Seager v. Copydex (No. 2)*[57]), and this would have given the defendant an unassailable right thereafter to propagate trees from the cuttings and sell them in competition with the plaintiff. The plaintiff sued for delivery up of all trees in the defendant's possession which had been propagated from the stolen cuttings and for injunctive relief, basing his claim on misuse of confidential material by the defendant.

If the defendant had been employed by the plaintiff to work in the orchard, there could be no doubt that the plaintiff would have been entitled to such relief. The case would have fallen squarely within such authorities as *Lamb v. Evans*[58] (misuse of printers' blocks for use in compiling a trade directory) and *Robb v. Green*[59] (surreptitious copying of the employer's customer list). The plaintiff's budwood was not for sale, precisely because he wished to preserve to himself the technique which he had developed for propagating Franklin Early White nectarines, as the defendant knew. By stealing the budwood the defendant acquired the ability to use that technique by dishonest means, just as if he had stolen a sheet of paper containing details of a secret formula. In the

---

[53] Cm. 819 (1989).
[54] In *R. v. Gold* [1988] A.C. 1063 the defendant hacked into British Telecom's electronic mail system and, among others, the Duke of Edinburgh's empty mailbox, using customer identification numbers without permission. His conduct was held not to fall within the Forgery and Counterfeiting Act 1981, and the Computer Misuse Act 1990 was passed in order to close the lacuna.
[55] [1913] 2 Ch. 469 at 475.
[56] [1978] Qd.R. 72.
[57] [1969] 1 W.L.R. 809 at 813.
[58] [1893] 1 Ch. 218.
[59] [1895] 2 Q.B. 315.

case of Franklin Early White nectarines, the formula was genetic, the result of cross-breeding, and was contained in (and inseparable from) the budwood.

The defendant relied on the absence of any consensual relationship between himself and the plaintiff, and he contended that an equitable obligation of confidence could only arise from the imparting of confidential matter by the plaintiff. It would be most unsatisfactory if that were so in relation to a formula of commercial value, which the plaintiff was not prepared to impart to the defendant, and which the defendant therefore resorted to dishonest means to obtain.

Dunn J. upheld the plaintiff's claim. After reference to *Prince Albert v.* **8–18** *Strange*,[60] *Saltman*[61] and *Argyll*,[62] he said[63]:

"[Counsel for the defendants] argued that the budwood twigs were not 'information confidentially imparted' and that therefore no obligation of confidence deserving of protection had arisen, challenging the proposition that 'it would be extraordinary if a defendant, who acquired by eavesdropping or other improper covert means the secrets of the plaintiff because he would not have been able to get them by consensual arrangement, could defend proceedings by the plaintiff on the ground that no obligation of confidence could arise without communication of the information by the plaintiff.' (Meagher, Gummow and Lehane's book, at page 719.)

I find myself quite unable to accept that a thief who steals a trade secret, knowing it to be a trade secret, with the intention of using it in commercial competition with its owner, to the detriment of the latter, and so uses it, is less unconscionable than a traitorous servant. The thief is unconscionable because he plans to use and does use his own wrong conduct to better his position in competition with the owner, and also to place himself in a better position than that of a person who deals consensually with the owner.

I have already expressed the opinion that, when the male defendant stole budwood from the plaintiff's orchard, what he got was a trade secret. The secret was the technique of propagating Franklin Early White nectarines, using budwood from the plaintiff's orchard. The technique of budding was no secret, but the budwood existed only in the plaintiff's orchard, where the plaintiffs guarded it by exercising general surveillance over fruit-pickers and visitors, and by bruiting it abroad that it was theirs and theirs alone. The 'information' which the genetic structure of the wood represented was of substantial commercial value, much time and effort had been expended by the male plaintiff in evolving it and it could not be duplicated by anybody whatsoever."

A comparable injunction was granted in *Shelley Films Ltd v. Rex Features* **8–19** *Ltd*,[64] on the ground of breach of an equitable duty of confidence, against use of photographs surreptitiously taken of a confidential costume design.

The plaintiffs were producers of a film, *Mary Shelley's Frankenstein*, starring the actor Robert De Niro as the Frankenstein "creature". He wore a highly distinctive costume made up of prostheses described as analogous to a rubber

[60] (1848) 1 Mac. & G. 25.
[61] (1948) 65 R.P.C. 203.
[62] [1967] Ch. 302.
[63] [1978] Qd.R. 72 at 79–80.
[64] [1994] E.M.L.R. 134.

sculpture. The plaintiffs, who had invested over $40 million in the film, were anxious that the appearance of the creature should remain a secret until the film was released. Filming took place in a secure area, manned by security guards and with notices stating that the taking of photographs was not permitted. A freelance photographer managed to gain access to the set and took photographs depicting the "creature" on the scaffold, which he supplied to the defendant photographic agency. A picture of the scene was published in the *Sunday People*.

Two days later the plaintiffs obtained, *ex parte*, an order against the defendants requiring them to disclose the identity of the photographer, but Rattee J. set aside the order on an *inter partes* hearing, on the ground that the information relating to the film which the plaintiffs sought to protect could not be said to have been communicated to the photographer in confidence, when it was the plaintiffs' case that he had obtained it clandestinely and without the plaintiffs' knowledge. The judge appears not to have been referred to any of the authorities showing that a duty of confidence may be owed by a person who obtains confidential information surreptitiously or by accident or mistake.

The plaintiffs continued with the action and applied for an interlocutory injunction restraining the defendants from publishing any photograph or reproduction depicting any costume design made for use in the film. The injunction was granted after fuller argument.

The judge, Martin Mann Q.C., cited *Franklin v. Giddins* and added:

> "Although Dunn J. characterised the information involuntarily imparted to the defendant as a trade secret, there is in my judgment no relevant distinction for present purposes between such information and less secret information similarly or analogously obtained provided always that it is properly to be regarded as confidential."

He further held that the steps taken by the plaintiffs to maintain security and prevent photography, the circumstances in which the photographs were taken, and the plaintiffs' evidence about the value which they attached to keeping the film costumes secret for commercial reasons, established against the defendant agency a serious issue to be tried that it was under an equitable obligation not to publish the photographs, sufficient for the grant of an interlocutory injunction.

Unconscionable use—*Weld-Blundell v. Stephens* revisited

8–20   Where a defendant uses improper means to obtain confidential material, the unconscionability of any attempted use of the material by him will ordinarily speak for itself. The same will not necessarily be so in the case of material received by mistake, even though the recipient realises that he has received it by mistake. The document might, for example, show that the recipient had suffered a serious wrong.

Consider the facts of *Weld-Blundell v. Stephens*[65] as told by Scrutton L.J.:

> "Mr Weld-Blundell ... instructed an accountant, one Stephens, ... to investigate the affairs of a company managed by one Hirst, which affairs he suspected were not in order. In the course of his letter he said that Hirst's

---

[65] [1919] 1 K.B. 520 at 537–538; aff'd. [1920] A.C. 959.

predecessor 'Lowe, an ingenious thief, with the help of the rest of the gang, B., H. A., and C. managed by just the same manoeuvres and pretexts to get two or three thousands.' Stephens accepted the employment for reward, and sent his partner to call on Hirst to make inquiries about the company. The partner, by what seems to me quite inexcusable carelessness, dropped or left the letter in Hirst's room. Hirst conceived himself to be justified in reading a private letter obviously not meant for him, and passed it on to Lowe and Comins, who immediately brought actions against Mr Weld-Blundell for libel, the publication alleged being the publication to Stephens."

If the same facts occurred today, would Mr Weld-Blundell succeed in an action against Messrs Hirst, Lowe and Comins claiming delivery up of the letter and an injunction against use of its contents, thus preventing the prosecution of actions against him for libel?

The letter was certainly confidential (and the Court of Appeal rejected the **8–21** accountants' argument that they owed no duty of confidentiality in respect of it because of its libellous nature). It was obviously dropped or left by mistake. Mr Hirst knew that it was a private letter and not meant for him. His conduct in reading the letter was no different from that of the person instanced by Sir Nicolas Browne-Wilkinson V.-C. in *English & American Insurance Ltd v. Herbert Smith*[66] who is handed in error a letter addressed to another marked "Private and Confidential", which he chooses to read. Mr Lowe's knowledge of the contents of the letter therefore stemmed from Mr Hirst's breach of an equitable obligation of confidence towards the writer of the letter, Mr Weld-Blundell.

Mr Weld-Blundell would no doubt feel aggrieved that a letter written by him in confidence, dropped by accident and leaked to Mr Lowe by a person who ought never to have read it, should be used to bring a libel action against him. Mr Lowe would no doubt feel aggrieved at the allegation made by Mr Weld-Blundell that he was an ingenious thief who had misappropriated company funds, and would wish to clear his reputation. Would it be unconscionable for him to seek to use the contents of the letter, and how should a court exercise its discretion whether to grant equitable relief in such circumstances?

It would seem that, prima facie, Mr Weld-Blundell should be entitled to an order for delivery up of the letter and an injunction restraining Mr Lowe (and other unintended recipients) from making use of its contents, but it is an interesting question whether the court might attach conditions to the granting of relief, such as requiring some form of withdrawal of the imputations contained in the letter (on the basis that, if he was seeking the assistance of equity to recover from X a document making a serious allegation against X, he should be willing to withdraw the allegation).

This example illustrates the importance, especially in cases where the relevant matter has not come to the knowledge of the recipient under a direct relationship with the confider, of concentrating on the particular circumstances in which the information was received in determining whether they were such as to impose on him a duty of confidence, as a matter of conscience, and the scope of such duty.

---

[66] [1988] F.S.R. 232 at 238.

CHAPTER IX

CONFIDENTIALITY AND PRIVACY

9–01   The Report of the Law Commission in 1981 on Breach of Confidence[1] was an indirect sequel to the 1972 Report of the Younger Committee on Privacy. The Younger Committee rejected proposals that there should be a general remedy for the protection of privacy, but they recommended new remedies to cover certain specific ways in which privacy might be invaded and they drew attention to the action for breach of confidence, which they considered was potentially capable of affording greater protection to privacy than had hitherto been realised. The Committee also recommended that the action for breach of confidence should be referred to the Law Commission.

The Younger Committee was particularly concerned at the covert use of surveillance devices and recommended the creation of a criminal offence of surreptitious surveillance by means of a technical device, *i.e.* an electronic or optical extension of the human senses.[2] This recommendation was not implemented.

9–02   The Law Commission considered the same subject in the context of civil liability for breach of confidence and commented as follows:[3]

"To turn now to the principles which in our view should govern the imposition of an obligation of confidence upon someone who obtains information by means of a surveillance device, we believe that a distinction must be made between (i) devices which are primarily designed *for the purpose of surveillance* and (ii) the wide range of devices which are not in themselves designed or adapted solely or primarily for that purpose, although they are *capable of being so used*. Examples of devices falling within the second category are ordinary binoculars, and an ordinary tape-recorder which may be used to record the conversation of participants at a meeting, either openly or secretly by hiding it under the table. There may be situations when surveillance devices of the latter kind are used to which those subject to that surveillance should not reasonably take exception, if they are or ought reasonably to be aware of it and if they could without undue inconvenience take precautions to avoid the surveillance in question. Thus, on the one hand, it may be thought that two people, who meet secretly in a secluded corner of a large railway station throughout which clear notices are displayed that television cameras are being used to detect criminal activities (such as malicious damage), cannot reasonably

---

[1] Cmnd. 8388 (1981), para. 1.2.
[2] Cmnd. 5012 (1972), paras. 503 and 563.
[3] Cmnd. 8388 (1981), paras. 6.37–6.38.

expect the fact of their meeting to be treated as confidential. On the other hand, it may well be that the use of an ordinary camera with a telephoto lens to obtain from the street a picture of a confidential document lying on a desk in a private house would go far beyond the reasonable expectations of the person who left it there, and that the taker of the picture should be subject to an obligation of confidence in respect of the information so obtained.

We can summarise our views on the use of surveillance devices as follows. We think that an obligation of confidence should cover information obtained by the use of *any* surveillance device, provided that such information would not have been acquired without the use of that device. However, in the case of devices which, though not designed or adapted primarily for surreptitious surveillance, enable information to be obtained which would not otherwise have been acquired, liability for the subsequent disclosure or use of that information should arise only if the person from whom the information has been obtained was not or ought not reasonably to have been aware of the use of the device, and ought not reasonably to have taken precautions to prevent the information from bring acquired in the way in question."

The Law Commission's draft Breach of Confidence Bill contained provisions to that effect,[4] but its recommendation that the law of breach of confidence should be made statutory was not adopted.

Since then there have been many calls for legislative protection of privacy.[5]   **9–03**
In *Kaye v. Robertson*[6] the Court of Appeal confirmed with regret that in English law there is no right to privacy and therefore no right of action for breach of privacy. Legatt L.J. said[7]:

"This right has so long been disregarded here that it can be recognised now only by the legislature."

In that case a journalist interviewed and took photographs of the plaintiff, a well-known actor, while he was in hospital suffering from severe brain injury and in no fit condition either to be interviewed or to give informed consent to be interviewed. The journalist ignored notices at the entrance to the hospital ward and on the plaintiff's door asking visitors to see a member of the medical staff before visiting. Bingham L.J. said[8]:

"This case ... highlights, yet again, the failure of both the common law of England and statute to protect in an effective way the personal privacy of individual citizens ... . If ever a person has a right to be let alone by strangers with no public interest to pursue, it must surely be when he lies in

---

[4] Clause 5.
[5] See the White Paper on "Privacy and Media Intrusion", July 1995, Cmnd. 2918. See also the observations of the House of Lords in *R. v. Khan*, July 2, 1996, where the question of the existence of a right to privacy in English law was left open.
[6] [1991] F.S.R. 62.
[7] *ibid.* at 71.
[8] *ibid.* at 70.

hospital recovering from brain surgery and in no more than partial command of his faculties. It is this invasion of his privacy which underlies the plaintiff's complaint. Yet it alone, however gross, does not entitle him to relief in English law."

The court granted limited relief, under the tort of malicious falsehood, in the form of an injunction prohibiting the defendants from publishing an article which implied that the plaintiff had been interviewed and photographed with his consent. The court also held that it could not, as a matter of law, grant an injunction prohibiting the publication of the photographs so as to prevent the defendants from profiting from their own trespass.

9–04 However, the fact that there is no right of action for breach of privacy, *eo nomine*, does not preclude the courts from providing protection, under the law of confidentiality, against certain forms of invasion of privacy. Indeed, that part of the purpose of the law of confidentiality is to protect personal privacy is clear, for example, from the speech of Lord Keith in the *Spycatcher* case where he said (in the context of considering whether detriment is a necessary ingredient of the cause of action for breach of confidence)[9]:

> "In other cases there may be no financial detriment to the confider, since the breach of confidence involves *no more than an invasion of personal privacy*. Thus in *Duchess of Argyll v. Duke of Argyll* [1967] Ch. 302 an injunction was granted against the revelation of marital confidences. *The right to personal privacy is clearly one which the law should in this field seek to protect*." (Emphasis added.)

9–05 There is no doubt that the law of confidentiality may apply to information and materials of a personal and private nature. They may include etchings made in private[10] and photographs taken in private.[11] Such materials have about them "the necessary quality of confidence" (in the words of Lord Greene M.R. in *Saltman*[12]) to be capable of protection by an equitable obligation of confidence.

When material has the necessary quality of confidence, equitable protection is not limited to cases in which it passes to a recipient under a consensual transaction, but is in principle available in cases in which the material is disclosed to the recipient under compulsion of law or is obtained by mistake known to the recipient or by improper means.[13] If private photographs were accidentally delivered to the wrong house, the recipient who knew that they were not meant for him would surely be under an obligation of conscience not, for example, to sell them to a magazine, just as much as the recipient of a letter meant for somebody else and marked "Private and Confidential" would be constrained by an equitable obligation of confidence (*per* Sir Nicolas Browne-Wilkinson V.-C. in *English & American Insurance v. Herbert Smith*[14]).

9–06 If, as is suggested, equitable protection is also available against a person who gleans private information by covert eavesdropping, including electronic eavesdropping, it should be equally available against the peeping Tom who

[9] [1990] 1 A.C. 109 at 255.
[10] *Prince Albert v. Strange* (1849) 2 De G. & S.M. 652.
[11] *Pollard v. Photographic Company* (1889) 40 Ch.D. 345.
[12] (1948) 65 R.P.C. 203 at 215.
[13] See Chap. VIII, above.
[14] [1988] F.S.R. 232.

obtains information or material of a private nature, by use of a telephoto lens.

This view is supported by the reasoning of Laws J. in *Hellewell v. Chief Constable of Derbyshire*.[15] The plaintiff sued for breach of confidence in relation to the use made by the police of a "mugshot" photograph of the plaintiff, taken while he was in police custody (acting under a code of practice issued by the Secretary of State under section 166 of the Police and Criminal Act 1984). The Chief Constable denied that the police owed any duty of confidence to the plaintiff in relation to the photograph. The judgment dealt with three connected issues: whether a photograph was capable of being the subject of a duty of confidence, whether the plaintiff was owed any such duty by the defendant, and what was the scope of the duty (although the judge also analysed the third issue in terms of the public interest defence).

In relation to the first matter the judge said[16]:

"I entertain no doubt that disclosure of a photograph may, in some circumstances, be actionable as a breach of confidence. If a photographer is hired to take a photograph to be used only for certain purposes but uses it for an unauthorised purpose of his own, a claim may lie against him (*Pollard v. Photographic Co.* (1888) 40 Ch.D. 345). That case concerned portrait photographs of a lady taken for her private use by a hired photographer who then used one of the pictures for a Christmas card which was put on sale in his shop. North J. upheld the plaintiff's claim, both in contract and breach of confidence. If someone with a telephoto lens were to take from a distance and with no authority a picture of another engaged in some private act, his subsequent disclosure of the photograph would, in my judgment, as surely amount to a breach of confidence as if he has found or stolen a letter or diary in which the act was recounted and proceeded to publish it. In such a case, the law would protect what might reasonably be called a right of privacy, although the name accorded to the cause of action would be breach of confidence."

As to the duty of the defendant, the judge held that the fact that the police took a photograph of the plaintiff, in custody and without freedom of choice, constrained them in the use to which they might lawfully put it. The circumstances in which they acted imposed a duty of confidence, breach of which would be actionable as a matter of private law. The scope of the duty was governed by consideration of what was reasonable.

The decision of the Court of Appeal in *Kaye v. Robertson*[17] was cited in **9–07** argument in *Hellewell*[18] but not referred to in the judgment, probably because the Court of Appeal as not concerned in the former case with an action for breach of confidence. Suppose, however, that *Kaye v. Robertson* had been argued under breach of confidence. The journalist took photographs of the plaintiff in private circumstances. If he had the plaintiff's true consent to publication, plainly he would be entitled to do so. But if the plaintiff was under such a disability as not to be able to give true consent, in principle he was surely

[15] [1995] 1 W.L.R. 804.
[16] *ibid.* at 807.
[17] [1991] F.S.R. 62.
[18] [1995] 1 W.L.R. 804.

as much entitled to protection in equity as if the defendant had climbed over the wall of his garden and secretly photographed him, or (in Laws J.'s example) had photographed him in private by use of a long range lens.

In *Shelley Films Ltd v. Rex Features Ltd*[19] an injunction was granted, on the ground of breach of an equitable duty of confidence, against use of a photograph of a film costume surreptitiously taken by a freelance photographer, who gained access to the film studio without invitation, in disregard of notices prohibiting photography. It would be surprising if the law of confidentiality accorded less protection to a patient in hospital.

In granting an injunction, the judge in *Shelley Films Ltd v. Rex Features Ltd* distinguished what he referred to as "the notorious case of *Kaye v. Robertson*", saying that:

> "... I venture that [Bingham L.J. at [1991] F.S.R. 70] was adverting solely to invasions of 'privacy' as a possible branch of the law of tort and not to predations of confidential information which is primarily an equitable doctrine and a very different question."

Professor Cornish has commented[20]:

> "Typically, the subject of protection exists as information before the obligation of confidence is assumed. But some cases have concerned events which the person bound by confidence had observed for himself. So far the courts have shown no inclination to treat the two cases differently and indeed to do so would be highly artificial. The consequence, however, is to broaden the role of the confidence action in the field of privacy."

So far this area remains undeveloped and the position of the high-tech eavesdropper and the peeping Tom with a long-range lens unresolved.

[19] [1994] E.M.L.R. 134. See Chap. VIII, above.
[20] *Intellectual Property: Patents, Copyright, Trade Marks and Allied Rights* (2nd ed., 1989) para. 8–011. See also David J. Siepp "English Judicial Recognition of a Right of Privacy" (1983), Oxford Journal of Legal Studies, Vol. 3, No. 3, 325.

CHAPTER X

REMEDIES

Injunction

A final injunction may be granted to a successful plaintiff in an action for **10–01** breach of confidence (whether arising in contract or from an equitable obligation of confidence) or for inducement of breach of contract, in order to prevent continuation of the wrongful conduct. It may also be granted, *quia timet*, to prevent threatened breach of confidence. In all such cases the court has a discretion whether to grant an injunction and, if so, on what terms and for what period. The question of duration arises particularly in "springboard" cases,[1] where the injunction should not normally extend beyond the period for which unfair advantage may reasonably be expected to continue.[2]

The question has arisen whether an injunction may be granted against a person whose past breach of confidence has resulted in the information ceasing to be protectable, to prevent him from profiting from his past wrong. In the *Spycatcher* case the point was discussed but left unresolved.[3]

In *Kaye v. Robertson*[4] the Court of Appeal held that an injunction could not in law be granted against a journalist prohibiting publication of photographs in order to prevent him from profiting from his wrong in taking them.[5] It would seem that an injunction cannot ordinarily be granted to prohibit conduct, not in itself unlawful, merely to prevent profit from previous wrongdoing.

An interlocutory injunction may be granted on the principles set out in *American Cyanamid v. Ethicon,*[6] but any such injunction must be framed in terms sufficiently specific to leave no uncertainty what the affected person is or is not allowed to do.[7,8,9,10] In *Times Newspaper Ltd v. MGN Ltd*, the Court of Appeal held that no injunction could be granted to prevent premature publication of a pirated version of Lady Thatcher's memoirs, because the plaintiffs had to concede that vital parts of the book would have to be excepted

---

[1] See Chapter IV, above.
[2] *Potters-Ballotini Ltd v. Weston-Baker* [1977] R.P.C. 202 at 206; *Roger Bullivant Ltd v. Ellis* [1987] F.S.R. 172 at 183–184.
[3] See para. 4–09, above.
[4] [1991] F.S.R. 62 at 69. See para. 4–10, above.
[5] No consideration appears to have been given to the question whether the plaintiff might be entitled to an order for delivery up of the photographs.
[6] [1975] A.C. 396.
[7] *Potters-Ballotini Ltd v. Weston-Baker* [1977] R.P.C. 202.
[8] *Lawrence David Ltd v. Ashton* [1991] 1 All E.R. 385.
[9] *PSM International plc v. Whitehouse* [1992] 1 I.R.L.R. 279.
[10] *Times Newspaper Ltd v. MGN Ltd* [1993] E.M.L.R. 442, see paras. 3–006 and 3–024.

from the scope of any injunction and the drafting of such an exception could not be satisfactorily achieved.

10–02 *Universal Thermosensor Ltd v. Hibben*[11] provides salutary warning against obtaining an interlocutory injunction in too wide terms. In that case the plaintiff succeeding in establishing breach of duty of confidence, but, having obtained an interlocutory injunction in excessively wide terms which led to the collapse of the defendants' business, it had to pay damages to the defendants on its cross undertaking. Sir Donald Nicholls V.-C. recognised that he had a discretion not to enforce the undertaking, and also found that the defendants had acted dishonestly, but he rejected the plaintiff's argument that the undertaking should for that reason not be enforced. He said[12]:

> "Punishment of the defendants is not my function. If the defendants have suffered material loss by reason of excessive width in the terms of the injunction sought and obtained by the plaintiff in July 1990, in my view they are entitled to look to the plaintiff for damages pursuant to its undertaking. Plaintiffs, and those who advise them, know or ought to know that there is a risk in obtaining interlocutory injunctive relief: the risk is that the plaintiff may have to pay compensation to the defendant if it turns out at the trial that, having regard to the facts and law as established at the trial, the effect of the injunction was to restrain a defendant from activities which it ought to have been at liberty to pursue."

Destruction or delivery up

The court has power to order delivery up or destruction of material containing confidential information or derived from misuse of confidential information, unless possibly the material has substantial intrinsic value independently of the misuse of confidential information.

10–03 In *Prince Albert v. Strange* the defendant opposed an order for delivery up or destruction of the catalogues and the impressions of the royal etchings which were in his possession. Knight-Bruce V.-C. said[13]:

> "It is then said that neither the copies of the catalogue, nor the impressions that have been taken, can be delivered, or be directed to be delivered up, inasmuch as the Defendant contends that he is entitled to the property in the materials on which they are printed. With regard to catalogues, no such question, I think, arises. They must be either cancelled or destroyed; and without destruction they can hardly be cancelled. With regard to the impressions, it might possibly be right to attend to the Defendant's claim, had the impressions been upon a material of intrinsic value—upon a material not substantially worthless, except for the impressions which, by the wrongful act of the Defendants, have been placed there. That case, however, does not arise. The material here is substantially worthless,

---

[11] [1992] 1 W.L.R. 840.
[12] *ibid.* at 858.
[13] (1849) 2 De G. & S.M. 652 at 716. The point does not appear to have been argued on the defendant's appeal before Cottenham L.C.

except for that in which the Defendant has no property. There consequently can be no reason why the effectual destruction of subject should not be directed by the Court."

This passage was cited and applied by Dunn J. in *Franklin v. Giddins*, where he ordered the delivery up for destruction of fruit trees propagated by the defendant from budwood cuttings stolen from the plaintiff's orchard.[14]

The court's power is discretionary. In *Saltman*, where the defendants misused confidential drawings of tools for the manufacture of leather punches, the report records that[15]:

"In the course of the discussion as to the relief to be given to the Plaintiffs, their Lordships expressed reluctance to make any order which would involve the destruction or sterilisation of tools which would serve a useful purpose, since under Lord Cairns's Act the Court could award damages, to cover both past and future acts, in lieu of an injunction."

The order finally agreed was that the defendants should deliver up the drawings, and that there should be an inquiry as to the damages suffered by the plaintiffs by reason of the defendants' conduct in using the drawings for the construction of leather punches for sale on their own account.

Where the successful plaintiff seeks an order for delivery up of material containing confidential information it will usually be granted, especially if the defendant cannot be relied on to destroy it.[16] In *Robb v. Green*,[17] for example, the defendant was ordered to deliver up for destruction a customer list which he had surreptitiously copied while employed by the plaintiff, and an injunction was granted restraining him from making use of the information so obtained.[18]

Account of profits

Account of profits is an established form of equitable relief. In the *Spycatcher*   **10–04**
case the *Sunday Times* was held liable to account to the Crown for profits from its breach of duty of confidence in publishing material from Mr Wright's memoirs, before the information had entered the public domain, knowing that Mr Wright was acting in breach of duty of confidence in disclosing the information. Lord Keith said[19]:

"An account of profits made through breach of confidence is a recognised form of remedy available to a claimant (*Peter Pan Manufacturing Corporation v. Corsets Silhouette Ltd* [1964] 1 W.L.R. 96; *cf. Reading v. Attorney-General* [1951] A.C. 507). In cases where the information disclosed is of a commercial character an account of profits may provide some compensation to the claimant for loss which he has suffered through the disclosure, but damages are the main remedy for such loss. The remedy

---

[14] [1978] Qd.R. 72 at 81–83. See para. 8–17, above.
[15] (1948) 65 R.P.C. 203 at 219.
[16] *Industrial Furnaces Ltd v. Reaves* [1970] R.P.C. 605 at 627.
[17] [1895] 2 Q.B. 315.
[18] See also *Reid & Sigrist Ltd v. Moss* [1932] 49 R.P.C. 461; and *Peter Pan Manufacturing Corporation v. Corsets Silhouette Ltd* [1964] 1 W.L.R. 96.
[19] [1990] 1 A.C. 109 at 262.

is, in my opinion, more satisfactorily to be attributed to the principle that no one should be permitted to gain from his own wrongdoing. Its availability may also, in general, serve a useful purpose in lessening the temptation for recipients of confidential information to misuse it for financial gain. In the present case 'The Sunday Times' did misuse confidential information and it would be naive to suppose that the prospect of financial gain was not one of the reasons why it did so. I can perceive no good ground why the remedy should not be made available to the Crown in the circumstances of this case, and I would therefore hold the Crown entitled to an account of profits in respect of the publication on 12 July, 1987."

10–05   Lord Goff expressed reservations about a general statement that a man is not to be allowed to profit from his own wrong and preferred to place the remedy of an account on a restitutionary basis. He said,[20]

"The statement that a man shall not be allowed to profit from his own wrong is in very general terms, and does not of itself provide any sure guidance to the solution of a problem in any particular case. That there are groups of cases in which a man is not allowed to profit from his own wrong, is certainly true. An important section of the law of restitution is concerned with cases in which a defendant is required to make restitution in respect of benefits acquired through his own wrongful act—notably cases of waiver of tort; of benefits acquired by certain criminal acts; of benefits acquired by certain criminal acts; of benefits acquired in breach of a fiduciary relationship; and, of course, of benefits acquired in breach of confidence. The plaintiff's claim to restitution is usually enforced by an account of profits made by the defendant through his wrong at the plaintiff's expense. This remedy of an account is alternative to the remedy of damages, which in cases of breach of confidence is now available, despite the equitable nature of the wrong, through a beneficent interpretation of the Chancery Amendment Act 1858 (Lord Cairns' Act), and which by reason of the difficulties attending the taking of an account is often regarded as a more satisfactory remedy, at least in cases where the confidential information is of a commercial nature, and quantifiable damage may therefore have been suffered."

The rule that the remedy of an account is an alternative remedy to damages was historically explained on the basis that by seeking an account the plaintiff adopted the defendant's acts,[21] and he therefore could not claim both. A better explanation is that both are forms of compensation for wrongful conduct at the plaintiff's expense and that to allow both would lead to over-compensation.

An account may be combined with other remedies apart from damages. In *Peter Pan Manufacturing Corporation v. Corsets Silhouette Ltd,*[22] where the defendants misused confidential design information to produce two styles of bra, Pennycuick J. granted an injunction restraining the defendants from manufacturing, using or distributing those styles, an order for destruction or delivery up of existing stocks and an account of profits made from those styles.

[20] *Spycatcher* [1990] 1 A.C. 109 at 286.
[21] *Sutherland Publishing Co. Ltd v. Caxton Publishing Co. Ltd* [1936] Ch. 323 at 336.
[22] [1964] 1 W.L.R. 96.

Constructive trust

A constructive trust may arise in a variety of situations, not confined to cases **10–06** of misappropriation of trust funds. In *Beatty v. Guggenheim Exploration Co.*[23] Cardozo J. said:

> "A court of equity in decreeing a constructive trust is bound by no unyielding formula. The equity of the transaction must shape the measure of relief."

In *Phipps v. Boardman*[24] the defendants bought shares in a company in which a trust had a substantial holding. They used their own money to buy the shares, but they were held to be in breach of fiduciary duty because they gained the opportunity to make the purchase from information acquired as agents of the trustees and they acted without full disclosure to the trustees. Wilberforce J. made an order declaring that they held the shares as constructive trustees, and his judgment was upheld by the House of Lords.[25]

In *U.S. Surgical Corporation v. Hospital Products International Pty Ltd*[26] the **10–07** defendants, who were exclusive distributors in Australia of surgical stapling instruments manufactured by the plaintiffs, marketed their own similar product in circumstances which were found by the trial judge, McLelland J., to amount to a breach of a fiduciary duty owed to the plaintiffs. The plaintiffs sought relief on the basis of a constructive trust over the defendants' assets. McLelland, J. said[27]:

> "Liability for breaches of equitable obligations may be of either a restitutionary or a compensatory nature. Restitutionary relief may be given by way of the imposition of a constructive trust over specific property (specific restitution) or by an accounting for profits. The imposition of a liability to acount for profits is essentially a personal rather than a proprietary remedy, but it may in some cases be appropriate to impose an equitable lien over specific property by way of security for such accounting. In the area of relief against what used to be called equitable fraud, of which profiting from a fiduciary position is one example, the precise form of relief must be moulded to satisfy the demands of justice and good conscience in the particular case: 'the court must look at the circumstances in each case to decide in what way the equity can be satisfied' (*Chalmers v. Pardoe* [1963] 1 W.L.R. 677 at 682; [1963] 3 All E.R. 552 at 555; 'the equity of the transaction must shape the measure of the relief': *Beatty v. Guggenheim Exploration Co* 122 N.E. 378 [1919], at 381; 225 N.Y. 380, at 389)."

He held that the assets of the defendants' manufacturing business were not

[23] (1919) 225 N.Y. 380 at 389, cited by Mason J. in *Hospital Products Ltd v. U.S. Surgical Corp.* (1984) 156 C.L.R. 41 at 108.
[24] [1967] 2 A.C. 46.
[25] See para. 2–04, above.
[26] [1982] 2 N.S.W.L.R. 766, reversed in the High Court on the ground that no fiduciary relationship existed between the parties ((1984) 156 C.L.R. 41).
[27] [1982] 2 N.S.W.L.R. 766 at 812–813.

property the obtaining or pursuing of which was or ought to have been an incident of the defendants' fiduciary duty, and therefore it would not be right to impose a constructive trust over those assets in favour of the plaintiffs.

Instead he ordered an account of profits from sales of the defendants' rival products. He also directed that the defendants' liability to account should be secured by an equitable lien over the defendants' assets, holding that the imposition of such a lien was a matter within the discretion of the court.[28]

10–08   In *LAC Minerals Ltd v. International Corona Resources Ltd*[29] the defendant acquired mining rights through misuse of information given to it in confidence by the plaintiff, which would otherwise have obtained the mining rights and developed the mine for itself. The trial judge declared that the defendant held the property on trust for the plaintiff, and he ordered it to deliver up the property on being compensated for the value of improvements it had made to the property in developing the mine. The order was upheld (by a majority) by the Supreme Court of Canada. La Forest J. said[30]:

> "The issue then is this. If it is established that one party (here LAC) has been enriched by the acquisition of an asset, the Williams property, that would have, but for the actions of that party, been acquired by the plaintiff (here Corona) and if the acquisition of that asset amounts to a breach of duty to the plaintiff, here either a breach of fiduciary obligation or a breach of a duty of confidence, what remedy is available to the party deprived of the benefit? In my view the constructive trust is one available remedy, and in this case it is the only appropriate remedy.
>
> In my view the facts present in this case make out a restitutionary claim, or what is the same thing, a claim for unjust enrichment. When one talks of restitution, one normally talks of giving back to someone something that has been taken from them (a restitutionary proprietary award), or its equivalent value (a personal restitutionary award). As the Court of Appeal noted in this case, Corona never in fact owned the Williams property, and so it cannot be 'given back' to them. However, there are concurrent findings below that, but for its interception by LAC, Corona would have acquired the property. In *Air Canada v. British Columbia* (judgment pronounced May 4, 1989 [now reported at 59 D.L.R. (4th) 161 at pp. 193–194, B.C.L.R. (2d) 145; [1989] 4 W.W.R. 97]), I said that the function of the law of restitution 'is to ensure that where a plaintiff has been deprived of wealth that is either in his possession *or would have accrued for his benefit*, it is restored to him. The measure of restitutionary recovery is the gain the [defendant] made at the [plaintiff's] expense.' In my view the fact that Corona never owned the property should not preclude it from the pursuing [of] a restitutionary claim: see Birks, *An Introduction to the Law of Restitution* (1985), at pp. 133–139. LAC has therefore been enriched at the expense of Corona."

The minority would have awarded damages as the appropriate remedy.

It remains to be seen whether English courts will go as far as the majority of

---

[28] Citing Goff and Jones, *The Law of Restitution* (2nd ed., 1978), pp. 47, 48 and 61, but see now Goff and Jones (4th ed., 1993) pp. 93–102.

[29] [1990] F.S.R. 441; (1989) 61 D.L.R. (4th) 14. See para. 2–22, above.

[30] [1990] F.S.R. 441 at 469.

the Supreme Court of Canada. But there seems no reason in principle why they should not, and that view is reinforced by the suggestions made, *obiter*, in several of the judgments in the *Spycatcher* case that Mr Wright held the copyright in his book on constructive trust for the Crown.[31]

Damages

Damages are available at common law for breach of a contractual duty of **10–09** confidence or inducement of breach of contract. Under the jurisdiction derived from Lord Cairns' Act 1858 (now contained in section 50 of the Supreme Court Act 1981) the court has a discretionary jurisdiction to award damages in addition to or in substitution for an injunction. It has been argued that the jurisdiction is available only in support of a legal right and not in the case of a claim based on a purely equitable obligation.[32] However, in *Saltman*,[33] which the Court of Appeal decided on the ground that there was a breach of an equitable duty of confidence, the court considered that it had jurisdiction under Lord Cairns's Act to award damages, to cover both past and future acts, in lieu of an injunction.

In *Malone v. Metropolitan Police Commissioner*[34] Sir Robert Megarry V.-C. said in relation to the right of confidentiality:

"This is an equitable right which is still in course of development, and is usually protected by the grant of an injunction to prevent disclosure of the confidence. Under Lord Cairns' Act 1858 damages may be granted in substitution for an injunction; yet if there is no case for the grant of an injunction, as when the disclosure has already been made, the unsatisfactory result seems to be that no damages can be awarded under this head: see *Proctor v. Bayley* (1889) 42 Ch.D. 390. In such a case, where there is no breach of contract or other orthodox foundation for damages at common law, it seems doubtful whether there is any right to damages, as distinct from an account of profits."

The Law Commission said in its Report on Breach of Confidence[35] that, so far as the repetition of a past, or anticipation of a future, breach of confidence is concerned, the courts have been empowered since Lord Cairns' Act to award damages in addition to or in substitution for an injunction. Lord Goff also referred in the *Spycatcher* case, in the passage cited above,[36] to damages being available under the Act for breach of an equitable duty of confidence.[37]

A more problematical question is the availability of damages in the situation **10–10** instanced by Megarry V.-C. where there is no case for the grant of an injunction. This is considered in Chapter II, dealing with the foundation[38] of the

---

[31] [1990] 1 A.C. 109 at 211 *per* Dillon L.J.; 263, *per* Lord Keith; 266, *per* Lord Brightman; 275–276 *per* Lord Griffiths; 288, *per* Lord Goff. See also Goff and Jones, *The Law of Restitution* (4th ed., 1993), pp. 694–695.

[32] Meagher, Gummow and Lehane on *Equity: Doctrines and Remedies* (3rd ed., 1992), para. 2321.

[33] (1948) 65 R.P.C. 203 at 219.

[34] [1979] 1 Ch. 344 at 360.

[35] Cmnd. 8388 (1981), para. 4.73.

[36] See para. 10–04, above.

[37] The same approach was taken by the Full Court of the Victorian Supreme Court in *Talbot v. General Television Corporation Pty Ltd* [1981] R.P.C. 1; [1980] V.R. 224.

[38] Where alternatives including a tortious theory of liability are discussed.

courts' jurisdiction in relation to breach of confidence. It is suggested that, quite apart from Lord Cairns' Act, compensation in equity (also known as equitable damages) may be awarded generally for breach of an equitable duty of confidence, just as for breach of duty by a fiduciary; and that the same compensatory principles underlie compensation or damages in equity as underlie damages at common law.[39] If this is correct, damages are available for breach of duty of confidence, whether in contract or in equity. These may in an appropriate case include loss of anticipated profits or "expectation damages".

In *United Scientific Holdings Ltd v. Burnley Borough Council*[40] Lord Diplock said:

> "Your Lordships have been referred to the vivid phrase traceable to the first edition of *Ashburner, Principles of Equity* where, in speaking in 1902 of the effect of the Supreme Court of Judicature Act he says (p. 23) 'the two streams of jurisdiction' (sc. law and equity)—'though they run in the same channel, run side by side and do not mingle their waters.' My Lords, by 1977 this metaphor has in my view become both mischievous and deceptive. The innate conservatism of English lawyers may have made them slow to recognise that by the Supreme Court of Judicature Act 1873 the two systems of substantive and adjectival law formerly administrated by courts of law and Courts of Chancery (as well as those administered by courts of admiralty, probate and matrimonial causes), were fused. As at the confluence of the Rhone and Saône, it may be possible for a short distance to discern the source from which each part of the combined stream came, but there comes a point at which this ceases to be possible. If Professor Ashburner's fluvial metaphor is to be retained at all, the waters of the confluent streams of law and equity have surely mingled now."

Lords Simon and Fraser made similar observations.[41]

10–11 In *Henderson v. Merrett Syndicates Ltd*,[42] Lord Browne-Wilkinson, dealing with the relationship of law and equity in a different context, warned of the need to ensure that the law did not "become again manacled by 'clanking chains'[43] this time represented by causes, rather than forms of action". Similarly it may be thought anachronistic today that the court's power to award damages for breach of confidence should differ according to whether the cause of action lies in contract or in an equitable obligation of confidence. But the issue is not yet firmly decided.

Other unresolved questions are whether damages may be awarded for mental stress or injury to feelings caused by breach of confidence, and whether exemplary or punitive damages may be awarded.[44]

Damages cannot ordinarily be recovered for injury to reputation or feelings[45] but there are exceptions. Defamation has always been an exception, because injury to reputation is the essence of the wrong. The courts have also

---

[39] *Royal Bank of Brunei v. Tan* [1995] 2 A.C. 378.

[40] [1978] A.C. 904 at 924.

[41] *ibid.* at 944 and 957.

[42] [1995] 2 A.C. 145 at 206.

[43] *United Australia Ltd v. Barclays Bank Ltd* [1941] A.C. 1 at 29, *per* Lord Atkin. "When these ghosts of the past stand in the path of justice clanking their mediaeval chains the proper course for the judge is to pass through them undeterred."

[44] For the comments of the Law Commission, see paras. 4.79–4.86 of its Report of Breach of Confidence (1981).

[45] *Addis v. Gramophone Co. Ltd* [1909] A.C. 488.

made an exception in cases of contract where the subject matter of the contract is the provision of pleasure[46] or protection from distress,[47] as distinct from other contracts where mental distress is a foreseeable consequence of breach.[48]

In *Williams v. Settle*[49] the defendant, a professional photographer, was **10–12** employed to take photographs of the plaintiff's wedding. The copyright in the photographs vested in the plaintiff. Two years later the plaintiff's father-in-law was murdered. The defendant sold some of the photographs to the press, one of which, showing a wedding group, was published prominently in national newspapers. The trial judge awarded damages of £1,000, and this was upheld by the Court of Appeal. Sellers L.J. said[50]:

"In the present action the judge was clearly justified, in the circumstances in which the defendant, in breach of the plaintiff's copyright, handed these photographs to the press knowing the use to which they were going to be put, in awarding substantial and heavy damages of a punitive nature. The power to do so, quite apart from the ordinary law of the land, is expressly given by statute."

He then referred to section 17(3) of the Copyright Act 1956, the forerunner of section 97(2) of the Copyright, Designs and Patents Act 1988, which now provides that:

"The court may in an action for infringement of copyright having regard to all the circumstances, and in particular to—
(a) the flagrancy of the infringement, and
(b) any benefit accruing to the defendant by reason of the infringement,
award such additional damages as the justice of the case may require."

The law as to exemplary or punitive damages is now that laid down by the House of Lords in *Rookes v. Barnard*.[51] The situations in which such damages may be awarded include conduct calculated to give the defendant a profit likely to exceed the compensation payable to the plaintiff.

The Court of Appeal of New Zealand has expressed the view in *Aquaculture* **10–13** *Corporation v. New Zealand Green Mussel Co. Ltd*[52] that there is no reason in principle why exemplary damages should not be awarded for actionable breach of confidence in a case where a compensatory award would not adequately reflect the gravity of the defendant's conduct, but there is a lack of English authority on the subject.

The problem is most likely to arise where confidential information of a personal nature is leaked to, or otherwise obtained by, the press in breach of a duty of confidence, in circumstances where the plaintiff may suffer considerable upset, but no monetary loss, and an account of profits may be an impracticable remedy. The questions which arise are, firstly, whether such a plaintiff is entitled to compensation for the non-pecuniary harm caused to him;

---

[46] *Jarvis v. Swan Tours Ltd* [1973] Q.B. 233.
[47] *Heywood v. Wellers* [1976] Q.B. 446.
[48] *Bliss v. South East Thames Regional Health Authority* [1987] I.C.R. 700 at 718; *Hayes v. Dodd* [1990] 2 All E.R. 815 at 826; *Watts v. Morrow* [1991] 1 W.L.R. 1421 at 1439.
[49] [1960] 1 W.L.R. 1072.
[50] *ibid.* at 1082.
[51] [1964] A.C. 1129 at 1226–1227.
[52] [1990] 3 N.Z.L.R. 299 at 301.

and secondly, whether he is entitled to claim exemplary damages on the basis that the conduct was calculated to generate a profit exceeding the amount of any compensatory damages (which, if the answer to the first question is negative, would *ex hypothesi* be nil). Professor Cornish has commented[53]:

> "There remains the question as yet unexplored in the case-law, whether damages for injury to feelings are available for breach of confidence, as they are for defamation and copyright infringement. All that can usefully be said is this. Breach of confidence is slowly becoming one of the ways in which the law accords protection to privacy and those aspects of personal reputation that are associated with it. Infringement of copyright and defamation fulfil the same function in ways that are differently limited. But since both allow damages for injured feelings, it would seem quixotic to bar this form of monetary compensation from the third field, for the sake of yet another historical point."

It may be argued that, in a case where a duty of confidentiality exists to protect personal privacy,[54] its object is to protect the feelings of the confider, and therefore it would be in accordance with principle to allow damages for injury to feelings caused by breach of that duty. But whether the courts will adopt that approach remains to be seen. If they do, the case for exemplary damages would be weakened, because the plaintiff would be entitled to compensation for the non-pecuniary injury caused to him as well as to an account.

Declaration

10–14   The court has a discretionary power to grant declaratory relief, and this may be an appropriate way of determining questions of confidentiality.[55] Such relief is normally sought by a person complaining of breach of confidence. However there is no reason in principle why a person who is threatened with proceedings for breach of confidence if he makes use of information alleged to be confidential should not bring proceedings for a declaration of non-confidentiality, just as a party threatened, for example, with an action for passing off may seek a declaration of non-liability.[56] In *Price Waterhouse v. BCCI Holdings (Luxembourg) SA*[57] the plaintiffs applied for, and were granted, a declaration that they were not precluded by confidence owed to the defendants from supplying information and documents to an inquiry into the supervision of BCCI.

Anton Piller order

10–15   *Anton Piller KG v. Manufacturing Processes Ltd*[58] was an action for infringement of copyright and misuse of confidential information. The action

---

[53] *Intellectual Property Patents, Copyright, Trade Marks and Allied Rights* (2nd ed., 1989) para. 8–042.

[54] See Chap. IX, above.

[55] See, for example, *Malone v. Metropolitan Police Commissioner* [1979] 1 Ch. 344 and *Hellewell v Chief Constable of Derbyshire* [1995] 1 W.L.R. 804.

[56] Compare *Bulmer Ltd v. Bollinger S.A.* [1974] Ch. 401; [1978] R.P.C. 79.

[57] [1992] BCLC 583. See para. 6–12, above.

[58] [1976] Ch. 55.

began with orders made *ex parte*, authorising the plaintiffs to inspect the defendants' premises and seize relevant documents. The procedure was approved by the Court of Appeal, with the warning that such an order was only to be made where it was essential so that justice could be done between the parties and when, if the defendant were forewarned, there would be grave danger that vital evidence would be destroyed or hidden.

Concern that such orders were being made too readily, and executed in a way which amounted to abuse, has led to stricter controls being imposed by the courts: see *Columbia Picture Industries Inc. v. Robinson*[59] per Scott J.; *Lock International plc v. Beswick*[60] per Hoffman J.; and *Universal Thermosensors Ltd v. Hibben*[61] per Nicholls V.-C.

In *Universal Thermosensors Ltd v. Hibben*, Nicholls V.-C. commented that the case illustrated both the virtues and the vices of Anton Piller orders. The plaintiff was enabled to recover stolen documents containing confidential information, which the judge considered would in all probability otherwise have been destroyed; but this result was achieved at a high price. Irregularities in the execution of the order led to claims against the plaintiff and the plaintiff's solicitors which were settled during the trial.

Anton Piller orders remain a valuable weapon, but one which requires the utmost care by the court and by the plaintiff both in making the application and in executing any order. The fact that such applications are usually made in a hurry makes it all the more important for the plaintiff to take care to ensure, as in any *ex parte* application, that all relevant matters are drawn to the attention of the court.

Action for discovery

A person whose confidence has been breached, but who does not know who **10–16** was responsible, may be able to bring an action against a recipient of the confidential information to compel him to disclose the identity of the informer. This form of action is derived from the ancient bill of discovery in equity, which was given new life by the decision of the House of Lords in *Norwich Pharmacal Co. v. Customs and Excise Commissioners*[62] and applied by the House of Lords in *British Steel Corporation v. Granada Television Ltd*[63] In the latter case an unknown senior employee of BSC, during a steel strike, supplied to Granada a number of highly confidential documents, which were used in a television programme. BSC issued a writ and notice of motion claiming, among other things, delivery up of the documents. They were returned by Granada, but with portions cut out to hide the identity of the mole. BSC then amended its writ and notice of motion to claim an order that Granada serve an affidavit disclosing the source of their information. This claim succeeded.

Granada had promised the mole that they would not reveal his identity. Confidentiality therefore came into the case at two stages; the mole owed a duty of confidence to BSC, and Granada promised confidentiality to the mole in breaching that duty. Granada conceded that an application for an injunction to

---

[59] [1987] Ch. 38.
[60] [1989] 1 W.L.R. 1268.
[61] [1992] F.S.R. 361.
[62] [1974] A.C. 133.
[63] [1981] A.C. 1096 at 1171.

prohibit use of the documents before the programme was shown would have succeeded, but denied that the bill of discovery procedure was available against newspapers.

10–17   The House of Lords rejected Granada's argument, but recognised that the remedy of an action for discovery, being equitable, was discretionary.[64] The court ought not to compel confidence bona fide given to be breached unless necessary in the interests of justice.[65] The plaintiff therefore had to show that it could not get all the relief it reasonably required without such discovery. Whereas in libel cases a plaintiff might be able to recover all he reasonably required in compensation for the libel by suing the newspaper without needing to know the source of its information, BSC was in the position of having an undetected mole in its higher ranks, causing suspicion and mistrust among others, and needed to know the mole's identity.

Following that decision, Parliament introduced qualified immunity from such an action by section 10 of the Contempt of Court Act 1981, which provides:

> "No court may require a person to disclose, nor is any person guilty of contempt of court for failing to disclose, the source of information contained in a publication for which he is responsible, unless it is established to the satisfaction of the court that disclosure is necessary in the interests of justice or national security or for the prevention of disorder or crime."[66]

Delay

10–18   In accordance with ordinary principles of equity, a person seeking equitable relief against breach of confidence will risk refusal if he fails to act with reasonable promptness once he knows of the breach. He cannot, for example, stand by while the party in breach exploits the information and then claim an account of profits. For actions based on breach of contract the limitation period is six years, subject to the provisions of section 32 of the Limitation Act 1980 relating to fraud, concealment or mistake.

---

[64] *British Steel Corporation v. Granada Television Ltd* [1981] A.C. 1096 at 1174, *per* Lord Wilberforce.
[65] *Science Research Council v. Nasse* [1980] A.C. 1028.
[66] For discussion of section 10, see para. 15–04, below.

CHAPTER XI

EUROPEAN CONVENTION ON HUMAN RIGHTS

ARTICLES 8 AND 10

Articles 8 and 10 of the European Convention for the Protection of Human **11–01** Rights and Fundamental Freedoms[1] provide as follows:

"*Article 8*
   (1) Everyone has the right to respect for his private and family life, his home and his correspondence.
   (2) There shall be no interference by a public authority with the exercise of this right except such as is in accordance with the law and is necessary in a democratic society in the interests of national security, public safety or the economic well-being of the country, for the prevention of disorder or crime, for the protection of health or morals, or for the protection of the rights and freedoms of others.

Article 10
   (1) Everyone has the right to freedom of expression. This right shall include freedom to hold opinions and to receive and impart information and ideas without interference by public authority and regardless of frontiers. This Article shall not prevent States from requiring the licensing of broadcasting, television or cinema enterprises.
   (2) The exercise of these freedoms, since it carries with it duties and responsibilities, may be subject to such formalities, conditions, restrictions or penalties as are prescribed by law and are necessary in a democratic society, in the interests of national security, territorial integrity or public safety, for the prevention of disorder or crime, for the protection of health or morals, for the protection of the reputation or rights of others, for preventing the disclosure of information received in confidence, or for maintaining the authority and impartiality of the judiciary."

The United Kingdom is a party to the Convention, but has not enacted it as part of domestic law. However, the courts have gradually taken increasing cognisance of it when they have felt it possible to do so.

[1] Cmnd. 8969 (1993).

Article 8 and English law

11–02   Article 8 was relied upon by the defendant in *R. v. Khan*.[2] He was charged with heroin smuggling. The evidence against him consisted of a tape recorded conversation, obtained clandestinely by the police having affixed a listening device to the outside wall of his house. The police had no statutory authority to do so, but acted within Home Office guidelines. The fixing of the device involved trespass and some physical damage to the property. The trial judge ruled that the evidence was admissible. The defendant then pleaded guilty, reserving his right to appeal. His appeal was dismissed. Lord Taylor C.J. said[3]:

> "As to the argument based on article 8 of the European Convention on Human Rights, counsel for the Crown rightly pointed out that it is not (as yet) part of the law of the United Kingdom since it has not been enacted into our statutory law. He referred us to *Chundawadra v. Immigration Appeal Tribunal* [1988] Imm.A.R. 161 and *Pan-American World Airways Inc. v. Department of Trade* [1976] 1 Lloyd's Rep. 257. From these authorities it is clear that it is permissible to have regard to the Convention, which is of persuasive assistance, in cases of ambiguity or doubt. In the circumstances of the present case the position is neither ambiguous nor doubtful; nor is it incumbent on us to consider whether there was a breach of article 8, and we do not propose to do so."

The House of Lords approved this approach with the qualification that the principles of the Convention could be taken into account in the exercise of the court's discretion to exclude evidence under section 78 of the Police and Criminal Evidence Act 1984.

Article 10 and English law

11–03   In relation to article 10 the courts have gone further. In *Rantzen v. Mirror Group Newspapers (1986) Ltd* Neill L.J., after noting[4] that the courts had no power to enforce Convention rights directly, but might refer to the Convention for assistance to resolve an ambiguity in English legislation[5] or when considering the exercise of a discretion,[6] went on to say[7]:

> "Where freedom of expression is at stake, however, recent authorities lend support for the proposition that article 10 has a wider role and can properly be regarded as an articulation of some of the principles underlying the common law."

---

[2] [1995] Q.B. 27. Affirmed by the House of Lords, July 2, 1996.
[3] *ibid.* at 40.
[4] [1994] Q.B. 670 at 690.
[5] *ex p. Brind* [1991] 1 A.C. 696 at 747.
[6] *Spycatcher No. 1* [1987] 1 W.L.R. 1248 at 1296. See also the judgment of Neill L.J. in *Re W (A Minor) (Wardship: Restrictions on Publication)* [1992] 1 W.L.R. 100 at 103.
[7] [1994] Q.B. 670 at 691.

He relied in particular on the speech of Lord Goff in the *Spycatcher* case where, after referring to the requirement that an injunction to restrain the disclosure of government secrets must be shown to be in the public interest, Lord Goff continued[8]:

"... I can see no inconsistency between English law on this subject and article 10 of the European Convention on Human Rights. This is scarcely surprising, since we may pride ourselves on the fact that freedom of speech has existed in this country perhaps as long as, if not longer than, it has existed in any other country in the world.... In any event I conceive it to be my duty, when I am free to do so, to interpret the law in accordance with the obligations of the Crown under this treaty. The exercise of the right to freedom of expression under article 10 may be subject to restrictions (as are prescribed by law and are necessary in a democratic society) in relation to certain prescribed matters, which include 'the interests of national security' and 'preventing the disclosure of information received in confidence'. It is established in the jurisprudence of the European Court of Human Rights that the word 'necessary' in this context implies the existence of a pressing social need, and that interference with freedom of expression should be no more than is proportionate to the legitimate aim pursued. I have no reason to believe that English law, as applied in the courts, leads to any different conclusion."

Neill, L.J. also cited *Derbyshire County Council v. Times Newspapers Ltd.*[9]

The position that article 8 may be looked at only in cases of ambiguity or doubt, but that article 10, although not part of domestic law, is found to be an articulation of common law principles, is clearly a somewhat unsatisfactory half way house.[10] It would seem, however, that in relation to article 10, at least, decisions of the European Court of Human Rights must be regarded as of persuasive authority, and the principles established by them are likely to be followed except where statutory provisions require a court to do otherwise.

Article 10 and the European Court

The words of article 10(2) "necessary in a democratic society" have been **11–04** interpreted as connoting something less than "indispensable", but stronger than "reasonable" or "desirable". There must be a "pressing social need" to interfere with the right to freedom of expression, and the interference must be proportionate to the legitimate aim pursued.[11]

In *Sunday Times v. United Kingdom (No. 2)*[12] the European Court of Human Rights amplified the general principles, with particular reference to the press, as follows:

"Argument before the Court was concentrated on the question whether the interference complained of could be regarded as 'necessary in a

---

[8] [1990] 1 A.C. 109 at 283–284.
[9] [1993] A.C. 534 at 551.
[10] Repeated calls by senior judges, including the present Lord Chief Justice and Master of the Rolls, for legislation to adopt the Convention as domestic law have, to date, not been followed.
[11] *Barthold v. Germany* (1985) 7 E.H.R.R. 283; *Spycatcher (No. 2)* [1990] 1 A.C. 109 at 283–284.
[12] (1991) 14 E.H.R.R. 229 at 241–242.

democratic society.' In this connection, the Court's judgments relating to Article 10—starting with HANDYSIDE,[13] concluding, most recently, with OBERSCHLICK[14] and including, amongst several others, SUNDAY TIMES[15] and LINGENS[16]—announce the following major principles.

(a) Freedom of expression constitutes one of the essential foundations of a democratic society; subject to paragraph (2) of Article 10, it is applicable not only to 'information' or 'ideas' that are favourably received or regarded as inoffensive or as a matter of indifference, but also to those that offend, shock or disturb. Freedom of expression, as enshrined in Article 10, is subject to a number of exceptions which, however, must be narrowly interpreted and the necessity for any restrictions must be convincingly established.

(b) These principles are of particular importance as far as the press is concerned. Whilst it must not overstep the bounds set, *inter alia*, in the 'interests of national security' or for 'maintaining the authority of the judiciary,' it is nevertheless incumbent on it to impart information and ideas on matters of public interest. Not only does the press have the task of imparting such information and ideas; the public also has a right to receive them. Were it otherwise, the press would be unable to play its vital role of 'public watchdog.'

(c) The adjective 'necessary', within the meaning of Article 10(2), implies the existence of a 'pressing social need.' The Contracting States have a certain margin of appreciation in assessing whether a need exists, but it goes hand in hand with a European supervision, embracing both the law and the decisions applying it, even those given by independent courts. The Court is therefore empowered to give the final ruling on whether a 'restriction' is reconcilable with freedom of expression as protected by Article 10.

(d) The Court's task, in exercising its supervisory jurisdiction, is not to take the place of the competent national authorities but rather to review under Article 10 the decisions they delivered pursuant to their power of appreciation. This does not mean that the supervision is limited to ascertaining whether the respondent State exercised its discretion reasonably, carefully and in good faith; what the Court has to do is to look at the interference complained of in the light of the case as a whole and determine whether it was 'proportionate to the legitimate aim pursued' and whether the reasons adduced by the national authorities to justify it are 'relevant and sufficient.'

For the avoidance of doubt, and having in mind the written comments that were submitted in this case by 'Article 19,' the Court would only add to the foregoing that Article 10 of the Convention does not in terms prohibit the imposition of prior restraints on publication, as such. This is evidenced not only by the words 'conditions,' 'restrictions,' 'preventing' and 'prevention' which appear in that provision, but also by the Court's SUNDAY TIMES judgment of 26 April 1979[17] and its MARKET INTERN VERLAG Gmbh

---

[13] *Handyside v. United Kingdom* (1976) 1 E.H.R.R. 737.
[14] *Oberschlick v. Austria*, Series A, No. 204.
[15] *Sunday Times v. United Kingdom* (1979) 2 E.H.R.R. 245.
[16] *Lingens v. Austria* (1986) 8 E.H.R.R. 103.
[17] *Sunday Times v. United Kingdom* (1979) 2 E.H.R.R. 245.

AND KLAUS BEERMANN judgment of 20 November, 1989.[18] On the other hand, the dangers inherent in prior restraints are such that they call for the most careful scrutiny on the part of the Court. This is especially so as far as the press is concerned, for news is a perishable commodity and to delay its publication, even for a short period, may well deprive it of all its value and interest."

It is important to stress that the requirement for the court to look at the **11–05** interference complained of in the light of the case as a whole, and to determine whether it is "proportionate to the legitimate aim pursued", is the final step in its process of reasoning and not the starting point. Otherwise, the decision could all too easily turn on matters of political or social viewpoint, upon which in any democracy opposing views may be held without being either "right" or "wrong", and this would itself be a denial of justice in a democratic society.

Article 8 (right to privacy) and article 10 (right to freedom of expression) are each subject to such exceptions as are "in accordance with the law" (*per* article 8) or "prescribed by law" (*per* article 10) and are "necessary in a democratic society". It is necessary in a democratic society that the principles of law should be clear and known in advance[19] and that applies to the exception to article 10 concerning restrictions "for preventing the disclosure of information received in confidence".

The content of the law in this area must be based on objective legal principles, rather than a general discretion to act upon the judge's view of the facts as a whole. There is an important distinction, recognised in English domestic law, between rights of confidentiality vested in the government and rights of confidentiality vested in its citizens. In the case of the former, the purpose is the protection of the public, and it would be irrational to enforce such rights unless the threatened disclosure would be harmful to the public.[20] Citizens' rights are for their own benefit (although there is a general public interest in maintaining respect for confidence in the same way as there is a general public interest in maintaining respect for freedom of contract) and should not be subject to dispensation on the mere basis that on the judge's view of the facts the public would be interested in disclosure or benefit from disclosure. There must be a higher test, and it is a matter of law what that test is. This subject is discussed in relation to domestic law in Chapter VI.

As the European Court's role is not to take the place of the competent domestic court, but to review its application of the law, it can only do so properly if the domestic court has itself identified the principles of law on which it has acted. It is in that context that the court has to consider whether the restriction resulting from the application of those principles to the facts of the case is proportionate to the legitimate purpose.

Spycatcher in Europe

In *Observer and Guardian v. United Kingdom*[21] the newspapers complained **11–06** of the interlocutory injunction granted by Millett J. in *Spycatcher (No. 1)*[22] in July 1986, and continued in force by the House of Lords in July 1987, by which

---

[18] *Markt Intern Verlag and Beermann v. Germany* (1990) 12 E.H.R.R. 161.
[19] In *Malone v. United Kingdom* (1984) 7 E.H.R.R. 14 the government lost for that reason.
[20] *Commonwealth of Australia v. John Fairfax & Sons Ltd* (1980) 147 C.L.R. 39 at 51–52 Mason J., cited in *Spycatcher* [1990] 1 A.C. 109 at 258, 270 and 283.
[21] (1991) 14 E.H.R.R. 153.
[22] [1987] 1 W.L.R. 1428.

they were restrained from publication of extracts from Peter Wright's book until the final determination of the case in October 1988.[23]

By the time of the House of Lords' first decision in July 1987 the book had been published in the U.S.A. and was freely obtainable in the United Kingdom by anyone who wanted to read it. In *Sunday Times v. United Kingdom (No. 2)*[24] complaint was made by the *Sunday Times* in respect of the period of the injunction from (but not before) the first decision of the House of Lords.

11–07   In *Spycatcher (No. 1)*[25] the House of Lords' decision to continue to restrain publication of extracts from the book, despite its widespread availability, was reached by a majority of three to two, with strong dissenting speeches from Lord Bridge and Lord Oliver. Lord Bridge said[26]:

> "But I can see nothing whatever, either in law or on the merits, to be said for the maintenance of a total ban on discussion in the press of this country of matters of undoubted public interest and concern which the rest of the world now knows all about and can discuss freely ....
>
> The maintenance of the ban, as more and more copies of the book *Spycatcher* enter this country and circulate here, will seem more and more ridiculous. If the Government are determined to fight to maintain the ban to the end, they will face inevitable condemnation and humiliation by the European Court of Human Rights in Strasbourg. Long before that they will have been condemned at the bar of public opinion in the free world."

Lord Bridge was right in his forecast that the government would lose before the European Court of Human Rights. It rejected the complaints that article 10 was violated by the granting of injunctions in the first place, when there was still confidentiality to protect, but it held that the continuation of those injunctions by the House of Lords after confidentiality had been lost did contravene article 10. The court said[27]:

> "As regards the interest of national security relied on, the Court observes that in this respect the Attorney General's case underwent, to adopt the words of Scott J., 'a curious metamorphosis.' As emerges from Sir Robert Armstrong's evidence, injunctions were sought at the outset, *inter alia*, to preserve the secret character of information that ought to be kept secret. By 30 July 1987, however, the information had lost that character .... By then, the purpose of the injunctions had thus become confined to the promotion of the efficiency and reputation of the Security Service, notably by: preserving confidence in that Service on the part of third parties; making it clear that the unauthorised publication of memoirs by its former members would not be countenanced; and deterring others who might be tempted to follow in Mr Wright's footsteps.
>
> The Court does not regard these objectives as sufficient to justify the continuation of the interference complained of. It is, in the first place, open to question whether the actions against O.G.[28] could have served to advance the attainment of these objectives any further than had already

---

[23] For the history of the *Spycatcher* case, see (1992) 14 E.H.R.R. 153 at 156–173.
[24] (1992) 14 E.H.R.R. 229.
[25] [1987] 1 W.L.R. 1248.
[26] *ibid.* at 1286.
[27] (1992) 14 E.H.R.R. 153 at 195–196.
[28] *Observer* and *The Guardian*.

been achieved by the steps taken against Mr. Wright himself. Again, bearing in mind the availability of an action for an account of profits, the Court shares the doubts of Lord Oliver of Aylmerton[29] whether it was legitimate, for the purpose of punishing Mr. Wright and providing an example to others, to use the injunctive remedy against persons, such as O.G., who had not been concerned with the publication of *Spycatcher*. Above all, continuation of the restrictions after July 1987 prevented newspapers from exercising their right and duty to purvey information, already available, on a matter of legitimate public concern."

The United Kingdom was ordered to pay £100,000 to the *Observer* and *The Guardian* and £100,000 to the *Sunday Times* for costs and expenses in the domestic proceedings and at Strasbourg.

Article 10 and Order for disclosure of a journalists source

This subject, which arose in *Goodwin v. United Kingdom*,[30] is considered in Chapter XV.[31]

---

[29] Lord Oliver said at [1987] 1 W.L.R. 1248 at 1318,
"I question whether the imposition of an injunction on A simply in order to punish B and to provide an example to C is a correct or permissible use of an injunctive remedy. The injunction was originally imposed in order to preserve the confidentiality of the then unpublished allegations. That confidentiality has now, without fault on the part of the appellants, been irrevocably destroyed and, no doubt, destroyed as a result of a calculated policy adopted by Mr Wright and those associated with him. ... But once that has occurred and the prescribed material is available for public ventilation and discussion by everybody except those subject to the existing restraint, I question whether it can be right to continue that restraint against parties in no way concerned with flouting the court's orders and to interfere with their legitimate business of publishing and commenting upon matters already in the public domain for the purpose, not of preventing that which can no longer be prevented, but of punishing Mr Wright and providing an example to others."
[30] *The Times*, March 28, 1996.
[31] See paras. 15–03 *et seq.*

Chapter XII

CONFIDENTIALITY AND FOREIGN LAW

12–01   A conflict of laws problem arises if the law of one country is invoked to obtain disclosure of documents or information within the jurisdiction of another, *a fortiori* if such disclosure would be contrary to the law of the country in whose jurisdiction they are.

There is generally accepted and well founded dislike of laws which have extra-territorial effect, both on grounds of respect for the jurisdiction of other countries and to avoid injustice in the form of a party being subject to mutually contradictory edicts. The risk is particularly great for companies, like banks, operating across frontiers. But there is another side to the picture. Neill L.J. observed in *Derby & Co. Ltd v. Weldon (Nos. 3 & 4)*[1] that "assets, like the Cheshire cat, may disappear unexpectedly", and that modern technology and the ingenuity of its beneficiaries can make assets depart at a speed which would make the disappearance of the Cheshire cat look sluggish.

12–02   There may therefore be cases in which strict adherence by the courts to the principle of territoriality may play into the hands of fraudsters.

The authorities may be divided into three groups:

> (1) cases where English courts are asked to make an order requiring production of documents of a confidential nature which are outside the jurisdiction;
>
> (2) cases where foreign courts make an order requiring production of documents of a confidential nature which are within the United Kingdom;
>
> (3) cases where English courts or regulatory authorities are asked to assist the courts or regulatory authorities of another country.

Cases where English courts are asked to order production of confidential documents outside the jurisdiction

12–03   It is necessary to distinguish between:

> (1) cases where the person against whom the order is sought is a party to litigation in the United Kingdom (otherwise than merely for the purpose of discovery under the *Norwich Pharmacal*[2] procedure); and

---

[1] [1990] Ch. 65 at 95.
[2] *Norwich Pharmacal Co. v. Customs & Excise Commissioners* [1974] A.C. 133.

(2) cases where the person against whom the order is sought is not a party to the litigation or has been joined in an action only for the purposes of discovery.

In the former class the ordinary rules of discovery make no distinction between documents inside and outside the jurisdiction, so long as they are within the possession, custody or power of the party against whom discovery is sought. This involves no breach of comity, because discovery in the ordinary course of litigation is a matter of procedure, not substance, and the principle that procedure is governed by the *lex fori* is of general application and universally admitted.[3]

In cases where the party against whom a production order is sought is not a party to the action, or has been joined for the purpose of discovery, an order for production is not merely an incidental matter of procedure but is the substance of the relief sought. In *R. v. Grossman*[4] an order was made, *ex parte*, against Barclays Bank Ltd at its London head office requiring it to allow the Inland Revenue to inspect and take copies of its books relating to the account of an Isle of Man company at its Isle of Man branch, under section 7 of the Bankers' Books Evidence Act 1879. The order was set aside by the Court of Appeal. Lord Denning M.R. said[5]:

> "I think that the branch of Barclays Bank in Douglas, Isle of Man, should be considered in the same way as a branch of the Bank of Ireland or an American Bank, or any other bank in the Isle of Man which is not subject to our jurisdiction. The branch of Barclays Bank in Douglas, Isle of Man, should be considered as a different entity separate from the head office in London. It is subject to the laws and regulations of the Isle of Man. It is licensed by the Isle of Man government. It has its customers there who are subject to the Manx laws. It seems to me that the court here ought not in its discretion to make an order against the head office here in respect of the books of the branch in the Isle of Man in regard to the customers of that branch. It would not be right to compel the branch—or its customers— to open their books or to reveal their confidences in support of legal proceedings in Wales. Any order in respect of the production of the books ought to be made by the courts of the Isle of Man—if they will make such an order. It ought not to be made by these courts. Otherwise there would be danger of a conflict of jurisdictions between the High Court here and the courts of the Isle of Man. That is a conflict which we must always avoid."

In *MacKinnon v. Donaldson, Lufkin and Jenrette Securities Corporation*[6] the **12–04** plaintiff in an action involving allegations of international fraud obtained an order *ex parte* under the Bankers' Books Evidence Act requiring an American

---

[3] Dicey & Morris, *The Conflict of Laws* (12th ed., 1993), p. 169, citing *Ailes* (1941) 39 Mich.L.Rev. 392; *The Consul Corfitzon* [1917] A.C. 550 at 555–556; *MacKinnon v. Donaldson, Lufkin & Jenrette Corp.* [1986] 1 Ch. 483 at 494–495, *per* Hoffman J.,

"I am not concerned with the discovery required by R.S.C., Ord. 24 from ordinary parties to English litigation who happen to be foreigners. If you join the game you must play according to the local rules. This applies not only to plaintiffs but also to defendants who give notice of intention to defend."

[4] (1981) 73 Cr.App.R. 302.

[5] *ibid.* at 307.

[6] [1986] 1 Ch. 482.

bank, which was not a party to the action, to produce books held at its head office in New York relating to one of the defendants, a defunct Bahamian company. The plaintiff also issued a *supoena duces tecum* against an officer of the bank at its London office. Hoffmann J. set aside both orders.

The plaintiff attempted to distinguish *Grossman* on the ground that in that case the Isle of Man court had previously refused a similar application and had granted an injunction restraining the bank from disclosing the information. It was also argued that the American bank, by carrying on business in London, had submitted to the jurisdiction of the English court and should be required to comply with the *subpoena* unless production would be unlawful by the law of the place where the documents were kept.

Hoffman J. rejected that argument. He said[7]:

> "I think that this argument confuses personal jurisdiction, *i.e.* who can be brought before the court, with subject matter jurisdiction, *i.e.* to what extent the court can claim to regulate the conduct of those persons. It does not follow from the fact that a person is within the jurisdiction and liable to be served with process that there is no territorial limit to the matters upon which the court may properly apply its own rules or the things which it can order such a person to do. As Dr Mann observed in a leading article "The Doctrine of Jurisdiction in International Law", (1964) 111 *Recueil de cours* 146,
>
> > 'The mere fact that a state's judicial or administrative agencies are internationally entitled to subject a person to their personal or 'curial' jurisdiction does not by any means permit them to regulate by their orders such person's conduct abroad. This they may do only if the state of the forum also had substantive jurisdiction to regulate conduct in the manner defined in the order. In other words, for the purpose of justifying, even in the territory of the forum, the international validity of an order, not only its making, but also its content must be authorised by substantive rules of legislative jurisdiction.'
>
> See also by the same author "The Doctrine of International Jurisdiction Revisited after Twenty Years" (1984) 196 *Recueil des cours* 9, 19.
>
> The content of the subpoena and order is to require the production by a non-party of documents outside the jurisdiction concerning business which it has transacted outside the jurisdiction. In principle and on authority it seems to me that the court should not, save in exceptional circumstances, impose such a requirement upon a foreigner, and, in particular, upon a foreign bank. The principle is that a state should refrain from demanding obedience to its sovereign authority by foreigners in respect of their conduct outside the jurisdiction."

The plaintiff also attempted to distinguish *Grossman* by arguing that he would be entitled to join the bank as a defendant under *Norwich Pharmacal*[8] and *Bankers Trust Co. v. Shapira*[9] and that the case should not therefore be regarded as an attempt to enforce discovery against a non-party.

12–05 Hoffman J. rejected that distinction, holding that for jurisdictional purposes such cases were much more akin to a *subpoena* directed to a witness than to

---

[7] *Mackinnon v. Donaldson, Lufkin and Jenrette Securities Corporation* [1986] 1 Ch. 482 at 493.
[8] [1974] A.C. 133.
[9] [1980] 1 W.L.R. 1274.

discovery required of an ordinary defendant, and that the court should recognise the same international jurisdictional limits in such cases as in cases of a *subpoena duces tecum* or an order under the Bankers' Books Evidence Act 1879. He accordingly held, following *Grossman*, that an order for production of documents held at a bank's foreign branch or head office should not be made save in very exceptional circumstances. He also expressed the opinion that, where alternative procedures were available (as by way of letters rogatory), an infringement of sovereignty could seldom be justified except perhaps on the grounds of urgent necessity relied upon by Templeman J. in *London and County Securities Ltd v. Caplan*.[10]

Cases where foreign courts have ordered production of confidential documents within the United Kingdom

The same reasoning applies in reverse in cases of orders by foreign courts for **12–06** production of confidential documents in the United Kingdom.

In *X AG v. A Bank*[11] a *subpoena* was issued in the United States District Court for the Southern District of New York against an American bank requiring it to produce documents relating to accounts maintained at its London branch by X, a Swiss corporation with no business in the United States, and Y, a subsidiary of X which was also incorporated in Switzerland, but had a major office in New York. The *subpoena* was returnable before a federal grand jury investigating alleged tax evasion. The bank declared its intention to comply with the *subpoena*. X and Y obtained an injunction in the English High Court restraining the bank from doing so on the ground that it would be in breach of duty of confidence. An order was then made by the New York District Court, *ex parte* and *in camera*, requiring the bank to comply with the *subpoena*. The bank applied to set aside the High Court injunction. Leggatt J. refused to do so.

Since the injunction was interlocutory, Leggatt J. decided the matter on *American Cyanamid* principles and did not have to reach a final determination of the points of law raised. However, he referred to the order enforcing the *subpoena* as "the exercise by the United States court in London of powers which, by English standards, would be regarded as excessive"[12] and stated that in relation to the merits he was firmly on the side of the plaintiffs.

After referring to the qualifications to the duty of banking confidentiality recognised in *Tournier v. National Provincial and Union Bank of England*,[13] the first being where disclosure is by compulsion of law, the judge observed that to apply foreign law in relation to banking business conducted in the City of London would be "to allow a fairly large cuckoo in the domestic nest".[14]

It was also argued by the bank that an English court would not enforce a **12–07** contract if performance required the doing of an act which violates the law of the place of performance (*Ralli Bros v. Compania Naviera a Sota y Aznar*[15]), and therefore the contract was unenforceable in so far as it sought to require confidentiality in New York.

[10] May 26 1978, unrep.
[11] [1983] 2 All E.R. 464.
[12] Cited by Hoffman J. in *Mackinnon v. Donaldson, Lufkin & Jenrette Corp.* [1986] 1 Ch. 482 at 494.
[13] [1924] 1 K.B. 461 at 473.
[14] [1983] 2 All E.R. 464 at 478.
[15] [1920] 2 K.B. 287.

If, following the approach in *Grossman*, a bank's London and overseas branches are to be regarded as separate entities, the performance which the English order was seeking to enforce was performance in England. Disclosure in New York could only happen if the London branch breached its duty of confidentiality in London by disclosure of documents to its New York branch for production in New York. The fact that a consequence of the contract being performed in its place of performance (England) was that the documents would not reach New York did not make the English order an extra-territorial order.[16]

Legatt J. rejected the argument that to continue the injunction would be to enforce a contract in a manner contrary to the law of the place of performance on a different ground, that the *subpoena* and order made without argument on the merits were not to be equated with legislation or a final judgment, and could not be said to have rendered the keeping of secrecy by the bank illegal, particularly since the evidence suggested the bank was most unlikely in the circumstances to be held in contempt by the New York court.

In *A v. B Bank*[17] Morland J. made an order both restraining the defendant bank from delivering up to a grand jury in New York any documents held at their London branch relating to the plaintiffs' accounts, and also requiring the bank to return to their London branch any documents already removed from the jurisdiction in connection with the grand jury *subpoena*.

Assistance by English courts or regulatory authorities to foreign courts or regulatory authorities

12–08   The United Kingdom is a party to the Hague Convention on the *Taking of Evidence Abroad in Civil and Commercial Matters* (1970)[18] and to a number of bilateral civil procedure conventions. English courts have jurisdiction to assist in obtaining evidence for foreign courts or tribunals under the Evidence (Proceedings in Other Jurisdictions) Act 1975 and Rules of the Supreme Court, Order 70.

The question of confidentiality arose in *Re State of Norway's Application*.[19] Norwegian proceedings involved an issue whether a deceased tax payer was the settlor of a trust. On the request of the Norwegian court an order was made by the English court for examination of two directors of the trust's London bank on a number of matters including the identity of the settlor. The Court of Appeal[20] held, by a majority, that the order should be set aside on the grounds that its terms were too wide and that the directors should not be required to disclose banking confidences, which might affect unknown people, in a case where there was no allegation of fraud or crime.

On a second request by the Norwegian court, in more limited terms, a further order was made and was upheld by the judge, with the qualification that the witnesses were not to be asked the identity of the settlor unless either of them first gave evidence that the settlor was the agent or nominee of the deceased tax

---

[16] Nor would an order requiring an English company to bring back documents relating to a domestic subject matter, which it had sent out of the jurisdiction (as in *Director of Public Prosecutions v. Channel Four Television* [1993] 2 All E.R. 517), be regarded as assuming extra-territorial subject matter jurisdiction.

[17] August 13, 1990, unreported. The order is recited in the later judgment of Hirst J. reported at [1993] Q.B. 311.

[18] Cmnd. 3991 (1970).

[19] [1990] 1 A.C. 723.

[20] [1987] 1 Q.B. 433.

payer. The judge's order was reversed by the Court of Appeal on a point of jurisdiction but restored by the House of Lords. On the issue of confidentiality, Woolf L.J. said[21] that in deciding whether to assist in obtaining the evidence requested in the proceedings, where a question of confidentiality arose, the English court should adopt the same approach as if the proceedings were taking place before the English court. That required a balancing exercise which the judge had properly performed. The judge's approach was approved in the House of Lords by Lord Goff, with whom the other members of the appellate committee agreed.

In relation to criminal law the United Kingdom is a party to the European **12–09** Convention on *Mutual Assistance* (1957) and the Vienna Convention *Against Illicit Traffic in Narcotic Drugs and Psychotic Substances* (1988), and to various bilateral agreements. Under section 7 of the Criminal Justice (International Co-operation) Act 1990, the powers of entry, search and seizure under the Police and Criminal Evidence Act 1984 are extended to enable evidence to be obtained at the request of a foreign court or prosecuting authority in cases which would be serious arrestable offences if they occurred in the United Kingdom. It has been emphasised by the Divisional Court that the issue of a search warrant under section 7 is a serious intrusion into the liberty of the subject and that the court must exercise great caution before such an application is granted.[22]

A regulatory body which has power to require disclosure of confidential **12–10** material may also have a right to disclose it to a foreign counterpart. In *A v. B Bank*,[23] after the U.S. Federal Reserve Board had failed to secure the documents which it wanted from the defendant bank by grand jury *subpoena* (because the bank was restrained from disclosing them by injunction), it approached the Bank of England with information which caused the latter to serve a notice on the defendant bank, under section 39 of the Banking Act 1987, requiring production of documents relating to the plaintiffs' accounts. Section 82 of the Act places restrictions on the Bank of England's power to disclose information which it obtains under the Act about a person's affairs to another person; but, by section 84, those restrictions do not preclude it from disclosing such information for the purpose of assisting an authority with corresponding functions in another country. So there was nothing to prevent the Bank of England from supplying the documents to the Federal Reserve Board.

Hirst J. rejected the plaintiffs' argument that the injunction previously granted by Morland J. precluded the defendant bank from complying with the Bank of England's notice. He also rejected the allegation that the notice was invalid because the Bank of England was acting for a collateral purpose, as an evidence gathering agency for a foreign supervisory body. For the notice to be valid the Bank of England must require the information specified in its notice for the performance of its functions under the Act. However, Hirst J.'s judgment suggests that the courts will incline to a broad view of its functions in matters involving international co-operation. He said[24]:

"[Counsel for the plaintiffs] seeks in effect to draw a line down the centre of the Atlantic, and to suggest that in some way the supervisory operations

---

[21] [1990] 1 A.C. 723 at 782.
[22] *R. v. Southwark Crown Court and H.M. Customs & Excise ex p. Sorsky Defries, The Independent* September 15, 1995.
[23] [1993] Q.B. 311. See para. 12–07, above.
[24] *ibid.* at p. 327.

of the Federal Reserve Board and those of the Bank of England are separate and unconnected. In fact, in the world of international banking today, supervisory authorities in various countries can, should, and no doubt do regularly co-operate on matters of mutual supervisory concern as sections 84(6) and 86 confirm."

PART 2

PARTICULAR RELATIONSHIPS

A list of all relationships, occupations and positions, likely to give rise to duties of confidence—if it were possible to compile—would be very long. It would include agents, trustees, partners and employees; professional people; holders of public and private offices; personal relationships, such as husband and wife; counsellors and mediators; and many others.

In this part of the book a small number are considered in further detail: medical advisers; bankers; broadcasters and journalists; employees; clergy, counsellors, mediators and teachers; and lawyers. They have been chosen either because there are important authorities relating to them, or because they are of particular interest, or for both reasons.

CHAPTER XIII

MEDICAL ADVISERS[1]

The modern version of the Hippocratic Oath introduced by the World Medical **13–01** Association as the Declaration of Geneva (as amended at Sydney in 1968) includes the statement:

"I will respect the secrets which are confided in me, even after the patient has died."

There is no doubt that the relationship of doctor[2] and patient carries with it a legal obligation of confidence in respect of confidential information concerning the patient gained by the doctor in his professional capacity,[3] whether directly from the patient or, for example, from medical records. The scope of the duty can present particularly difficult questions. Guidance to doctors is given by the General Medical Council in the so-called "Blue Book"[4] and in further booklets entitled "Confidentiality" and "HIV and Aids: The Ethical Considerations".[5]

A doctor may wish, or feel that he may be under a duty, to disclose **13–02** information about a patient for a wide variety of purposes. They include:

(1) diagnosis, advice and treatment;
(2) advancement of medicine;
(3) protection of others;
(4) protection of himself;
(5) management and record keeping;
(6) compliance with a requirement of law.

He is plainly at liberty to disclose information if required by law or with consent properly given.

The "Blue Book" states, at paragraph 77:

"Where a patient, or a person properly authorised to act on a patient's

---

[1] On confidentiality and the medical profession, see Kennedy and Grubb, *Medical Law* (2nd ed., 1994), pp. 637–673 and Mason and McCall Smith, *Law and Medical Ethics* (4th ed., 1994), pp. 167–190. See also "How to Keep a Clinical Confidence", HMSO, 1994.
[2] This chapter concentrates on doctors, but duties of confidentiality are owed by all concerned in advising and treating patients.
[3] *Hunter v. Mann* [1974] Q.B. 767 at 772. *W. v. Egdell* [1990] Ch. 359.
[4] The full title is "Professional Conduct and Discipline: Fitness to Practice", December 1993.
[5] Published in October 1995 as part of a group of booklets on duties of a doctor.

behalf, consents to disclosure, information to which the consent refers may be disclosed in accordance with that consent."

That accords with the general law. Consent may be express or implied. Whether it is to be implied will depend on the nature and purpose of the disclosure. But there may be situations in which, for one reason or another, the doctor acts deliberately without consent.

Difficulties may also arise in relation to minors or persons under a disability and disclosures within the family. Medical confidence is one incident of the relationship between the doctor and his patient and exists for the benefit of the patient. It is not absolute, not only because it would defeat the object for which it exists if it precluded the doctor from making disclosure in circumstances where, in the exercise of a proper professional judgment, he considered it in the patient's best interests to do so, but also because its preservation could in some circumstances be harmful for other reasons.

13–03   The fullest judicial statement is to be found in *Duncan v. Medical Practitioner's Disciplinary Committee*, where Jeffries J. attempted to summarise both the principle of medical confidence and certain qualifications. He said[6]:

> "The Court now addresses directly what is medical confidence? It is not difficult to grasp the broad concept of professional confidence for it is fundamental to the relationship of a professional man with a lay person. On a strict analysis of legal relationships, it is probably contractually based, as several cases have suggested ....
>
> Without trust [the doctor/patient relationship] would not function properly so as to allow freedom for the patient to disclose all manner of confidences and secrets in the practical certainty that they would repose with the doctor. There rests with a doctor a strong ethical obligation to observe a strict confidentiality by holding inviolate the confidences and secrets he receives in the course of his professional ministerings. If he adheres to that ethical principle then the full scope of his ability to administer medical assistance to his patient will develop.
>
> The foregoing embodies the principle of medical confidence, but it cannot be left there without identifying the existence of qualifications and modifications for I have described, not defined exhaustively the concept. Confidentiality is not breached by private discussions with colleagues in pursuance of treatment, but this may require full disclosure and consent. The confidentiality may be waived by the patient. The doctor may be required by law to disclose. A doctor may be in a group practice where common filing systems are used. Staff who have access to information must be impressed with the requirement of confidence. Limited information to some outside agencies may be made available by a doctor from his files for statistical, accounting, data processing or other legitimate purposes. A doctor may be treating more than one person that requires, or mandates, exchange of information, but here caution and prudence must be carefully observed and consents obtained. As this very case demonstrates a doctor may reveal confidences and secrets if he is required to defend himself, or others, against accusations of wrongful conduct. There may be occasions, they are fortunately rare, when a doctor receives information involving a patient that another's life is immediately endangered and urgent action is

---

[6] [1986] 1 N.Z.L.R. 513 at 520, N.Z. High Court.

required. The doctor must then exercise his professional judgment based upon the circumstances, and if he fairly and reasonably believes such a danger exists then he must act unhesitatingly to prevent injury or loss of life even if there is to be a breach of confidentiality. If his actions later are to be scrutinised as to their correctness, he can be confident any official inquiry will be by people sympathetic about the predicament he faced. However, that qualification cannot be advanced so as to attenuate, or undermine, the immeasurably valuable concept of medical confidence. If it were applied in that way it would be misapplied, in my view, because it would be extravagant with what is essentially a qualification to the principle. Some might say that is line-drawing and if they do then so be it. The line-drawing is not arbitrary but based upon reason and experience, and is the exercise of professional judgment which is part of daily practice for a doctor. The foregoing, either in the description or the qualifications, is not advanced as anything but an outline."

Diagnosis, advice and treatment

In *Sidaway v. Board of Governors of the Bethlem Royal Hospital and the*   **13–04**
Maudsley Hospital[7] the plaintiff underwent an elective operation which carried a very small risk of damage to the spinal column. This occurred. The surgeon had not advised her of the risk. The judge found that in refraining from doing so he was following a practice which would have been accepted as proper by a responsible body of skilled and experienced neuro-surgeons, and, applying the test formulated in *Bolam v. Friern Barnet Management Committee*,[8] he held that the surgeon was not liable. His judgment was upheld by the House of Lords.

It was argued by the plaintiff that the surgeon's failure to inform should be regarded as a breach of duty, independently of any medical opinion or practice. The House of Lords preferred to view the matter in the context of the doctor's professional duty to his patient. Lord Bridge said that a doctor's professional functions may broadly be divided into three phases: diagnosis, advice and treatment, each requiring the exercise of professional judgment. He also said,[9]

"A very wide variety of factors must enter into a doctor's clinical judgment not only as to what treatment is appropriate for a particular patient, but also as to how best to communicate to the patient the significant factors necessary to enable the patient to make an informed decision whether to undergo the treatment. He may take the view, certainly with some patients, that the very fact of his volunteering, without being asked, information of some remote risk in the treatment proposed, even though he described it as remote, may lead to that risk assuming an undue significance in the patient's calculations."

For purposes of diagnosis, advice or treatment, a doctor might wish to discuss a patient's case with colleagues or to have tests done. Investigative procedures involving the taking of samples or invasive techniques clearly require the patient's consent, whether they are performed for the purpose of routine

[7] [1985] A.C. 871.
[8] [1957] 1 W.L.R. 582.
[9] [1985] A.C. 871.

screening (as in pregnancy) or for the more specific purpose of differential diagnosis.

13–05   A more difficult question is to what extent the patient's explicit consent is needed for a sample to be tested in a particular way which the patient may not appreciate is intended. A doctor might not wish to go into the precise forms of testing with his patient in advance, for reasons similar to those referred to by Lord Bridge, *i.e.* to avoid causing possibly undue alarm.

It is suggested that, in general, a patient who consults a doctor impliedly consents to the doctor disclosing such information about the patient to other appropriately skilled staff (whether by sending a sample for analysis or otherwise) as may be necessary to enable the doctor to decide how best to perform the three phases of diagnosis, advice and treatment. But that is a general, not a universal, proposition. It may be displaced by other considerations, for example, in relation to HIV testing about which there has been particular controversy.[10]

Performing a venepuncture without consent would be an assault. But, assuming that consent is given for the procedure, the question arises whether sending a sample for HIV testing without informing the patient of the proposed nature of the test would involve a breach of the doctor's duty towards his patient.

The GMC's guidance on this subject is explicit. It recognises that, regrettably, "serious social and financial consequences ... may exist for the patient from the mere fact of having been tested for the condition" of HIV infection, and that there is therefore:

> "a strong argument for each patient to be given the opportunity, in advance, to consider the implications of submitting to such a test and deciding whether to accept or decline it."[11]

It therefore advises that,

> "Only in the most exceptional circumstances, where a test is imperative in order to secure the safety of persons other than the patient, and where it is not possible for the prior consent of the patient to be obtained,[12] can testing without explicit consent be justified."[13]

It would be difficult for a doctor who ignored that advice to rely on a defence of implied consent to a claim by the patient for breach of confidence in using his specimen for HIV testing without his actual consent.

Advancement of medicine

13–06   In *W. v. Egdell* Bingham L.J. said[14]:

> "It has never been doubted that the circumstances here were such as to

[10] See the discussion in Mason and McCall Smith, *Law and Medical Ethics* (4th ed., 1994), pp. 231–234.

[11] "Confidentiality", para. 12.

[12] If the patient were too ill even to be consulted, then the need for a proper diagnosis for purposes of his own treatment would be a justification.

[13] "Confidentiality", para. 13.

[14] [1990] 1 Ch. 359 at 419.

impose on Dr Edgell a duty of confidence owed to W. He could not lawfully sell the contents of his report to a newspaper, as the judge held .... Nor could he, without a breach of the law as well as professional etiquette, discuss the case in a learned article or in his memoirs or in gossiping with friends, unless he took appropriate steps to conceal the identity of W."

The same principle must apply to the use of patient information for medical research unless with the patient's consent.

The GMC's booklet, "Confidentiality" gives the following advice[15]:

"Where, for the purposes of medical research there is a need to disclose information which it is not possible to anonymise effectively, every reasonable effort must be made to inform the patients concerned, or those who may properly give permission on their behalf, that they may, at any stage, withhold their consent to disclosure.

Where consent cannot be obtained, this fact should be drawn to the attention of a research ethics committee which should decide whether the public interest in the research outweighs patient's rights to confidentiality. Disclosure to a researcher may otherwise be improper, even if the researcher is a registered medical practitioner."

There may be circumstances where a breach would be so technical as to cause no damage and where a court would not think it appropriate to grant equitable relief in any form. For example, a researcher who is given access to medical records may have no interest in the identity of the patients, and have no intention of publishing information from which any patient could possibly be identified. But it may be difficult, if not impossible, to remove the patient's names from the material to which the researcher is given access.

In such a case it may be that there would be no cause of action at all, because the disclosure would involve no detriment to the patients.[16] In reality, of course, it is unlikely that such a case would give rise to any complaint which would ever come before a court, and, if it did, it is improbable that the court would intervene to stop such research.

On the other hand, where the research would involve publication of the identity of patients, or of information which would enable their identification, it is doubted whether the advancement of medical knowledge could ever afford a defence in law to an action for breach of confidence; and it cannot be too strongly emphasised that no research ethics committee, however medically distinguished, has authority to dispense with a patient's legal rights.

Protection of others

It is clear from *W. v. Egdell*[17] that disclosure of information about a patient, **13–07** even contrary to his wishes and contrary to his interests, may be lawful for the protection of others potentially at risk. It is equally clear that the risk must be grave. Reference was made both by the trial judge and in the judgments of Sir Stephen Brown P. and Bingham L.J. (with which the third member of the court agreed) to the advice of the GMC that:

[15] "Confidentiality", paras. 15 and 16.
[16] See Chap. VI, above.
[17] [1990] 1 Ch. 359.

"Rarely, disclosure may be justified on the ground that it is in the public interest which, in certain circumstances such as, for example, investigation by the police of a grave or very serious crime, might override the doctor's duty to maintain his patient's confidence."

The current version reads[18]:

"Rarely, cases may arise in which disclosure in the public interest or in the interests of an individual may be justified, for example, a situation in which the failure to disclose appropriate information would expose the patient, or someone else, to a risk of death or serious harm."

13–08   American courts have gone further. In *Tarasoff v. Regents of the University of California*[19] the parents of a girl killed by a man, who two months earlier told a psychologist employed at the university of his intention to kill her, were held to have an arguable claim against the university authorities for negligent failure to warn the deceased of the danger, although they did warn the police. It is unlikely that an English court would entertain such a claim.[20]

It is not only violent criminals who may present a serious risk to the life or health of others. A motorist who suffers from blackouts obviously ought not to drive and is under a duty to inform the licensing authority of his disability. What is the position of his doctor if he advises the patient of his duty, but the patient ignores his advice and continues to drive? A motorist who drives in disregard of a serious disability is an obvious danger to the life of others, and it would be surprising if the doctor's duty of confidentiality extended to keeping secret the fact that he was doing so.[21]

13–09   A controversial question is whether a specialist who diagnoses HIV infection or AIDS is at liberty to inform other health care professionals, who are or may be involved in the patient's care, and the patient's spouse or other sexual partner.

The GMC's booklet "HIV and AIDS: The Ethical Considerations" recommends that the patient should be encouraged to give his consent to such disclosure, but advises that in the last resort it would not be improper to make such disclosure, without the patient's consent, where the doctor judges that failure to disclose would put the health of a specific individual at serious risk.[22]

This advice is consistent with the principle that a doctor's duty of confidentiality is subject to the qualification that a doctor who learns in his professional capacity of matters which cause serious risk to others is not prevented from making such disclosure as may be necessary to safeguard those at risk.

In *X v. Y*[23] the plaintiff health authority obtained injunctions against a

---

[18] "Blue Book" (December 1993) para. 86. The paragraph is substantially repeated in the booklet on "Confidentiality" at para. 18.

[19] (1976) Sup., 131 Cal. Rptr. 14.

[20] Compare also the position of the psychologist with that of the police, against whom it is improbable that a claim would lie: see *Hill v. Chief Constable of West Yorkshire* [1989] A.C. 53.

[21] This accords with the GMC's advice to doctors in the booklet on "Confidentiality", para. 19 and Appendix 1, which states that a doctor should inform the medical adviser of the Driver and Vehicle Licensing Authority if a patient continues to drive, against medical advice when unfit to do so.

[22] Paras. 17 and 19.

[23] [1988] 2 All E.R. 648.

newspaper reporter and the publishers of a newspaper, restraining publication of information about two doctors in general practice suffering from AIDS, which was supplied to the reporter by an employee or employees of the health authority from access to hospital records. Both doctors had sought medical advice and were being properly and effectively counselled. The judge found that the small theoretical risk of their infecting a patient was, in practice, removed by counselling. The sole justification sought to be advanced by the defendants for publication was not that it was necessary to protect individuals at risk, but that the subject was one of public interest and that publication would contribute to public debate. This was no defence.

Self-protection

If a patient sues a doctor or makes a complaint about him, for example, to the **13–10** Health Services Commissioner or the GMC, he would no doubt be taken to waive confidentiality to the extent necessary to enable the doctor to defend himself.[24]
A doctor might have equal need to use information gained about a patient in his professional capacity for the protection of his own position in circumstances not resulting from a complaint by a patient, but, for example, from allegations by other staff. Just as the Court of Appeal has recognised an implied qualification of the implied duty of confidence owed by a banker to his customer where disclosure is required in the interests of the banker,[25] it would be surprising if there was no similar qualification in the case of a doctor and if he had to rely simply on a discretion of the court to enable him to safeguard his own professional position.[26]

Management and record keeping

General practitioners and hospitals have to maintain records. Increasingly **13–11** they are computerised. The storing of information, whether manually or on computer, to which as a matter of practical reality others may have access involves actual or potential loss of secrecy. Moreover information may be stored not merely for medical but for management purposes, *e.g.* in the case of a private hospital patient so that the accounting department bills the patient correctly. The legal justification may be put in alternative ways. Since no medical practice or hospital could operate properly or efficiently without maintaining medical records, it may be said that the patient impliedly consents to it. Alternatively it may be said that the keeping of records is in part for the purpose of the patient's present or future treatment and in part for the protection of the doctor's or hospital's proper interests, and therefore does not in itself infringe upon any duty of confidentiality to the patient. Infringement will occur if records are leaked for other purposes, for example, by disclosure to the press (as in *X v. Y*[27]).

---

[24] Compare *Lillicrap v. Nalder* [1993] 1 W.L.R. 94 (claim against solicitor).
[25] *Tournier v. National Provincial and Union Bank of England* [1924] 1 K.B. 461.
[26] See *Duncan v. Medical Practitioner's Disciplinary Committee* [1986] 1 N.Z.L.R. 513, *per* Jeffries J.
("As this very case demonstrates a doctor may reveal confidences and secrets if he is required to defend himself, or others, against accusations of wrongful conduct.")
[27] [1988] 2 All E.R. 648.

Paragraph 78 of the "Blue Book" states:

"Doctors carry prime responsibility for the protection of information given to them by patients or obtained in confidence about patients. They must therefore take steps to ensure, as far as lies in their control, that the records, manual or computerised, which they keep, to which they have access, or which they transmit, are protected by effective security systems with adequate procedures to prevent improper disclosure."[28]

A patient who is concerned what may be in his medical records has a right of access to them, subject to certain exceptions, under the Access to Health Records Act 1990.

Disclosure required by law

13–12   A number of statutory provisions compel disclosure of otherwise confidential information and material. Some apply specifically to doctors; others apply more generally but would include doctors. The following are examples:

(1) Road Traffic Act 1988, s.172.
    Under this section any person may be required to give information which may lead to the identification of a driver alleged to be guilty of certain offences. In *Hunter v. Mann*[29] a doctor who refused to give such information under the equivalent section of the previous Act on grounds of confidentiality was held by the Divisional Court to have been rightly convicted.
(2) Supreme Court Act 1981, ss.33(2) and 74(2).
    Orders may be made for discovery of medical records in, or in anticipation of, actions involving claims in respect of personal injuries or death. In other classes of action there are no equivalent statutory provisions, but production of medical records may be obtained at trial by *subpoena.*
(3) Police and Criminal Evidence Act 1984, ss.8 to 12.
    Medical records are excluded from powers of search under a magistrates' warrant, but a constable may obtain access to such records for the purposes of a criminal investigation by order of a circuit judge.
(4) Public Health (Control of Diseases) Act 1984 and Public Health (Infectious Diseases) Regulations 1988 (S.I. 1988 No. 1546).
    These require a doctor to notify actual or suspected cases of patients suffering various forms of infectious disease to the proper officer of the local authority.
(5) Reporting of Injuries, Diseases and Dangerous Occurrences Regulations 1985 (S.I. 1985 No. 2023).
    These require notification of industrial accidents and diseases.
(6) Misuse of Drugs (Notification and Supply to Addicts) Regulations 1973 (S.I. 1973 No. 799).
    These concern registration of addicts.

---

[28] This advice is repeated in summary in the booklet, "Confidentiality", para. 1.
[29] [1974] Q.B. 767.

A doctor may also be required as a witness to answer questions about matters learned confidentially in his professional capacity.[30]

Children

The relationship and rights of parent and child in connection with medical **13–13** treatment and advice, and the duties of the doctor, were considered by the House of Lords in *Gillick v. West Norfolk Area Health Authority*.[31]

The Department of Health and Social Services issued to health authorities a memorandum of guidance on family planning services, including a section on contraceptive advice and treatment for young people. It recommended that clinics should be available for people of all ages; that if a girl under 16 wanted contraception the doctor should do his best to persuade her to inform her parents or guardian; but that if she refused, the doctor might exceptionally, in the exercise of his clinical judgment, prescribe contraceptive treatment, without parental knowledge or consent; and the document referred to the doctor's duty of confidentiality to patients, including those under 16.

The Court of Appeal declared that the advice was unlawful, but the House of Lords (by a majority) reversed the decision. The central reasoning of the majority was that parental rights existed only for the benefit of the child and diminished gradually as the child acquires the ability to make decisions for himself. The pace of that development will vary from child to child. Lord Scarman said[32]:

> "The law relating to parent and child is concerned with the problems of the growth and maturity of the human personality. If the law should impose upon the process of 'growing-up' fixed limits where nature knows only a continuous process, the price would be artificiality and a lack of realism in an area where the law must be sensitive to human development and social change."

It was held that the parental right to decide whether or not a child under 16 should have medical treatment terminates if and when the child has sufficient understanding and intelligence to enable him or her to understand fully what is involved.

The doctor's duty is to act in accordance with what he believes to be in the patient's best interest. That duty involves satisfying himself whether the patient has a sufficiently mature understanding to have the capacity to consent to the treatment in question. In assessing whether the patient has such capacity and what is in his or her best interests, the doctor must exercise his professional judgment.

The same considerations must govern the doctor's approach to the question of confidentiality. The doctor stands in a confidential relationship to every patient of whatever age including a baby,[33] but the purpose of the relationship is the welfare of the patient. Information relevant to matters within the parent's

---

[30] *Duchess of Kingston's Case* (1776) State Trials 355 at 571–572; see also at 586–591; *Garner v. Garner* (1920) 36 T.L.R. 196.

[31] [1986] A.C. 112.

[32] *ibid.* at 186.

[33] *Re C (A Minor) (Wardship: Medical Treatment) (No. 2)* [1990] Fam 39. See also *Re Z (A Minor) (Identification Restrictions on Publication)* [1996] 2 W.L.R. 88.

responsibility for decision-making can and should ordinarily be disclosed to the parent in the child's interests, and to do so would not involve a breach of duty.

13–14   Special considerations would arise if the doctor had reason to believe that the parent was abusing the child, or neglecting the child, or that disclosure to the parent would for some reason be harmful to the child. In those cases it might be the doctor's duty not to inform the parent but, for example, to inform the police or the social services department. Paragraph 83 of the "Blue Book" states:

> "Deciding whether or not to disclose information is particularly difficult in cases where a patient cannot be judged capable of giving or withholding consent to disclosure. One such situation may arise where a doctor believes that a patient may be the victim of abuse or neglect. In such circumstances the patient's interests are paramount and will usually require the doctor to disclose relevant information to an appropriate, responsible person or an officer of a statutory agency."[34]

In matters where the doctor is satisfied that the patient has sufficient responsibility to make his or her own judgment, the doctor should respect the patient's confidentiality and should accordingly not disclose information to the patient's parent against the patient's wishes, save in the most exceptional circumstances.[35]

Because development is a continuous process, there may be grey areas in which the doctor can only be guided by his professional judgment in considering whether the interests of the patient require that information should or should not be disclosed.

Persons under a disability

13–15   The relationship between persons suffering from disability through age, illness or accident, and those who care for them will obviously vary according to the nature and extent of the disability, but the same general principles must apply in relation to invalid and carer as in relation to minor and parent or guardian.

Disclosure to a relative

13–16   Aside from patients of limited capacity, disclosure of information gained by the doctor in his professional capacity should in normal circumstances only be made to another member of the patient's family with the patient's express or implied consent. But there may be cases where a doctor believes that it would be in the patient's interests, for example, to inform the patient's husband or wife of something unknown to the patient. It is likely that the courts would regard that as a matter for the doctor's professional judgment, and would not hold him to be in breach of duty to the patient provided that he acted in what he reasonably believed to be in the patient's best interest.

[34] Similar advice is given in the booklet "Confidentiality", paras. 10 and 11.
[35] See paragraphs 13–16.

Paragraph 12 of the GMC's booklet "Confidentiality" states:

"Rarely, you may judge that seeking consent to the disclosure of confidential information would be damaging to the patient, but that disclosure would be in the patient's medical interests. For example, you may judge that it would be in a patient's interests that a close relative should know about the patient's terminal condition, but that the patient would be seriously harmed by the information. In such circumstances information may be disclosed without consent."[36]

The principle is not confined to disclosure within the circle of the patient's family, but that is where it is most likely to apply.

The circumstances would have to be still more exceptional to justify a doctor disclosing confidential information about a patient from concern for his best medical interests but contrary to the patient's express wishes. However, it is difficult to say that this could never be justified.

In *Weld-Blundell v. Stephens*[37] Bankes L.J. took the example of a patient informing his doctor that he intended to commit suicide at a particular place and time, and he implied that a contract to keep that communication secret would be an illegal contract. Attempted suicide was then a criminal offence, and a different justification would now be required for the doctor to warn others if forbidden by the patient to do so, although it is still an offence to assist in another's suicide. Suppose that the patient was suffering from clinical depression. The doctor might well feel that it was his duty to warn someone close to the patient in order to try to avert the possibility of suicide. It is suggested that a court would be unlikely to hold that the doctor's duty of confidentiality extended to prevent him from taking what he believed to be necessary action for the purpose of saving the patient's life.

The Dead

The ethical obligation recognised in the Declaration of Geneva ("I will **13–17** respect the secrets which are confided in me, even after the patient has died") is repeated in the "Blue Book" at paragraph 91[38]:

"The fact of a patient's death does not of itself release a doctor from the obligation to maintain confidentiality."

Equity may impose a duty of confidentiality towards another after the death of the original confider.[39] The question is not one of property (whether a cause of action owned by the deceased has been assigned) but of conscience.

It is open to the courts to regard divulgence by a doctor of information supplied in confidence by a patient who has since died as being unconscionable as well as unprofessional. If so, there is no reason in principle why equity should not regard the doctor as owing a duty of confidence to the deceased's estate, consonant with the maxim that equity will not suffer a wrong to be without a remedy.

---

[36] This repeats in substance para. 82 of the "Blue Book".
[37] [1919] 1 K.B. 520 at 527.
[38] And in the booklet "Confidentiality", para. 13.
[39] *Morison v. Moat* (1851) 9 Hare 241; affirmed (1852) 21 L.J. Chanc. 248.

It is possible also that a doctor might owe a duty in conscience towards others. A patient might disclose to his doctor information about X, another member of his family (who might or might not also be his patient), publication of which would be damaging or embarrassing to X, in the understandable belief that there was no risk to X of the doctor making the information public. It would be most unsatisfactory if, on the patient being killed the next day, the doctor became free to make disclosure.

A professional man may owe a duty to persons other than his client, provided that such duty does not conflict with his duty to the client. If the doctor knew that the patient was concerned for X and did not want the information to get out for X's sake, it would be open to a court to hold that publication by the doctor on the patient's death would be unconscionable conduct towards X. *White v. Jones*,[40] although not a case on confidentiality, nevertheless provides an interesting parallel. If under concepts derived from *Nocton v. Lord Ashburton*[41] a solicitor may owe a duty in respect of the economic well being of his client's surviving intended beneficiary,[42] so should the doctor's conscience move him to continue to respect his former patient's confidence on behalf of X.

---

[40] [1995] 2 A.C. 207.
[41] [1914] A.C. 932.
[42] *White v. Jones* [1995] 2 A.C. 207 at 270–272 and 275–276, *per* Lord Browne-Wilkinson.

CHAPTER XIV

BANKERS

Tournier v. National Provincial and Union Bank of England[1]

Tournier is the leading authority on the duty of confidence owed by a bank to **14–01** its customer. The Court of Appeal held that a bank owes to its customer an implied contractual duty to keep his affairs secret, but that the duty is qualified. The duty arises at the commencement of the relationship and continues after the customer has closed his account in relation to information gained during the period of the account. It covers information about the customer's affairs gained by virtue of the banking relationship and is not limited to information from or about the account itself.[2]

The appeal in *Tournier* arose from a jury trial, in which the judge had directed the jury that disclosure of the state of a customer's account by a banker to a third party was not a breach of contract if made "justifiably, that is to say, if, under the circumstances of the particular case, it was reasonable and proper that he should make the communication". This was held to be an inadequate explanation of a difficult area of law. Atkin L.J. commented that[3]:

> "... to leave to the jury what is 'justifiable' or 'proper' is merely to tell them that the bank may not divulge information except on occasions when they may divulge it, and that of what those occasions are the jury are the judges. This appears to me to treat as fact what is matter of law ... ."

The fullest judgment on the qualifications to the implied obligation of **14–02** secrecy is that of Bankes L.J. who said[4]:

> "At the present day I think it may be asserted with confidence that the duty is a legal one arising out of contract, and that the duty is not absolute but qualified. It is not possible to frame any exhaustive definition of the duty. The most that can be done is to classify the qualification, and to indicate its limits. ...
> On principle I think that the qualifications can be classified under four

---

[1] [1924] 1 K.B. 461.

[2] See also *Barclays Bank plc v. Taylor* [1989] 1 W.L.R. 1066 at 1070 *per* Lord Donaldson M.R., "The banker–customer relationship imposes upon the bank a duty of confidentiality in relation to information concerning its customer and his affairs which it acquires in the character of his banker."

[3] *Tournier v. National Provincial and Union Bank of England* [1924] 1 K.B. 461 at 485.

[4] *ibid.* at 471–472 and 473.

heads: (a) Where disclosure is under compulsion by law; (b) where there is a duty to the public to disclose; (c) where the interests of the bank require disclosure; (d) where the disclosure is made by the express or implied consent of the customer."

These four qualifications were reaffirmed by the Court of Appeal in *Barclays Bank plc v. Taylor*.[5]

The true effect of the qualifications is not to excuse a breach of duty, but to identify certain limits to the duty itself. In this regard the judgment of Lord Donaldson M.R. in *Barclays Bank plc v. Taylor* is to be preferred to that of Croom-Johnson L.J. Lord Donaldson M.R. said[6]:

"The duty to maintain confidentiality is not all-embracing, subject to exceptions. It does not exist in four exceptional circumstances ... ."

Croom-Johnson L.J. said[7]:

"Faced with those order [under section 9 of the Police and Criminal Evidence Act 1984], the banks complied with them, thereby necessarily breaching the duties of confidence which they owed to Mr and Mrs Taylor.
The four circumstances in which a banker is justified in breaking that duty are set out in *Tournier v. National Provincial and Union Bank of England* [1924] 1 K.B. 461, 473 in the judgment of Bankes, L.J. The first is 'disclosure ... under compulsion by law'. That means that, in complying with the orders under section 9, the banks were not in breach of that implied term in their contracts with Mr Taylor."

It is contradictory to speak of the banks "necessarily breaching their duty of confidence" owed to the customer, and at the same time to say that "the banks were not in breach of that implied term of their contracts".

In *El Jawhary v. BCCI*[8] Sir Donald Nicholls V.-C. followed the approach taken by Lord Donaldson, saying:

"Where the case is within one of the qualifications to the duty of confidence, the duty, ex hypothesi, does not exist ... ."

14–03 In *Barclays Bank plc v. Taylor* it was argued by the customer that a bank served with notice of an application for an order under the Police and Criminal Evidence Act, requiring disclosure of documents relating to his affairs, owed him a duty to resist the application and to inform him. The court held that the contract between banker and customer did not contain any such implied duty on the part of the bank; and that, once an order valid on its face was made, the bank was obliged to comply with it.

The same principle applies after disclosure as before it. In *El Jawhary v. BCCI* Sir Donald Nicholls V.-C. held that, where a bank disclosed information to a third party in circumstances within one of the qualifications to the duty of confidence, there was no basis for implying an obligation on the bank to tell the customer what it had done.

[5] [1989] 1 W.L.R. 1066 at 1070, *per* Lord Donaldson M.R.
[6] *ibid.* at 1074.
[7] *ibid.* at 1075.
[8] [1993] BCLC 396 at 400.

In *Robertson v. Canadian Imperial Bank of Commerce*[9] a *subpoena* was served on a bank requiring it to give evidence and produce bank statements in an action to which the customer was not a party. The bank manager, having tried unsuccessfully to contact the customer before complying with the *subpoena*, produced the bank statements and gave evidence as required, without protest and without informing the court that he had been unable to contact the customer. The customer sued the bank, alleging breach of confidence in disclosing the information without having first consulted the client or voiced objection. At first instance the judge found that the defendant had breached its duty, but that the action failed because the bank manager's evidence, including the production of the information, was covered by absolute privilege.

The Privy Council held that the first of the *Tournier* qualifications applied (disclosure under compulsion by law), so that there was no duty, and expressed no opinion whether the bank, if it had been in breach of duty, would have been protected by the absolute immunity which attaches to the testimony of witnesses.

In concluding that the first of the *Tournier* qualifications applied, the Board **14–04** left unanswered a number of questions. Lord Nolan said that the Board had much sympathy with the argument by the customer that he should have been notified of the issue of the *subpoena*. He added[10]:

> "In the ordinary way a customer in good standing could reasonably expect, *if only as a matter of courtesy and good business practice*, to be told by his bank that a subpoena had been received ... . Their Lordships accept that the bank was compelled by law to produce the bank statement to the court, but it was under no compulsion to withhold knowledge of the subpoena from the customer." (Emphasis added.)

Although observing that there was no compulsion to withhold knowledge, the Board refrained from holding that there was a duty to inform. Lord Nolan recognised that it would be difficult to formulate the terms of any duty to be implied, and that it could not go beyond a duty to use best endeavours, in which case on the judge's findings there had been no breach.

On the question of the bank's failure to object to production, Lord Nolan said that there was no head of privilege which the customer, or the bank, could have claimed, and that it would be difficult to formulate the terms of any contractual duty to inform the court that the bank was producing the bank statement without the customer's consent. In any event, the customer had not established that the bank's omission to do so had caused him any loss, but Lord Nolan added[11]:

> "Their Lordships would not exclude the possibility that a particular banker/customer relationship would include some such implied term or duty of care as that for which the customer has contended, and that damages might be recoverable as a result of its breach by the bank concerned, but this is not such a case."

[9] [1994] 1 W.L.R. 1493.
[10] *ibid.* at 1498.
[11] *ibid.* at 1500.

14–05   There is no reason to differentiate between a bank given notice of an intention to apply for an order for discovery[12] and a bank served with a *subpoena. Barclays Bank plc v. Taylor* was cited in argument in *Robertson.*[13] but regrettably is not referred to in the judgment. The judgment of the Privy Council leaves open the question whether a bank served with notice requiring production of documents owes any, and if so what, duty to try to inform the customer, or to object to the order (if there are potential grounds for objection), or to inform the court of the absence of the customer's consent.

In *Tournier* Atkin L.J. emphasised that it would not be right to imply an obligation of secrecy into the contract between a bank and its customer merely because it would be a reasonable term to include, but only if it was a necessary term; and that, whilst it was necessary to imply some term, there must be "important limitations" to the term required to be implied, one being that it was "plain that there is no privilege from disclosure enforced in the course of legal proceedings."[14]

That limitation plainly applies to documents produced under *subpoena* or other compulsory process. That being so, as Lord Donaldson M.R. said in *Barclays Bank plc v. Taylor*[15]:

> "The real question is whether, in order to give business efficacy to the relationship of banker and customer, there must be an implied obligation to contest a section 9 application or to probe it or to inform its customer."

It may be that a customer in good standing would reasonably expect, "as a matter of courtesy and good business practice", to be informed by the bank of any notice requiring it to produce documents regarding the customer's affairs. Courtesy and good business practice are no doubt the basis on which many commercial relationships are expected to be conducted, and in fact conducted, but they are not the basis for the imposition of an implied term. Although a customer might be displeased at his bank complying with an order for discovery without informing him or seeking to oppose the order, it is difficult to see how a term requiring the bank to do so could be said to be necessary. Moreover the difficulty which the Privy Council recognised about any attempt to formulate such an implied contractual term is argument against it.

Compulsion by law

14–06   Apart from obligations of disclosure which are of general application (*e.g.* to answer questions in the witness box[16]), compulsion may arise in various ways particularly relevant to banks. They include the following,[17]

  (1) *Bankers' Books Evidence Act 1879*, under which orders for inspection may be made in civil or criminal proceedings.

[12] *Barclays Bank v. Taylor* [1989] 1 W.L.R. 1066.
[13] [1994] 1 W.L.R. 1493.
[14] [1924] 1 K.B. at 483 and 486.
[15] [1989] 1 W.L.R. at 1074.
[16] *Loyd v. Freshfield* (1826) 2 Car. & P. 325 at 329; *Parry-Jones v. Law Society* [1969] 1 Ch. 1 at 9; *Robertson v. Canadian Imperial Bank of Commerce* [1994] 1 W.L.R. 1493.
[17] See Paget, *Law of Banking* (10th ed., 1989) pp. 312–315 and 346–358.

(2) *Taxes Acts*. Banks may be compelled to disclose certain information to the Inland Revenue under the Taxes Management Act 1970, section 24 or the Income and Corporation Taxes Act 1988, s.745.

(3) *Drug Trafficking Offences Act 1986*. A bank which knows or suspects that funds in a customer's account or with which the bank is involved in dealing represent, directly or indirectly, proceeds of drug trafficking is required to inform the police under section 24.

(4) *Insolvency Act 1986*. A bank may be compelled to disclose information about the affairs of insolvent customers under sections 236 (companies) and 366 (individuals).

(5) *Financial Services Act 1986*. Under section 177 a bank may be required to disclose information about the affairs of a person suspected of insider dealing.

(6) *Companies Act 1985*. Inspectors appointed under the Act may require a bank to disclose information or produce documents relating to the affairs of a customer, where the customer is the company under investigation, or where the requirement is authorised by the Secretary of State, or where the bank is itself under investigation: section 452(1A), (1B).

(7) *Police and Criminal Evidence Act 1984*. Under section 9 and schedule 1, a bank may be ordered to produce documents for the purposes of a criminal investigation, as illustrated by *Barclays Bank plc v. Taylor*.[18]

(8) *Banking Act 1987*. Under section 39 a bank may be required by notice from the Bank of England to produce documents, and the section has been construed as intended to override any duty of confidence otherwise owed to a customer.[19]

(9) Discovery orders may be made in support of a tracing claim in equity, or in support of a Mareva injunction, requiring a bank to disclose information relating to its customer.[20]

Confidentiality and foreign law is considered in Chapter XII.

Duty to the public

In *Tournier* Banks L.J. said[21]:   **14–07**

> "Many instances ... might be given. They may be summed up in the language of Lord Finlay in *Weld-Blundell v. Stephens*,[22] where he speaks of cases where a higher duty than the private duty is involved, as where 'danger to the State or public duty may supercede the duty of the agent to his principal'."

Scrutton L.J. thought it clear that the bank might disclose the customer's account and affairs to prevent fraud or crimes.[23]

Atkin L.J. also thought it safe to say that the bank's obligation was subject to

---

[18] [1989] 1 W.L.R. 1066.
[19] *A v. B Bank* [1993] Q.B. 311; *Price Waterhouse v. B.C.C.I.* [1992] BCLC 583.
[20] *A v. C (Note)* [1981] Q.B. 956; *Banker's Trust Co. v. Shapira* [1980] 1 W.L.R. 1274; *A.J. Bekhor & Co. Ltd v. Bilton* [1981] Q.B. 923.
[21] [1924] 1 K.B. 461 at 473.
[22] [1920] A.C. 956 at 965.
[23] [1924] 1 K.B. 461 at 481.

the qualification that it had the right to disclose information relating to its customer's affairs when and to the extent to which it was reasonably necessary for protecting the bank, or other interested persons, or the public, against fraud or crime.[24]

14–08   In *Price Waterhouse v. B.C.C.I.*[25] Millett J. had to consider banking confidence at one remove. The issue was whether Price Waterhouse was at liberty to disclose information, obtained in the course of acting for B.C.C.I. as auditors and professional advisers, to an inquiry set up by the Government and the Bank of England, under the chairmanship of Bingham L.J., to investigate the supervision of B.C.C.I. under the Banking Act and to make recommendations.

On the subject of banking confidentiality and public duty of disclosure, Millett J. said that[26]:

> "... there seems no reason to doubt the general correctness of the statement in Paget's *Law of Banking* (10th ed., 1989) p. 256, based on a remark of Bankes L.J. in the *Tournier* case [1924] 1 K.B. 461 at 474 ... that
> 'The giving of information to the police, for instance in regard to a customer suspected of a crime would be unwarranted.' "

What Bankes L.J. said in *Tournier* was[27]:

> "I cannot think that the duty of non-disclosure is confined to information derived from the customer himself or from his account. To take a simple illustration. A police officer goes to a banker to make an inquiry about a customer of the bank. He goes to the bank, because he knows that the person about whom he wants information is a customer of the bank. The police officer is asked why he wants the information. He replies, because the customer is charged with a series of frauds. Is the banker entitled to publish *that* information? Surely not. He acquired the information in his character of banker." (Emphasis added.)

The point which Bankes L.J. was making was that in his simple illustration the banker would not be entitled to publish to the world the information which he gained about his customer *from* the police that the customer was charged with a number of frauds, because he acquired that information "in his character of banker" (albeit not from the customer himself). Bankes L.J. was not there addressing the scope of the public duty qualification and whether the banker would be entitled to assist the police.

An express undertaking by a bank to a customer to keep secret the fact that the customer was presently engaged, or intending to engage, in a criminal or fraudulent course of conduct would be unenforceable as contrary to public policy; and a bank would not be under an implied obligation to keep such information secret (see the judgments of Scrutton and Atkin L.JJ. in *Tournier* referred to above).[28] The situation may be very different where a customer discloses the commission of a past offence. In *Weld-Blundell v. Stephens*[29] the

---

[24] *Tournier v. National Provincial and Union Bank of England* 1 K.B. 461 at 486.
[25] [1992] BCLC 583. For a fuller discussion, see paras. 6–012-6–015, above.
[26] *ibid.* 583 at 598.
[27] [1924] 1 K.B. 461 at 474.
[28] *ibid.* at 481 and 486; See also *Gartside v. Outram* [1857] 26 L.J.Ch. (NS) 113; *Initial Services Ltd v. Patterill* [1968] 1 Q.B. 396.
[29] [1919] 1 K.B. 521 at 527, *per* Bankes L.J. and 544–545, *per* Scrutton L.J.

Court of Appeal drew a strong distinction between confiding in a professional man an intention to commit a crime and confessing a past crime, and between voluntary disclosure and disclosure under process of law. By the same reasoning a bank would ordinarily have no right to make voluntary disclosure of information acquired in the character of banker about criminal or fraudulent conduct by a customer, except for the purposes of prevention or protection.

The subject of public interest is considered further in Chapter VI.

Interest of the bank

In *Tournier* Bankes and Scrutton L.JJ. instanced disclosure in collecting or suing for an overdraft.[30] Atkin L.J. referred to the bank having the right to disclose information when, and to the extent to which, it is reasonably necessary for the protection of the bank's interests, either as against its customer or as against third parties in respect of transactions of the bank for or with its customer.[31]   **14–09**

In *Sunderland v. Barclays Bank Ltd*[32] the defendants dishonoured a cheque drawn by the plaintiff in favour of her dressmaker at a time when her account was overdrawn. The bank manager's real reason was not the fact of the account being overdrawn, but that most of the cheques drawn on it had been to bookmakers. The plaintiff complained about the return of the cheque to her husband, who spoke to the bank manager. He told the plaintiff's husband about the cheques to the bookmakers. The plaintiff sued for breach of duty of confidence. Du Parcq L.J. dismissed her claim, holding that when the bank received an implied demand for an explanation of its apparent discourtesy in dishonouring the cheque, it was entitled in its own interests to explain the circumstances.

Consent

In *Sunderland v. Barclays Bank Ltd*, Du Parcq L.J. also held that there was implied consent to disclosure in that when the plaintiff's husband took over the conduct of the matter of the dishonoured cheque, the plaintiff impliedly consented to the bank giving him the explanation.   **14–10**

Lee Gleeson Pty Ltd v. Sterling Estates Pty Ltd[33] provides another example of implied consent. A builder entered into a contract with a site owner for the development of a site. The owner ran into financial difficulties and the builder stopped work for non-payment. Negotiations took place involving the builder, owner and owner's bank. The builder and the owner came to an arrangement for the builder to complete the work and for the owner to pay by staged instalments. At the owner's request, the bank wrote to the builder confirming that the owner had authorised the bank to make payments in accordance with the arrangement. The owner subsequently countermanded the bank's instructions. The bank did not inform the owner. The owner sued the bank under an Australian statutory provision relating to misleading or deceptive conduct in trade or commerce.

---

[30] [1924] 1 K.B. 461, at 473 and 481.
[31] *ibid.* at 486.
[32] *The Times*, November 24, 1938, 5 Legal Decisions Affecting Bankers 163.
[33] [1992] 1 Bank L.R. 342 (New South Wales Supreme Court).

The bank contended that it could not have informed the builder of the revocation of the owner's instructions without placing itself in breach of confidence to its customer. Brownie J. rejected the bank's argument, holding that by authorising the bank to write to the builder, making a statement as to its authority to make payments to the builder, the customer impliedly authorised the bank to inform the owner of the change to those instructions.

CHAPTER XV

BROADCASTERS AND JOURNALISTS

The law of confidentiality affects the media in two separate ways—(1) in **15–01** limiting their freedom to publish, and (2) in providing qualified protection against disclosure of sources.

Freedom to publish

There are innumerable dicta which emphasise the importance in a democ- **15–02** racy of a free press, but also that it must operate within the rule of law.[1] The principles of the law of confidentiality therefore apply to the press as they apply to others.[2]

A more recent development is the recognition by English courts of article 10 of the European Convention on Human Rights[3] as articulating some of the principles underlying the common law in relation to freedom of expression.[4]

The European Court of Human Rights has emphasised the particular importance of the principles of article 10 in relation to the press[5]:

> "Whilst it must not overstep the bounds set, *inter alia*, in the 'interests of national security' or for 'maintaining the authority of the judiciary', it is nevertheless incumbent on it to impart information and ideas on matters of public interest. Not only does the press have the task of imparting such information and ideas: the public also has a right to receive them. Were it otherwise, the press would be unable to play its vital role of 'public watch dog'."

---

[1] *e.g. British Steel Corporation v. Granada Television* [1981] A.C. 1096 at 1168 *per* Lord Wilberforce,
"First, there were appeals, mde in vigorous tones to such broad principles as the freedom of the press, the right to a free flow of information, the public's right to know. In Granada's printed case we find quotations from pronouncements of Sheridan in Parliament and from declarations of eminent judges in cases where the freedom of the press might be involved. I too would be glad to be counted among those whose voice was raised in favour of this great national possession—a free press: who indeed would not? ... Freedom of the press imports, generally, freedom to publish without pre-censorship, subject always to the laws relating to libel, official secrets, sedition and other recognised inhibitions."
[2] *Francome v. Mirror Group Newspapers Ltd* [1984] 1 W.L.R. 892.
[3] Cmnd. 8969 (1953).
[4] *Rantzen v. Mirror Group Newspapers Ltd* [1994] Q.B. 670 at 691. See Chapter XI, above.
[5] *Observer and Guardian v. United Kingdom* (1991) 14 E.H.R.R. 153 at 191; *Sunday Times v. United Kingdom (No. 2)* (1991) 14 E.H.R.R. 229 at 241.

Article 10(2) recognises that the exercise of freedom of expression may be subject to such restrictions as are prescribed by law and are necessary in a democratic society, *inter alia*, for preventing the disclosure of information received in confidence.

The principles on which a duty of confidence may be negated or reduced by public interest considerations are discussed in Chapter VI.

Of particular importance in relation to the press is the requirement that the interference with freedom of expression should be no more than is proportionate to the legitimate aim pursued.[6]

Article 10 is discussed more fully in Chapter XI.

Disclosure of sources

15–03   A journalist who receives information from an informant in confidence will on ordinary principles owe an obligation of confidence to the informant not to reveal his identity; but that duty, like any other duty of confidence, is subject to qualifications, in particular where disclosure is required by law. Such disclosure may be required by statute.

The Police and Criminal Evidence Act 1984, for example, contains special provisions under which an order may be made by a circuit judge for journalistic material held in confidence to be produced to the police in cases where they are investigating a serious offence, subject to various conditions.[7]

Similarly, the Prevention of Terrorism (Temporary Provisions) Act 1989 contains provisions under which an order may be made for the production of such material for the purposes of investigation of terrorist activities.[8]

15–04   At common law a journalist could be compelled to disclose otherwise confidential information, including his sources, if required to do so in the witness box or by an action for discovery,[9] although the court would only order such disclosure if it considered it necessary.

Section 10 of the Contempt of Court Act 1981 now provides:

> "No court may require a person to disclose, nor is any person guilty of contempt of court for refusing to disclose, the source of information contained in a publication for which he is responsible, unless it be established to the satisfaction of the court that disclosure is necessary in the interests of justice or national security or for the prevention of disorder or crime."

Publication means any speech, writing, television or sound broadcast or other communication in whatever form, which is addressed to the public at large or to any section of the public.[10]

In applying section 10, no assistance is to be gained from authorities preceding the Act.[11] The section applies not only to direct orders to disclose the

---

[6] *Spycatcher* [1990] 1 A.C. 109 at 284; *Observer and Guardian v. United Kingdom* (1991) 14 E.H.R.R. 153; *Sunday Times v. United Kingdom (No. 2)* (1991) 14 E.H.R.R. 229 at 242.
[7] PACE 1984, s.9 and Sched. 1.
[8] Prevention of Terrorism (Temporary Provisions) Act 1989, s.17 and Sched. 7.
[9] *Attorney-General v. Clough* [1963] 1 Q.B. 773; *Attorney-General v. Foster and Mulholland* [1963] 2 Q.B. 477; *British Steel Corporation v. Granada Television Ltd* [1981] A.C. 1096; *Attorney-General v. Lundin* (1982) 75 Cr.App.R. 90.
[10] Contempt of Court Act 1981, s.2; Broadcasting Act 1990, s.201. *Secretary of State for Defence v Guardian Newspapers Ltd* [1985] A.C. 339 at 348, *per* Lord Diplock.
[11] *X Ltd v. Morgan-Grampian (Publishers) Ltd* [1991] 1 A.C. 1 at 40–41.

identity of a source but also to any order for disclosure of material which will indirectly identify the source, and it applies notwithstanding that the enforcement of the restriction may operate to defeat rights of property vested in the party who seeks to obtain the material.[12]

In *Re An Inquiry under the Company Securities (Insider Dealing) Act 1985*[13] **15–05** the House of Lords held that the word "necessary" did not denote an absolute concept, *i.e.* did not mean "indispensable", but could most nearly be paraphrased as "really needed" and involved making a value judgment on the facts of the case.

In *X Ltd v. Morgan-Grampian (Publishers) Ltd*[14] the House of Lords emphasised the need to look to both sides of the picture, particularly in cases involving the "interests of justice" exception. Lord Bridge, with whose speech the other members of the Appellate Committee agreed, said that[15]:

> "... if non-disclosure of a source of information will imperil national security or enable a crime to be committed which might otherwise be prevented, it is difficult to imagine that any judge would hesitate to order disclosure. These two public interests are of such overriding importance that once it is shown that disclosure will serve one of those interests, the necessity of disclosure follows almost automatically; though even here if a judge were asked to order disclosure of a source of information in the interests of the prevention of crime, he 'might properly refuse to do so if, for instance, the crime was of a trivial nature'.
> But the question whether disclosure is necessary in the interests of justice gives rise to a more difficult problem of weighing one public interest against another."

In *Secretary of State for Defence v. Guardian Newspapers Ltd*[16] Lord Diplock had interpreted the "interests of justice" exception narrowly as being used "in the technical sense of the administration of justice in the course of legal proceedings in a court of law or ... before a tribunal or body exercising the judicial power of the state". Rose J. followed that interpretation in refusing to order disclosure of a newpaper's source in *X v. Y.*[17]

However, in *X Ltd v. Morgan-Grampian (Publishers) Ltd* it was held that **15–06** Lord Diplock's dictum was too narrow, and that it is "in the interests of justice", within the meaning of section 10:

> "that persons should be enabled to exercise important legal rights and to protect themselves from serious legal wrongs whether or not resort to legal proceedings in a court of law will be necessary to obtain these objectives."[18]

Lord Bridge added, as an "obvious" example, that if an employer of a large

---

[12] *X Ltd v. Morgan-Grampian (Publishers) Ltd* [1991] 1 A.C. 1.
[13] [1988] A.C. 660 at 704 and 708–709.
[14] [1991] 1 A.C. 1.
[15] *ibid.* at 43.
[16] [1985] A.C. 339 at 350.
[17] [1988] 2 All E.R. 648.
[18] [1991] 1 A.C. 1 at 43.

staff was suffering grave damage from the activities of an unidentified disloyal servant, it was in the interests of justice that he should be able to identify him in order to terminate his contract of employment, notwithstanding that no legal proceedings might be necessary to achieve that end.

This example was not far removed from the facts. Two companies wished to raise additional capital and were preparing, with the help of their accountants, a corporate plan to put to lenders. Publication of the information in the plan, prior to completion of the negotiations, was likely to cause the companies severe damage. A draft of the plan, marked strictly confidential, was stolen from the company's premises. On the next day a source telephoned Mr Goodwin, a journalist on an engineering magazine, with information which it was reasonable to assume must have come from the missing plan. An injunction was granted against Mr Goodwin and others prohibiting publication. Mr Goodwin was also ordered to disclose his notes, which would have revealed his source. He refused to comply, having given a promise of confidentiality. There was no suggestion of misconduct by the companies.

The House of Lords upheld the order for disclosure. Lord Bridge suggested, as illustrations and not as a code, the kind of factors to be taken into consideration when deciding whether disclosure was necessary in the interests of justice[19]:

"In estimating the importance to be given to the case in favour of disclosure there will be a wide spectrum within which the particular case must be located. If the party seeking disclosure shows, for example, that his very livelihood depends upon it, this will put the case near one end of the spectrum. If he shows no more than that what he seeks to protect is a minor interest in property, this will put the case at or near the other end. On the other side the importance of protecting a source from disclosure in pursuance of the policy underlying the statute will also vary within a wide spectrum. One important factor will be the nature of the information obtained from the source. The greater the legitimate public interest in the information which the source has given to the publisher or intended publisher, the greater will be the importance of protecting the source. But another and perhaps more significant factor which will very much affect the importance of protecting the source will be the manner in which the information was itself obtained by the source. If it appears to the court that the information was obtained legitimately this will enhance the importance of protecting the source. Conversely, if it appears that the information was obtained illegally, this will diminish the importance of protecting the source unless, of course, this factor is counterbalanced by a clear public interest in publication of the information, as in the classic case where the source has acted for the purpose of exposing iniquity.

On the facts of the case itself, it was held that disclosure was necessary in the interests of justice because of the substantial continuing threat to the companies' business while the source remained unknown; because to prevent an employer, engaged in proceedings to restrain a breach of confidence, the opportunity to discover and proceed against a treacherous employee, who was causing him damage, was a denial of justice; and because the importance of protecting the journalist's source was much diminished by the source's

[19] *X Ltd v. Morgan-Grampian (Publishers) Ltd* [1991] 1 A.C. 1.

complicity, at least, in a gross breach of confidentiality, not counterbalanced by any legitimate interest which publication was calculated to serve.[20]

Mr Godwin continued to refuse to comply with the disclosure order and was fined £5,000 for contempt.

The European Court of Human Rights, by a majority of 11 to 7,[21] held that **15–07** the order and fine were a violation of article 10 of the European Convention on Human Rights on the grounds that there was not a reasonable relationship of proportionality between the legitimate aim pursued by the disclosure order (the protection of the companies' rights) and the means deployed to achieve that aim, and that the disclosure order and fine were not "necessary in a democratic society" for the protection of the companies' rights under English law.

The court recognised as a matter of general principle that, without protection of journalistic sources, such sources could be deterred from assisting the press in informing the public on matters of public interest, and as a result the vital public watchdog role of the press could be undermined. Therefore, limitations on the confidentiality of journalistic sources called for the most careful scrutiny by the court.

On the facts of the case itself, the justification for the disclosure order had to be considered in the wider context of the injunction which had been granted prohibiting publication and which had largely neutralised the threat of damage to the companies. The court considered that their further interest in unmasking the dishonest employee was insufficient to outweigh the vital public interest in the protection of the journalist's source.

There is a curious anomaly in this decision. The court recognised that protection of the anonymity of a journalist's source is likely to encourage the supply of information to the press. If information is of a kind which in the public interest should be published, there is an axiomatic public interest in not stifling its supply. To that end it may be regarded as desirable that persons should not be deterred from providing information which, acting in good faith, they believe should be published.

However, there was no suggestion that any public interest would have been served, or could reasonably have been thought to be served, by the unauthorised disclosure of the information in the companies' plan, and the propriety of the injunction against publication was undisputed. On the premise that the source was party, at least, to a gross breach of confidentiality, not counterbalanced by any legitimate interest which publication was intended to serve, it is hard to see why the protection of that source should be regarded as a matter of "vital public interest", unless all suppliers of information to the press are to be considered alike. That would be strange, for it is difficult to see why it should be regarded as desirable, still less a matter of vital public interest, to encourage persons, acting in bad faith, to supply information which there is no arguable public interest in publishing.

In *Director of Public Prosecutions v. Channel Four Television Co. Ltd*[22] **15–08** Channel Four broadcast a television programme made by Box Productions Ltd, in which it was alleged that there was widespread and systematic collusion between members of the Royal Ulster Constabulary and loyalist terrorists, which had resulted in at least 20 sectarian murders in Northern Ireland in the

---

[20] *X Ltd v. Morgan-Grampian (Publishers) Ltd* [1991] 1 A.C. 1. at 44–45 and 54.
[21] *Goodwin v. United Kingdom, The Times*, March 28, 1996.
[22] [1993] 2 All E.R. 517.

previous two years. A central role in the programme was played by source A, who revealed information to the programme researcher only under an explicit undertaking given by Box and Channel Four not to reveal his identity. At the end of the programme production, sensitive material was sent out of the jurisdiction, its precise whereabouts being known only to the researcher, who also left the jurisdiction.

After the programme was broadcast, an order was made in the Crown Court on the application of an officer of the Metropolitan Police Special Branch, under Schedule 7 to the Prevention of Terrorism (Temporary Provisions) Act 1989, requiring Channel Four and Box to produce documents relating to it. A subsequent order was made that the material which had been taken out of the jurisdiction should be brought back and produced to the police. The companies refused to comply, because of the promise of confidentiality given to A and because of fears for the life of A and the researcher.

The Director of Public Prosecutions brought contempt proceedings against the companies in the Divisional Court. It was held that the orders of the Crown Court had to be obeyed unless and until they were set aside, but that the court was satisfied in any event that the judge's discretion had been properly exercised. The court accepted that the companies were motivated by what they regarded as proper motives, and that they now found themselves in a real dilemma, caught between their express, unqualified promises to A and their duty in law. The court was nevertheless strongly critical of the companies. Woolf L.J. said[23]:

> "Whether they were aware of this at the time or not, both Box and Channel Four should have appreciated that, because of the provisions of the 1989 Act, they should not have given an unqualified undertaking to source A. They could properly give an undertaking that they would not disclose source A's identity unless they were ordered to do so by the court and that they would do everything in their power to protect his identity, but they were not in the position to give the totally unqualified undertaking which they did unless they were intending to break an order of the court to disclose if an order was made."

The companies were fined £75,000.

---

[23] *Director of Public Prosecutions v. Channel Four Television Co. Ltd* [1993] 2 All E.R. 517 at 531; see too at 534–535.

CHAPTER XVI

EMPLOYEES

Contract

The relationship between an employer and employee is contractual and, **16–01** whilst the existence of a contract does not prevent concurrent application of the equitable doctrine of confidence,[1] the scope of the employee's duty of confidence is governed by the contract,[2] whether express or implied, for as long as the parties remain bound by the contract.[3]

Although the function of implied terms is to "dot the i's and cross the t's of the express terms or to fill in some lacuna left by the contracting parties which must properly be filled by the implied term in order to give business efficacy",[4] it is convenient for present purposes to consider first what obligation of confidentiality the court will imply into a contract of employment before considering express terms.

Implied obligation during employment

The court will imply into any contract of employment a general obligation on **16–02** the part of the employee not to use or disclose confidential information or materials acquired in his capacity as an employee, except for the purposes of his employment.

This principle goes back at least to *Tipping v. Clarke*, in which Sir James Wigram V.-C. said[5]:

> "... it is clear that every clerk employed in a merchant's counting-house is under an implied contract that he will not make public that which he learns in the execution of his duty as clerk."

Wigram V.-C's words were quoted with express approval by Lord Cottenham L.C. in *Prince Albert v. Strange*[6] and the principle has been applied in many subsequent cases.[7]

---

[1] *Lamb v. Evans* [1893] 1 Ch. 218; *Printers & Finishers Ltd v. Holloway* [1965] R.P.C. 239; *Thomas Marshall (Exports) Ltd v. Guinle* [1979] 1 Ch. 227.
[2] *Robb v. Green* [1895] 2 Q.B. 315; *Faccenda Chicken Ltd v. Fowler* [1987] 1 Ch. 117 at 135.
[3] The special position which arises after termination by repudiatory breach is considered at para. 16–09 below.
[4] *Initial Services Ltd v. Putterill* [1968] 1 Q.B. 396 at 411.
[5] (1843) 2 Hare 383 at 393.
[6] (1849) 1 Mac. & G. 25 at 45.
[7] *Merryweather v. Moore* [1892] 2 Ch. 518; *Robb v. Green* [1895] 2 Q.B. 315; *Reid & Sigrist Ltd v. Moss* (1932) 49 R.P.C. 461.

171

The obligation is subject to usual qualifications, for example, where disclosure is required by law or in cases of serious wrongdoing.[8]

Implied obligation after termination

16–03   The scope of an employee's obligation of confidence after termination of his employment is more difficult. In *Lamb v. Evans*[9] it was suggested that the duty was limited to not using materials acquired in the course of his employment and did not prevent him from using his knowledge.

Subsequent authorities have made it clear that the duty is not so confined. In *Printers & Finishers Ltd v. Holloway*[10] Cross J. said:

"The mere fact that the confidential information is not embodied in a document but is carried away by the employee in his head is not, of course of itself a reason against the granting of an injunction to prevent its use or disclosure by him. If the information in question can fairly be regarded as a separate part of the employee's stock of knowledge which a man of ordinary honesty and intelligence would recognise to be the property of his old employer, and not his own to do as he likes with, then the court, if it thinks that there is a danger of the information being used or disclosed by the ex-employee to the detriment of the old employer, will do what it can to prevent that result by granting an injunction. Thus an ex-employee will be restrained from using or disclosing a chemical formula or a list of customers which he has committed to memory."[11]

Customer lists have presented particular difficulties, to which further reference is made below.

The reference to the information being "a separate part of the employee's stock of knowledge" is important and echoes what was said by the House of Lords in *Herbert Morris Ltd v. Saxelby*,[12] the fundamental principle of which is that a person is not to be fettered from making proper use of his skills, both for his own benefit and for that of the public.

In so far as knowledge gained in confidence has become part of the employee's general skill and knowledge, he owes no duty after the termination of his employment to refrain from using it in other employment. Such knowledge is to be distinguished from the type of information referred to by Cross J. in the passage cited above, *i.e.* trade secrets and the like.

16–04   The distinction between knowledge which is, and knowledge which is not, to be regarded as part of an ex-employee's general skill and knowledge has been a fruitful source of litigation, and drawing the line can be difficult.[13]

---

[8] *Gartside v. Outram* (1857) 26 L.J.Ch. (NS) 113; *Initial Services Ltd v. Putterill* [1968] 1 Q.B. 396; *In re a Company's Application* [1989] 1 Ch. 477; see also Chap. VI.

[9] [1893] 1 Ch. 218 at 236; see paras. 1–14–1–15, above.

[10] [1965] R.P.C. 239 at 255.

[11] See also *Johnson & Bloy (Holdings) Ltd v. Wolstenholme Rink plc* [1987] I.R.L.R. 499 at 502, *per* Parker L.J.,

"Somebody may hit upon the combination of two ingredients after many years of research, which produce an immensely valuable result wholly unknown to anybody else. An employee would have no difficulty in holding that knowledge in his head and inevitably carrying it away with him. But it cannot ... be regarded as part of the ordinary skill and experience of the particular employee. It is a secret, whether or not it is carried away in his head ... ."

[12] [1916] A.C. 688.

[13] For examples, see Brearley and Bloch, *Employment Covenants and Confidential Information* (1993), pp. 78–82.

In *Faccenda Chicken Ltd v. Fowler*[14] Neill L.J., delivering the judgment of the Court of Appeal, said:

"In our judgment the information will only be protected [after the employment has ceased] if it can properly be classed as a trade secret or as material which, while not properly to be described as a trade secret, is in all the circumstances of such a highly confidential nature as to require the same protection as a trade secret eo nomine ... . It is clearly impossible to provide a list of matters which will qualify as a trade secret or their equivalent. Secret processes of manufacture provide obvious examples, but innumerable other pieces of information are *capable* of being trade secrets, though the secrecy of some information may be only short-lived."

There is no universal formula for determining what is a trade secret or item of equivalent confidentiality. In *PSM International plc v. Whitehouse*[15] Lloyd L.J. described it as a question of degree. In *Lansing Linde Ltd v. Kerr*[16] Staughton L.J. considered that "trade secret" embraced information used in a trade, restricted in its dissemination, and the disclosure of which would be liable to cause real or significant harm to the party claiming confidentiality. That is very close to Sir Robert Megarry, V.-C.'s criteria in *Thomas Marshall Ltd v. Guinle*[17] for identifying information protectable *during* a contract of employment.

Since the underlying reason for a distinction being drawn between the duty of confidentiality owed during a contract of employment, and the duty which continues to subsist after it, is that the ex-employee should not be prevented from using his general skill and knowledge in subsequent employment, it is suggested that this should guide the court in deciding whether the post-termination duty extends to a particular piece of information. If the effect of holding that it does would be to put an unreasonable restriction on the ex-employee's ability to find or carry out work in the sector in which he is skilled, the duty should not extend to it. If it would not, there is no reason why the duty of confidentiality should not continue to apply.

This approach fits logically with the opinion expressed by the Court of Appeal in *Faccenda Chicken Ltd v. Fowler*,[18] that confidential information other than a trade secret or equivalent could not be protected by an express restrictive covenant. In other words, a guide whether the post-termination implied duty of confidentiality extends to a particular item is whether an express covenant to the same effect would be upheld. If the answer is doubtful, the issue should be resolved in favour of the ex-employee for reasons given by Scott J. in *Balston Ltd v. Headline Filters Ltd*[19] and echoed by Mummery J. in *Ixora Trading Inc. v. Jones*[20]:

"Technologically based industries abound. All have what they regard as secrets. Employees, particularly those employed on the scientific or technical side of the manufacturing business, necessarily acquire knowledge of the relevant technology. They become associated with technological advances and innovations. Their experience, built up during their years

---

[14] [1987] 1 Ch. 117 at 137–138.
[15] [1992] I.R.L.R. 279 at 282.
[16] [1991] 1 W.L.R. 251.
[17] [1979] 1 Ch. 227.
[18] [1987] 1 Ch. 117 at 137.
[19] [1987] F.S.R. 330 at 351.
[20] [1990] 1 F.S.R. 251 at 261.

of employment, naturally equips them to be dangerous competitors if and when their employment ceases. The use of confidential information restrictions in order to fetter the ability of these employees to use their skills and experience after determination of their employment to compete with their ex-employer is, in my view, potentially harmful. It would be capable of imposing a new form of servitude or serfdom, to use Cumming-Bruce L.J.'s words on technologically qualified employees. It would render them unable in practice to leave their employment for want of an ability to use their skills and experience after leaving. Employers who want to impose fetters of this sort on their employees ought in my view to be expected to do so by express covenant. The reasonableness of the covenant can then be subjected to the rigorous attention to which all employee covenants in restraint of trade are subject. In the absence of an express covenant, the ability of an ex-employee to compete can be restricted by means of an implied term against use or disclosure of trade secrets. But the case must, in my view, be a clear one. An employee does not have the chance to reject an implied term. It is formulated and imposed on him subsequently to his initial entry into employment. To fetter his freedom to compete by means of an implied term can only be justified, in my view, by a very clear case."

Customer lists

16–05   In the absence of a valid, express covenant to the contrary, an ex-employee may ordinarily solicit business from customers of his former employer after his employment has ended. He will, however, be in breach of duty to his employer if he solicits the employer's customers before the end of his employment with a view to obtaining their future business.[21]

The employee will also be in breach of duty if, during his employment, he copies his employer's customer list with a view to using it to compete against the employer later. In *Robb v. Green*[22] an order was made in those circumstances against the ex-employee requiring him to deliver up the list for destruction and restraining him from making use of the information obtained by copying it.

The same principle would apply if the employee had instead committed the list to his memory.[23]

The injunction granted in *Robb v. Green* did not prohibit the defendant from sending out circulars to customers whose names he could remember apart from having copied the plaintiff's list. Maugham L.J. noted this point in *Wessex Dairies Ltd v. Smith* adding[24]:

"It follows, in my opinion, that the servant may, while in the employment of the master, be as agreeable, attentive and skilful as it is in his power to be to others with the ultimate view of obtaining the customers' friendly feelings when he calls upon them if and when he sets up business for himself."

In *Roger Bullivant Ltd v. Ellis*[25] Nourse L.J. also noted the point that the

---

[21] *Wessex Dairies Ltd v. Smith* [1935] 2 K.B. 80.
[22] [1895] 2 Q.B. 315.
[23] *Printers & Finishers Ltd v. Holloway* [1965] R.P.C. 239 at 255.
[24] [1935] 2 K.B. 80 at 89.
[25] [1987] F.S.R. 172 at 182–183.

injunction in *Robb v. Green* did not prevent the defendant from contracting with any of the plaintiff's customers if he was able to do so without using the information which he had unlawfully acquired, and he commented that the form of order made in that case might not be satisfactory in relation to names of customers, because it might be difficult to know whether it had been breached. In those circumstances it was legitimate for the court to grant instead a springboard injunction, restraining the ex-employee from dealing with any customers on the list whom he had approached while the list was in his possession, provided that the term of the injunction was no longer than the period for which he was likely to obtain an unfair advantage from use of the list.

Use of confidential information after termination for purposes other than use of the ex-employee's skills

It is one thing for the implied obligation of confidentiality to be qualified so as   **16–06**
not to impede an ex-employee's proper use of his general skill and knowledge in subsequent employment, whether for himself or others. It is a different matter for him to disclose such information for other purposes.

In *Mainmet Holdings plc v. Austin*[26] the plaintiffs specialised in heating systems. The defendant was their former managing director. After his departure he sent to customers copies of internal reports about defects in the customers' systems, including one by himself marked "highly confidential". On an application for an interlocutory injunction it was held that there was no serious issue to be tried on the question of breach of confidence, because the reports did not come into the category of trade secrets or information of equivalent confidentiality, and therefore the defendant owed no continuing duty in respect of them.

It is suggested that the judge misdirected himself. Although the reports were not trade secrets, there was a strong prima facie case that they were confidential; they could not be regarded as part of the defendant's general skill and knowledge of the business of heating systems; nor was he attempting to use them as such. His use was conceded on the application to have been malicious.

Express terms

In *Faccenda Chicken Ltd v. Fowler*[27] the plaintiffs bred and sold chickens.   **16–07**
The defendant, during his employment as their sales manager, introduced an operation of selling freshly killed chickens from refrigerated vans. He left their employment to set up a similar business of his own in the same area, and several of the plaintiffs' van salesmen went to work for him. The plaintiffs claimed an injunction and damages for misuse of confidential "sales information", including the names and addresses of customers, their usual requirements, the prices charged to them, and the van salesmen's delivery routes.

Goulding J. found that the information came into the category of confidential information which the defendant was required to use only for the plaintiffs' benefit while he remained in their employment, but which became part of his general skill and knowledge, so that he was permitted to use it after the end of the contract for his own benefit in competition with the plaintiffs. He also

---

[26] [1991] F.S.R. 538.
[27] [1987] 1 Ch. 117.

suggested that an employer could protect information in that category by an express covenant. The Court of Appeal disagreed on that point, adding[28]:

> "In our view the circumstances in which a restrictive covenant would be appropriate and could be successfully invoked emerge very clearly from the words used by Cross J. in *Printers & Finishers Ltd v. Holloway* [1965] 1 W.L.R. 1 of 6 ...,
>> 'If the managing director is right in thinking that there are features in the plaintiffs' process which can fairly be regarded as trade secrets and which their employees will inevitably carry away with them in their heads, then the proper way for the plaintiffs to protect themselves would be by exacting covenants from their employees restricting their field of activity after they have left their employment not by asking the court to extend the general equitable doctrine to prevent breaking confidence beyond all reasonable bounds.' "

16–08 Consistently with this reasoning, an express term may be effective to *identify* what is, properly, regarded as confidential information or information falling in the narrower category of a trade secret or the equivalent. It is well established that for information to be treated as confidential or a trade secret it must be defined with sufficient precision,[29] and an express contractual term may have that effect. The fact that the contract specifies that certain information is to be treated as a trade secret and kept confidential after the end of the employment does not compel a court to recognise it as such, for unreasonable restraints of trade cannot gain validity by being dressed up as clauses protecting trade secrets, if they are not.[30] But the terms of the contract may be a relevant factor in considering whether the man of ordinary honesty and intelligence, referred to by Cross J. in *Printers & Finishers Ltd v. Holloway*, would think he was doing anything wrong in using some piece of information gained during his previous employment.

So, for example, in *United Sterling Corporation Ltd v. Felton and Mannion*[31] Brightman J. said:

> "In my judgment there is no evidence that Mr Mannion was given any special information which he ought to have regarded as a separate part of his stock of knowledge of polystyrene plants, information which an honest and intelligent man would have recognised as the property of the employer and not of the employee. There is no evidence that anything was expressly disclosed to Mr Mannion in confidence. He was never asked to sign any restrictive covenant. There is no evidence that he has done more during the years of his employment than add to his general stock of knowledge and experience of polystyrene plants in the ordinary way that any intelligent employee would naturally do. I see no basis for suggesting that Mr Mannion's conscience was affected during the period of his employment so as to place him under an obligation not to make use of that which he inevitably learned during his years with the plaintiff company."

[28] *Faccenda Chicken Ltd v. Fowler* [1987] 1 Ch. 117 at 137–138.
[29] See para. 3–24 above.
[30] *Balston Ltd v. Headline Filters Ltd* [1987] F.S.R. 330 at 351.
[31] [1974] R.P.C. 162 at 173.

Termination as a result of repudiatory breach

Where termination of employment occurs as a result of repudiatory breach **16–09** by the employer, typically by wrongful summary dismissal, the employee is relieved from further performance of his own contractual obligations, including restrictive post-employment covenants.[32] But the bringing to an end of all primary contractual obligations may leave the parties in a relationship in which duties are owed by operation of law.[33] It is suggested, therefore, that while termination of employment through wrongful repudiation by the employer[34] brings to an end any contractual obligation of confidence owed by the employee to the employer, it does not ipso facto bring to an end the employee's equitable duty in respect of trade secrets or information of equivalent confidentiality.

Employer's obligation

An employer or prospective employer may also owe a duty of confidence to **16–10** an employee or prospective employee. In *Smith, Kline & French Laboratories (Australia) Ltd v. Department of Community Services*[35] the court observed:

"Confidential information is commonly supplied without payment: for example, by a prospective employee (or his referee) to support an application for employment. The understanding ordinarily would be that the prospective employer would not disclose the information to any third party; but it would hardly be expected that its use would necessarily be confined to the employment application itself. If that application were successful, the employee would not act on the assumption that material in the relevant file would be destroyed. He would surely be inclined to assume that it might be resorted to later to assist the employer in making decisions relevant to the employee—for example, as to whether the employee (rather than another) should be promoted, or dismissed."

Where the information is supplied by the prospective employee in response to an advertisement or request by the prospective employer, the obligation of confidence could be regarded as arising under an implied contract, the consideration for which would be the provision of the information,[36] or in equity. Such a duty would be owed to the prospective employee in respect of any information of a confidential nature concerning himself, whether it came from the prospective employee personally or from the referee acting on his request. An additional duty of confidence might be owed to the referee if the reference contained matters of a confidential nature relating to the referee. If the information was unsolicited, it is suggested that there would still be an equitable obligation of confidence.

On the formation of a contract of employment, the nature of the relationship

---

[32] *General Billposting Co. Ltd v. Atkinson* [1909] A.C. 118.

[33] In *Photo Production Ltd v. Securicor Transport Ltd* [1980] A.C. 827 at 850, Lord Diplock gave the example of bailor and bailee.

[34] An employee cannot bring to an end his own contractual obligation by wrongful repudiation if not accepted by the employer: *Thomas Marshall Ltd v. Guinle* [1979] Ch. 227, approved in *Gunton v. Richmond Borough Council* [1981] Ch. 448.

[35] (1991) 28 F.C.R. 291 at 303 (Full Court of the Federal Court of Australia).

[36] *Mechanical and General Inventions Co. v. Austin* [1935] A.C. 346 at 370.

would change, but the employer would continue to owe a duty of confidentiality to the employee, whether under an implied term of the contract or in equity, in respect of personal information about the employee gained by the employer in that capacity, subject to usual qualifications.[37]

16–11   The obligation not to disclose personal information about an employee to a third party without his consent will ordinarily continue after the employment has ended. An ex-employer who is asked for information about a former employee by a prospective employer should therefore be cautious. It is suggested that he would be free to express his views about the qualities of the former employee, because that would be a matter of his own opinion, but that he would not be free to divulge facts which would fairly be regarded as personal to the former employee, for example, his health record.

In *Prout v. British Gas plc*[38] the defendants operated a scheme for employees to make suggestions, promising confidentiality so long as the employee wished and that his interests would be protected if his suggestion was worth patenting. The plaintiff suggested a form of bracket designed to prevent warning lamps being vandalised. The defendants indicated that they were not interested in it, and the plaintiff then applied for a patent himself. He subsequently sued for breach of confidence and patent infringement. The claim for breach of confidence was put forward on alternative bases of breach of contract or of an equitable obligation. It was held that the plaintiff was entitled to succeed on either ground, and that the duty of confidence continued until the publication of the patent application, when the plaintiff thereby voluntarily put his invention in the possession of the public. The court directed an inquiry as to damages or an account of profits, at the plaintiff's option.

---

[37] An obvious example would be an employer's obligation to supply details of an employee's earnings to the Inland Revenue.
[38] [1992] F.S.R. 478.

CHAPTER XVII

CLERGY, COUNSELLORS, MEDIATORS AND TEACHERS

CLERGY

The ecclesiastical law of the Church of England requires a minister not to reveal or make known to any person any crime or offence revealed to him by confession "except they be such crimes as by the laws of this realm his own life may be called into question for concealing the same".[1]   **17–01**

The modern position in civil law was stated by Lord Denning M.R. in *Attorney-General v. Mulholland and Foster*[2] as follows:

> "The only profession I know which is given a privilege from disclosing information to a court of law is the legal profession, and then it is not the privilege of the lawyer but of his client.
>
> Take the clergyman, the banker or the medical man. None of these is entitled to refuse to answer when directed to by a judge. Let me not be mistaken. The judge will respect the confidence which each member of these honourable professions receives in the course of it and will not direct him to answer unless not only it is relevant but also it is a proper and, indeed, necessary question in the course of justice to be put and answered."

This passage was approved by the House of Lords in *British Steel Corporation v. Granada Television Ltd.*[3]

The doctor with his medical responsibility and the clergyman with his pastoral responsibility are each concerned for the personal welfare of those to whom they minister, and should owe similar obligations of confidentiality to those under their care.

By the same reasoning the clergyman's duty of confidence should be subject to similar qualifications as obtain in the case of a doctor,[4] that is, not only where disclosure is required by law, but also where he reasonably believes disclosure to be necessary to prevent serious harm to others; or (exceptionally) for the protection of the person concerned (*e.g.* a seriously disturbed parishioner who

---

[1] *Canons Ecclesiastical* (1603), Canon 113 proviso, which remains unrepealed. *Halsbury's Laws of England* (4th ed.), Vol. 14, para. 308, n. 1.
[2] [1963] 2 Q.B. 477 at 489.
[3] [1981] A.C. 1096. Lord Wilberforce (with whom Lord Russell agreed) described it at 1169–1170 as a "classic passage". Viscount Dilhorne cited it at 1181. Lord Fraser referred to it at 1196.
[4] See Chap. XIII.

may be in need of medical attention); or to enable the clergyman to protect himself against accusations of misconduct.

COUNSELLORS

17–02   There are many forms of counselling. Much important help is provided by voluntary organisations. Some, like the Samaritans, cope with emergencies. Other specialise in particular areas such as marriage breakdown. Within the state system counselling is provided by probation officers, social workers[5] and many others.

Those who provide such services, whether voluntarily or otherwise, clearly do so on a tacit assumption of confidentiality, and therefore owe an obligation of confidence to those who consult them, subject to the same general qualifications as apply to doctors or clergymen. In some cases the obligation may also be limited by particular public duties. Probation officers, for example, are responsible for providing reports to courts and for supervising the performance of court orders. Any duty of confidentiality owed by them in private law must therefore be subject to their duty in public law to the court. The same must apply to social workers when acting under the control of the court, for example, in wardship or adoption proceedings.[6]

MEDIATORS

17–03   Counselling, conciliation and mediation shade into each other, and the terms are sometimes used without discrimination, although they can take very different forms.[7] Mediation as a means of alternative dispute resolution may vary in its degree of formality.

The most formal type of alternative dispute resolution is arbitration, although there is an important difference between an arbitrator, who makes a decision and a mediator, who tries to help the parties to reach an agreement.

In *Dolling-Baker v. Merrett*[8] it was held that parties to an arbitration agreement are under an implied obligation not to disclose or to use for any other purpose documents prepared for or disclosed in the arbitration, or to disclose in any way any evidence given in the arbitration, except with the consent of the other party or leave of the Court.[9]

17–04   The same logic, whether in support of an implied contractual term or an equitable obligation, must apply as much, if not more strongly, in the case of mediation. For it would destroy the basis of mediation if, in the case of the mediation failing, either party could publicise matters which had passed between themselves or between either of them and the mediator for the purposes of mediation. An obligation of confidence would also be owed to both parties by the mediator.

In the case of *Theodoropoulas v. Theodoropoulas*,[10] it was held that, where a

---

[5] Guidance to social workers is included in "How to Keep a Clinical Confidence", HMSO 1994.
[6] See paras. 23–07—23–08, below.
[7] For a discussion of the differences in the context of divorce, see the Law Commission, "The Ground for Divorce", 1990.
[8] [1990] 1 W.L.R. 1205 at 1213, *per* Parker L.J.
[9] For a fuller discussion, see Chap. XXIV.
[10] [1964] P. 311.

husband and wife were trying to effect a reconciliation in the presence of a conciliator, neither of the parties, nor the conciliator, could give evidence of the conversation in subsequent divorce proceedings without the consent of the other party. Simon P. said[11]:

"No doubt, when a probation officer or an SSAFA representative or a clergyman is approached, the court will readily infer that the parties have gone to him with a view to reconciliation and on the tacit understanding that nothing said should afterwards be used against them; but, equally, where it is proved that any private individual is enlisted specifically as a conciliator, in my judgment the law will aid his or her efforts by guaranteeing that any admissions or disclosures by the parties are privileged in subsequent matrimonial litigation."

In *Re D.*[12] the Court of Appeal held that in proceedings made under the Children Act 1989 statements made by a party in the course of meetings held for the purposes of reconciliation, mediation or conciliation were privileged from production, by analogy with "without prejudice" correspondence, except if a statement was made clearly indicating that the maker had in the past caused or was likely in the future to cause serious harm to the well-being of a child. However, the court emphasised that it was concerned in that case only with a question of admissability of evidence, and not with duties of confidence. In order that the parties should know where they stand, it is preferable that any formal mediation agreement should contain a confidentiality clause.[13]

It is also obviously important that a mediator who is given information by one party should establish with that party whether he is at liberty to disclose it to the other party.

TEACHERS

Schools keep records on every pupil's academic achievements, other skills **17–05** and abilities and progress at school.[14] Such records, like medical records or the

---

[11] *Theodoropoulas v. Theodoropoulas* [1964] P. 311 at 313–314.
[12] *Re D (Minors) (Conciliation: Disclosure of Information)* [1993] Fam. 231.
[13] CEDR Centre for Dispute Resolution uses a clause which provides:
  "By taking part in the Mediation the Parties undertake to each other and agree that:
    (i) the entire Mediation is and will be kept confidential;
    (ii) the Parties, the Representatives and their advisers and the Mediator shall keep all statements and all other matters whether oral or written including any settlement agreement relating to the Mediation confidential except insofar as disclosure is necessary to implement and enforce such settlement agreement;
    (iii) the entire process of the Mediation shall be treated as privileged and will be conducted on the same basis as without prejudice negotiation in an action in the courts or similar proceedings. All documents, submissions and statements made or produced for the purposes of the Mediation whether oral or written shall be inadmissible and not subject to discovery in any arbitration, legal or other similar proceedings except that evidence which is otherwise admissible or discoverable shall not become inadmissible or non-discoverable by reason of its use in connection with this Mediation."
[14] Schools maintained by a local education authority, special schools and grant-maintained schools are required to keep and update such records under the Education (School Records) Regulations 1989 (S.I. 1989 No. 1261). The parents or pupil (depending on the pupil's age) have a right to disclosure.

records kept on an employee by an employer, are confidential, but may be used for the purpose of the pupil's welfare, for example, in assisting a child care officer to prepare a report for a court. There would also be no objection to their use for preparing references or reports to a prospective employer or university or another school, for in such cases consent by the pupil, or by his parents on his behalf, would be implied.

A teacher may also learn confidential information about a child or his family from the child or from other sources. A teacher has a quasi-parental responsibility for a child in his care and owes a duty to the child to keep such information confidential, except in so far as to do so would conflict with his proper appreciation of the child's best interests. Here the position of a teacher *vis-à-vis* the pupil and the pupil's parents is similar to that of a doctor and can present similar difficulties.

17–06 Education should be a shared responsibility between teacher, parent and pupil. Ordinarily it would be in the pupil's interest that a teacher should feel free to discuss matters concerning the pupil with the pupil's parents. But there are situations where that will not be so.

One example is where an older pupil confides in a teacher about matters which he or she does not want his or her parents to know, in which case the teacher must respect that confidence unless he has good reason to believe that it would be damaging to the pupil to do so.

Another is where a teacher makes a promise of confidentiality to a pupil. It may be necessary in the interests of the pupil that the teacher should break that promise, but he should do so only if satisfied for good reasons that it is.

There is also the difficult area of suspected child abuse. A teacher is not required to act as a detective, nor is he qualified to make medical judgments about the cause of injuries. Reporting a case of suspected child abuse, which turns out to be unfounded, may cause immense distress. Nevertheless where a teacher is in possession of information from which he has real ground to suppose that a child is the subject of abuse, his paramount concern must be the interests of the child, and he will not be in breach of any duty of confidentiality if he reports his concern to an appropriate responsible person or authority such as the local authority's social services department.

CHAPTER XVIII

LAWYERS

Even before any broad development of the law of confidence, it was recognised **18–01** that the relationship between a lawyer and his clients imported obligations of confidentiality. In *Taylor v. Blacklow*,[1] for example, Gaselee J. said that:

> "... the first duty of an attorney is to keep the secrets of his client. Authority is not wanted to establish that proposition ... ."

The duty of confidence owed by a solicitor or barrister to his client is governed by the same general principles of law as apply to any other professional person. In the case of a solicitor the duty will arise both by contract and under the equitable doctrine of confidence; in the case of the barrister (unless he is instructed by direct access) the duty is equitable.[2] But there are, in addition, two special features which affect lawyers, arising from the central role performed by lawyers in the administration of justice.

The first is that confidential information obtained by a lawyer for the purpose of advising his client is ordinarily subject to legal professional privilege.[3] The second is that solicitors and barristers are officers of the court, and as such they owe duties to the court and are subject to its supervisory jurisdiction. This may give rise to restrictions beyond those which would be imposed under normal principles of confidence, as the decision of the Court of Appeal in *Re a Firm of Solicitors*[4] illustrates. The court (by a majority) upheld an injunction restraining a firm of solicitors from acting for a defendant in an action brought by a company which, although not a former client of the firm, had previously supplied the firm with confidential information about matters relevant to the later action. The firm had put in place a Chinese wall to prevent any risk of leakage of such information to those acting for the defendant.

Parker L.J. and Sir David Croom-Johnson held that the test to be applied in **18–02** determining whether the firm should be permitted to act for the defendant was whether a reasonable person in the position of the objector would anticipate a

---

[1] (1836) 3 Bing. (N.C.) 235.
[2] For the rules of professional conduct, see the Law Society's "Guide to the Professional Conduct of Solicitors" (1993), Chap. 16, and the "General Council of the Bar's Code of Conduct", para. 501(f), 603 and 604.
[3] See Chap. XX, below.
[4] [1992] 1 Q.B. 959. See also *Re a Solicitor* (1987) 131 S.J. 1063; *David Lee & Co. (Lincoln) Ltd v. Coward Chance* [1991] 1 Ch. 259; *Re a Firm of Solicitors* [1995] 3 All E.R. 482; *MacDonald v. Martin* [1990] 3 S.C.R. 1235 (Supreme Court of Canada): *Ablitt v. Mills & Reeve, The Times* October 25, 1995.

danger of confidential information being used against him, in which case the court should intervene to prevent a situation of apparent unfairness, and they quoted the words of Cozens-Hardy M.R. in *Rakusen v. Ellis, Munday & Clarke*[5]:

> "We expect and indeed we exact from solicitors, who are our officers, a higher standard of conduct than we can enforce against those who are not our officers."

Staughton L.J., dissenting, held that, so far as concerned the law on confidential information, an injunction could only be granted on a *quia timet* basis where there was an actual likelihood of mischief, but he acknowledged that the court's power to control solicitors might cause it to intervene if there was an apparent risk of mischief.

18–03 Although a lawyer's duty of confidentiality is ordinarily owed to his client, such a duty may be owed to a third person. A barrister, for example, may send a document to his opponent on a "counsel only" basis, in which case the recipient would owe a duty of confidence not to disclose it to anyone else without the sender's consent.

The duty owed by a lawyer to his client will extend to all confidential information obtained in that capacity during the period of his retainer, irrespective of its source,[6] and it continues after the termination of the retainer.

In *Wilson v. Rastell*[7] (a case on privilege) Buller J., referring to a decision by him in an earlier case, said:

> "... I thought that the privilege of not being examined to such points was the privilege of the party, and not of the attorney: and that the privilege never ceased at any period of time. In such a case it is not sufficient to say that the cause is at an end; the mouth of such a person is shut for ever."

"For ever" may be an overstatement, for information can lose the quality of confidence, but the duty of confidence will continue for as long as the information retains that quality.

18–04 When considering the duties of a lawyer to his client, no practical distinction can be drawn between the limits of confidence and the limits of privilege. (The subject here discussed is the duty of a lawyer to his client, as opposed to the difficult subject of the relationship of privilege and confidentiality as between a client and another party about which see Chapter XX.) For confidentiality is a pre-requisite of legal professional privilege; and, conversely, if information is recognised to be privileged, the decision whether to disclose it belongs to the client and not to the lawyer.

This is consistent with the approach taken, for example, by Scrutton L.J. in *Weld-Blundell v. Stephen*,[8] where he said:

> "But take the case of a solicitor. Under the decision in *Reg. v. Cox and Railton*[9] when the accused has consulted his solicitor after the commission

[5] [1912] 1 Ch. 831 at 834–835.
[6] See the Law Society's "Guide to the Professional Conduct of Solicitors" (1993), para. 16.02.
[7] (1792) 4 T.R. 753 at 759. Cited by Lord Taylor C.J. in *R. v. Derbyshire Magistrates Court, ex parte B* [1995] 3 W.L.R. 681 at 693.
[8] [1919] 1 K.B. 520 at 544–545.
[9] (1884) 14 Q.B.D. 153 at 175.

of a crime for the legitimate purpose of being defended the communication is *privileged*, the *privilege* being that of the client. If then the solicitor in breach of this *confidence and privilege* announced his intention of informing the prosecution of the contents of his client's communication, I cannot believe that the Court would not restrain him before communication or give damages against him for breach of his contract of employment after communication ... ." (Emphasis added.)

Under the rubric of privilege the courts have accorded greater protection to confidences imparted to lawyers than to doctors, priests or journalists,[10] for reasons explained by Sir George Jessel M.R. in *Anderson v. Bank of British Columbia*[11] and by Taylor L.J. in *Balabel v. Air India*[12]:

"It is common ground that the basic principle justifying legal professional privilege arises from the public interest requiring full and frank exchange of confidence between solicitor and client to enable the latter to receive necessary legal advice. Originally it related only to communications where legal proceedings were in being or in contemplation. This was the rationale which distinguished the solicitor and client relationship from that between any other professional man and his client."

The scope of legal professional privilege has been expanded so that it now generally embraces all confidential communications between a lawyer and his client for the purposes of obtaining legal advice, including information passed by one to the other "as part of the continuum aimed at keeping both informed so that advice may be sought and given as required".[13]

Where legal professional privilege applies, its nature is absolute and the court has no discretion whether to enforce it. This was emphasised by the House of Lords and by the High Court of Australia in the similar cases of *R. v. Derby Magistrates' Court ex parte B*[14] and *Carter v. Managing Partner, Northmore, Hale, Davy & Leake*.[15] In each case a defendant in criminal proceedings sought to compel production by witnesses of documents which had been brought into existence by legal practitioners for the purpose of giving confidential legal advice. The defendant was charged in one case with murder and in the other with conspiracy to defraud. Each asserted that the documents sought were likely to assist him in his defence. It was held in each case that production could not be ordered for essentially the same reasons, namely that legal professional privilege was a fundamental principle of the administration of justice, for the purpose of enabling a person to seek and obtain legal advice in confidence, and that where such privilege attached, no exception to it should be permitted (unless compelled by statute).

In *R. v. Derby Magistrates' Court ex parte B* the magistrate, following a decision of the Court of Appeal[16] which the House of Lords overruled, had

---

[10] *Attorney-General v. Mulholland and Foster* [1963] 2 Q.B. 477 at 489. *British Steel Corporation v. Granada Television Ltd* [1981] A.C. 1096 at 1169–1170, 1181 and 1196.
[11] [1876] 2 Ch.D. 644 at 648–649.
[12] [1988] 1 Ch. 317 at 324.
[13] *ibid.* at 330.
[14] [1995] 3 W.L.R. 681.
[15] (1995) 69 A.L.J.R. 572.
[16] *R. v. Ataou* [1988] Q.B. 798.

directed himself that he must balance the public interest which protects confidential communications between a solicitor and his client against the public interest in securing that all relevant and admissible evidence was made available to the defence, and had concluded that the balance came down firmly in favour of production. The House of Lords held that no such balancing exercise was to be performed or that:

> "Putting it another way, if a balancing exercise was ever required in the case of legal professional privilege, it was performed once and for all in the 16th Century, and since then has applied across the board in every case, irrespective of the client's individual merits."[17]

In *Carter v. Northmore Hale Davy & Leake* the High Court of Australia expressed the same view. Deane J. said[18]:

> "Where legal professional privilege attaches, there is no question of balancing the considerations favouring the protection of confidentiality against any considerations favouring disclosure in the circumstances of the particular case. The privilege itself represents the outcome of such a balancing process and reflects the common law's verdict that the considerations favouring the 'perfect security' of communications and documents protected by the privilege must prevail. The common law's verdict in that regard was explained by Knight Bruce V.-C. in a judgment[19] which Lord Selborne L.C. was later to describe[20] as 'one of the ablest judgments of one of the ablest Judges who ever sat in this Court':
>
> > 'The discovery and vindication and establishment of truth are main purposes certainly of the existence of Courts of Justice; still, for the obtaining of these objects, which, however valuable and important, cannot be usefully pursued without moderation, cannot be either usefully or creditably pursued unfairly or gained by unfair means, not every channel is or ought to be open to them. . . . Truth, like all other good things, may be loved unwisely—may be pursued too keenly— may cost too much. And surely the meanness and the mischief of prying into a man's confidential consultations with his legal adviser, the general evil of infusing reserve and dissimulation, uneasiness, and suspicion and fear, into those communications which must take place, and which, unless in *a condition of perfect security*, must take place uselessly or worse, are too great a price to pay for truth itself.' "

There are, however, limits to the circumstances in which legal professional privilege attaches. The information must itself be confidential. So, for example, legal professional privilege cannot attach to extracts from public records made by a solicitor for the purposes of a defence, nor to communications with an opposing party,[21] nor to copies of documents which were not brought into existence in circumstances covered by legal professional privilege even where the copies were obtained for the purposes of litigation.[22]

---

[17] [1995] 3 W.L.R. 681, per Lord Taylor C.J. at 696.
[18] (1995) 183 C.L.R. 121, 133–134.
[19] *Pearse v. Pearse* (1846) 1 De G. & Sm. 12 at 28–29.
[20] *Minet v. Morgan* (1873) 8 Ch.App. 361 at 368.
[21] *Lyell v. Kennedy (No. 3)* (1884) 27 Ch.D. 1.
[22] *Ventouris v. Mountain* [1991] 1 W.L.R. 607.

Crime or fraud

Privilege does not attach to communications between a client and legal adviser, **18–05** or documents brought into existence, as a step in a criminal or fraudulent enterprise, or for the purpose of stifling or covering up a crime or fraud, whether the legal adviser is himself a party to the plot or innocent,[23] for, as Stephen J. said in *R. v. Cox and Railton*,[24] a communication in furtherance of a criminal purpose does not "come into the ordinary scope of professional employment" and "the protection of such communications cannot possibly be otherwise than injurious to the interests of justice."

In *Bullivant v. Attorney-General for Victoria*, Lord Halsbury L.C. said[25]:

"... for the perfect administration of justice and for the protection of confidence which exists between a solicitor and his client, it has been established as a principle of public policy that those confidential communi-cations shall not be subject to production. But to that, of course, this limitation has been put, that no court can be called upon to protect communications which are in themselves part of a criminal or unlawful proceeding."

A serious problem for an honest solicitor is what to do when the facts are not **18–06** clear. Drawing a line between proper defence of a client and improper concealment of wrongdoing may be difficult. So is the position of a solicitor who begins to suspect that a transaction in which he has been retained involves fraud. Terminating his retainer may be a solution in some cases, but not in others, particularly where the solicitor is in possession of funds which may represent the proceeds of fraud. This problem arose in *Finers v. Miro*.[26] The plaintiffs had acted for the defendant in setting up a complex corporate scheme to hold assets on his behalf. Secrecy was a primary aim of the scheme. Subsequently, reasonable grounds arose for suspicion that many of the assets represented the proceedings of fraud carried out on an insurance company, now in liquidation.

The solicitors were in a dilemma what to do and concerned that they might be liable as constructive trustees of the assets held under their control. They accordingly applied to the court, by an originating summons under Order 85 of the Rules of the Supreme Court, for directions in relation to the assets. The Court of Appeal held that the insurance company's liquidator should be given notice of the solicitors' application, notwithstanding the defendant's conten-tion that such notice would constitute a breach of the legal professional privilege to which he was entitled. Dillon L.J. said[27]:

"It was urged for the defendant that the advice obtained by the defendant from Mr Stein [a partner in the firm of solicitors] was not advice on how to commit a fraud but advice after the fraud, if there was one, had been

[23] *R. v. Cox and Railton* (1884) 14 Q.B.D. 153; *Bullivant v. Attorney-General for Victoria* [1901] A.C. 196 at 201, *per* Lord Halsbury; 206, *per* Lord Lindley; *O'Rourke v. Darbishire* [1920] A.C. 581; *Gamlen Chemical Co. (UK) Ltd v. Rochem* (unreported) December 7, 1979, C.A. (Civil Division) Transcript No. 777 of 1979; *Finers v. Miro* [1991] 1 W.L.R. 35.
[24] (1884) 14 Q.B.D. 153 at 167.
[25] [1901] A.C. 196 at 201.
[26] [1991] 1 W.L.R. 35.
[27] *ibid.* at 40.

committed. I note, however, that in *O'Rourke v. Darbishire*[28] Lord Sumner refers, at p. 613, to a party consulting a solicitor 'in order to learn how to plan, execute, or stifle an actual fraud'. The privilege cannot, in my judgment, apply if the solicitor is consulted—even though he does not realise this and is himself acting innocently—to cover up or stifle a fraud."

But how well established must a client's wrongdoing be in order to absolve a lawyer of his prima facie duty of confidence? In *Finers*, Dillon L.J. continued:

"On the material before us I conclude that *it does seem probable* that the defendant may have consulted Mr Stein for the purpose of being guided and helped, albeit unwittingly on the part of Mr Stein, in covering up or stifling *a fraud on the insurance company of which there is a prima facie case resting on solid grounds*."[29] (Emphasis added.)

18–07   If the test used by Dillon L.J. in *Finers* is an appropriate one for the court, is it also suitable for a lawyer to use when exercising his own judgment about a client? Suppose that a solicitor, acting for both prospective mortgagor and prospective mortgagee, discovers information that leads him to suspect that the mortgagor is planning to defraud the mortgagee and that he, the solicitor, is to be the mortgagor's unwitting tool in this fraud.

The Law Society's guidance in such cases is that the solicitor can no longer continue to act for either the mortgagor or the mortgagee. This may well be correct if the solicitor's suspicion remains merely an unsubstantiated suspicion. If it seems to him probable, however, that the purpose of his retainer is the furtherance of a fraud of which "there is a prima facie case on solid grounds", the question arises (a) whether there is any duty to the mortgagor which prevents the solicitors from informing the mortgagee of the fraud, and indeed (b) whether it is not the solicitor's *duty* to inform the mortgagee.

18–08   In *Mortgage Express Ltd v. Bowerman & Partners*[30] the Court of Appeal held that where a solicitor acting for both borrower and mortgagee in a property purchase discovered, on investigating title, information about recent prior sales, which might have caused the mortgagee to suspect that the valuation with which he had been provided was excessive, the solicitor owed a duty to disclose that information to the mortgagee as well as to the borrower.

Sir Thomas Bingham M.R. stressed that it was not a case in which a solicitor acting for two parties received information confidential to one of them. He observed, *obiter*, that in such a case it might be necessary for the solicitor to obtain the consent of the client whose information it was to disclose it to the other, and that if consent were refused the solicitor might be obliged to cease to act for that other party or both.

If a solicitor continues to act for a party who he suspects may be using him in a fraudulent or criminal enterprise, he plainly does so at his peril.[31] But whether he is permitted or under a duty to reveal the information to the potential victim is another matter.

If his suspicions are correct, then there can be no privilege or confidence in

[28] [1920] A.C. 581.
[29] A test derived from an amalgam of what was said by Lord Wrenbury in *O'Rourke v. Derbyshire* [1920] A.C. 581 at 632–644 and by Templeman L.J. in *Gamlen Chemical Co. (UK) Ltd v. Rochem Ltd*.
[30] *The Times*, August 1, 1995.
[31] See *Royal Brunei Airlines SDN BHD v. Tan* [1995] 3 W.L.R. 64.

the matter, and the solicitor cannot therefore be in breach of duty to his client by revealing what he knows. If, however, his suspicions turn out to be incorrect, then he will have acted in breach of confidence if he has voluntarily disclosed information obtained by him confidentially.

This factor is important when considering what, if any, duty of disclosure he **18–09** may owe. It is suggested that such a duty could in any event only arise if the other party were a client or in a position closely analogous to that of a client (*i.e.* someone placing reliance on the solicitor in the transaction). But further, it may be difficult, if not impossible, for the solicitor to act as judge between his clients whether one is defrauding the other, and the courts should not impose on him a duty which would have the effect of requiring him to do so. He ought therefore not to be under a duty to disclose to one client his suspicion that the other is defrauding him, unless possibly the facts known to him go beyond suspicion and admit of no honest explanation. In any case the fact of the solicitor ceasing to act, without giving any explanation, should itself ordinarily be a warning to the other party that there may be matters to investigate.

Use of information in defence of the lawyer's own interests

It is established by a number of Court of Appeal dicta[32] that a lawyer is not **18–10** entitled to reveal confidential information in order to oppose the making of a wasted costs order against him pursuant to Order 62, rule 11 of the Rules of the Supreme Court. It is doubtful whether this restriction can be ascribed to equitable principles of confidence,[33] since professional persons are entitled in general to use information imparted to them confidentially, if it is reasonably necessary for them to do so in protection of their own legitimate interests.[34]

Rather, the restriction must arise as a result of the privileged nature of the information, or from the court's supervision of solicitors and barristers as officers of the court. Since orders for costs are within the discretion of the court, the court is unusually well placed to avoid any injustice in considering a wasted costs application by making proper allowance for this restriction upon respondent lawyers. In the leading case of *Ridehalgh v. Horsefield*,[35] the Court of Appeal observed:

> "The respondent lawyers are in a different position. The privilege is not theirs to waive. In the usual case where a waiver would not benefit their client they will be slow to advise the client to waive his privilege, and they may well feel bound to advise that the client should take independent advice before doing so. The client may be unwilling to do that, and may be unwilling to waive if he does. So the respondent lawyers may find themselves at a grave disadvantage in defending their conduct of proceedings, unable to reveal what advice and warnings they gave, what

[32] See, *e.g. Orchard v. South Eastern Electricity Board* [1987] 1 Q.B. 565, *per* Donaldson M.R. at 572 and *per* Dillon L.J. at 580; *Ridehalgh v. Horsefield* [1994] Ch. 205, at 236 to 237.

[33] *pace* Donaldson M.R. in *Orchard*: his comments are not supported by the approach adopted by Dillon L.J. in that case, or by the Court of Appeal in *Ridehalgh*.

[34] *Tournier v. National Provincial and Union Bank of England* [1924] 1 K.B. 461 (bankers); *Duncan v. Medical Practitioner's Disciplinary Committee* [1986] 1 N.Z.L.R. 513 (doctors); *R. v. Institute of Chartered Accountants of England and Wales, ex p. Brindle* [1994] B.C.C. 297, 312 (accountants).

[35] [1994] Ch. 205, at 237.

instructions they received. In some cases this potential source of injustice may be mitigated by reference to the taxing master, where different rules apply, but only in a small minority of cases can this procedure be appropriate. Judges who are invited to make or contemplate making a wasted costs order must make full allowance for the inability of respondent lawyers to tell the whole story. Where there is room for doubt, the respondent lawyers are entitled to the benefit of it. It is again only when, with all allowances made, a lawyer's conduct of proceedings is quite plainly unjustifiable that it can be appropriate to make a wasted costs order."

18–11   The question arises whether this restriction upon lawyers opposing wasted costs applications extends to lawyers facing other civil claims or criminal sanctions. The Law Society's "Guide to the Professional Conduct of Solicitors"[36] states that:

> "A solicitor may reveal confidential information concerning the client to the extent that it is reasonably necessary to establish a defence to a criminal charge or civil claim against the solicitor or where the solicitor's conduct is under investigation by the Solicitors Complaints Bureau or the Solicitors' Disciplinary Tribunal."

This passage is consistent with principles of confidence as applied to other professional people,[37] but what about privilege?

If the proceedings have been brought, or have resulted from a complaint, by the client, clearly the client cannot assert privilege to prevent the solicitor from deploying previously confidential material to the extent reasonably necessary to defend himself.[38] If the proceedings have been brought by somebody else,[39] the problem is more difficult.

It can be argued that the wasted costs jurisdiction of the court is exceptional in a number of respects: both the procedure adopted and the relief sought are within the discretion of the court.[40] Furthermore, the application for a wasted costs order is part of the very proceedings in which privilege has been claimed for the material concerned: the client's interest in the maintenance of his privilege is therefore likely to be strong. Most importantly, the court is able to make express allowance in the solicitor's favour for the prohibition which it has itself imposed on the solicitor from telling the full story. In those circumstances it might therefore be considered reasonable that restrictions should apply to lawyers resisting an application for wasted costs that would not necessarily apply to lawyers facing separate and independent proceedings.

Nonetheless it is doubtful whether the broad statement in the Law Society's guide is correct. In *R. v. Derby Magistrates' Court ex parte B*[41] Lord Taylor C.J. said that:

---

[36] At p. 333.
[37] *Duncan v. Medical Practitioner's Disciplinary Committee* [1986] 1 N.Z.L.R. 513. *R. v. Institute of Chartered Accountants of England and Wales, ex p. Brindle* [1994] B.L.C. 297 at 312.
[38] *Lillicrap v. Nalder* [1993] 1 W.L.R. 94.
[39] See the example at para. 18–07, above, of a claim by a mortgage lender. If the loan was fraudulent, no question of privilege would arise, but it might be the defendant's case that the loan was *not* fraudulent and he might need to disclose confidential documents with a view to establishing the innocence of the transaction and his own innocence.
[40] *Ridehalgh v. Horsefield* [1994] Ch. 205 at 238–239.
[41] [1995] 3 W.L.R. 681 at 697.

"... no exception should be made to the absolute nature of legal professional privilege, once established ..."

If the information given to a solicitor was originally privileged, and if there has been no express or implied waiver of privilege by the client, it is difficult to see how the solicitor may use such information to defend himself even against a criminal charge. It may be that if the solicitor could show to the court with jurisdiction over the criminal proceedings that the effect of his inability to use the information would be seriously to impede his ability to defend himself, the court would have an inherent jurisdiction to stay the criminal proceedings, but even that solution presents difficulties, for it would be likely to involve the solicitor revealing to the court that which, *ex hypothesi*, he is not authorised to reveal.

Disclosure required by law

A lawyer who discloses confidential information under compulsion of law **18–12** commits no breach of confidence. In *Parry-Jones v. Law Society*,[42] Diplock L.J. said of a solicitor's contractual duty of confidence:

"Such a duty exists not only between solicitor and client, but, for example, between banker and customer, doctor and patient and accountant and client. Such a duty of confidence is subject to, and overridden by, the duty of any party to that contract to comply with the law of the land."

Examples include the following:

(1) *The Legal Aid Board.* A lawyer acting for a client who is legally aided owes a **18–13** duty not only to the client, but also to the Legal Aid Board. A number of the Civil Legal Aid (General) Regulations 1989 concern the duty of lawyers in certain circumstances to provide information to the Area Director. Much, if not all, of such information would prima facie be regarded as confidential to the client, but it is clear that this confidentiality does not prevent the making of reports required by the regulations—or, indeed, the provision of information which may enable the Legal Aid Board to perform its functions under the Act.[43]

(2) *Money laundering.* Sections 93A and 93B of the Criminal Justice Act 1988 **18–14** create offences relating to: assisting another to retain the benefit of criminal conduct (93A) and the acquisition, possession or use of the proceeds of criminal conduct (93B).

There are statutory defences, including defences based upon prompt disclosure to a constable (as defined in the Act), and it is provided that "the disclosure shall not be treated as a breach of any restriction upon the disclosure of information imposed by statute or otherwise".

(3) *Drug trafficking.* Sections 23A and 24 of the Drug Trafficking Offences Act **18–15** 1986 contain similar provisions in relation to the laundering of the proceeds of

---

[42] [1969] 1 Ch. 1, at 9.
[43] See in particular, in relation to legal professional privilege, reg. 73.

drug trafficking, including provisions that disclosure to a constable or suspicion or belief that property or funds are derived from drug trafficking shall not be treated as a breach of any restriction upon the disclosure of information.

Children

18–16 In *Ramsbotham v. Senior*,[44] Malins V.-C. said:

> "... no person, be he solicitor or not, can have any privilege whatever in doing, or abstaining from doing, that which has the effect of concealing the residence of a ward of this Court, and thereby preventing the Court exercising its due control over the ward."

In that case the mother of wards of court had absconded with them and her solicitor was ordered to produce envelopes of letters which he had received from her, with the object of discovering her residence from the postmarks. She was in grave, continuing contempt of court and therefore had no privilege in concealing her whereabouts from the court; and since she had no privilege in keeping the information confidential, the solicitor had none to protect.

18–17 In *Re L*[45] the House of Lords, by a majority of three to two, held that in care proceedings under the Children Act 1989 privilege did not attach to an expert's report, which was obtained by a party under an order of the court giving leave to the expert to study the court papers. The parents were drug addicts. The child became ill after ingestion of methadone. An order was made giving leave to disclose the court papers to a medical expert and requiring his report to be filed. The mother's solicitors instructed a chemical pathologist, whose report cast doubt on the mother's explanation of the incident. The judge ordered disclosure of the report to the police.

The mother appealed against the order, arguing that the report was the subject of legal professional privilege and that the court ought not to have made an order compelling its disclosure to other parties either at the time of the original order requiring the report to be filed or at the time of the order under appeal.

Lord Jauncey, delivering the opinion of the majority, distinguished *R. v. Derby Magistrates Court ex parte B*[46] on two grounds: care proceedings were of a special non-adversarial nature unlike ordinary litigation, and the expert's report was not a communication between solicitor and client but a report by a third party prepared on the instructions of the client for the purposes of the proceedings. He concluded that care proceedings were:

> "so far removed from normal actions that litigation privilege has no place in relation to reports obtained by a party thereto which could not have been prepared without the leave of the court to disclose documents already filed or to examine the child."

It follows that the question of the court's power to impose a disclosure condition when giving leave for the court papers to be shown to an expert did

---

[44] (1869) L.R. 8 Eq. 575.
[45] *The Times*, March 22, 1996.
[46] [1995] 3 W.L.R. 681.

not arise, because in the absence of privilege the report would be disclosable to other parties to the proceedings in any event.

The House of Lords did not go so far as to hold that no legal professional privilege arose in care proceedings. On the contrary, Lord Jauncey not only distinguished the expert's report under consideration from communications between solicitor and client, but he said that his view that litigation privilege never arose in relation to the expert's report did not affect privilege arising between solicitor and client.

It is uncertain whether privilege would attach to a report by an expert, a **18–18** statement from a witness, or other communications between a solicitor and a third party for the purpose of care proceedings, made without need for leave of the court to examine court documents or to examine the child.

Behind this issue lies the unresolved question whether a party to care proceedings is under a duty of disclosure of matters adverse to his or her case.

In *Essex County Council v. R.*[47] Thorpe J. after holding that the court, when **18–19** considering the welfare of the child, has power to override legal professional privilege, continued:

> "For my part, I would wish to see case law go yet further and to make it plain that the legal representatives in possession of such material relevant to determination but contrary to the interests of their client, not only are unable to resist disclosure by reliance on legal professional privilege, but have a positive duty to disclose to the other parties and to the court."

In *Oxfordshire County Council v. P*[48] Ward J. said: **18–20**

> "In all cases where the welfare of children is the court's paramount consideration, there is a duty on all parties to make full and frank disclosure of all matters material to welfare whether those matters are favourable to or adverse to their own particular case."

In *Re L* Lord Jauncey cited the passages above and said that he preferred to **18–21** wait until the point arose directly for decision before determining whether such a duty exists and if so what is its scope.

The premise to Thorpe J's. approach in *Essex County Council v. R* (that the court has power to override legal professional privilege when considering the welfare of a child) is not consistent with the reasoning of the House of Lords in *R. v. Derby Magistrates Court ex parte B*, as to the absolute nature of legal professional privilege when established, or in *Re L*, which was based on the view that legal professional privilege never arose in relation to the expert's report rather than that it could be overridden.

If there is a duty on a party to care proceedings to disclose all material matters, whether favourable or adverse to their case, it must follow that they would have no privilege to withhold from other parties or the court any relevant evidence obtained by their solicitor on their behalf. If on the other hand they are under no such duty, it is suggested that there is no good reason to deny them the right to claim privilege in respect of such material obtained by their solicitor on their behalf.

---

[47] [1994] Fam. 167 at 168.
[48] [1995] Fam. 161 at 166.

PART 3

CONFIDENTIALITY AND THE LEGAL PROCESS

Confidentiality is not in itself a bar to disclosure of information or documents in legal proceedings. Nevertheless there are a number of rules and practices by which the courts accord a greater or lesser degree of protection to confidential information, or certain kinds of confidential information, either by excluding it altogether, or by restricting the manner in which it is disclosed, or by restricting the use thereafter made of it. This part of the book looks at these rules and their relationship with principles of confidentiality.

195

CHAPTER XIX

GENERAL PRINCIPLE AND EXCEPTIONS

The general principle

Generally speaking, confidentiality is not a bar to disclosure of documents or **19–01** information in the process of litigation, but the court will only compel such disclosure if it considers it necessary for the fair disposal of the case. This principle was recognised by the House of Lords in a trio of cases: *D. v. National Society for the Prevention of Cruelty to Children*,[1] *Science Research Council v. Nassé*[2] and *British Steel Corporation v. Granada Television Ltd*[3] The principle applies whether the person making the disclosure claims confidentiality for himself or is under a duty of confidentiality to another.

If a litigant wishes to withhold production of a relevant document on grounds of confidentiality, he should include it in his list of documents but object to its production. The court is entitled to inspect the document when considering whether to order production.

Exceptions

The principle that information necessary for the fair disposal of disputes **19–02** should be disclosed, even if it is confidential, is subject to statutory and common law exceptions.

Statutory exceptions

Various statutes which give powers to obtain information of a confidential **19–03** information also impose restrictions on the disclosure of such information.[4] In such cases the recipient cannot be compelled by *subpoena* to make disclosure which is prohibited by statute.

---

[1] [1978] A.C. 171.
[2] [1980] A.C. 1028.
[3] [1981] A.C. 1096.
[4] For example, the Banking Act 1987, ss.82–87.

Common law exceptions

19–04   The general principle does not apply in cases of:

(1) "without prejudice" communications and communications to mediators and conciliators;
(2) legal professional privilege; or
(3) public interest immunity,

the rationale being that the public interest in maintaining secrecy in such cases outweighs the general principle in favour of disclosure.[5]

"WITHOUT PREJUDICE" COMMUNICATIONS AND COMMUNICATIONS TO MEDIATORS AND CONCILIATORS

"Without prejudice" communications

19–05   Negotiations genuinely aimed at a settlement are inadmissible in evidence, not only in the litigation in the course of which they take place, but also in any subsequent litigation connected with the same subject-matter. Moreover, such negotiations are not discoverable to third parties—nor indeed to the negotiators themselves (though the point may only be of theoretical importance).[6]

In the leading case of *Rush & Tompkins Ltd v. Greater London Council*,[7] Lord Griffiths cited with approval the words of Oliver L.J. in *Cutts v. Head*[8]:

> "That the rule rests, at least in part, upon public policy is clear from any authorities, and the convenient starting point of the inquiry is the nature of the underlying policy. It is that parties should be encouraged so far as possible to settle their disputes without resort to litigation and should not be discouraged by the knowledge that anything that is said in the course of such negotiations (and that includes, of course, as much the failure to reply to an offer as an actual reply) may be used to their prejudice in the course of the proceedings. They should, as it was expressed by Clauson J. in *Scott Paper Co. v. Drayton Paper Works Ltd* (1927) 44 R.P.C. 151, 156, be encouraged fully and frankly to put their cards on the table ... . The public policy justification, in truth, essentially rests on the desirability of preventing statements or offers made in the course of negotiations for settlement being brought before the court of trial as admissions on the question of liability."

In *Cutts v. Head*[9] Oliver L.J. took the view that this public policy justification came to an end once the trial of the issues in the action had taken place, and that the rationale of protection thereafter must therefore be "an implied agreement imported from the marking of a letter 'without prejudice' that it shall not be referred to at all".

---

[5] Privilege against self-incrimination is omitted. Although one of the factors underlying the existence of the privilege is personal privacy (*per* Lord Mustill in *R. v. Directors of Serious Fraud Office, ex p. Smith* [1993] A.C. 1, at 31), it is unconnected with the general law of confidentiality which is the subject of this book.

[6] *Rush & Tompkins Ltd v. Greater London Council* [1989] 1 A.C. 1280, esp. at 1301 and 1304A.

[7] [1989] 1 A.C. 1280, at 1299.

[8] [1984] Ch. 290, at 306.

[9] *ibid.* at 307.

This part of his judgment was not cited by the House of Lords in *Rush & Tompkins Ltd* and his premise was indeed contradicted in the speech of Lord Griffiths.[10] Nevertheless, it is suggested that he was correct in his view that a person participating in "without prejudice" negotiations owes to his opponent a private law duty of confidentiality, and that this must be so whether or not the document is formally marked "without prejudice", although the duty must be subject to qualifications.

A legally aided litigant, for example, may owe a duty to the Legal Aid Board to disclose a "without prejudice" offer made by the opposing party, which might cause the Legal Aid Board to consider whether legal aid should be continued in the event of the offer being refused.

Similarly, a company being supported in litigation by its bank may wish, or feel under an obligation, to disclose to the bank a settlement offer which it has received (or made). Its auditors may also need to know the state of outstanding litigation for the purpose of reporting on the company's accounts pursuant to the statutory requirements of the Companies Act 1985.

However, if no duty of confidentiality were owed at all, a party to "without prejudice" negotiations would be at liberty to publicise them at large. This would be inimical to the object to such negotiations and contrary to the assumption on which they are ordinarily conducted.

Statements to mediators and conciliators[11]

In matrimonial cases privilege has been held to extend to statements made by   **19–06**
the parties with the aim of effecting a reconciliation. The privilege covers both communications between the parties themselves, or their agents, and also communications to any private individual specifically enlisted as a conciliator. The earlier authorities were reviewed in *Theodoropoulas v. Theodoropoulas*[12] by Sir Jocelyn Simon P.

Similarly, in *Re D. (Minors) (Conciliation: Disclosure of Information)*,[13] the Court of Appeal held that in proceedings under the Children Act 1989 privilege analogous to "without prejudice" privilege applied to prevent evidence being given of a statement made by a party in the course of meetings held or communications made for the purpose of conciliation (except in the very unusual case where a statement is made clearly indicating that the maker has in the past caused or is likely in the future to cause serious harm to the well-being of a child).

There is no logical reason to confine this approach to cases involving spouses or children and, particularly in view of increasing emphasis on alternative methods of dispute resolution, statement to mediators specifically appointed and recognised by both parties should in general be treated as privileged.

Legal professional privilege and public interest immunity

These subjects are considered in the following chapters.   **19–07**

---

[10] [1989] 1 A.C. 1280, at 1300–1301.
[11] See also paras. 17–01—17–04, above.
[12] [1964] P. 311.
[13] [1993] Fam. 231, at 241. See also *D. v. N.S.P.C.C.* [1978] A.C. 171, *per* Lord Hailsham at 226 and *per* Lord Simon at 237.

CHAPTER XX

LEGAL PROFESSIONAL PRIVILEGE AND CONFIDENCE

Origins and basis of legal professional confidence

20–01   Communications between a person and his legal adviser, or (once litigation is contemplated or pending) between either of them and a third party, are protected from discovery if they were created for the purposes (broadly interpreted) of legal advice.[1]

Legal professional privilege, as it is now called, has its origins in the concept of confidence. At first its rationale was the protection of the honour of the professional man, but this approach was eventually rejected by the courts. As Lord Simon said in *D. v. N.S.P.C.C.*[2]:

> "A man of honour would not betray a confidence, and the judges as men of honour themselves would not require him to. Thus originally legal professional privilege was that of the legal adviser, not the client. (For the foregoing, see *Wigmore, Evidence*, secs. 2286, 2290.) But, with the decline in the ethos engendering the rule, the law moved decisively away from it. The turning point was the *Duchess of Kingston's Case* (1776) 20 State Tr. 355 at 386–391, where both the duchess's surgeon and a personal friend, Lord Barrington, were compelled to give evidence in breach of confidence."

20–02   In the case of legal advisers, however, the courts, under their inherent jurisdiction to control their own rules of procedure and evidence, developed the special doctrine of legal professional privilege.[3] The foundation of the modern doctrine of legal privilege was summarised by Sir George Jessel M.R. in *Anderson v. Bank of British Columbia*[4]:

> "The object and meaning of the rule is this: that as, by reason of the complexity and difficulty of our law, litigation can only be conducted by professional men, it is absolutely necessary that a man, in order to prosecute his rights or to defend himself from an improper claim, should have recourse to the assistance of professional lawyers, and it being so

[1] This statement is deliberately general. Fuller treatment of the sub-divisions of legal professional privilege into "advice privilege" and "litigation privilege" is outside the scope of this book. Qualifications to the general principle have been considered in the context of qualifications to the lawyer's duty of confidence to his client in Chap. XVIII, above.

[2] [1978] A.C. 171 at 238.

[3] The principle has also been recognised by the European Court of Justice: see *Australian Mining & Smelting Europe Ltd v. E.C. Commission* [1982] 2 C.M.L.R. 264.

[4] (1876) 2 Ch.D. 644 at 649.

absolutely necessary, it is equally necessary, to use a vulgar phrase, that he should be able to make a clean breast of it to the gentleman whom he consults with a view to the prosecution of his claim, or the substantiating his defence against the claim of others; that he should be able to place unrestricted and unbounded confidence in the professional agent, and that the communications he so makes to him should be kept secret, unless with his consent (for it is his privilege, and not the privilege of the confidential agent), that he should be enabled properly to conduct his litigation."

In *R. v. Derbyshire Magistrates Court, ex p. B*[5] Lord Taylor C.J. described legal professional privilege as much more than an ordinary rule of evidence, but as a fundamental condition on which the administration of justice as a whole rests.

Legal professional privilege and the private law duty of confidence owed by a **20–03** lawyer to his client are twins, but not identical twins. The doctrines are similar in that legal professional privilege is founded upon the public interest in upholding the confidential relationship which exists between a lawyer and his client, and it is a prerequisite of legal professional privilege that the information for which privilege is claimed is confidential.[6]

The doctrines are different in that the source of the private law duty of confidence is to be found either in contract or in the equitable doctrine of confidence, and breach of such duty gives rise to a cause of action, although the court has a discretion whether to grant equitable relief in support of the duty. Legal professional privilege does not found a cause of action; it is an evidential rule, and where privilege exists the court has no power to override it.

The duty of confidence owed by a lawyer to his client has been discussed in more detail in Chapter XVIII, and the subject of legal professional privilege has been considered in that context.

In litigation, no party is entitled to compel the disclosure of documents or information in respect of which another person is entitled to claim legal professional privilege. However, it may happen that a party in fact obtains such information, and the question may arise whether he is entitled to deploy it in evidence.

Since the rules of evidence exist to govern the conduct of litigation, it may be supposed that the answer to that question should depend on those rules. Logic might also suggest that where those rules permit one party to deploy in evidence a document belonging to the opposing party, it cannot be unconscionable for that party to do so, and accordingly the equitable doctrine of confidence cannot operate to prevent him.

Nevertheless, equitable principles of confidence have sometimes been prayed in aid in order to protect parties to litigation who have lost the benefit of the privilege to which they were entitled. In cases where the courts have had to deal with concepts both of confidence and privilege, there has sometimes been confusion, much of which has stemmed from the unfortunate decision of the Court of Appeal in *Calcraft v. Guest*[7] and subsequent attempts to obviate its consequences by reference to the doctrine of confidence.

Calcraft v. Guest

In *Calcraft v. Guest*, certain documents had been created to assist in the **20–04** preparation of the defence of an action for assault (*Fry v. Stevens*) tried at the

---

[5] [1995] 3 W.L.R. 681 at 695.
[6] *Kennedy v. Lyall* (1881) 23 Ch.D. 387 at 404–405, *per* Cotton L.J.
[7] [1898] 1 Q.B. 759.

Dorchester Assizes in 1787. Privilege in the documents belonged to a Mr John Calcraft. After the action, the documents were retained by Mr John Calcraft's solicitor, a Mr Thomas Bartlett. In due course, the documents came into the possession of Mr Bartlett's great-great-grandson, a Mr C. L. O. Bartlett.

More than 100 years after *Fry v. Stevens*, Mr John Calcraft's successor-in-title (also named Calcraft) commenced an action against a Mrs Drax to which the documents were relevant. Judgment was given in his favour. Shortly after-wards, the existence of the documents was discovered by Mr C. L. O. Bartlett. Before returning them to Mr Calcraft, he showed them to the solicitors acting for Mrs Drax, who had instructed Mr Bartlett's firm in other matters (though not on this occasion). Mrs Drax's solicitors took copies of the documents and sought to put them in evidence in an appeal. Mr Calcraft objected as Mr John Calcraft's successor-in-title, arguing that privilege in the documents had not been destroyed by Mr C. L. O. Bartlett's wrongful disclosure of the documents to Mrs Drax's solicitors.

Lindley M.R. (with whom Rigby and Vaughan Williams L.JJ. concurred) held that "the mere fact that documents used in a previous litigation are held and have not been destroyed does not amount to a waiver of the privilege."[8] He continued:

> "Then comes the next question. It appears that the appellant has obtained copies of some of these documents, and is in a position to give secondary evidence of them; and the question is whether he is entitled to do that."

Lindley M.R. cited a dictum of Parke B. in *Lloyd v. Mostin*[9]:

> "... Where an attorney intrusted confidentially with a document com-municates the contents of it, or suffers another to take a copy, surely the secondary evidence so obtained may be produced. Suppose the instrument were even stolen, and a correct copy taken, would it not be reasonable to admit it?"

Lindley M.R. concluded that the case came within the scope of Parke B.'s dictum and that secondary evidence of the privileged documents was therefore admissible.

Is *Calcraft v. Guest* right?

20–05   It is an odd proposition that one party could break into the offices of the opposing party's solicitors, take copies of privileged documents, and then introduce them at trial. Suppose that, instead of producing documents, one party chose to call a solicitor, who had previously acted for the other party, to give evidence of privileged matters. One would expect it to be said that his evidence would not be admissible without the consent of his former client.[10]

It seems that in *Calcraft v. Guest*, the court viewed privilege (1) as attaching to documents themselves, rather than to the information contained in them, and (2) as being a legitimate reason for refusing to produce material documents, but nothing more than that.

---

[8] *Calcraft v. Guest* [1898] 1 Q.B. 759 at 761–762.
[9] (1842) 10 M. & W. 478.
[10] *pace* Sir John Strange in *Bishop of Winchester v. Fournier* (1752) 2 Ves. Sen. 445, at 447. See *Wilson v. Rastell* (1792) 4 T.R. 753, *per* Buller J. at 759, and *Bate v. Kinsey* (1834) 1 C.M. & R. 38, *per* Lyndhurst C.B. at 43 and *R. v. Derby Magistrates Court, ex parte B* [1995] 3 W.L.R. 681, *per* Lord Taylor C.J. at 693.

There is a certain logic (though no merit) to the decision if, but only if, privilege is restricted to a rule exonerating a party from producing a document which is in his possession and satisfies the requirements of privilege.[11] On that basis, a copy document actually in the possession of the opposing party cannot be privileged, no matter how it was obtained.

The principle in *Calcraft v. Guest* has been closely examined and rejected in New Zealand in the case of *R. v. Uljee*.[12] In England, it has been criticised and distinguished (not always satisfactorily) but not overruled. In *English & American Insurance Co. Ltd v. Herbert Smith*,[13] Browne-Wilkinson V.-C. said:

> "I think that when this or some other case reaches the House of Lords it may well be that the absolute rule laid down in *Calcraft v. Guest* is the suspect decision ... ."

As authority binding on the Court of Appeal and on lesser courts, *Calcraft v. Guest* has thrown a long shadow over subsequent cases.

Ashburton v. Pape

Mrs Drax's leading counsel in *Calcraft v. Guest* was Herbert Cozens-Hardy **20–06** Q.C. He was also a member of the Court of Appeal which considered the consequences of that decision 15 years later, in the case of *Lord Ashburton v. Pape*.[14] Pape was a bankrupt who sought discharge. Lord Ashburton, one of his creditors, opposed his discharge. In answer to a *subpoena*, a clerk from the firm of solicitors retained by Lord Ashburton attended court with a number of privileged letters from Lord Ashburton to his solicitors. Complaining of illness, he handed the letters over to Mr Pape's solicitors, who took copies and passed the originals to their client.

Lord Ashburton issued separate proceedings and obtained by interlocutory motion an order, both that Pape deliver up the original letters and that he, with various others, be restrained "until judgment or further order from publishing or making use of any of the copies of such letters or any information contained therein except for the purpose of the bankruptcy and subject to the direction of the Bankruptcy Court". Lord Ashburton appealed, seeking to vary the order so as to remove from it the specified exception. His appeal succeeded.

Interpretation of the Court of Appeal's decision is made more difficult by textual discrepancies between the various reports of it.[15] Nevertheless, it is most often read as doing much to mitigate the effects of the earlier decision in *Calcraft v. Guest* by making it possible for a party claiming privilege in respect of a document to obtain an injunction restraining another party from deploying it (or a copy) in evidence, notwithstanding that it (or a copy) would otherwise be admissible.

Cozens-Hardy M.R. said[16]:

---

[11] But see *Minter v. Priest* [1930] A.C. 558, *per* Lord Atkin at 579.
[12] [1982] 1 N.Z.L.R. 561.
[13] [1988] F.S.R. 232 at 236–237.
[14] [1913] 2 Ch. 469; 109 L.T. 381; 82 L.J.Ch. 527; 29 T.L.R. 623; 57 S.J. 644.
[15] See, *e.g.* C. Tapper, "Privilege and Confidence" (1972) 35 M.L.R. 83, at 85ff., and N. H. Andrews, *The Influence of Equity upon the Doctrine of Legal Professional Privilege* (1989) 105 L.Q.R. 608 at 615ff.
[16] [1913] 2 Ch. 469 at 473.

"The rule of evidence as explained in *Calcraft v. Guest* merely amounts to this, that if a litigant wants to prove a particular document which by reason of privilege or some circumstance he cannot furnish by the production of the original, he may produce a copy as secondary evidence although that copy has been obtained by improper means, and even, it may be, by criminal means. The court in such an action is not really trying the circumstances under which the document was produced. That is not an issue in the case and the Court simply says 'Here is a copy of a document which cannot be produced; it may have been stolen, it may have been picked up in the street, it may have improperly got into the possession of the person who proposes to produce it, but that is not a matter which the Court in the trial of the action can go into.' But that does not seem to me to have any bearing upon a case where the whole subject-matter of the action is the right to retain the originals or copies of certain documents which are privileged."

Swinfen Eady L.J. said,[17]

"The principle upon which the Court of Chancery has acted for many years has been to restrain the publication of confidential information improperly or surreptitiously obtained or of information imparted in confidence which ought not to be divulged.... There is here a confusion between the right to restrain a person from divulging confidential information and the right to give secondary evidence of documents where the originals are privileged from production, if the party has such secondary evidence in his possession. The cases are entirely separate and distinct."

Comparison of *Calcraft* and *Ashburton*

20–07   *Ashburton v. Pape* appears to set up a clear distinction between privilege, which is lost or rendered useless by disclosure, and confidentiality, which may continue to protect privileged communications which have come into the possession of the other party as a result of a breach of confidence or by accident. But although the courts have recognised that *Calcraft* and *Ashburton* exemplify separate principles and they have been explained on that basis,[18] this separation has not always been observed.

Particular difficulties have arisen where it has been suggested that privilege has been waived by some step taken by the party entitled to privilege, and the question has arisen whether the party alleged to have waived privilege can in such a situation recover his position by relying on the principle in *Ashburton v. Pape*.[19]

One solution would be to say that ordinary principles of confidentiality may still apply at any time until the documents are produced in evidence at trial. If the party receiving the documents knew at the time that they were confidential

---

[17] *Ashburton v. Pape* [1913] 2 Ch. 469 at 475–476.

[18] *Goddard v. Nationwide Building Society* [1987] 1 Q.B. 670, *per* May L.J. at 679–683; *English & American Insurance Co. Ltd v. Herbert Smith* [1988] F.S.R. 232; *Webster v. James Chapman & Co.* [1989] 3 All E.R. 939.

[19] Privilege may also be lost by the use made of documents, even if they are not directly disclosed to the opposing party. See, *e.g.*, *Great Atlantic Insurance Co. v. Home Insurance Co.* [1981] 1 W.L.R. 529; *Lillicrap v. Nalder & Son* [1993] 1 W.L.R. 94. Contrast *British Coal Corporation v. Dennis Rye Ltd* [1988] 1 W.L.R. 1113; *Goldman v. Hesper* [1988] 1 W.L.R. 1238.

and disclosed in error, or subsequently learns this without in the meantime having changed his position to his detriment, the mistaken party should still be able to assert a duty of confidentiality.

An alternative solution would be to say that, if, according to the rules governing the conduct of litigants, privilege has been waived, there can be nothing unconscionable in the opposing party using the information or documents concerned, and that there is therefore no room for the application of the doctrine of confidence. The question what constitutes a waiver of privilege would remain, but would fall to be determined by common law rules and not by reference to equitable principles.

The approach adopted by the courts

The courts have not consistently adopted either of these two logical **20–08** alternatives, but have steered a somewhat meandering course between the two, and their reasoning has shown at times a confusion between the concepts of privilege and confidence.

Two cases which maintained clearly the distinction between privilege and confidence were *Butler v. Board of Trade*[20] and *Webster v. James Chapman & Co.*[21]

In *Butler*, the plaintiff sought a declaration that the Board of Trade, which had brought a prosecution against him, was not entitled to make any use of a letter written to him by his solicitor. A copy of the letter, together with other documents, had been handed over by his solicitor to the Official Receiver of a company in compulsory liquidation.

Goff J., having found that the original letter was privileged and the copy confidential, declined to grant relief on the principle in *Ashburton* because:

> "In my judgment it would not be a right or permissible exercise of the equitable jurisdiction in confidence to make a declaration at the suit of the accused in a public prosecution in effect restraining the Crown from adducing admissible evidence relevant to the crime with which he is charged. It is not necessary for me to decide whether the same result would obtain in the case of a private prosecution, and I expressly leave that point open."[22]

Goff J.'s distinction between private litigation and public prosecution was subsequently approved by the Criminal Division of the Court of Appeal in *R. v. Tompkins*,[23] but has not been followed in New Zealand and was criticised by Nourse L.J. in *Goddard v. Nationwide Building Society*.[24]

In *Webster v. James Chapman & Co.*,[25] Scott J.'s consideration whether to **20–09** grant relief to the plaintiff was governed by his view of the principles applicable to actions for breach of confidence. In that case, the plaintiff was injured at work and brought an action against his employer. A report by a firm of expert engineers was obtained by his solicitors, who requested the firm to reconsider

---

[20] [1971] 1 Ch. 680.
[21] [1989] 3 All E.R. 939.
[22] [1971] Ch. 680 at 690.
[23] (1978) 67 Cr.App.R. 181.
[24] [1987] 1 Q.B. 670 at 686.
[25] [1989] 3 All E.R. 939.

some elements of its opinion. The plaintiff's solicitors inadvertently sent a copy of the unrevised report to the defendant's solicitors.

The plaintiff sought an order that the defendant deliver up any copies of the unrevised report and be restrained from using its contents in any way. Scott J. held[26]:

> "If a document has been disclosed, be it by trickery, accident or otherwise, the benefit and protection of legal privilege will have been lost ... . The question then will be what protection the court should provide given that the document which will have come into the possession of the other side will be confidential, and that use of it will be unauthorised."

Scott J. took the view that he was required to give broad consideration to all the circumstances of the case, and concluded that the balance came down against granting the relief sought.[27]

20–10 However, the distinction between the law of privilege and principles of confidence has not been so clearly drawn in other cases. In *Goddard v. Nationwide Building Society*,[28] a solicitor acted for both the plaintiff mortgagor and the defendant mortgagee in relation to the purchase of a property by the plaintiff with the assistance of a loan from the defendant. The plaintiff subsequently sued the defendant in respect of alleged defects in the property. The solicitor had made a file note while the transaction was proceeding of conversations he had had with the plaintiff following receipt of information from the defendant.

After the plaintiff had commenced proceedings, the solicitor sent the file note to the defendant, which pleaded the substance of its contents in its defence. The plaintiff sought an injunction ordering that the defendant should deliver up the file note and all copies thereof, and restraining the defendant from using or relying upon it in any manner.

Having held that privilege in the document belonged to the plaintiff and that it should therefore not have been sent to the defendant, May L.J. and Nourse L.J. went on to hold that the plaintiff was entitled to the relief sought.

May L.J. appeared to subscribe to a view of *Ashburton* which placed the relief granted in that case within the scope of ordinary principles of confidentiality.[29] Nourse L.J., on the other hand, made a number of obser- vations which suggested that the relief granted to Lord Ashburton was not simply to be equated with the injunctive relief available in an action for breach of confidence. He began by suggesting that it was no longer necessary for a party seeking *Ashburton* relief in ongoing litigation to initiate separate proceedings. He then stated that principles of confidentiality would assist a party seeking *Ashburton* relief only where the material was (or had been) privileged:

> "It cannot be the function of equity to accord a de facto privilege to communications in respect of which no privilege can be claimed. Equity follows the law."

---

[26] *Webster v. James Chapman & Co.* [1989] 3 All E.R. 939 at 946–947.
[27] *ibid.* at 947.
[28] [1987] 1 Q.B. 670.
[29] *e.g.* at 680A–B, though see the observations of Vinelott J. in *Derby & Co. Ltd v. Weldon (No. 8)* [1991] 1 W.L.R. 73, at 79.

He continued:

"... the right of the party who desires the protection to invoke the equitable jurisdiction does not in any way depend on the conduct of the third party into whose possession the record of the confidential communication has come ... equity gives relief against all the world, including the innocent, save only a bona fide purchaser for value without notice."

Moreover, he observed that:

"... once it is established that a case is governed by *Lord Ashburton v. Pape* [1913] 2 Ch. 469 there is no discretion in the court to refuse to exercise the equitable jurisdiction according to its view of the materiality of the communication, the justice of admitting or excluding it or the like. The injunction is granted in aid of the privilege which, unless and until it is waived, is absolute."

This is a difficult passage. The usual rationalisation of *Calcraft v. Guest* and *Ashburton v. Pape* has been that, when a document has been mistakenly disclosed to the opposing party, the benefit of privilege is lost, but that the court has a discretion to grant equitable relief so as to enable the mistaken party to recover his position. That was the approach adopted by May L.J. and followed in *Webster v. James Chapman & Co.*[30] by Scott J., who treated this passage in Nourse L.J.'s judgment as *obiter*.

On the other hand, Nourse L.J. appears to suggest that the mere disclosure of a document does not involve the loss of privilege, and that a person has an absolute right to have the document treated as privileged unless and until there is some "waiver" of privilege in respect of it. This approach was followed in *Derby v. Weldon (No. 8)*[31] by Vinelott J., who disagreed with Scott J.'s approach in *Webster v. Chapman*.

In *English & American Insurance Co. Ltd v. Hubert Smith*[32] Browne-Wilkinson V.-C. took a broad view of the jurisdiction recognised in *Ashburton v. Pape* and *Goddard v. Nationwide Building Society*, holding that the equitable right to restrain the use of confidential information could be enforced at any time before the information was tendered in evidence. He also rejected the argument that the jurisdiction was confined to cases in which the person seeking to use the information was improperly implicated in obtaining it. **20–11**

In *Guinness Peat Properties Ltd v. Fitzroy Robinson Partnership*,[33] a professional negligence action against architects, the defendants accidentally disclosed in a supplementary list of documents a letter sent by them to their insurers, containing their views as to the merits of the allegations made against them. The plaintiffs' solicitor inspected the letter, copied it and sent a copy to the plaintiffs' expert, who referred to it in his report. The defendants sought an injunction restraining the plaintiffs from using or relying upon the copy of the letter, and for the delivery up of all copies of the letter in the plaintiffs' possession or control. The defendants succeeded, both at first instance and in the Court of Appeal.

[30] [1989] 3 All E.R. 939.
[31] [1991] 1 W.L.R. 73, at 84; see also *per* Dillon L.J. at 99.
[32] [1988] F.S.R. 232.
[33] [1987] 1 W.L.R. 1027.

The plaintiffs argued, first, that:

"... privilege is essentially privilege from compulsory disclosure ... once a privileged document has not only been disclosed but also inspected in the course of discovery, it is too late to put the clock back; the privilege is lost."

Secondly, they distinguished the *Goddard* and *Herbert Smith* cases, on the grounds that neither of those two cases dealt with a loss of privilege occurring as a result of a step taken in the litigation by the party entitled to the privilege.

20–12   Slade L.J., delivering the leading judgment, accepted these submissions with one important reservation,

"My one reservation is this. I do not think that after inspection has taken place in the course of discovery, the court is inevitably and invariably powerless to intervene by way of injunction in exercise of the equitable jurisdiction exemplified by the *Ashburton, Goddard* and *Herbert Smith* cases if the particular circumstances warrant such intervention on equitable grounds."

He then set out the principles which, in his view, should govern the court's deliberations:

"In my judgment, the relevant principles may be stated broadly as follows:
  (1) where solicitors for one party to litigation have, on discovery, mistakenly included a document for which they could properly have claimed privilege in Part 1 of Schedule 1 of a list of documents without claiming privilege, the court will ordinarily permit them to amend the list under R.S.C., Ord. 20, r. 8, at any time before inspection of the document has taken place;
  (2) however, once in such circumstances the other party has inspected the document in pursuance of the rights conferred on him by R.S.C., Ord. 24, r. 9, the general rule is that it is too late for the party who seeks to claim privilege to attempt to correct the mistake by applying for injunctive relief ...
  (3) if, however, in such a last mentioned case the other party or his solicitor either (a) has procured inspection of the relevant document by fraud, or (b) on inspection, realises that he has been permitted to see the document only by reason of an obvious mistake, the court has the power to intervene for the protection of the mistaken party by the grant of an injunction in exercise of the equitable jurisdiction ... . Furthermore, in my view it should ordinarily intervene in such cases, unless the case is one where the injunction can properly be refused on the general principles affecting the grant of a discretionary remedy ... ."[34]

While the second and third of the principles set out in the last passage above may provide a workable rule, they are not derived from any conventional application of the equitable doctrine of confidentiality. The general law of confidence, as it is usually applied, would not limit the intervention of equity to cases where there had been fraud or a mistake which was obvious at the time of

---

[34] *Guinness Peat Properties Ltd v. Fitzroy Robinson Partnership* [1987] 1 W.L.R. 1027 at 1045–1046; see also the judgment of the Court of Appeal in *Mainwaring v. Goldtech Investments Ltd, The Times*, February 19, 1991.

receipt, but would also extend to cases where the mistake was discovered afterwards.[35]

In *Derby & Co. Ltd v. Weldon (No. 8)*,[36] the plaintiffs' solicitors inadvertently **20–13** allowed the defendants' solicitors to inspect a number of privileged documents. Despite the advice of counsel to the effect that they should first ascertain whether privilege had been intentionally waived, the defendants' solicitors requested and obtained copies of some of the privileged material. Subsequently the plaintiffs applied for an order requiring the defendants to deliver up all copies of some 14 documents and restraining the defendants from relying on any information contained in them.

At first instance, Vinelott J. acceded to the plaintiffs' application, except in the case of three documents which, as he held, were not on their face clearly privileged. The Court of Appeal upheld his judgment, except that it allowed the plaintiffs' appeal in respect of the three documents which he had held to be beyond the scope of the relief sought.

Dillon L.J. gave the leading judgment in the Court of Appeal. Although finding in the plaintiffs' favour, on the authority of *Guinness Peat* he rejected[37] the plaintiffs' broad submission that the court could always intervene in a case of mistaken disclosure.

He distinguished *Goddard v. Nationwide Building Society*[38] and *English & American Insurance Co. Ltd v. Herbert Smith*,[39] which were relied on by the plaintiffs in support of that proposition, on the grounds that they did not involve any question of waiver of privilege:

> "The documents in question had got into the hands of the other party to the litigation, despite the wishes of the person entitled to privilege and in circumstances which could not amount to waiver of privilege."

He further held that the documents which the defendants were obliged to return should not be limited to those that were clearly privileged on their face, since the defendants were seeking to take advantage of an obvious general breakdown in the plaintiffs' system for excluding privileged documents from discovery.

He saw this as a critical factor, drawing an analogy from rectification of a contract, where a species of equitable estoppel operates to prevent one party to a contract from relying on what he knows to be a mistake in his favour in the text of the contract.

He concluded[40]:

> "I see no reason why the first and second defendants should not be deprived of all the benefit from their having in those circumstances knowingly taken advantage of an obvious mistake."

It is not, however, clear whether he regarded the case as one in which the

---

[35] See, for example, *Webster v. James Chapman & Co.* [1989] 3 All E.R. 939. The fact that the confidentiality of the material is not apparent at the time of receipt may (as in *Webster*) make the refusal of equitable relief more likely on other grounds—for example, because the recipient has changed his position to his detriment.

[36] [1991] 1 W.L.R. 73.

[37] *ibid.* at 95.

[38] [1987] Q.B. 670.

[39] [1988] F.S.R. 232.

[40] *Derby & Co. Ltd v. Weldon (No. 8)* [1991] 1 W.L.R. 73 at 100.

inspecting party was estopped from asserting that there had been a loss of privilege, or simply as an application of *Ashburton v. Pape* in a case where there had been loss of privilege.

20–14   The "obvious mistake" approach was taken a further stage by the Court of Appeal in *Pizzey v. Ford Motor Co. Ltd*,[41] which was followed by Aldous J. in *International Business Machines Corp. v. Phoenix International (Computers) Ltd*.[42] In these cases the question arose whether an injunction was obtainable if the person to whom the privileged material was disclosed in the course of inspection did not realise that it was privileged, but a reasonable solicitor would have so realised.

The Court of Appeal held that "the law ought not to give an advantage to obtusity and if the recipient ought to have realised that a mistake was evident then the exception applies." Aldous J. followed this test, but his decision illustrates the difficulties involved in applying it.

The reality is that in modern cases discovery is often on a voluminous scale, carried out by large teams. Not only are mistakes likely to be made, but there are many cases where the notion that each document is individually scrutinised at the time of inspection by a solicitor, evaluating in the context of his knowledge of the case whether the document is intended to be disclosed, is wholly unrealistic.

20–15   Conceptually, the position has become muddled. In summary, the rule at present appears to be that the equitable jurisdiction in *Ashburton v. Pape* can be invoked, even after a document has been disclosed as the result of a positive step taken in the proceedings. However, once a document has been formally inspected under the Rules, the court will only allow the equitable jurisdiction to be invoked if the disclosure was procured by fraud, or if either the inspecting party knew or it would have been obvious to a hypothetical reasonable solicitor that the disclosure was by mistake.

One further complication in the present case law must be mentioned. Although *Calcraft v. Guest* has been outflanked to a large extent by the fashioning of relief under *Ashburton*, in *ITC Film Distributors Ltd v. Video Exchange Ltd*[43] Warner J. was doubtful whether he could grant relief on that basis, but arrived at the same result by applying a version of the doctrine of public interest immunity.

One of the defendants had obtained possession of privileged documents, which had been left in the court. He exhibited copies of certain of the documents to a long affidavit, which was later read in part to the judge, and some of the documents were referred to and used for the purpose of cross-examining a witness. Warner J. found as a fact that the defendant concerned had obtained possession of the documents by a trick.

Warner J. considered that there were difficulties in granting *Ashburton* relief at that stage, but he accepted the plaintiff's alternative submission that he must:

> "balance the public interest that the truth should be ascertained, which is the reason for the rule in *Calcraft v. Guest* ... against the public interest that litigants should be able to bring their documents into court without fear that they may be filched by their opponents, whether by stealth or by a trick, and then used by them in evidence."[44]

[41] *The Times*, March 8 1993.
[42] [1995] 1 All E.R. 413.
[43] [1982] 1 Ch. 431.
[44] *ibid.* at page 440.

He held that documents obtained in such circumstances were exempt from forensic scrutiny as a matter of public interest and fell within the continuum of relevant evidence (in the words of Lord Simon[45]):

> "... which may be excluded from the forensic scrutiny. This extends from that excluded in the interest of the forensic process itself as an instrument of justice ... through that excluded for such and also for cognate interests ... through again that excluded in order to facilitate the avoidance of forensic contestation ... to evidence excluded because its adduction might imperil the security of that civil society which the administration of justice itself also subserves ... ."

However, Warner J. took the view that it was impossible for him to exclude those documents at which he had already looked, since they had been used in evidence, and it would be impossible for him to disregard the answers given by the witness when the documents had been put to him. Warner J.'s judgment was cited with approval by Nourse L.J. in *Goddard*.[46]

The present position needs to be simplified. It is clearly seen by the courts as **20–16** desirable to afford a measure of protection to privileged material inadvertently disclosed to the opposing party, for reasons stated by Browne-Wilkinson V.-C. in *English & American Insurance Ltd v. Herbert Smith*[47]:

> "Legal professional privilege is an important safeguard of a man's legal rights. It is the basis on which he and his advisers are free to speak as to matters in issue in litigation and otherwise without fear that it will subsequently be used against him. In my judgment, it is most undesirable if the security which is the basis of that freedom is to be prejudiced by mischances which are of every day occurrence leading to documents which have escaped being used by the other side."

The first step towards a satisfactory solution would be to overrule *Calcraft v. Guest*. The right to privilege should be more than a right not to give compulsory disclosure (as it was interpreted in *Calcraft v. Guest* and as was accepted in *Guinness Peat Properties Ltd v. Fitzroy Robinson Partnership*). It should be a right not to have privileged information used in legal proceedings without the consent of the person entitled to privilege. The next step would be to clarify the concept of waiver of privilege.

Deliberate and unqualified waiver of privilege obviously terminates any privilege. There may be limited waiver for a specific purpose only, which would not amount to a general waiver of privilege.[48] In addition to cases of intentional waiver, there may also be cases of implied or imputed waiver. So, a party who puts in evidence part of a privileged document, even accidentally, cannot prevent the whole document going in, unless there are points which relate to a different subject, in which case privilege may still be asserted in respect of the unrelated parts. The rationale is that the holder of the privilege should not be able to abuse it by using it to create an inaccurate or incomplete perception of the protected document.[49] Another example of implied or imputed waiver

---

[45] *D. v. National Society for the Prevention of Cruelty to Children* [1978] A.C. 171 at 233.
[46] [1987] 1 Q.B. 670 at 685.
[47] [1988] F.S.R. 232 at 239.
[48] *British Coal Corporation v. Dennis Rye (No. 2) Ltd* [1988] 1 W.L.R. 1113, *Goldman v. Hesper* [1988] 1 W.L.R. 1238.
[49] *Attorney-General v. Maurice* (1986) 161 C.L.R. 475 at 487–488.

would be where an opposing party has in good faith prepared his case on the basis that there was no dispute about the admissibility of the disclosed material, and its subsequent exclusion would cause that party embarrassment or prejudice. The test of implied or imputed waiver should be whether the party claiming privilege has behaved in such a way that to allow him to assert privilege would tend to give him an unfair advantage over the opposing party or to place the latter at an unfair disadvantage. This is similar to the test applied in Australia.[50]

Disclosure by mischance of privileged material should not cause loss of a right of privilege unless either the right has become empty (as where the material has become so widely circulated as to lose the quality of confidence, or where it has been not merely disclosed but used in evidence) or there has been implied or imputed waiver.

---

[50] *Attorney-General v. Maurice* (1986) 161 C.L.R. 475 481 at 488. *Goldberg v. Ng*, High Court of Australia, November 3, 1995 (unreported). (On the facts, the judgments of the minority may be considered more persuasive.)

Chapter XXI

PUBLIC INTEREST IMMUNITY

Origins and basis

Confidentiality is not by itself a ground of immunity from disclosure of **21–01** information or documents in the course of litigation, whether by a party or by a non-party; but the desirability in the public interest that confidentiality in the relevant subject-matter should be preserved may give rise to public interest immunity.

The origin of this lies in the doctrine of Crown privilege, which is of considerable antiquity. However, the immunity is not a matter of privilege, nor is it confined to the Crown.[1] It is a protection given by the courts to documents and information whose disclosure in legal proceedings would be damaging to the public interest.

The corner-stone of the modern law is *Conway v. Rimmer*,[2] in which the House of Lords departed from its own unanimous decision, 25 years earlier, in the case of *Duncan v. Cammell, Laird & Co. Ltd.*[3] It is necessary to regard with caution any case pre-dating *Conway v. Rimmer.*[4]

Confidentiality and public interest immunity

Confidentiality is a necessary, but not a sufficient, basis for a claim for public **21–02** interest immunity.

In *Alfred Crompton Amusement Machines Ltd v. Customs & Excise Commissioners*[5] Lord Cross said:

" 'Confidentiality' is not a separate head of privilege, but it may be a very material consideration to bear in mind when privilege is claimed on the ground of public interest."

Lord Cross was speaking in the context of a claim for privilege in respect of

---

[1] See, *e.g. per* Lord Pearson in *R. v. Lewes Justices, ex p. Home Secretary* [1973] A.C. 388 at 406, and *per* Lord Simon in *D. v. N.S.P.C.C.* [1978] A.C. 171 at 235H.
[2] [1968] A.C. 910. See, *e.g. Air Canada v. Secretary of State for Trade* [1983] 2 A.C. 394, *per* Lord Fraser of Tullybelton at 432.
[3] [1942] A.C. 624.
[4] Even of *Conway v. Rimmer*, it was observed by Lord Keith of Kinkel in *Burmah Oil Co. Ltd v. Governor and Company of the Bank of England* [1980] 1 A.C. 1090 at 1131 that "no definitive body of binding rules universally applicable to future cases in the field is to be gathered from the speeches delivered."
[5] 1974 A.C. 405 at 433.

documents of a confidential nature obtained from third parties, to whom a duty of confidence would be owed. That fact did not of itself make the documents privileged but was highly pertinent. Lord Cross's statement is not to be read as implying that public interest immunity could attach to documents which were not of a confidential character at all.

The object of a claim for public interest immunity is to prevent a document being placed before the court because its public disclosure would be damaging to the public interest. That cannot apply if the document itself does not warrant being treated as secret, for example because it has already lost all secrecy. So, in *Sankey v. Whitlam*[6] Gibbs A.C.J. said:

"... it may be necessary for the proper functioning of the public service to keep secret a document of a particular class, but once the document has been published to the world there no longer exists any reason to deny to the court access to that document, if it provides evidence that is relevant and otherwise admissible."

It would be different if, despite some prior publication, disclosure of the documents would still be capable of causing harm, for example, to national security.[7]

21–03 The additional ingredient which has to be established is that the public interest in preserving the secrecy of a particular document or class of documents overrides the public interest in the administration of justice, which ordinarily requires that the parties should not be obstructed from placing relevant evidence before the court. As Lord Templeman said in *R. v. Chief Constable of West Midlands Police, ex p. Wiley*[8]:

"A claim to public interest immunity can only be justified if the public interest in preserving the confidentiality of the document outweighs the public interest in securing justice."

Class and contents claims

21–04 A common categorisation[9] of claims to immunity is to classify them as either contents claims or class claims. The former assert that the disclosure of a document is objectionable because the public interest will be damaged by the disclosure of the contents of that particular document. The latter, in practice considerably more common, assert that the disclosure of a document is objectionable because it belongs to a class of documents whose disclosure would damage the public interest.[10]

It has been said that there is no distinction in principle between a contents

---

[6] [1978] 142 C.L.R. 1 at 45 (High Court of Australia).
[7] *Thorburn v. Hermon, The Times*, May 14, 1992.
[8] [1995] 1 A.C. 274 at 280.
[9] Described in *Burmah Oil Co. Ltd v. Governor and Company of the Bank of England* [1980] A.C. 1090, by Lord Wilberforce at 1111, as "rough but accepted", and by Lord Scarman at 1143, as "good working, but not logically perfect"; see also the exposition of the categories by Lord Edmund-Davies at 1124. Some dissatisfaction with the categories has been expressed by, for example, Lord Hodson in *Conway v. Rimmer* [1968] A.C. 910 at 979, and by Lord Keith in *Burmah Oil*, at 1132.
[10] The possibility that such a claim might be valid was denied by MacNaughton J. in *Spigelman v. Hocken* (1934) 150 L.T. 256 at 262, but his view must yield to subsequent authority.

claim and a class claim,[11] but in practice class-based claims attract a particularly high degree of judicial scrutiny. It is not possible, for example, for a class claim in respect of a number of documents to be based upon the administrative burden of checking individual documents to ascertain whether a contents claim could be made in respect of any of them.[12]

Although "the privilege is a narrow one, most sparingly to be exercised",[13] in *D. v. National Society for the Prevention of Cruelty to Children*[14] Lord Hailsham said:

> "The categories of public interest are not closed, and must alter from time to time whether by restriction or extension as social conditions and social legislation develop."

In *R. v. Chief Constable of West Midlands Police, ex p. Wiley*,[15] however, Lord Woolf, though stating his agreement with Lord Hailsham's dictum, observed that,

> "The recognition of a new *class-based* public interest immunity requires clear and compelling evidence that it is necessary."[16] (Emphasis added.)

Reasons for immunity

It is impossible to compile a list of all reasons advanced for immunity, but **21–05** they include the following:

(1) that disclosure would be prejudicial to national security or foreign relations[17];

(2) that disclosure would create or fan ill-informed or captious public or political criticism of the inner workings of government,[18] and increase the difficulties of the decision-making process;

(3) that disclosure would impede the flow of information necessary in the public interest, in particular by discouraging candour in communications by or to persons with public responsibilities[19] or by discouraging informants from coming forward[20];

(4) that immunity is required to set a limit on the State's invasion of an individual's privacy.[21]

These reasons have provoked varying degrees of controversy, with the

---

[11] In *Conway v. Rimmer* [1968] A.C. 910, *per* Lord Morris at 971.
[12] *per* Lord Woolf in *R. v. Chief Constable of West Midlands, ex p. Wiley* [1995] 1 A.C. 274 at 293.
[13] *Robinson v. State of South Australia* [1931] A.C. 704, P.C., at 714.
[14] [1978] A.C. 171 at 230.
[15] [1995] 1 A.C. 274 at 305.
[16] See also *R. v. Lewes Justices, ex p. Home Secretary* [1973] A.C. 388 at 412, *per* Lord Salmon—"This immunity should not lightly be extended to any other class of document or information, but its boundaries are not to be regarded as immutably fixed."
[17] *e.g. Burmah Oil Co. Ltd v. Governor and Company of the Bank of England* [1980] A.C. 1090, *per* Lord Salmon at 1121; *Balfour v. Foreign and Commonwealth Office* [1994] 1 W.L.R. 681.
[18] *per* Lord Reid in *Conway v. Rimmer* [1968] A.C. 910 at 952.
[19] *Burmah Oil Co. Ltd v. Governor and Company of the Bank of England* [1980] A.C. 1090, *per* Lord Wilberforce at 1112, and *per* Lord Scarman at 1145.
[20] *D. v. N.S.P.C.C.* [1978] A.C. 171, *per* Lord Diplock at 218.
[21] *Re Joseph Hargreaves Ltd* [1900] 1 Ch. 347, as explained by Lord Reid in *Conway v. Rimmer* [1968] A.C. 910, at 946F; *Lonrho plc v. Fayed (No. 4)* [1994] Q.B. 775, at 787, *per* Bingham M.R.

argument based on the encouragement of candour, in particular, being the subject of much judicial scepticism. While it is generally acknowledged that confidentiality may encourage frankness on the part of informants, doubts have often been expressed about the candour argument as applied to public officials or ministers.[22]

21–06   In *Conway v. Rimmer*[23] Lord Reid, in a much quoted passage, said:

> "Virtually everyone agrees that Cabinet minutes and the like ought not to be disclosed until such time as they are only of historical interest. But I do not think that many people would give as the reason that premature disclosure would prevent candour in the Cabinet. To my mind the most important reason is that such disclosure would create or fan ill-formed or captious public or political criticism. The business of government is difficult enough as it is, and no government could contemplate with equanimity the inner workings of the government machine being exposed to the gaze of those ready to criticise without adequate knowledge of the background and perhaps with some axe to grind."

Doubts have in turn been expressed whether the avoidance of "ill-informed or captious criticism" constitutes a satisfactory explanation for the protection of government documents.

In *Commonwealth of Australia v. John Fairfax & Sons Ltd*,[24] Mason J. said:

> "... it can scarcely be a relevant detriment to the government that publication of material concerning its actions will merely expose it to public discussion and criticism. It is unacceptable in our democratic society that there should be a restraint on the publication of information relating to government when the only vice of that information is that it enables the public to discuss, review and criticize government action."

Moreover, it might reasonably be said that the problem of ill-informed public criticism of the government is more likely to be cured by a greater degree of openness in the inner workings of government than it is by the withholding of information on grounds of public interest immunity.

It is nevertheless generally agreed that the business of government must be attended by a degree of confidentiality, especially at high level. But if so, what is the basis and how does it explain the immunity that would attach to Cabinet minutes from, say, before the last election?

21–07   Perhaps the best answer is that given by Mason J. in *Sankey v. Whitlam*.[25] After setting out the relevant passage from Lord Reid's speech in *Conway v. Rimmer*, he continued:

---

[22] *Conway v. Rimmer* [1968] A.C. 910, *per* Lord Reid at 952, *per* Lord Morris at 957, *per* Lord Pearce at 985 and *per* Lord Upjohn at 994; *Burmah Oil Co. Ltd v. Governor and Company of the Bank of England* [1980] A.C. 1090, *per* Lord Keith at 1132; *Sankey v. Whitlam* (1978) 142 C.L.R. 1, *per* Stephen J. at 63 and *per* Mason J. at 97. But see also *Conway v. Rimmer, per* Lord Hodson at 974; *Burmah Oil Co. Ltd v. Governor and Company of the Bank of England, per* Lord Wilberforce at 1112; *Air Canada v. Secretary of State for Trade* [1983] 2 A.C. 394, *per* Lord Fraser at 433; *Sankey v. Whitlam* (1978) 142 C.L.R. 1, *per* Gibbs A.C.J. 40.
[23] [1968] A.C. 910 at 952.
[24] (1980) 147 C.L.R. 39 at 52, approved in *Attorney-General v. Guardian Newspapers Ltd (No. 2)* [1990] 1 A.C. 109, *per* Lord Keith at 258, Lord Griffiths at 270 and Lord Goff at 283. See para. 5–03.
[25] (1978) 142 C.L.R. 1, at 97–98.

"I agree with his Lordship that the possibility that premature disclosure will result in want of candour in cabinet discussions or in advice given by public servants is so slight that it may be ignored, despite the evidence to the contrary which was apparently given and accepted in *Attorney-General v. Cape (Jonathan) Ltd.* I should have thought that the possibility of future publicity would act as a deterrent against advice which is specious or expedient. I also agree with his Lordship that the efficiency of government would be seriously compromised if Cabinet decisions and papers were disclosed whilst they or the topics to which they relate are still current or controversial. But I base this view, not so much on the probability of ill-formed criticism with its inconvenient consequences, as upon the inherent difficulty of decision making if the decision-making processes of cabinet and the materials on which they are based are at risk of premature publication."

Since it is the power and duty of the court, as Lord Reid stated in *Conway v. Rimmer*[26]:

"to hold a balance between the public interest, as expressed by a Minister, to withhold certain documents or other evidence, and the public interest in ensuring the proper administration of justice",

it is not bound by any ministerial certificate, although in the exercise of its judgment the court will normally attach considerable, and in some cases (those involving national security being the classic example) conclusive, weight to a ministerial certificate.

The court's ultimate responsibility was emphasised in *Air Canada v.* **21–08** *Secretary of State for Trade* by Lord Fraser, with whom Lord Edmund Davies and Lord Templeman agreed, when he said[27]:

"I do not think that even Cabinet minutes are completely immune from disclosure in a case where, for example, the issue in a litigation involves serious misconduct by a Cabinet Minister. Such cases have occurred in Australia (see *Sankey v. Whitlam* (1978) 21 A.L.R. 505) and in the United States (see *United States v. Nixon* (1974) 418 U.S. 683) but fortunately not in the United Kingdom: see also the New Zealand case of *Environmental Defence Society Inc. v. South Pacific Aluminium Ltd (No. 2)* [1981] 1 N.Z.L.R. 153. But while Cabinet documents do not have complete immunity, they are entitled to a high degree of protection from disclosure."

In order to adjudicate on a claim for public interest immunity the court has power to inspect the disputed material, but where the claim is supported by a ministerial certificate courts have been very sparing in the exercise of that power. In *Air Canada v. Secretary of State for Trade* Lord Fraser expressed the view of the majority of the House of Lords that:

"... in order to persuade the court even to inspect documents for which public interest immunity is claimed, the party seeking disclosure ought at least to satisfy the court that the documents are very likely to contain

---

[26] [1968] A.C. 910 at 952.
[27] [1982] A.C. 394 at 432.

material which would give substantial support to his contention on an issue which arises in the case, and that without them he might be 'deprived of the means of ... proper presentation' of his case ... ."[28]

This presents a party with the difficult task of persuading the court as to the likely effect of a document which neither he nor the court has seen. This may be thought an unsatisfactory position but it can be changed only by the House of Lords. The impetus for its reconsideration may be provided by the *Matrix Churchill* trial and the report of the inquiry conducted by Sir Richard Scott, V.-C. following the collapse of the prosecution in that case.[29]

In *Matrix Churchill* the defendants were charged with export control offences based on the alleged deception of the government as to the intended use of machine tools for which licences had been sought for export to Iraq. The prosecution advanced class claims, supported by ministerial certificates, for public interest immunity in respect of a wide range of documents relating to communications between officials, between ministers and officials, and between ministers, and relating to the defendants' contacts with the security and secret intelligence services. The judge inspected the disputed documents and ordered the disclosure of a large number of them. The disclosed documents were used as the basis for cross-examination of two officials of the Department of Trade and Industry and a former minister at the department. On the conclusion of the evidence of the former minister, the prosecution was abandoned and the defendants were acquitted.

Air Canada v. Secretary of State for Trade was a civil action, and the reasoning of Lord Fraser's speech shows that he was directing himself towards the adversarial system of civil justice practised in the United Kingdom. *Matrix Churchill* was a criminal case, and since the *Air Canada* rule did not apply, the judge was able to inspect the documents and a miscarriage of justice was avoided. However its facts illustrate the potential injustice which may be caused by a rule prohibiting a court from inspecting documents unless persuaded in advance by a party, who has not seen them, that they are very likely to contain material substantially supporting his case.

It should be recognised that the application to the reported authorities of the reasons for immunity listed above[30] is in many cases an exercise in *ex post facto* rationalisation, since claims to Crown privilege in the past were rarely scrutinised as carefully as they are today. It was often successfully asserted on behalf of the Crown that production of specified documents would be contrary to the public interest, without any further explanation. Nevertheless, the categories remain a convenient basis for the examination of the classes of documents for which claims to immunity have been made.

Documents whose disclosure would be prejudicial to national security or foreign relations

21–09   A question of national security or foreign relations is recognised as the most compelling basis for a claim to public interest immunity, whether the claim is made on a class or a contents basis.

---

[28] [1983] 2 A.C. 394 at 435.
[29] Report of the Inquiry into the Export of Defence Equipment and Dual-Use Goods to Iraq and Related Prosecutions, presented to the House of Commons on February 15, 1996.
[30] See para. 21–05, above.

In *Balfour v. Foreign and Commonwealth Office*,[31] a former employee of the Foreign Office claimed that he had been unfairly dismissed by his former employer. In proceedings before an industrial tribunal, he sought discovery of certain documents from the Foreign Office. The Foreign Secretary and Home Secretary each signed certificates raising objection to:

"the production of any evidence, documentary or otherwise, about the organisation of the security and intelligence services, their theatres of operation or their methods. Express reference was made to foreign powers and terrorist organisations and the threat to national security of disclosure."[32]

The certificates were held to be conclusive and Russell L.J. cited the dictum of Lord Diplock in *Council of Civil Service Unions v. Minister for the Civil Service*[33]:

"National security is the responsibility of the executive government; what action is needed to protect its interests is, as the cases cited by my learned friend, Lord Roskill, establish and common sense itself dictates, a matter upon which those upon whom the responsibility rests, and not the courts of justice, must have the last word. It is par excellence a non-justiciable question. The judicial process is totally inept to deal with the sort of problems which it involves."

Interestingly, however, in Sir Richard Scott's inquiry into Matrix Churchill and other cases the legal adviser to the secret intelligence and security services gave evidence that those services had experienced no real difficulties in protecting their sensitive information by contents claims and that a class claim was an unnecessary and confusing addition.[34]

National security, or the public safety, may also be one justification for the **21–10** immunity traditionally bestowed upon "documents pertaining to the general administration of the naval, military and air force services".[35] However, most of the cases are more immediately explicable by reference to one of the other categories dealt with below.

The protection of specific military secrets clearly falls within the national security category. Although the House of Lords departed in *Conway v. Rimmer* from their decision in *Duncan v. Cammell, Laird & Co.*,[36] their lordships were in no doubt that the decision in that case had been right on its facts.

The case arose from the loss of 99 lives at the sinking of the new submarine *Thetis* during trials in Liverpool bay in June 1939. Representatives and dependants of the deceased commenced an action against Cammell, Laird & Co., the makers of the submarine, claiming damages for negligence. The defendants declined to produce a number of documents included in their discovery, on the basis that the First Lord of the Admiralty objected to their production. These documents included the contract for the *Thetis*, correspon-

---

[31] [1994] 1 W.L.R. 681.
[32] *ibid.* at 684.
[33] [1985] A.C. 374 at 412.
[34] Report of the Inquiry into the Export of Defence Equipment and Dual-Use Goods to Iraq and Related Prosecutions, paragraphs G18–39 and G18–102.
[35] *Conway v. Rimmer* [1968] A.C. 910, *per* Lord Upjohn at 993.
[36] [1942] A.C. 624.

dence relating to the vessel's trim, reports as to the submarine's condition when raised, various plans and specifications and the notebook of a foreman painter employed by the defendants.

The First Lord duly swore an affidavit stating that in his opinion the disclosure of these documents to any person would be injurious to the public interest and his certificate was held to be conclusive.

Similar protection is given to diplomatic secrets and confidential communications between British authorities and other states. In *R. v. Governor of Brixton Prison, ex p. Osman*,[37] Osman, who had been committed to custody to await return to Hong Kong to face criminal charges, applied for a writ of *habeas corpus* and sought discovery of various Government documents. In his certificate claiming immunity, the Minister of State for Foreign and Commonwealth Affairs divided them into three categories, including:

> "(A) Communications exchanged between ministers and/or officials of the Crown either in the United Kingdom or overseas concerning matters of policy, advice, judgment, action or prospective action within government. (B) Communications or reports of communications between British authorities (both in the United Kingdom and Hong Kong) and another sovereign state concerning matters of policy, advice, judgment, action or prospective action within government ... ."[38]

The reasons given by the Minister for his belief that production of these documents would be detrimental to foreign relations were set out at length by Mann L.J., who observed[39] that:

> "It does not seem to be in dispute that the documents in categories (A) and (B) are documents eligible for a public interest claim. Were there such a dispute it could be given its quietus by examining the speeches of Lord Upjohn in *Conway v. Rimmer* [1968] A.C. 910, 933, of Lord Salmon in *Burmah Oil Co. Ltd v. Governor and Company of the Bank of England* [1980] A.C. 1090, 1121C and of Lord Keith of Kinkel and Lord Scarman in the same case at pp. 1132B and 1144G."

Documents whose disclosure would expose the inner workings of government to ill-informed and captious criticism and increase the difficulties of the decision-making process

21–11   It has been suggested above that mere avoidance of ill-informed criticism is no satisfactory basis for a claim for immunity, and that the real question is whether disclosure would be sufficiently detrimental to the decision-making process to justify a claim for immunity. The courts are unlikely to accept a class-based claim on this ground except at high level. There is a great difference between documents relating to high affairs of state and more mundane communications between officials.

In *Re Grosvenor Hotel, London (No. 2)*,[40] Salmon L.J. said:

> "Again there may be classes of documents such as communications at a

---

[37] [1991] 1 W.L.R. 281.
[38] *ibid.* at 286.
[39] *ibid.* at 287.
[40] [1965] 1 Ch. 1210 at 1258–1259; cited by Lord Morris in *Conway v. Rimmer* [1968] A.C. 910 at 973.

very high level, *e.g.*, cabinet minutes, minutes of discussions between heads of departments, despatches from ambassadors abroad and the like which any right-minded person would say clearly ought not to be subject to protection in an action."

He continued:

"I can see no reason, unless compelled by authority to do so, for extending this privilege to routine communications between one civil servant and another."

This ground of public interest immunity can be used to protect only **21–12** documents created for purposes of state, which in this context must mean national government rather than the broader apparatus referred to as the state by Lord Simon in *D. v. National Society for the Prevention of Cruelty to Children*[41]:

"The state is the whole organisation of the body politic for supreme civil rule and government—the whole political organisation which is the basis of the civil government. As such it certainly extends to local—and, as I think, also statutory—bodies in so far as they are exercising autonomous rule."

Lord Reid observed in *Conway v. Rimmer*[42]:

"There are now many large public bodies, such as British Railways and the National Coal Board, the proper and efficient functioning of which is very necessary for many reasons including the safety of the public. The Attorney-General made it clear that Crown privilege is not and cannot be invoked to prevent disclosure of similar documents made by them or their servants even if it were said that this is required for the proper and efficient functioning of that public service."

It is equally difficult to imagine a court upholding a class-based claim for immunity on the ground that it was necessary to protect the decision-making processes of local government or other statutory autonomous bodies.

In *R. v. Chief Constable of West Midlands Police, ex p. Wiley*[43] Lord Woolf **21–13** said of the decision in *D. v. National Society for the Prevention of Cruelty to Children*:

"The significance of that case is that it made clear that the immunity does not only exist to protect the effective functioning of departments or organs of central government or the police, but also could protect the effective functioning of an organisation such as the N.S.P.C.C. which was authorised under an Act of Parliament to bring legal proceedings for the welfare of children."

[41] [1978] A.C. 171 at 236.
[42] [1968] A.C. 910 at 941.
[43] [1995] 1 A.C. 274 at 291.

But the public interest recognised in that case was the public interest in protecting the free flow of information about child abuse *to* the NSPCC, rather than the public interest in protecting the internal decision-making processes *of* the NSPCC.

The scope of this category of immunity is particularly liable to change over time. Lord Keith noted in *Burmah Oil Co. Ltd v. Governor and Company of the Bank of England*,[44] that:

> "There can be discerned in modern times a trend towards more open governmental methods than were prevalent in the past. No doubt it is for Parliament and not for courts of law to say how far that trend should go."

It should not be assumed that the trend is irreversible. Lord Pearce commented in *Conway v. Rimmer*[45]:

> "In theory any general legal definition of the balance between individual justice in one scale and the safety and well-being of the state in the other scale, should be unaffected by the dangerous times in which it is uttered. But in practice the flame of individual right and justice must burn more palely when it is ringed by the more dramatic light of bombed buildings. And the human mind cannot but be affected subconsciously, even in generality of definition, by such a contrast since it is certainly a matter which ought to influence the particular decision in the case."

Documents whose disclosure would discourage the free flow of information communicated for official purposes

21–14   Some kinds of official reports and records attract immunity. The scope of this category must now be regarded as uncertain in the light of the numerous judgments rejecting arguments that immunity is required to encourage candour in official reports; in recent years, its extent has certainly been greatly reduced.

In *Ankin v. London and North Eastern Railway Company*,[46] objection was successfully made to the production of a report furnished by the defendant to the Ministry of Transport pursuant to section 6 of the Railways Regulation Act 1871 following a railway accident. The case would unquestionably be decided differently today. Lord Reid said in *Conway v. Rimmer*[47]:

> "*Ankin's* case is a good example of what happens if the courts abandon all control of this matter. It was surely far fetched and indeed insulting to the managements of railway companies to suggest that in performing their statutory duty they might withhold information from the Minister because it might be disclosed later in legal proceedings."

The armed forces

21–15   The earlier cases often involved military matters and include claims to immunity successfully made for the minutes and proceedings of Army courts of

---

[44] [1980] A.C. 1090 at 1134. See also *per* Mason J. in *The Commonwealth of Australia v. John Fairfax & Sons Ltd* (1980) 147 C.L.R. 39, at 52, cited above at paras. 5–03 and 21–06.
[45] [1968] A.C. 910 at 982.
[46] [1930] 1 K.B. 527.
[47] [1968] A.C. 910 at 947.

enquiry,[48] Admiralty collision reports[49] and naval and military medical records.[50]

These cases should be regarded with particular caution in the light of *Conway v. Rimmer* and more recent case-law. In *Barrett v. Ministry of Defence*,[51] a naval airman died after a bout of heavy drinking. His widow commenced proceedings against the Ministry of Defence claiming damages for negligence and, prior to the service of a statement of claim, sought discovery of the report of a naval board of enquiry that had been convened to enquire into her husband's death.

On appeal, Popplewell J. refused her application but considered *obiter* a claim to immunity in respect of the report, which was made by the Ministry of Defence and backed by ministerial certificate. Dismissing this claim, he held that the absence of the alleged immunity would affect neither the candour of witnesses at future boards of enquiry nor the morale, discipline or safety of those in the service.

Although it appears from *Barrett* that there is no longer any blanket immunity in respect of all military boards of enquiry, it can easily be seen that different considerations might govern, on the one hand, an investigation into the death of an individual and, on the other hand, an investigation into matters of, say, potential technical significance. On the basis of *Barrett*, however, it appears that protection of the latter would result not so much from the need for candour as from considerations of national security.

Official medical records

Official medical records have in the past been protected by the courts. For **21–16** example, a doctor's report made to the Home Office after the exhumation and examination of a murder victim was held to be immune from production in *Williams v. Star Newspaper Company Ltd.*[52]

Similarly, medical reports on the mental condition of a man confined in the hospital wing of a prison were held to be immune from production in an action brought against the Home Office by another prisoner attacked and injured by that man.[53] However, the case caused both Devlin J. and the Court of Appeal great concern, and it is likely that it would be decided differently today.[54]

A better guide to the modern approach is provided by *R. v. Secretary of State for the Home Department, ex p. Benson.*[55]

It was held that no immunity attached to a medical report produced in

---

[48] *Home v. Bentinck* (1820) 2 Brod. & B. 130, at 162ff.; *Beatson v. Skene* (1860) 5 H. & N. 838; *Dawkins v. Lord Rokeby* (1873) L.R. 8 Q.B. 255 at 270. A claim for immunity was refused in *Dickson v. The Earl of Wilton* (1859) 1 F. & F. 419.

[49] *The Bellerophon* (1875) 44 L.J.Adm. (N.S.) 5.

[50] *Gain v. Gain* [1961] 1 W.L.R. 1469; *Anthony v. Anthony* (1919) 35 T.L.R. 559.

[51] *The Times*, January 24, 1990.

[52] (1908) 24 T.L.R. 297. Darling J. apparently made his decision on the strength of the existence of the minister's certificate alone, without consideration of the grounds for it. By way of contrast, see *Leigh v. Gladstone* (1909) 26 T.L.R. 139: Lord Alverstone C.J. held that a prison doctor's report to the prison's Governor was not immune from production, though it does not appear that the objection to production in this case was backed by a ministerial certificate.

[53] *Ellis v. Home Office* [1953] 2 Q.B. 135.

[54] See the comments of Lord Reid, in *Conway v. Rimmer* [1968] A.C. 910, at 948; compare, also, the result in *Campbell v. Tameside Metropolitan Borough Council* [1982] 1 Q.B. 1065, referred to at para. 23–10, below.

[55] (November 1, 1988, unreported); cited in *R. v. Secretary of State for the Home Department, ex p. Duggan* [1994] 3 All E.R. 277 at 285.

connection with the Home Secretary's consideration of the length of the term to be served by a person sentenced to life imprisonment, when production of the report was sought by its subject. The argument, advanced to protect the report of a prison doctor, that liability to production would result in a lack of candour was rejected.

The police

21–17   Police reports have been the subject of a number of decisions relating to public interest immunity. As Lord Reid said in *Conway v. Rimmer*[56]:

> "The position of the police is peculiar. They are not servants of the Crown and they do not take orders from the Government. But they are carrying out an essential function of government, and various Crown rights, privileges and exemptions have been held to apply to them."

Here too, the law has developed over the years. Reports on road traffic accidents produced by the police were held to be immune from disclosure in civil proceedings in the Scottish case of *McKie v. The Western Scottish Motor Traction Co. Ltd.*[57] Earlier, in England, Macnaghten J. had rejected in *Spigelman v. Hocken*[58] a class claim advanced in respect of a statement made to a police officer after a road accident by one of the defendants who was involved in the accident, but observed that there might be grave objections in the public interest to producing the police officer's actual report.

21–18   In *Conway v. Rimmer*,[59] however, Lord Pearce said:

> "One may perhaps take police reports of accidents as an extreme example of the malaise that can be produced by a total acceptance of the theory that all documents should be protected whenever the Minister says so on the basis that candour will be injured if there is production ... . When one considers the large public interest in a just decision of road accident cases, and the absence of any possible corresponding injury to the candour of police reports on accident cases, one realises to what a complete lack of common sense a general blanket protection of wide classes may lead. And it would be an equal departure from common sense to suppose that no great public injury could result from disclosure of police reports concerning their war on really serious crime."

In fact, police reports on accidents on the road or accidents on government premises, or involving government employees, were among categories of documents in respect of which the Lord Chancellor announced in a statement in the House of Lords in 1956 that class-based immunity would no longer be claimed.[60]

Conway v. Rimmer itself concerned the status of police reports. A former probationary police constable sued a police superintendent for damages for malicious prosecution. The superintendent had been instrumental in bringing a charge of larceny against the plaintiff of which the plaintiff had been acquitted.

---

[56] [1968] A.C. 910 at 953.
[57] (1952) S.C. 206.
[58] (1933) 150 L.T. 256.
[59] [1968] A.C. 910, at 985–986.
[60] See also the observations of Dillon L.J. in *Marcel v. Commissioner of Police of the Metropolis* [1992] Ch. 225 at 256E–F.

Shortly after his acquittal, the plaintiff had been dismissed. The plaintiff sought discovery of five confidential police reports, of which four were standard probationary or training reports and one was a report submitted by the defendant to his chief constable for submission to the Director of Public Prosecutions. The defendant was willing to release these documents, but the Home Secretary swore an affidavit objecting to their production.

The speeches in the House of Lords focused primarily on the duties and powers of a judge when faced with a ministerial certificate claiming immunity, and there was relatively little direct consideration of the question whether the documents in question were in a class that prima facie attacted immunity. The majority view appears to have been that the class claim in respect of the pro-bationary reports clearly failed, but that the class claim in respect of the report to the chief constable might have more substance in it.[61]

In *Evans v. Chief Constable of Surrey*,[62] the plaintiff alleged wrongful arrest **21–19** and false imprisonment by the police following the murder of one of his friends. The plaintiff sought an order for the production of a report made by the police to the Director of Public Prosecutions, on the strength of which the Director of Public Prosecutions had advised that there was a prima facie case against the plaintiff and that he should be charged with the murder. The Attorney-General intervened and certified that it was in the public interest that the report should not be disclosed.

Wood J. held that the plaintiff had not shown that the discovery sought was relevant to his case, but he added[63]:

> "It seems to me important, and very important in the functioning of the criminal process of prosecution, that there should be freedom of communi-cation between police forces around the country and the Director of Public Prosecutions in seeking his legal advice without fear that those documents will become subject to inspection, analysis and detailed investigation at some later stage ... I find the arguments in the Attorney-General's certificate to be convincing."

There is an obvious distinction between a police road accident report, which will be largely factual and will contain names and addresses of witnesses and what they said to the police, and communications between the police and the Director of Public Prosecutions containing legal analysis and advice.

A similar distinction has been drawn in the case of complaints made to the **21–20** Police Complaints Authority under the Police and Criminal Evidence Act 1984. Reports on the investigation of such complaints are immune from production in civil proceedings: *Taylor v. Anderton*.[64] Witness statements taken in the course of the investigation and transcripts of disciplinary hearings are not immune.[65]

R. v. Chief Constable of West Midlands Police, ex p. Wiley illustrates the risk that public interest immunity can sometimes defeat its own purpose. In a line of cases beginning with *Neilson v. Laugharne*[66] the Court of Appeal had

---

[61] See *per* Lord Reid at 954, Lord Morris at 972, Lord Hodson at 980, Lord Pearce at 988–989 and Lord Upjohn at 996.

[62] [1988] 1 Q.B. 588.

[63] *ibid.* at 600.

[64] [1995] 1 W.L.R. 447; see also *O'Sullivan v. Commissioner of Police of the Metropolis, The Times,* July 3, 1995.

[65] *R. v. Chief Constable of West Midlands Police, ex p. Wiley* [1995] 1 A.C. 274.

[66] [1981] Q.B. 736.

previously held that statements taken under the statutory police complaints procedure were immune from production in civil proceedings. In *Wiley* two complainants sought undertakings from the police, before providing statements in support of their complaints, that the files created in the investigation of their complaints would not be used in civil proceedings which the complainants had either issued or intended to issue. On the police refusing to give such undertakings, the complainants challenged the lawfulness of the refusal by proceedings for judicial review. The heart of their complaint was that since, under *Neilson*, they would be unable to make use in the civil proceedings of information obtained by the police in the complaint investigations, the police should be put in a reciprocal position as regards information supplied by the complainants for the purpose of the complaint proceedings. The House of Lords held that *Neilson* and the cases that followed it had been wrongly decided. Lord Woolf observed[67] that the applicants' non co-operation in the complaints procedure was the direct result of the immunity recognised in *Neilson*, contrary to the very object which it was designed to achieve.

Financial Regulator

21–21   *Wiley* was applied by Arden J. in *Kaufmann v. Credit Lyonnais Bank*,[68] In this case, the plaintiff sought an order for the production of confidential reports, which had been made voluntarily on behalf of the defendant to the Security and Futures Authority ("the SFA"), its regulator for the purposes of the Financial Services Act 1986, together with assorted correspondence with the SFA. The defendant resisted the plaintiff's application, and an assertion of public interest immunity in respect of the documents was made both by the SFA and by the Bank of England, which had received copies of the documents in its capacity as the supervisory board of the defendant as a banking institution.

The claim to public interest immunity was class-based and the class was defined as documents containing:

> "information which was (i) disclosed to a regulator voluntarily and in confidence (ii) other than as a matter of routine (iii) brought into being for the purpose of enabling the regulator more effectively to discharge its functions or duties (iv) save where the disclosure of that information by the regulator was necessary for the proper performance of its functions and duties."

Arden J. declined to accept this class-based claim, observing:

> "Given the object of the 1986 Act is, so far as material, the protection of investors, the need for a class based immunity claim to public interest immunity which would result in the withholding of information from investors must in my judgment be clearly demonstrated."

Informants

21–22   In some circumstances, not only reports by officials, but also communications made to officials may attract immunity. The most prominent example of this is

---

[67] [1995] 1 A.C. 274 at 305.
[68] *The Times*, February 1, 1995.

the immunity attaching to documents whose disclosure would identify informants. This category is of very long standing. In *Home v. Bentinck*,[69] Dallas C.J. said:

> "It is agreed, that there are a number of cases of a particular description, in which, for reasons of state and policy, information is not permitted to be disclosed. To begin with the ordinary cases, and those of a common description in the courts of justice. In these courts, for reasons of public policy, persons are not to be asked the names of those from whom they receive information as to the frauds on the revenue. In all the trials for high treason of late years, the same course has been adopted; and, if parties were willing to disclose the sources of their information, they would not be suffered to do it by the judges."[70]

In *Marks v. Beyfus*[71] the plaintiff alleged that the defendants had maliciously conspired to have groundless criminal charges brought against him. The plaintiff called as a witness the Director of Public Prosecutions, who said in evidence that the prosecution had been instituted by himself and not the defendants. He had initiated it upon receipt of a written statement, but he declined to produce the statement or to reveal the identity of its author.

The Court of Appeal held that he had acted correctly. Lord Esher M.R. affirmed the rule that in a public prosecution a witness could not be asked (or permitted, even if willing, to answer) questions tending to disclose the informant, whether the informant was himself or a third person, but he added the important *caveat*:

> "I do not say it is a rule which can never be departed from; if upon the trial of a prisoner the judge should be of opinion that the disclosure of the name of the informant is necessary or right in order to shew the prisoner's innocence, then one public policy is in conflict with another public policy, and that which says that an innocent man is not to be condemned when his innocence can be proved is the policy that must prevail."[72]

In *R. v. Keane*[73] the Court of Appeal observed that this passage was not a **21–23** departure from, but an example of, the balancing exercise required where the application of public interest immunity would result in the withholding of relevant material in a criminal case. The court added:

> "If the disputed material may prove the defendant's innocence or avoid a miscarriage of justice, then the balance comes down resoundingly in favour of disclosing it."[74]

The Court of Appeal has also warned of the need for careful scrutiny of the nature of the material and its potential significance to the defendant's case before concluding whether its non-disclosure might result in a miscarriage. In *R. v. Turner*,[75] it was said:

[69] (1820) 2 Brod. & B. 130.
[70] *ibid.* at 162.
[71] (1890) 25 Q.B.D. 494.
[72] *ibid.* at 498.
[73] [1994] 1 W.L.R. 746.
[74] *ibid.* at 751–752.
[75] [1995] 1 W.L.R. 264 at 267.

"We wish to alert judges to the need to scrutinise applications for disclosure of details about informants with very great care. They will need to be astute to see that assertions of a need to know such details, because they are essential to the running of the defence, are justified. If they are not so justified, then the judge will need to adopt a robust approach in declining to order disclosure. Clearly, there is a distinction between cases in which the circumstances raise no reasonable possibility that information about the informant will bear upon the issues and cases where it will. Again, there will be cases where the informant is an informant and no more; other cases where he may have participated in the events constituting, surrounding, or following the crime. Even when the informant has participated, the judge will need to consider whether his role so impinges on an issue of interest to the defence, present or potential, as to make disclosure necessary."

Although public interest immunity may result in a litigant or would-be litigant losing, or being unable to bring, a civil action which he would otherwise have won, it would be an affront to the most basic principles of liberty that public interest could in any circumstances justify a person being wrongly convicted of a criminal offence, or that the doctrine of public interest immunity should ever be used in such a way as to have that effect. This principle is inherent in the judgments of Lord Esher M.R. in *Marks v. Beyfus* and of Lord Taylor C.J. in *R. v. Keane*. The subject of public interest immunity claims in criminal cases was considered in detail by Sir Richard Scott in his report of his inquiry into Matrix Churchill and other cases.

He observed that the balancing exercise referred to in *R. v. Keane* and other criminal cases[76] is different from the balancing exercise in civil cases in that if the document may be of assistance to the defendant in a criminal trial, no other considerations could outweigh that factor, and therefore the determinative question is whether the document might be of assistance to the defence.[77] A wider balancing exercise could only be performed if the document related to an issue or possible issue in the case but was not apparently of potential assistance to the defence.[78]

He also recommended that class claims for public interest immunity ought not to be made in criminal cases.[79] Consideration whether a document may assist the defence cannot be done on a class basis but depends on its contents.

Extension of the immunity of informants

21–24   The rule protecting informants in criminal cases has been extended by analogy to other fields. In *R. v. Lewes Justices, ex p. Secretary of State for Home Department*,[80] it was held by the House of Lords to apply to persons supplying information to the Gaming Board when it was considering whether to grant a gaming licence. Lord Salmon said[81]:

---

[76] *R. v. Clowes* [1992] 3 A.E.R. 440 at 454, *per* Phillips J. and *R. v. Brown* [1994] 1 W.L.R. 1599 at 1608, *per* Steyn L.J.

[77] "Report of the Inquiry into the Export of Defence Equipment and Dual-Use Goods to Iraq and Related Prosecutions", paragraph K6.14.

[78] *ibid.* para. K6.15.

[79] *ibid.* paras. K6.16, 6.18(ii).

[80] [1973] A.C. 388.

[81] *ibid.* at 413.

"When one considers the grievous social ills which will undoubtedly be caused by gaming clubs if they get into the wrong hands, it is obviously of the greatest public importance that the law should give the board all its support to ensure that this does not occur. In my view, any document or information that comes to the board from whatever source and by whatever means should be immune from discovery. It is only thus that the board will obtain all the material it requires in order to carry out its task efficiently. Unless this immunity exists many persons, reputable or disreputable, would be discouraged from communicating all they know to the board."

This last sentence shows that the need to protect sources of information is not confined to cases where the moral fibre of potential informants is questionable. Nor indeed is it confined to cases where sources require protection from a possible threat posed by underworld elements.

In *D. v. National Society for the Prevention of Cruelty to Children*,[82] the rule **21–25** was applied in relation to an informant who reported to the defendants that the plaintiff was beating her child. Lord Diplock said:

"I would extend to those who give information about neglect or ill-treatment of children to a local authority or the N.S.P.C.C. a similar immunity from disclosure of their identity in legal proceedings to that which the law accords to police informers. The public interests served by preserving the anonymity of both classes of informants are analogous; they are of no less weight in the case of the former than in that of the latter class, and in my judgment are of greater weight than in the case of informers of the Gaming Board to whom immunity from disclosure of their identity has recently been extended by this House."[83]

Documents created for the purpose of a private inquiry established by the Secretary of State for Foreign and Commonwealth Affairs, whose aim was to investigate the continuing supply of oil into Rhodesia notwithstanding the imposition of sanctions, were held to be immune by the House of Lords in *Lonrho Ltd v. Shell Petroleum Co. Ltd.*[84]

Lord Diplock, giving the only speech, said[85]:

"Even without the Minister's certificate I should not have needed evidence to satisfy me that the likelihood of success of an inquiry of this kind in discovering the truth as to what happened is greatly facilitated if those persons who know what happened come forward to volunteer information rather than waiting to be identified by the inquiry itself as likely to possess relevant information and having it extracted from them by question and answer. Nor would I need any evidence to satisfy me that without an assurance of complete confidentiality information is less likely to be volunteered; particularly where the inquiry is directed to matters that are

---

[82] [1978] A.C. 171.
[83] *ibid.* at 219.
[84] [1980] 1 W.L.R. 627.
[85] *ibid.* at 637.

the subject matter of a pending civil action to which the possessor of the information is a defendant."

The same rule has been applied in relation to persons providing information to the Audit Commission (which has responsibilities under the Local Government Finance Act 1982 with regard to the auditing of local government expenditure) about alleged wasted expenditure by a local authority.[86]

21–26   There is, however, an important distinction between information supplied voluntarily and that supplied under compulsion, as was emphasised by the House of Lords in *Re Arrows Ltd (No. 4)*.[87] A liquidator seeking to obtain information about the affairs of an insolvent company has a choice of routes under the Insolvency Act 1986. He will generally try to elicit information informally by relying on section 235, under which a wide class of persons owe a duty to provide information reasonably required by him. Or he may obtain an order from the court for the formal examination of a witness under section 236. The House of Lords held that no public interest immunity applied to information provided under the latter procedure. The question whether public interest immunity would attach to information provided under section 235 did not arise for decision, but Lord Browne-Wilkinson observed that the public interest in ensuring the free flow of such informally obtained information was much greater, and that if liquidators could be compelled to disclose such information to the Serious Fraud Office there would be a severe impairment of their ability to obtain necessary information.[88]

Documents whose disclosure would be oppressive

21–27   *Re Joseph Hargreaves Ltd*[89] concerned a summons for discovery under section 115 of the Companies Act 1862. The liquidators of an insolvent company sought to recover damages from the directors and auditors of the company. The summons was served on the local tax surveyor, requiring him to produce balance sheets submitted by the company. The Inland Revenue objected to production of the documents, and its objection was upheld by Wright J. and the Court of Appeal.
Lord Reid, commenting on the case in *Conway v. Rimmer*,[90] observed:

> "If the state insists on a man disclosing his private affairs for a particular purpose it requires a very strong case to justify that disclosure being used for other purposes."

Questions concerning the applicability of public interest immunity to tax documents arose again in *Lonrho plc v. Fayed (No. 4)*.[91] The plaintiff in an action for damages for conspiracy obtained an order against the defendants for discovery of financial documents including tax documents. The defendants

---

[86] *Bookbinder v. Tebbit (No. 2)* [1992] 1 W.L.R. 217.
[87] [1995] 2 A.C. 75. See para. 8–05, above.
[88] See also, *Re Barlow Clowes Gilt Managers Ltd* [1992] Ch. 208, where Millett J. expressed the view that there was strong public interest in attaching immunity to such information.
[89] [1900] 1 Ch. 347.
[90] [1968] A.C. 910 at 946.
[91] [1994] Q.B. 775.

appealed unsuccessfully, arguing that (a) such documents attracted public interest immunity when in the hands of the Inland Revenue (*Re Joseph Hargreaves Ltd*) and (b) public interest immunity must therefore also attach to such documents when in the hands of the tax payer.

Sir Thomas Bingham M.R. accepted the first part of the argument. In so doing, he adopted Lord Reid's explanation of *Re Joseph Hargreaves Ltd*. But he rejected the second part of the argument, saying[92]:

21–28

> "There are some fields in which, if immunity covers a document in the hands of party A, it would be absurd to order production of a copy in the hands of B or to permit oral evidence of the contents of the document by C. In fields such as national security or the conduct of international relations, production of B's copy or the admission of C's evidence would injure the very public interest which the immunity exists to protect. But it does not follow that that need be so in all fields. It all depends on the facet of the public interest which is in question. Mr Sumption was, I think, right to pose the question: what is for present purposes the relevant public policy?
>
> The answer to that question must be that which Lord Reid gave in commenting on *Re Joseph Hargreaves Ltd* [1900] 1 Ch. 347. The state must not, backed by compulsory powers, obtain information from the citizen for one purpose and use that information for another. It does not matter whether this is seen as a principle of good administration or statutory construction or ordinary morality or all three. That is the ratio which Lord Reid gave, as I understand him, and I do not think it bears on whether the taxpayer himself can be required to produce the documents or not."

He accordingly held that there was no public interest which entitled the defendants to claim immunity for the tax documents in their own possession.

Roch L.J., while concurring in the result, disagreed with the first part of the defendants' argument. He held that the Inland Revenue would have a duty of confidentiality in respect of the defendants' tax documents, but that they would not have attracted public interest immunity.

Leggatt L.J., in a short judgment, came somewhere between the other two opinions. He said:

> "... a person makes a truthful tax return not on the faith that the Inland Revenue will keep it confidential but because if he gives false information or conceals any part of his income, he can be prosecuted. The confidentiality is itself exacted by statute. So there is no need to introduce the concept of what is now called public interest immunity with its cornucopia of legal argument. But because for nearly a century communications with the revenue have been regarded as the subject of immunity, it is convenient to continue doing so, and it may indeed be too late for this court to put the clock back."

Four comments may be made. First, the fact that disclosure of confidential information is obligatory does not prevent the equitable doctrine of confidence from applying; on the contrary, it affords reason for it to do so.[93] Secondly, establishing a duty of confidentiality does not make otiose the question of public interest immunity, because a mere duty of confidentiality would not

---

[92] *Lonrho plc v. Fayed (No. 4)* [1994] Q.B. 775 at 788–789.
[93] See para. 8–02 above.

231

prevent disclosure in the course of legal proceedings. Thirdly, a majority of the court accepted that the documents did attract public interest immunity in the hands of the Inland Revenue. Fourthly, there is an interesting contrast between the reasoning of *Lonrho plc v. Fayed (No. 4)* and the reasoning of *Marcel v. Commissioner of Police of the Metropolis.*[94]

21–29   The effect of *Lonrho plc v. Fayed (No. 4)* is that the Inland Revenue could not have been compelled to produce the defendants' tax documents on *subpoena*, although the defendants could themselves be required to produce copies of the same documents in their own possession. In *Marcel* the Court of Appeal held that the police owed a duty of confidentiality towards a citizen from whom documents were seized, but that the police might be required to produce them on *subpoena* in circumstances where the owners of the seized documents might themselves be required to produce them on *subpoena*.

It is not a satisfactory explanation to say that in *Marcel* the documents were merely subject to a duty of confidentiality, whereas in *Lonrho plc v. Fayed (No. 4)* it was recognised that tax documents in the hands of the Inland Revenue could be the subject of public interest immunity; for, whilst that is correct, it does not explain the underlying question why confidential documents seized from a citizen by the police, and confidential documents supplied by the citizen to the Inland Revenue under compulsion, should have a different status.

It is an important question whether documents of a private nature obtained by the state by compulsory powers should be the subject merely of a duty of confidentiality or should attract public interest immunity.

In *Re Arrows Ltd (No. 4)*[95] the House of Lords rejected a claim for public interest immunity based on the public interest in ensuring that information extracted by statutory powers should be used only for the purpose for which the statutory power was conferred. Furthermore *Lonrho plc v. Fayed (No. 4)* is an uncertain authority in that whilst Sir Thomas Bingham M.R. was in favour of according public interest immunity to tax documents in the hands of the Inland Revenue on grounds of authority and principle, Roch L.J. was opposed to it on principle and Leggatt L.J. supported it lukewarmly on grounds of authority alone.

Each case will require its own examination, but it may be that in this area *Re Arrows (No. 4)* and *Marcel* will be seen in the future as providing more general guidance than *Lonrho plc v. Fayed (No. 4)*.

The nature of the protection afforded by immunity

21–30   In the nineteenth century, it was held that a document either attracted immunity in its entirety or not at all: it was not possible for arguably unobjectionable passages in immune documents to be received in evidence.[96] This may have been because the objection to disclosure generally affected every part of the document equally. In any event, it is now accepted that parts of a document may be disclosed while other parts are withheld.[97]

---

[94] [1992] Ch. 225; see para. 8–02, above.

[95] [1995] 2 A.C. 75.

[96] *per* Ellenborough C.J. in *Anderson v. Hamilton* (1816), cited in *Home v. Bentinck* (1820) 2 Brod. & B. 130, at 156n; *Stace v. Griffith* (1869) L.R. 2 P.C. 420, *per* Lord Chelmsford in the course of argument at 425.

[97] See *Burmah Oil Co. Ltd v. Governor and Company of the Bank of England* [1980] A.C. 1090, *per* Lord Edmund-Davies at 1124; *R. v. Chief Constable of West Midlands Police, ex p. Wiley* [1995] 1 A.C. 274, *per* Lord Templeman at 282 and *per* Lord Woolf at 307.

If immunity attaches to a document, its contents are protected from discovery and from production in court. The document's immunity does not necessarily prevent it from being used in other ways by the party in whose hands it is.

In *R. v. Commissioner of Police of the Metropolis, ex p. Hart-Leverton*,[98] the applicant sought judicial review of the Commissioner's decision to allow documents obtained in the course of a police complaints investigation and disciplinary hearing to be used by police legal advisers for purposes such as advising on evidence and taking statements from witnesses, so as to assist in the preparation of the defence to legal proceedings against the police commenced by the complainant. It was conceded by the Commissioner that the documents could not be used for the purpose of cross-examination.

Nolan J. held that the guiding principle of immunity was to ensure that the protected material did not go before the court. There was nothing in the use of the documents by the police or their legal advisers which conflicted with the immunity. This view was departed from by the Court of Appeal in *Halford v. Sharples*[99] and *R. v. Chief Constable of West Midlands Police, ex p. Wiley*,[1] but its authority was restored by the House of Lords in the latter case.[2]

One question is whether the concession made by the Commissioner in *ex p. Hart-Leverton* was unnecessary: is it possible to use immune documents in cross-examination? In *Alfred Crompton Amusement Machines Ltd v. Customs & Excise*,[3] Lord Cross of Chelsea remarked *obiter*[4] in relation to information for which immunity was claimed that:

21–31

"No doubt it will form part of the brief delivered to counsel for the commissioners and may help him to probe the appellants' evidence in cross-examination; but counsel will not be able to use it as evidence to controvert anything which the appellants' witnesses may say."

The point was considered in some detail by the House of Lords in *R. v. Chief Constable of West Midlands Police, ex p. Wiley*.[5] Lord Woolf, delivering the leading speech, quoted the statement of Lord Cross set out above and observed that his speech on that aspect of the case represented the unanimous view of the House of Lords. He also stated as a matter of principle that,[6]

"In general, the immunity is provided against disclosure of documents or their contents. It is not, at least in the absence of exceptional circumstances, an immunity against the use of knowledge obtained from the documents. It is impractical and artificial to erect barriers between a party and his legal advisers in an attempt to avoid that party having an advantage in the proceedings."

Lord Woolf went on to say that the legal advisers of a party in possession of material which is immune from disclosure should assist the court and the opposing party to mitigate any disadvantage as best they can by disclosing such

---

[98] *The Times*, February 6, 1990.
[99] [1992] 1 W.L.R. 736.
[1] [1994] 1 W.L.R. 114.
[2] [1995] 1 A.C. 274.
[3] [1974] A.C. 405.
[4] *ibid.* at 434, cited by Oliver L.J. in *Neilson v. Laugharne* [1981] Q.B. 736, at 753.
[5] [1995] 1 A.C. 274 at 301.
[6] *ibid.* at 306.

information as is possible without production of the document; but that, in so far as this is not possible, the courts should not try to create a level playing field by orders of the kind made in that case (*i.e.* restricting internal use of the document by the party in possession of it).

It follows from this reasoning that the concession made by the Commissioner in *ex p. Hart-Leverton* was too broad. He would have been entitled to use the material (even if it had been immune from production) for the purpose of cross-examination, provided that this was not done in such a way as to destroy the object of its immunity (for example, by putting the document to the witness).

The question has also arisen whether evidence about matters contained in a document, which is the subject of public interest immunity, may be adduced by other means, for example, by producing a copy of the document.

In many instances, a copy of an immune document will itself be immune, but this is not always the case, as is shown by *Lonrho plc v. Fayed (No. 4)*,[7] where Sir Thomas Bingham M.R. observed that it depends in each case on identifying the aspect of the public interest which the immunity is intended to serve.

If, for example, the reason for the grant of immunity is not that the release of the information would be harmful in itself, but only that the provision of that information from a particular source would be against the public interest, because it would tend to dry up the free flow of information on matters of public importance, there would be no objection to the provision of the same information from another source.

Raising the objection

21–32   A claim to public interest immunity will often be made by ministerial certificate or certificate given by the Permanent Secretary of the relevant government department.

However, in the absence of any governmental intervention,[8] an objection to production may be raised either by the holder or the owner of the document of which production is sought, or by any interested person, or by the court of its own motion.[9]

In *Re Barlow Clowes Gilt Managers Ltd*,[10] Millett J., holding that there was a public interest in protecting from production the transcripts of interviews carried out by liquidators, observed,[11]:

> "If the liquidation of insolvent companies were entrusted to the executive branch of government, the foregoing would be embodied in a certificate by the appropriate minister. As it is entrusted to the judicial branch, the place of the certificate must be taken by the doctrine of judicial notice."

The procedure to be adopted in criminal cases when the prosecution is in possession of information which it believes to be immune on the grounds of

---

[7] [1994] Q.B. 775 at 788. See para. 21–27 above.
[8] Unless the relevant authority has already taken the decision not to pursue a claim to immunity (see below).
[9] See *Marcel v. Commissioner of Police of the Metropolis* [1992] Ch. 225, *per* Dillon L.J. at 253; *R. v. Lewes JJ., ex p. Home Secretary* [1973] A.C. 388, *per* Lord Reid at 400; *Hennessy v. Wright* (1888) 21 Q.B.D. 509, esp. at 519 and 521.
[10] [1992] Ch. 208.
[11] *ibid.* at 223.

public interest from disclosure to the defence was considered by the Court of Appeal in *R. v. Davis*.[12] The Court held that in most cases the prosecution should give notice to the defence of its intention to apply to the court for a ruling and should give an indication of the category of the material concerned, and that the defence should generally have the opportunity to make representations to the court.

If it would be against the public interest to disclose even the category of the material for which immunity is claimed, the Crown's application should be made *ex parte*, on notice to the defence, though, in exceptional circumstances, the *ex parte* application might if necessary be made without notice to the defence. On any *ex parte* application, the court should consider whether or not the normal *inter partes* procedure would be more appropriate.

In general, issues of public interest immunity should be dealt with in the proceedings in which they arise, and not by way of an application for injunctive or declaratory relief in ancillary proceedings. Where a summary trial is to be conducted by magistrates who have decided against the defendant on an issue of public interest immunity, the magistrates have a discretion to grant the defendant a hearing before a new bench.[13]

Waiver

It has often been said that a claim to public interest immunity, in an appropriate case, is not a right but a duty, and therefore cannot be waived in the same manner as, for example, legal professional privilege.[14] This statement requires substantial qualification.   **21–33**

First, in cases where the immunity is based upon a duty of confidence owed to a person, a waiver of confidence by that person may operate as a negation of the immunity. As Lord Woolf said in *R. v. Chief Constable of West Midlands, ex p. Wiley*[15]:

> "If the purpose of the immunity is to obtain the co-operation of an individual to the giving of a statement, I find it difficult to see how that purpose will be undermined if the maker of the statement consents to it being disclosed."

Secondly, in many instances, the courts will not query a decision by the executive or other relevant authority not to pursue a claim to immunity. This may occur for different reasons. On the one hand, it may be that the relevant authority decides that there is no public interest to be served by protection from disclosure because, for example, the proposed revelations pose no threat to national security.[16]

Alternatively, an argument for public interest in immunity may exist, but the

---

[12] [1993] 1 W.L.R. 613.

[13] *R. v. South Worcestershire Magistrates, ex p. Lilley, The Times*, February 22, 1995, D.C.

[14] See, *e.g., D. v. N.S.P.C.C.* [1978] A.C. 171, *per* Lord Simon at 234; *R. v. Lewes JJ.* [1973] A.C. 388, *per* Lord Salmon at 412; *Re S. and W. (Minors) (Confidential Reports)* (1983) 4 F.L.R. 290 *per* Eveleigh L.J. at 292; *Makanjuola v. Commissioner of Police of the Metropolis* [1992] 3 All E.R. 617, *per* Bingham L.J. at 623.

[15] [1995] 1 A.C. 274, *per* Lord Woolf at 299. See also *Lonrho Plc. v. Fayed (No. 4)* [1994] Q.B. 775, *per* Sir Thomas Bingham M.R. at 786F, and *Campbell v. Tameside Metropolitan Borough Council* [1982] 1 Q.B. 1065, *per* Lord Denning M.R. at 1073.

[16] See, *e.g., A. v. Hayden* [1984] 156 C.L.R. 532.

executive or other authority may be able to decide the contest between (a) the aspect of the public interest supporting the immunity and (b) the aspect of the public interest supporting disclosure, in favour of the latter, without reference to the court.

Thus, in *R. v. Chief Constable of West Midlands, ex p. Wiley*,[17] Lord Woolf said:

> "If a Secretary of State on behalf of his department as opposed to any ordinary litigant concludes that any public interest in documents being withheld from production is outweighed by the public interest in the documents being available for purposes of litigation, it is difficult to conceive that unless the documents do not relate to an area for which the Secretary of State was responsible, the court would feel it appropriate to come to any different conclusion from that of the Secretary of State."

He later referred to[18]:

> "a well known part of the speech of Lord Simon of Glaisdale in *R. v. Lewes Justices, ex parte Secretary of State for the Home Department* [1973] A.C. 388 at 407, which is in these terms,
>> 'It is true that the public interest which demands that the evidence be withheld has to be weighed against the public interest in the administration of justice that courts should have the fullest possible access to all relevant material ... but once the former public interest is held to outweigh the latter, the evidence cannot in any circumstances be admitted. It is not a privilege which may be waived by the Crown ... or by anyone else.'
> It will be observed from that passage that when Lord Simon said that the privilege was one which could not be waived, he was referring to the situation after it had been determined that the public interest against disclosure outweighed that of disclosure in the administration of justice."

21–34　　Secretaries of State and the Attorney-General are capable of this form of disposal of the issue of immunity, but the situation may be different when parties other than government departments are involved.[19] It has been said that chief constables, once they have consulted with other chief constables and/or the Home Secretary or Attorney-General, are able to disclose documents which might have a prima facie claim to immunity. When there is a doubt as to whether immunity can properly be waived, the prudent approach is to leave the matter to the court.[20]

It is as yet unsettled whether an official's power to waive a claim to immunity where he decides that the public interest in immunity is outweighed by the public interest in the administration of justice brings with it a concomitant *duty* to make a claim *only* after taking this latter public interest into account. In *Bennett v. Commissioner of Police of Metropolis*,[21] Rattee J., without deciding

---

[17] [1995] 1 A.C. 274 at 296; see also *Sankey v. Whitlam* (1978) 142 C.L.R. 1 at 44–45 and 68.

[18] *ibid.* at 298.

[19] See Lord Woolf's observations in *R. v. Chief Constable of West Midlands Police, ex p. Wiley* [1995] 1 A.C. 274 at 297.

[20] *ibid.* at 297–298. In *Evans v. Chief Constable of Surrey* [1988] 1 Q.B. 588, the Chief Constable was not entitled to waive the immunity attaching to a report relating to a murder suspect sent by him to the Director of Public Prosecutions in the face of objection made by the Attorney-General.

[21] [1995] 1 W.L.R. 488 at 495ff. See also Ganz, *Matrix Churchill and Public Interest Immunity: A Postcript* (1995) 58 M.L.R. 417.

the matter, expressed the view that the existence of such a duty was arguable. The alternative view is that the responsible official is entitled to leave considerations of the administration of justice for the court to take into account to the extent that it chooses to do so.

Sir Richard Scott's report of his inquiry into Matrix Churchill and other cases included recommendations that a public interest immunity claim should not be made in a criminal case unless, in the opinion of the minister or person putting forward the claim, disclosure would cause substantial harm; nor should it be made if the minister formed the opinion that notwithstanding the sensitivity of the documents the public interest required that the documents should be disclosed.[22]

---

[22] *Report of the Inquiry into the Export of Defence Equipment and Dual-Use Goods to Iraq and Related Prosecutions*, para. K6.18(iv)(v).

Chapter XXII

METHODS OF PARTIAL PROTECTION

Restrictions on the manner in which confidential information is required to be disclosed

22–01   The courts may give partial protection to the confidentiality of information disclosed in litigation by ordering special restrictions on the circumstances and manner of its disclosure. These restrictions, most commonly to be found in cases concerning trade secrets and children,[1] fall into two broad categories:

(1) restrictions operating during pre-trial discovery;
(2) restrictions operating during trial.

Controls on the form of discovery

22–02   The earlier authorities on this topic were reviewed by the Court of Appeal in *Warner-Lambert Co. v. Glaxo Laboratories Ltd*[2] Buckley L.J. concluded[3]:

> "None of these cases purports to lay down a form of order suitable for universal use. Nor, I think, does any of them indicate that the court might not in appropriate circumstances at a later stage in the action have directed disclosure to a wider class of persons or on different terms. In my judgment, the court must in each case decide what measure of disclosure should be made, and to whom, and upon what terms, having regard to the particular circumstances of the case, bearing in mind that, if a case for disclosure is made out, the applicant should have as full a degree of appropriate disclosure as will be consistent with adequate protection of any trade secret of the respondent."

One possible control is to impose a restriction on the persons allowed to carry out inspection. In some circumstances, only a party's solicitors and a specified person or persons will be permitted to inspect documents, and then only on an undertaking not to disclose their content to any other persons. The

---

[1] In relation to children, see Chap. XXIII.
[2] [1975] R.P.C. 354.
[3] *ibid.* at 358.

238

specified person may sometimes be an independent expert, but often inspection will need to be made by a person more familiar with the business of the parties.[4]

Other possible controls include orders as to where the documents are to be inspected and stored, provision for the attendance at inspection of a representative of the party giving discovery, and restrictions on the making of copies or notes.

In deciding what condition to impose, the court may take into account its view of such factors as the susceptibility of the confidential information to memorisation.[5] The court may also take judicial notice of the standing of the party seeking discovery, if it is, for example, a reputable and well-known company.[6]

Restrictions operating during trial

Under ordinary court procedure, a large number of matters are dealt with in chambers. Broadly speaking, however, these are either preliminary hearings, or relate to family and domestic matters. Contested hearings at which there is a final determination on the merits are heard in open court.[7] Indeed, if a point of public importance arises in a matter proceeding in chambers, it is common practice for the hearing to be adjourned into open court for judgment. **22–03**

Exceptionally, however, a party wishing to protect confidential material may seek an order restricting public attendance at, or public reporting of, proceedings that would normally be held in open court. This relief will be granted only as a last resort and if absolutely necessary in the interests of justice. The reasons for this reluctance were set out by the House of Lords in *Scott v. Scott*.[8] Lord Shaw of Dunfermline cited among various passages from the works of Bentham:

> "Publicity is the very soul of justice. It is the keenest spur to exertion and the surest of all guards against improbity. It keeps the judge himself, while trying, under trial."[9]

This passage was also cited by Lord Diplock in *Harman v. Home Office*.[10]

Scott v. Scott was considered by the Court of Appeal more recently in *R. v. Chief Registrar of Friendly Societies, ex p. New Cross Building Society*.[11] Sir John Donaldson M.R., with whom Griffiths and Slade L.JJ. on this point expressly indicated their agreement, said[12]: **22–04**

> "The guidance which I get from their Lordships' speeches can be

---

[4] See, *e.g. Atari Incorporated v. Philips Electronics and Associated Industries Ltd* [1988] F.S.R. 416; *Format Communications MFG Ltd v. ITT (United Kingdom) Ltd* [1983] F.S.R. 473, C.A.; *Centri-Spray Corporation v. Cera International Ltd* [1979] F.S.R. 175.

[5] *Centri-Spray Corporation v. Cera International Ltd* [1979] F.S.R. 175 at 180–181.

[6] *Format Communications MFG Ltd v. ITT (United Kingdom) Ltd* [1983] F.S.R. 473 at 486.

[7] Whether or not a hearing has taken place in open court may be a finely balanced issue of fact: see, *e.g. McPherson v. McPherson* [1936] A.C. 177.

[8] [1913] A.C. 417.

[9] *Benthamia, or Select Extracts from the works of Jeremy Bentham* (1843) p. 115.

[10] [1983] 1 A.C. 280 at 303.

[11] [1984] 1 Q.B. 227.

[12] *ibid.* at 235.

summarised as follows. The general rule that the courts shall conduct their proceedings in public is but an aid, albeit a very important aid, to the achievement of the paramount object of the courts which is to do justice in accordance with the law. It is only if, in wholly exceptional circumstances, the presence of the public or public knowledge of the proceedings is likely to defeat that paramount object that the courts are justified in proceeding in camera. These circumstances are incapable of definition. Each application for privacy must be considered on its merits, but the applicant must satisfy the court that nothing short of total privacy will enable justice to be done. It is not sufficient that a public hearing will create embarrassment for some or all of those concerned. It must be shown that a public hearing is likely to lead, directly or indirectly, to a denial of justice."

In the case before it, a judicial review of the Chief Registrar's adverse decision as to the suitability of a building society to continue to be a repository of trust funds and to accept moneys for investment, the Court of Appeal considered that publicity during the first instance hearing and subsequent appeal would have resulted in a loss of public confidence such that the society would have had to close even if it had proved successful (which, in the event, it was not). The hearings had therefore been rightly held *in camera*.

The court will reduce to a minimum the length of time spent *in camera*.[13] Arrangements may be made between the parties so that it is unnecessary for the public to be excluded at all.[14]

Restrictions on the use of confidential information

22–05 A person who obtains information as the result of a disclosure made by his opponent under compulsion in the course of litigation does so under an obligation not to use that information for any "ulterior or collateral purpose".[15] Included within this principle is information obtained on discovery under Order 24, rule 10 of the Rules of the Supreme Court, under an Anton Piller Order, under a Mareva Order, or under an order made pursuant to section 7 of the Bankers' Books Evidence Act 1879.[16] Also protected are affidavits of means sworn under compulsion in the course of matrimonial proceedings.[17]

A party cannot claim the same protection in respect of documents disclosed voluntarily. Nor, it appears, can a party claim protection in respect of documents referred to in an affidavit voluntarily sworn, merely because he subsequently produces them only pursuant to an order under Rules of the Supreme Court, Order 24, rules 10 and 11.[18]

The obligation is owed to the court[19] by way of an implied undertaking.[20] The

---

[13] For example, only while details of some secret chemical process are revealed: *Badische Anilin und Soda Fabrik v. Levinstein* [1883] 24 Ch.D. 156.

[14] *Andrew v. Raeburn* (1874) 9 Ch.App. 522: privacy not required since it was unnecessary to read out the contents of the confidential letters concerned.

[15] *Alterskye v. Scott* [1948] 1 All E.R. 469.

[16] *Bhimji v. Chatwani* [1992] 1 W.L.R. 1158.

[17] *Medway v. Doublelock Ltd* [1978] 1 W.L.R. 710.

[18] *ibid.*

[19] It may be that the obligation is also owed to the parties personally: *Dory v. Richard Wolf GmbH* [1990] 1 F.S.R. 266 at 269. But see further below.

[20] The merits of the use of an undertaking to the court were described by Hobhouse J. in *Prudential Assurance Co. Ltd v. Fountain Page Ltd* [1991] 1 W.L.R. 756 at 764–765.

reasons for imposing the obligation were set out by Megaw L.J. in *Halcon International Inc. v. The Shell Transport and Trading Co.*[21]:

"... documents belonging to a party are their own property ... it is in general wrong that one who is thus compelled by law to produce documents for purposes of particular proceedings should be in peril of having these documents used by the other party for some purpose other than the purpose of those particular legal proceedings and, in particular, that they should be made available to third parties who might use them to the detriment of the party who has produced them on discovery. And there is the further, practical, reason ... that it is important, for the administration of justice, that there should not be a disincentive to parties to make proper discovery, so that they are minded to hold back, and seek to avoid the disclosure of documents which may tell against themselves in litigation."

The distinction between voluntary and involuntary discovery may seem straightforward, but deciding what is to be considered as "voluntary" can be problematical, especially where disclosure by one party is occasioned by a step taken by his opponent. In *Derby & Co. Ltd v. Weldon (No. 2)*, it was held by Sir Nicholas Browne-Wilkinson V.-C. that there is no obligation implied in respect of evidence voluntarily adduced in order to oppose an application for Mareva relief.[22]

By contrast, in *Lubrizol Corporation v. Esso Petroleum Company Ltd (No. 2)*[23] it was held by Hugh Laddie Q.C. that the third defendants, who had adduced documents in evidence in order to have set aside the leave given to the plaintiffs for service of proceedings on them outside the jurisdiction, were not true volunteers: the plaintiffs had served evidence referring to the documents, after which it was inevitable that the third defendants would have to rely upon the documents in question if service was to be set aside.

In *Prudential Assurance Co. Ltd v. Fountain Page Ltd*,[24] Hobhouse J. **22–06** proposed the following test:

"There is distinction between orders, the breach of which is a contempt of court and those orders or rules breach of which merely gives rise to a default. The principle of compulsion applies to the former category only."

This test cannot be regarded as comprehensive, however, since it would not be met by discovery under Order 24 or answers to interrogatories under Order 26, both of which are clearly protected.

Limitation of the principle to cases of compulsory disclosure in the strictest sense may also be a disincentive to co-operation. It frequently happens that one party to litigation requests documents which the opposing party considers that it is entitled to withhold, because the request is too wide or the documents are not strictly relevant to the issues, but the opposing party may, and quite often

---

[21] [1979] R.P.C. 97 at 121.
[22] *The Times*, October 20, 1988, 132 S.J. 1755.
[23] [1993] F.S.R. 53.
[24] [1991] 1 W.L.R. 756 at 765.

will, nevertheless produce the documents; or a party may waive privilege (on request or otherwise); or discovery may take place before the rules strictly require it. It is in the public interest to encourage co-operation between the parties and voluntary disclosure of each party's case at the earliest possible stage.

There is logic in the implied undertaking to the court being limited to documents whose disclosure is compelled by rules or orders of the court, but that does not necessarily exclude the existence of an obligation of confidentiality between the parties which need not be so limited. But the present law on this subject is far from clear.

22–07 In *Harman v. Secretary of State for the Home Department*,[25] a solicitor allowed a journalist to have access to documents obtained on discovery from the Home Office in an action commenced by her client. She was held to be in contempt of court. She appealed on the basis that the documents provided to the journalist had all been read out in open court, that they had thereby entered the public domain and that her obligations under her implied undertaking had at that time come to an end. The finding of contempt was upheld by the House of Lords by a majority of three to two. It was accepted on behalf of the Home Secretary that once the documents were read in open court the person giving discovery lost any right of confidentiality sufficient to mount a claim for breach of confidence against someone using the documents. There was therefore no issue as to the existence or scope of any private law duty of confidentiality, but opinions were divided as to the relationship between the law of confidentiality and the implied undertaking to the court.

Lord Scarman and Lord Simon in a joint dissenting speech said:

> "... Once the litigant's private right to keep his documents to himself has been overtaken by their becoming public knowledge, we can see no reason why the undertaking given when they were confidential should continue to apply to them ... . Notwithstanding the manner of its enforceability, the confidence imposed upon the party upon whom the duty is laid is in no way different from that which the law requires in other situations or relationships giving rise to a duty of confidence."[26]

Lord Keith, on the other hand, stated:

> "The implied obligation not to make improper use of discovered documents is, however, independent of any obligation existing under the general law relating to confidentiality. It affords a particular protection accorded in the interests of the proper administration of justice. It is owed not to the owner of the documents but to the court, and the function of the court in seeing that the obligation is observed is directed to the maintenance of those interests, and not to the enforcement of the law relating to confidentiality."[27]

Lord Diplock and Lord Roskill approached the matter in terms of the court's inherent power to prevent abuse of its own process.

---

[25] [1983] 1 A.C. 280.
[26] *ibid.* at 313.
[27] *ibid.* at 308.

As a result of a compromise by the United Kingdom reached when Ms **22–08** Harman's case was taken to the European Court of Human Rights, the Rules of the Supreme Court were amended by the introduction of Order 24, rule 14A, which provides that:

> "Any undertaking, whether express or implied, not to use a document for any purposes other than those of the proceedings in which it is disclosed shall cease to apply to such document after it has been read to or by the Court, or referred to, in open Court, unless the Court for special reasons has otherwise ordered on the application of a party or of the person to whom the document belongs."

The effect of that change (whatever its precise scope[28]) is to overrule the result, but not the reasoning, of *Home Office v. Harman*, and leaves the law in an anomalous position. A document may lose its confidentiality by other means than by being read out in open court. It may, for example, be leaked to the press and published, but that would not bring the undertaking to an end; application would have to be made for permission to use the document (unless the party giving discovery consented to its use). On that application the fact that its confidential nature had vanished would be a factor to be given "due weight", whatever that may be.[29]

In *EMI Records Ltd v. Spillane*[30] Sir Nicolas Browne-Wilkinson V.-C. held that the implied undertaking is not an absolute undertaking not to use the documents or permit their use for purposes other than the action in which discovery is given, but is an undertaking not without the consent of the party who gave discovery so to do.

This makes sense, because that party supplied the document in the first place, and if it no longer wishes the document to be treated as confidential, there is no reason why the court should require it to be treated as confidential (subject to third party considerations, which are referred to below). Conversely it is unsatisfactory that the receiving party should remain under an obligation to the court to treat a document as confidential even when the discovering party would have no personal right to require him to do so, subject only to the exception created by Order 24, rule 14A.

The solution is to accept the views expressed by Lords Scarman and Simon as a correct statement of law, but that solution is open only to the House of Lords.

In the meantime there remains the vexed question whether a private law **22–09** duty of confidentiality is owed by a person obtaining discovery of confidential documents in the course of litigation. In *Derby & Co. Ltd v. Weldon (No. 2)*,[31] Sir Nicholas Browne-Wilkinson V.-C. said:

> "I have the greatest doubts whether such a separate duty of confidence can exist . . . . But even assuming (contrary to my inclination) that there is such a separate duty of confidence, such duty can only be implied from the circumstances of the case. Such private duty of confidence cannot, in my judgment, be wider than that imposed by the implied undertaking."

---

[28] As to which there has been doubt. See *Singh v. Christie, The Times*, November 11, 1993, discussed at para. 22–13, below.
[29] *Sybron Corporation v. Barclays Bank plc* [1985] Ch. 299 at 322–323, *per* Scott J.
[30] [1986] 1 W.L.R. 967.
[31] *The Times*, October 20, 1988; 132 S.J. 1755.

This passage was cited and followed by Hobhouse J. in *Prudential Assurance Co. Ltd v. Fountain Page Ltd.*[32] He expressed his conclusion in yet stronger terms:

> "It is clear that where documents are produced in the course of legal proceedings, or information provided, the further use of that material must be governed by the legal principles or rules of court which relate to the use of such material and not by any private law rights. It is of course an *a fortiori* position where there were no antecedent private law rights in respect of that material; the use of material in litigation cannot itself give rise to that class of right."

Ferris J. followed these two decisions in *Apple Corps Ltd v. Apple Computer Inc.*[33] In doing so, he was obliged to consider the problematic decision of the Court of Appeal in *Mainwaring v. Goldtech Investments Ltd.*[34]

In this case the defendants' solicitors had lodged various documents, including privileged papers, with the taxing master following an order for interlocutory costs made in the defendants' favour. The defendants' solicitors subsequently came off the record for the defendants and the taxation was abandoned. The taxing master did not return the papers to the defendants or their former solicitors, but handed them to the Master who was the master in charge of the interlocutory proceedings between the parties.

The plaintiffs applied for and obtained an order against the defendants for the production of various documents. When the defendants failed to comply with the order for production, the Master looked through the documents in his possession and supplied those that fell within the terms of his order to one of the plaintiffs to enable her to take copies.

The defendants' counterclaim was dismissed when they failed to provide security for the plaintiffs' costs, and judgment was also entered for the plaintiffs in default of defence. The plaintiffs issued a summons seeking an order that the defendants' former solicitors should personally bear the costs of the plaintiffs' actions. The Master subsequently permitted the same plaintiff to inspect and to take copies of any of the documents in his possession, notwithstanding representations made on behalf of the defendants' former solicitors.

In due course, the plaintiffs' application for costs against the defendants' former solicitors was dismissed and the defendants' former solicitors obtained an order from Hoffman J. restraining the plaintiffs from making further use of the copy documents lodged by them for taxation purposes. One of the plaintiffs appealed from this order.

22–10 The Court of Appeal was of the view that any benefit of privilege in the documents had been lost, bearing in mind the circumstances in which they came into the possession of Miss Mainwaring. However, it also held that the plaintiffs had obtained the taxation documents subject to an obligation of confidentiality owed, not only to the defendants, but also to the defendants' former solicitors, and that Hoffmann J. had exercised his discretion correctly in favour of the solicitors.

Ferris J. took the view in *Apple Corps Ltd v. Apple Computer Inc.* that the continuing duty of confidentiality referred to by the Court of Appeal in

---

[32] [1991] 1 W.L.R. 756 at 766–767.
[33] [1992] 1 C.M.L.R. 969. See also *per* Millett J. in *Bank of Crete S.A. v. Koskotas* [1992] (No. 2) 1 W.L.R. 919 at 925.
[34] *The Times*, February 19, 1991.

Mainwaring was none other than that embodied in the plaintiffs' implied undertaking to the court. The fact that the Court of Appeal was told by counsel that the application to Hoffmann J. had been an application under Order 24, rule 14A supports Ferris J.'s interpretation, but there are two difficulties with it.

First, the Court of Appeal agreed with Hoffmann J. that the basis of the solicitors' right to keep the documents confidential was their status "as constituting confidential communications between themselves and counsel or themselves and their client, and that, as against the rest of the world, they were entitled to preserve their confidentiality." Secondly, the authorities referred to by the Court of Appeal—*Marcel v. Commissioner of Police of the Metropolis*[35] and *Webster v. James Chapman & Co.*[36]—suggest that the proper test to be applied, in the Court's view, was that applicable to the general law of confidence, rather than that applicable to undertakings impliedly given to the court on discovery.

If no private law duty of confidentiality is owed in respect of confidential **22–11** documents obtained during and for the purposes of litigation, and if the implied undertaking to the court is confined to documents disclosed by compulsion, the result is doubly unhappy.

It leaves unprotected the co-operative party, in the examples given above, who responds to a request by an opposing party for disclosure to which that party is not, as he believes, strictly entitled; or who gives voluntary discovery of privileged documents; or who gives discovery before he is required to do so. Again, someone who is not a party to litigation, but is threatened with a *subpoena*, may agree to produce documents without the formality of service and attendance at court; but in the absence of any private law duty of confidentiality he will be similarly unprotected.

Where documents of a confidential nature are disclosed in the ordinary course, and for the purpose of, litigation (and, *a fortiori*, where they are disclosed at the recipient's request) the recipient ought to be under a general obligation, either by implied contract or under the equitable doctrine of confidence, not to use them for other purposes.

In the case of arbitration, the voluntary nature of the proceedings has not precluded the courts from recognising such an obligation; on the contrary, it has caused them to do so.[37]

Third parties

Third parties who have given no undertaking, express or implied, cannot **22–12** themselves be bound by such undertakings as may be given by a party to the action.[38] On the other hand, an injunction will be granted against third parties intending to use documents obtained from a party in breach of his undertaking.[39] This may be explained on the basis either of contempt or of confidence.

In *Prudential Assurance Co. Ltd v. Fountain Page Ltd*,[40] Hobhouse J. said that:

---

[35] [1992] Ch. 225.
[36] [1989] 3 All E.R. 939.
[37] *Dolling-Baker v. Merrett* [1990] 1 W.L.R. 1205.
[38] *Sybron Corporation v. Barclays Bank Plc.* [1985] 1 Ch. 299 at 321–322.
[39] *Distillers Co. (Biochemicals) Ltd v. Times Newspapers Ltd* [1975] 1 Q.B. 613, cited with approval by the Court of Appeal in *Riddick v. Thames Board Mills Ltd* [1977] 1 Q.B. 881.
[40] [1991] 1 W.L.R. 756 at 765.

"any person who knowingly aids a contempt or does acts which are inconsistent with the undertaking is himself in contempt and liable to sanctions."

He cited as authority for this proposition *Distillers Co. (Biochemicals) Ltd v. Times Newspapers Ltd.*[41]

However, Talbot J. in the *Distillers* case in fact proceeded on the basis of confidentiality rather than contempt of court. It is suggested that a litigant may not only be owed a duty of confidentiality by third parties, but may also, in certain circumstances, himself owe a duty of confidentiality to third parties. A party may be required to disclose records in respect of which he owes a duty of confidence to a third party, if such records are relevant to the issues in the action. The law would be deficient if the receiving party did not in such circumstances owe an obligation to the third party not to use those documents otherwise than for the purpose for which they were provided. The implied undertaking to the court would be an undertaking not to use the discovered documents otherwise than for the purpose of the action without the consent of the party who gave the discovery, but that party might not mind what the recipient did with them. The recipient's duty to the third party, it is suggested, would be a duty arising under the equitable doctrine of confidence.

22–13   In *Singh v. Christie*[42] the court was faced with the problem in a slightly different form. The plaintiff brought a number of actions against solicitors and firms of solicitors for defamation. The actions were based on a telephone conversation between two solicitors, one of whom had been acting for the plaintiff and the other for the plaintiff's opponent in previous litigation. The solicitor for the plaintiff's opponent had made an attendance note of the conversation, which had been disclosed on discovery in another action, in which the plaintiff was a party and read in open court. It is not clear from the report, but is to be assumed, that the conversation was intended to be private and confidential between the solicitors. Drake J. struck out the defamation actions.

The plaintiff argued that, on the plain wording of Order 24, rule 14A, his implied undertaking not to use the document otherwise than for the purposes of the action in which it was disclosed ceased as soon as it was read in open court, unless the court had for special reasons ordered otherwise on the application of a party or the person to whom the document belonged (which it had not). Further, most of the defendants were not people who were entitled to make such an application, since they had neither been parties to the previous action nor were owners of the document.

Troubled by the injustice of this situation, Drake J. adopted the solution of interpreting Order 24, rule 14A as providing only a very limited release from the plaintiff's undertaking. He held that the effect of the rule was to permit the plaintiff to make known the contents of the document, but not to use it for any purpose he wished, and that the implied undertaking remained effective to prevent him from using the attendance note for the purpose of bringing defamation proceedings.

22–14   There are two problems about that approach. First, his ruling that the undertaking continued to apply in relation to the document contradicts the plain words "any undertaking ... shall cease to apply to such document ...".

[41] [1975] Q.B. 613.
[42] *The Times*, November 11, 1993.

Secondly, if the words of rule 14A do not mean what they say, it is completely unclear what is or is not permitted. Since breach of an undertaking is contempt, a party should not be left in doubt what he may or may not do.

A preferable way of solving the problem in that case would be to recognise that, independently of any implied undertaking to the court, the plaintiff owed an equitable duty of confidence to the third parties whose confidential conversation was revealed to him on discovery. The question whether reading of the attendance note in open court had the effect of making it so publicly known as to destroy its confidential quality would be essentially a question of fact. Information contained in a document may continue to have the quality of confidence as long as it possesses relative secrecy.[43] Its reading on one occasion in public, whether in court or elsewhere, would not necessarily as a matter of fact prevent it from continuing to have relative secrecy.

The scope of the implied undertaking

22–15 The implied undertaking is considered to have been given by all those to whom the documents are disclosed for the purposes of the litigation, including the parties to the litigation, their solicitors and, where appropriate, expert witnesses instructed by the parties.[44]

The undertaking applies to documents obtained from third parties on *subpoena* as it does to documents obtained from a litigant. It applies not only to documents, but also to the contents of those documents.[45] Further, when discovery is given by list, the undertaking extends to the list of documents itself.[46]

What purposes are ulterior or collateral is essentially a question of fact. In *Crest Homes Plc. v. Marks*,[47] the Court of Appeal expressed the view, uncontradicted in the House of Lords (though regarded, on the facts of the case, as a technicality), that:

> "the use of documents disclosed in one action for the purposes of another action will usually, perhaps invariably, be a collateral or ulterior purpose."[48]

In *Sybron Corporation v. Barclays Bank Plc.*,[49] the plaintiffs had commenced an action, in which they wished to involve further parties. For procedural reasons, they chose to commence a new action, rather than to add the new parties to the existing action. Although the causes of action in the two sets of proceedings were identical, Scott J. held that the implied undertaking still operated to prevent the plaintiffs without the leave of the court from using

---

[43] *Franchi v. Franchi* [1967] R.P.C. 149 at 152–153. See para. 3–09, above.

[44] See, *e.g. Distillers Co. (Biochemicals) Ltd v. Times Newspapers Ltd* [1975] 1 Q.B. 613.

[45] *Sybron Corporation v. Barclays Bank plc.* [1985] 1 Ch. 299 at 318. See also *Crest Homes Plc. v. Marks* [1987] 1 A.C. 829, *per* Lord Oliver at 854.

[46] *Dory v. Richard Wolf GmgH* [1990] 1 F.S.R. 266.

[47] [1987] 1 A.C. 829 at 837.

[48] An action based on such documents will be struck out as an abuse of process: *Riddick v. Thames Board Mills Ltd* [1977] 1 Q.B. 881.

[49] [1985] 1 Ch. 299 at 318.

documents obtained in the first action for the purposes of the second action. The required leave was given.

Different considerations apply when a primary purpose of the proceedings in which discovery is obtained is to facilitate the conduct of other proceedings. There is no breach of the implied undertaking involved in the use of documents obtained (for example) by means of a *Norwich Pharmacal* or *Anton Piller* Order for the purpose of pursuing claims against third parties. However, the undertaking is still effective, inasmuch as the use to which the documents are put must still not be ulterior or collateral to the purpose for which the discovery was obtained.[50] A party executing an *Anton Piller* order is not necessarily obliged, however, to disregard all information incidentally acquired in the course of its execution.[51]

It is not a breach of the undertaking to use documents disclosed on discovery for the purpose of an interlocutory application for committal for contempt of court. As Lord Oliver said in *Crest Homes Plc. v. Marks*[52]:

> "The proper policing and enforcement or [of?] observance of orders made and undertakings given to the court in an action are, in my judgment, as much an integral part of the action as any other step taken by the plaintiff in the proper prosecution of his claim."

Release from the implied undertaking

22–16 In *Crest Homes Plc. v. Marks*,[53] Lord Oliver stated that it was for a party seeking release to demonstrate "cogent and persuasive reasons why it should be released". Referring to the authorities cited to the House of Lords in relation to this question, he said:

> "I do not, for my part, think that it would be helpful to review these authorities for they are no more than examples and they illustrate no general principle beyond this, that the court will not release or modify the implied undertaking given on discovery save in special circumstances and where the release or modification will not occasion injustice to the person giving discovery."[54]

The issue will only arise where the party seeking release is unable to obtain consent to his proposed use of the discovered material from the person giving discovery. The question whether such release will occasion injustice to that person will involve similar considerations to those which would arise if the question was whether the proposed disclosure should be restrained as a breach of an obligation of confidence.

---

[50] *Bank of Crete S.A. v. Koskotas (No. 2)* [1992] 1 W.L.R. 919; *Wilden Pump & Engineering Co. v. Fusfield* [1985] F.S.R. 581.

[51] *Sony Corporation v. Time Electronics* [1981] 1 W.L.R. 1293.

[52] [1987] 1 A.C. 829 at 860.

[53] *ibid.* at 859.

[54] *ibid.* at 860. For later examples, see *Derby & Co. Ltd v. Weldon (No. 2)*, *The Times*, October 20, 1988; *Bibby Bulk Carriers Ltd v. Cansulex Ltd* [1989] 1 Q.B. 155; *Dory v. Richard Wolf GmbH* [1990] 1 F.S.R. 266; *Tassilio Bonzel & Schneider (Europe) A.G. v. Intervention Ltd* [1991] R.P.C. 43; *Bank of Crete v. Koskotas (No. 2)* [1992] 1 W.L.R. 919; *Apple Corps Ltd v. Apple Computer Inc.* [1992] 1 C.M.L.R. 969; *A v. B Bank (Governor and Company of Bank of England intervening)* [1993] Q.B. 311; *Omar v. Omar* [1995] 1 W.L.R. 1428.

CHAPTER XXIII

CHILDREN

Children have no general right of privacy or anonymity merely by virtue of **23–01** being children,[1] but because of their special vulnerability they are afforded special protection by the courts in certain circumstances. The nature and extent of this protection were reviewed by the Court of Appeal in *Re Z. (A Minor) (Identification: Restrictions on Publication).*[2] In that case it was established, broadly, that there are four bases of jurisdiction under which the court may be enabled to grant protection to a child:

(1) in the exercise of its inherent parental jurisdiction (as exemplified by the institution of wardship), which is directed at the welfare of the child and the child's upbringing[3];

(2) in the exercise of an inherent ancillary jurisdiction, directed at the protection of the integrity and effectiveness of the court's own proceedings;

(3) in the enforcement of the child's own private law right to confidentiality;

(4) in the exercise of statutory powers, *e.g.* section 8 of the Children Act 1989.[4]

A separate issue, not arising in *Re Z.*, is the extent to which child care or similar records may be the subject of public interest immunity. This last issue is considered further below.[5]

The restrictions which a court may impose may conveniently be divided into: **23–02**

(1) restrictions on publicity relating directly to its own proceedings; or

(2) restrictions on publicity relating to a child (whether or not the subject of other proceedings).

---

[1] *per* Ward L.J. in *Re Z. (A Minor) (Identification: Restrictions on Publication)* [1996] 2 W.L.R. 88, at 105, citing Waite L.J. in *R. v. Central Independent Television Plc.* [1994] Fam. 192, at 207.
[2] [1996] 2 W.L.R. 88.
[3] Though see *per* Hoffman L.J. in *R. v. Central Independent Television Plc.* [1994] Fam. 192, at 204, and *per* Waite L.J. at 207.
[4] Under this section the court may, among other things, make a "prohibited steps order", preventing a step which could be taken by a parent in meeting his parental responsibility for a child from being taken without the court's consent.
[5] At paras. 23–17 ff.

Publicity relating directly to the court's own proceedings

23–03   In court proceedings, the privacy of children may be protected by:

   (a) the exclusion of the public from hearings;
   (b) restrictions on the publication of proceedings; and
   (c) restrictions on the use of documents relating to the proceedings.

Exclusion of the public

23–04   At common law, it is recognised that the general rule as to the importance of open justice does not apply to the court when it is exercising its jurisdiction over wards. The reason for this was set out by Lord Shaw of Dumferline in *Scott v. Scott*[6]:

> "... the jurisdiction over wards and lunatics is exercised by the judges as representing His Majesty as parens patriae. The affairs are truly private afairs; the transactions are transactions truly intra familiam; and it has long been recognised that an appeal for the protection of the Court in the case of such persons does not involve the consequence of placing in the light of publicity their truly domestic affairs."

23–05   Recognition has also been given to this principle by various statutory provisions. Proceedings under the Children Act 1989 are required by the Family Proceedings Rules 1991, rule 4.16(7), to be held in chambers, unless the court otherwise directs. The public is excluded from family proceedings in the magistrates' courts under the provisions of section 69 of the Magistrates' Courts Act 1980.[7] Under section 64 of the Adoption Act 1976, proceedings under the Act are required to be disposed of *in camera*, if in the County Court, and may be heard in chambers, if in the High Court.

Restrictions on the publication of proceedings

23–06   Newspaper reporting of any case may be limited by an order under section 39(1) of the Children and Young Persons Act 1933, which provides that:

> "In relation to any proceedings in any court the court may direct that—
> (a) no newspaper report of the proceedings shall reveal the name, address, or school, or include any particulars calculated to lead to the identification, of any child or young person concerned in the proceedings, either as being the person by or against or in respect of whom the proceedings are taken, or as being a witness therein;
> (b) no picture shall be published in any newspaper as being or including a picture of any child or young person so concerned in the proceedings as aforesaid;
> except in so far (if at all) as may be permitted by the direction of the court."[8]

---

[6] [1913] A.C. 417, at p. 483; see also *per* Viscount Haldane L.C. at pp. 436–437.
[7] See also section 97 of the Children Act 1989.
[8] See also section 49 of the Children and Young Persons Act, which restricts reporting of the proceedings of juvenile courts.

Further restrictions on publication are common in proceedings where the **23–07** court is acting in its parental role. A consequence at common law of the privacy of such proceedings was that a person who published details of the proceedings exposed himself to liability for contempt of court.[9] Statutory notice of this has been taken in section 12(1) (as amended) of the Administration of Justice Act 1960[10]:

> "The publication of information relating to proceedings before any court sitting in private shall not of itself be contempt of court except in the following cases, that is to say—
>   (a) where the proceedings—
>   (i) relate to the exercise of the inherent jurisdiction of the High Court with respect to minors;
>   (ii) are brought under the Children Act 1989; or
>   (iii) otherwise relate wholly or mainly to the maintenance or upbringing of a minor..."

The scope of this statutory exception is confined to the actual proceedings of the court and does not extend to other information relating to the child concerned.[11]

Restriction on the use of documents relating to the proceedings

In exceptional circumstances in adoption proceedings or family proceedings, **23–08** confidential reports, or parts of them, may be withheld from the parties themselves (though available to the court). The principles on which the court should act were set out by the House of Lords in *Re D. (Minors) (Adoption Reports: Confidentiality)*.[12] Lord Mustill, giving the only speech, said that there must be a strong presumption in favour of disclosure on grounds of natural justice:

> "... the court should first consider whether disclosure of the material would involve a real possibility of significant harm to the child.
> If it would, the court should next consider whether the overall interests of the child would benefit from non-disclosure, weighing on the one hand the interest of the child in having the material properly tested, and on the other both the magnitude of the risk that harm will occur and the gravity of the harm if it does occur.
> If the court is satisfied that the interests of the child point towards non-disclosure, the next and final step is for the court to weigh that consideration, and its strength in the circumstances of the case, against the interest of the parent or other party in having an opportunity to see and respond to the material. In the latter regard the court should take into account the importance of the material to the issues in the case.
> Non-disclosure should be the exception and not the rule. The court

---

[9] *Re Martindale* [1894] 3 Ch. 193. See also *per* Lloyd L.J. in *Attorney-General v. Newspaper Publishing Plc.* [1988] 1 Ch. 333, at p. 380, citing *Arlidge and Eady, The Law of Contempt* (1982), at 244.

[10] For a full discussion of the proper interpretation of the legislative purpose of this section, see *Re F. (Orse. A.) (A Minor) (Publication of Information)* [1977] Fam. 58, C.A.

[11] See *per* Butler-Sloss L.J. in *Re M. and N. (Minors) (Wardship: Publication of Information)* [1990] Fam. 211, at 221–222. See also section 97(2) of the Children Act 1989.

[12] [1995] 3 W.L.R. 483.

should be rigorous in its examination of the risk and gravity of the feared harm to the child and should order non-disclosure only when the case for doing so is compelling."[13]

23–09   Rule 4.23(1) of the Family Proceedings Rules 1991 provides that:

"Notwithstanding any rule of court to the contrary, no document, other than a record of an order, held by the court and relating to proceedings to which this Part[14] applies shall be disclosed, other than to:
(a) a party;
(b) the legal representative of a party;
(c) the guardian *ad litem*;
(d) the Legal Aid Board;
(e) a welfare officer;
without leave of the judge or district judge."

A similar restriction applies at common law to wardship proceedings. The restriction may extend to prevent a party showing documents to a witness who is to give evidence in the course of the proceedings.[15] In *Oxfordshire County Council v. P.*,[16] Ward J. expressed the view that no breach of duty was committed by a guardian *ad litem* who disclosed information to the duty welfare officer of the local authority involved in care proceedings under the Children Act 1989:

"The cloak of confidentiality is not lifted when there is an exchange of information relating to the proceedings passing between the parties in the proceedings if the information remained confidential to the proceedings."[17]

The rule applies only to documents held by the court and does not operate so as to prevent a social worker from disclosing to the police oral statements made to the social worker for the purposes of care proceedings. However, it may be that a guardian *ad litem*, whose functions are more limited, is subject to more severe restrictions.[18]

23–10   The test adopted by the courts as to whether to permit disclosure is the same whether wardship proceedings or proceedings under the Children Act are concerned. Ward J. said in *Oxfordshire County Council v. P.*[19]:

"There is ... clear authority that the proceedings in wardship are confidential and confidentiality covers reports, statements, proofs of evidence, as well as documents filed and evidence given. I see no reason why the same treatment should not be accorded to proceedings under the Children Act 1989. The paramountcy of the child concerned in both proceedings ensures parity of reasoning. That was accepted in *Oxfordshire County Council v. M.* [1994] Fam. 151. It was accepted by Booth J. in *Kent*

---

[13] At 496–497.
[14] *i.e.* proceedings under the Children Act 1989.
[15] *R. v. Sunderland Juvenile Court, ex parte G. (A Minor)* [1988] 1 W.L.R. 398.
[16] [1995] 2 W.L.R. 543.
[17] At 552.
[18] *Re G. (Minor) (Social worker: Disclosure) The Times*, November 14, 1995.
[19] [1995] 2 W.L.R. 543, at 551.

County Council v. K. [1994] 1 W.L.R. 912. I am of the same view that the importance of confidentiality and the frankness of evidence it engenders must be protected in proceedings under the Children Act 1989 just as in wardship proceedings."

A number of reported decisions deal with the approach to be adopted by the court when considering applications to disclose confidential material. The considerations affecting the exercise of the court's discretion may be rather different when one of the parties to proceedings, or a third party, wishes to use documents relating to the proceedings for a private collateral purpose, rather than for publication in the public interest. In all cases, there is a balancing exercise to be carried out and the court has an unfettered discretion.[20] Where the material is relevant to criminal proceedings, leave to disclose is often given. In *Re D. (Minors) (Wardship: Disclosure),*[21] Sir Stephen Brown P. said:

"In relation to criminal proceedings it is clear that the wardship court should not, as it were, seek to erect a barrier which would prejudice the operation of another branch of the judicature. There have been a number of cases where the discretion of the judge has been exercised to give leave to disclose to the Crown Prosecution Service matters which are part of the wardship file. Similar considerations will apply to defendants because it is in the interests of justice that a defendant in a criminal trial should have available all relevant and necessary material for the proper conduct of his or her defence."[22]

The same approach is likely to be adopted in cases of criminal investigations as in cases of criminal proceedings.[23]

An application for disclosure made in respect of his own file by a ward who had attained his majority and wished to pursue a claim in negligence against Leeds Area Health Authority succeeded in *Re Manda.*[24] The significance of the decision lies in the consideration given by the Court of Appeal to the general principles applicable to the disclosure of material used in cases relating to children, the foremost of which is that the interests of the child concerned will always be the most important factor, since it is to protect those interests that the court imposes the curtain of privacy. This remains the case even after the child has attained its majority, but in that situation he or she alone, unless mentally incompetent, is entitled to decide what are his or her interests.

23–11

It is open to a third party to apply for disclosure of the wardship file and the court's power to order disclosure is not restricted to the assistance of litigants exercising some public function.[25] However, a party seeking disclosure should do what is possible to inform the judge as to the importance of the disclosure by:

---

[20] *Re R. (M.J.) (A Minor) (Publication of Transcript)* [1975] Fam. 89, at 98 (a trustee in bankruptcy given leave to use a transcript of evidence given by the bankrupt in wardship proceedings in order to assist the examination of the bankrupt under section 25 of the Bankruptcy Act 1925); cited in *Re F. (Minors) (Police Investigation)* [1989] Fam. 18, at 25–27.

[21] [1994] 1 F.L.R. 346, at 351.

[22] See also *Kent County Council v. K.* [1994] 1 W.L.R. 913 and *Cleveland County Council v. F.* [1995] 1 W.L.R. 785.

[23] See, for example, *Re F. (Minors) (Wardship: Police Investigation)* [1989] Fam. 18; *Re S. (Minors) (Wardship: Police Investigation)* [1987] Fam. 199.

[24] [1993] Fam. 183.

[25] *Re X. (Minors) (Wardship: Disclosure of Documents)* [1992] Fam. 124, at 128—documents sought for defence of libel action; application dismissed in absence of satisfactory evidence.

"... setting out in precise terms what documents he has already, what other documents in the same category he believes to be in existence, including his grounds for that belief, and by making a clear statement as to the extent to which justice would be at risk if he were to be denied access to the undisclosed material."[26]

Other publicity relating to children

23–12   A child may have a private law right of confidentiality no less than may an adult. In the normal course of events, the child's right to waive confidentiality is a right to be exercised by the child's parents on its behalf.[27] Any such waiver, however, is an exercise of parental responsibility, which the court is ultimately able to control—even in the face of parental opposition—by virtue of the provisions of the Children Act 1989.[28]

23–13   The court has an inherent jurisdiction, exercising the powers of the Crown as *parens patriae*, to prevent the publication of information which would be harmful to a child; but while the jurisdiction is theoretically unlimited, the courts have recognised various categories of case in which it will not be exercised. Such categories include where the child is under the supervision of another competent authority responsible for making decisions about the well-being and future of the child.[29]

23–14   In *Re Z. (A Minor) (Identification: Restrictions on Publication)*,[30] Ward L.J. said:

"There is now an established category of case, of which *Re X. (A Minor) (Wardship: Jurisdiction)* [1975] Fam. 47 and *R. v. Central Independent Television Plc.* [1994] Fam. 192 are examples, where the freedom to publish information has been set beyond the limit of the exercise of the jurisdiction. I would define that category as the case where:

(a) the child is not already under the court's protective wing in that the court is not exercising some supervisory role over some aspect of the child's care and upbringing but where, on the contrary, the originating summons is issued for the express purpose of seeking the injunctive relief;

(b) crucially, the material to be published is not material directly about the child or material directed at the manner of the child's upbringing. In this category the material is only indirectly or incidentally or inferentially referable to the child."

It is suggested that the second of these two factors should indeed be the crucial one. It is not easy to see why a child's right to protection from indirect or incidental publicity should depend upon the history of the court's involvement in its upbringing.

[26] *Re X (Minors (Wardship: Disclosure of Documents)* [1992] Fam. 124 at 138.
[27] *Re Z. (A Minor) (Identification: Restrictions on Publication)* [1996] 2 W.L.R. 88, at 106 *per* Ward L.J., who also observed that parents themselves owe their children a duty of confidentiality of uncertain ambit. In relation to medical treatment and advice, see para. 13–13, above.
[28] *ibid.* at 107–108.
[29] *A. v. Liverpool City Council* [1982] A.C. 363.
[30] [1996] 2 W.L.R. 88 at 104.

In cases in which the jurisdiction may be exercised, an important distinction **23–15** is to be drawn between those where the welfare of the child is paramount and those where it is not.

The child's welfare is the paramount consideration where the court determines any question with respect to the upbringing of a child or the administration of a child's property or the application of any income arising from it: section 1 of the Children Act 1989. *Re Z. (A Minor) (Identification): Restrictions on Publication)*[31] was such a case. Z. was a child with particular educational needs. A television company wished to make a programme about the unusual and successful treatment she was receiving from a specialised foreign institution. To this end, Z.'s mother applied to the court for discharge or variation of earlier injunctions, which had restricted publicity relating to Z.'s education. The Court of Appeal dismissed her appeal from Cazalet J.'s refusal of her application. Ward L.J. distinguished other cases concerning minors and publicity, saying[32]:

> "In my judgment a question of upbringing is determined whenever the central issue before the court is one which relates to how the child is being reared... This case is one where the mother wishes her child to perform for the making of the film. This mother wishes to bring up her child as one who will play an active part in a television film ... The court is, therefore, required to determine a question with respect to the upbringing of the child."

Where the child's welfare is not the paramount consideration, the court has **23–16** to balance the interests of the child, and the public interest in the protection of children, against the public interest in favour of publication. The following guidelines were extracted from a consideration of the authorities[33] by the Court of Appeal in *Re W. (A Minor) (Wardship: Restrictions on Publication)*[34]:

> "(1) The court will attach great importance to safeguarding the freedom of the press....
> (2) The court will also take account of article 10 of the Convention for the Protection of Human Rights and Fundamental Freedoms (1953) (Cmd. 8969) which is designed to safeguard the 'freedom to hold opinions and to receive and impart information and ideas without interference by public authority...'
> (3) These freedoms, however, are subject to exceptions which include restrictions upon publication which are imposed for the protection of children.
> (4) In considering whether to impose a restriction upon publication to protect a ward of court the court has to carry out a balancing exercise. It is to be noted, as Butler-Sloss L.J. pointed out in *Re M. and N.*

---

[31] [1996] 2 W.L.R. 88. See also *Re X. (A Minor) (Wardship: Jurisdiction)* [1975] Fam. 47, *per* Sir John Pennycuik at 62.

[32] *ibid.* at 110–111.

[33] *Re X. (A Minor) (Wardship: Jurisdiction)* [1975] Fam. 47; *Re C. (A Minor) (Wardship: Medical Treatment) (No. 2)* [1990] Fam. 39; *Re M. and N. (Minors) (Wardship: Publication of Information)* [1990] Fam. 211. See also *Re H.-S. (Minors) (Protection of Identity)* [1994] 1 W.L.R. 1141.

[34] [1992] 1 W.L.R. 100.

(Minors) (Wardship: Publication of Information) [1990] Fam. 211, 223, that 'in this situation the welfare of the child is not the paramount consideration'.

(5) In carrying out the balancing exercise the court will weigh the need to protect the ward from harm against the rights of the press (or other outside parties) to publish or to comment. An important factor will be the nature and extent of the public interest in the matter which it is sought to publish. A distinction can be drawn between cases of mere curiosity and cases where the press are giving information or commenting about a subject of genuine public interest.

(6) It is to be anticipated that in almost every case the public interest in favour of publication can be satisfied without any identification of the ward to persons other than those who already know the facts. It seems to me, however, that the risk of *some* wider identification may have to be accepted on occasions if the story is to be told in a manner which will engage the interest of the general public.

(7) Any restriction on publication which is imposed is intended to protect the ward and those who care for the ward from the risk of harrassment. The restraint must therefore be in clear terms and no wider than is necessary to achieve the purpose for which it is imposed. It also follows that, save perhaps in an exceptional case, the ward cannot be protected from any distress which may be caused by reading the publication himself."[35]

Public interest immunity of child care records

23–17   Child care records kept by local authorities have been held to be immune from production, even at the suit of their subject. The rationale of this is not the right of the child to confidentiality, but the necessity of such immunity if the child care services are to function properly. The leading authorities are the Court of Appeal's decisions in *Re D. (Infants)*[36] and *Gaskin v. Liverpool City Council*,[37] though the nature of the principle expressed in these cases has subsequently been the source of some doubts in the Court of Appeal.

In the Court of Appeal in *D. v. N.S.P.C.C.*[38] Scarman L.J. expressed the view that *Re D.* was a very special case which turned on its special facts. However, it was cited in all the speeches given in the House of Lords overturning the decision of the Court of Appeal, without any expression of apparent disapproval or reservation.[39]

In *Campbell v. Tameside Metropolitan Borough Council*,[40] the discovery of documents relating to a violent child, which were in the possession of a local educational authority, was in issue. The documents included records made by and for the use of psychologists, and preliminary discovery was sought by a teacher who had been attacked by the child and believed that she might as a result have a cause of action against the local education authority. The Court of Appeal ordered that the disclosure sought should be given.

Lord Denning took the view that the documents were protected by public

---

[35] *per* Neill L.J. at page 103.
[36] [1970] 1 W.L.R. 599.
[37] [1980] 1 W.L.R. 1549.
[38] [1978] A.C. 171 at 198.
[39] At 220, 227, 236 and 245.
[40] [1982] 1 Q.B. 1065.

interest immunity, but held that the public interest in the immunity was outweighed by the public interest in disclosure. Ackner L.J. distinguished *Re D.* as a case that turned on its own special facts and clearly took the view that there was no public interest to set in the balance against the public interest in disclosure. O'Connor L.J. stated that he rejected the defendants' submission that these were confidential documents closely analogous to those in the child care cases in which the courts had given immunity "for the reasons given by Lord Denning M.R. and Ackner L.J."

It is therefore unclear whether the majority of the Court of Appeal accepted or rejected the notion that the documents were prima facie entitled to immunity.

In *Brown v. Matthew*,[41] Ralph Gibson L.J. stated his view (expressly *obiter*) **23–18** that the protection afforded to child care records was not to be regarded as a matter of public interest immunity proper, apparently on the basis that:

> "To hold that public interest immunity applied here would mean that, whatever the attitude of the parties concerned, it could never be waived and would indeed have to be raised by the ... judge himself if not taken by the parties or the Crown."[42]

It is respectfully suggested that his reasoning ascribes too rigid a structure to the protection offered by public interest immunity. To say merely that public interest immunity can in no circumstances be waived, and that protection which can be waived is therefore not public interest immunity, is to oversimplify. Much may depend on the nature of the public interest underlying the immunity.[43]

Certainly, the protection of local authorities' case records was seen as a matter of public interest immunity by Booth J. in *Re S. (Minors) (Wardship: Police Investigation).*[44]

The scope of the immunity was considered by Hollings J. in *Re A. (Minors)* **23–19** *(Child Abuse: Guidelines) Practice Note*,[45] which dealt with wardship proceedings instituted by a local authority in a number of cases of suspected sexual and ritual abuse. He cited the judgment of Butler-Sloss L.J. in *Re M. (A Minor)*[46] and said:

> "The only further guidance that I feel able to give ... is to say that in disputed cases such as these, both in the interests of the children and of justice to the parties, discovery ought to be given of original material recording matters of fact in relation to the children, their parents or other relevant persons, other than social workers, especially, of course, transcripts and records of matters in issue, but not unless expressly and voluntarily waived by the local authority notes or records of case conferences or meetings or similar meetings, where those attending should

---

[41] [1990] 1 Ch. 662, at 675.
[42] *per* Lord Edmund-Davies in *Science Research Council v. Nasse* [1980] A.C. 1028, at 1074.
[43] See *Lonrho Plc. v. Fayed (No. 4)* [1994] Q.B. 775, *per* Sir Thomas Bingham M.R., at 786F. Though Roch L.J. expressed the opposite view at 793–4, it is suggested that the reasoning of the Master of the Rolls is to be preferred.
[44] [1987] Fam. 199, at 205.
[45] [1991] 1 W.L.R. 1026, at 1031–2.
[46] (1990) 88 L.G.R. 841.

feel able to express their opinion freely without having to look over their shoulder. Disclosure of case conference and similar notes therefore would normally be very much for the decision of the local authority. Application can always be made to the court if a refusal is considered unjustified, for, as Butler-Sloss L.J. has emphasised, while social work and analogous records kept by a local authority are in a special category, there is no absolute immunity against discovery.

I myself would expect in a normal disputed case, if there is such a thing, that disclosure would be made of documents recording facts, but not those recording opinion or advice, including advice received from third parties."

The effect of the use of these documents in wardship proceedings or proceedings under the Children Act 1989 was considered by Booth J. in *Re S. (Minors) (Wardship: Police Investigation).*[47]

Her tentatively expressed conclusion was that the local authority's right to confidentiality which formed the basis of the immunity had been waived only to the extent that extracts from the records had been put in evidence before the court: the remaining part of the records, which had not been put directly in evidence, continued to be protected by immunity.[48] It was only in respect of the extracts actually put before the court that the court had an unfettered discretion to allow disclosure to other parties.

---

[47] [1987] Fam. 199.
[48] See also *Re S. and W. (Minors) (Confidential Reports)* (1983) 4 F.L.R. 290.

CHAPTER XXIV

ARBITRATIONS

The duty in English law

In *Dolling-Baker v. Merrett*[1] Parker L.J., giving the leading judgment in the **24–01**
Court of Appeal, stated:

> "As between parties to an arbitration, although the proceedings are
> consensual and may thus be regarded as wholly voluntary, their very
> nature is such that there must, in my judgment, be some implied obligation
> on both parties not to disclose or use for any other purpose any documents
> prepared for and used in the arbitration, or disclosed or produced in the
> course of the arbitration, or transcripts or notes of the evidence in the
> arbitration or the award, and indeed not to disclose in any other way what
> evidence had been given by any witness in the arbitration, save with the
> consent of the other party, or pursuant to an order or leave of the court.
> That qualification is necessary just as it is in the case of the implied
> obligation of secrecy between banker and customer."

The court was not concerned in that case to identify the nature or extent of any
qualifications to the duty.

Disclosure reasonably necessary for the protection of a party's rights

In *Hassneh Insurance v. Mew*[2] Colman J. held that the duty was subject to the **24–02**
qualification that it did not prevent disclosure of an arbitrator's award if it was
reasonably necessary for the establishment or protection of an arbitrating
party's legal rights vis-a-vis a third party, and that in such a case the party
wishing to make disclosure did not require to seek the approval of the court. In
so holding, Colman J. based himself on the judgments in *Tournier v. National
Provincial and Union Bank of England*.[3]

The extent of this qualification was again considered by Colman J. in **24–03**
Insurance Company v. Lloyd's Syndicate.[4] The case arose out of a reinsurance

---

[1] [1990] 1 W.L.R. 1205 at 1213.
[2] [1993] 2 Lloyd's Rep. 243 at 249.
[3] [1924] 1 K.B. 461.
[4] [1995] 1 Lloyd's Rep. 272.

dispute between a Lloyd's syndicate and certain excess of loss reinsurers. The plaintiff reinsurers were the leading insurers on a slip subscribed also by five companies, who were not parties to the arbitration. In the arbitration between the syndicate and the leading insurers an interim award was issued in the syndicate's favour. The syndicate wished to disclose the award to the following market in order to persuade the following market to accept liability. Colman J. held that it was not entitled to do so, because as between the syndicate and the following market the award had no more status than if it had been an independent counsel's opinion. Disclosure might have been helpful to the syndicate in attempting to persuade the following market to accept its claim, but was not necessary to enable the syndicate to establish or enforce its rights against the following market.

This may be thought a harsh decision. When the leading insurers subscribed the slip, they had no knowledge on what terms other companies would subscribe, but as a matter of practicality it is common for the following market to follow the leader in matters such as settlements. If the following market had agreed to be bound by the leading underwriter's claims, settlements, decisions or arbitration awards, there is no doubt that the syndicate would have been entitled to disclose the arbitration award to the following market. If the leader had agreed to settle the syndicate's claim, the syndicate would have been entitled to tell the following market. If the arbitration had resulted in a decision that the leading underwriter was entitled to avoid the policy for non-disclosure, it would be surprising if the syndicate would have been entitled to prevent the following market from being told. It would in the circumstances seem not unreasonable to imply a qualification to the duty of confidentiality entitling the syndicate to inform the following market of the outcome of any claims made by it against the leaders of the slip as a step reasonably necessary to protect the syndicate's interest in obtaining prompt settlement and avoiding multiplicity of proceedings.

24-04   There is at present a lack of English authority on other possible qualifications.

The law in Australia

24-05   The subject of confidentiality in arbitrations was considered by the High Court of Australia in *Esso Australian Resources Ltd v. Plowman.*[5] The appellants, *Esso Australian Resources Ltd*, made or were assignees of contracts with two public utilities for the sale of natural gas. The price was to be adjusted by taking into account the effect of any changes in taxes. The contracts required the sellers to provide the buyers with details of any price changes and the calculations on which they were based. Disputes between the sellers and the buyers were referred to arbitration. The Minister for Energy and Minerals had substantial powers to require the supply of information by the utilities. The Minister brought actions against the appellants and the utilities claiming declarations that information disclosed by the appellants to the utilities in the arbitrations was not subject to any obligation of confidence. The appellants cross claimed for declarations that the arbitrations were to be held in private and that any documents or information supplied by any party to any other party for the purpose of the arbitrations was to be treated in confidence between the parties and the arbitrators.

---

[5] [1994–1995] 183 C.L.R. 10. For a copy of the judgments together with editorial comment, the salient parts of the experts' reports provided in the case by Stewart Boyd, Q.C. and others, and other learned articles, see *Arbitration International* [1995] Vol. 11, No. 3, pp. 231–340.

The trial judge decided in the Minister's favour. An appeal to the Supreme Court of Victoria was allowed in part, but the court upheld declarations to the effect that the utilities were not restricted from disclosing information to the Minister and others by reason only that it was obtained from the appellants in the arbitration and had not otherwise been published. On further appeal by the sellers the High Court remitted the declarations to the Supreme Court of Victoria for reformulation but otherwise dismissed the appeals.

The sellers argued that it was an implied term of the arbitration agreements that the arbitrations should be conducted in private, and that the buyers were under an implied contractual, and equitable, obligation of confidence not to disclose, except for the purposes of the arbitration, information and documents provided to them for the purposes of the arbitration by the sellers, unless authorised by statute.

Mason C.J., with whom Dawson and McHugh JJ. agreed, recognised that **24–06** (subject to any manifestation of a contrary intention arising from the arbitration agreement) an arbitration was to be held in private. He preferred to describe the privacy attaching to an arbitration as an incident of the subject-matter of the agreement to arbitrate, rather than to attribute it to an implied term of the agreement, although he did not consider that it mattered greatly.

This may be considered a false distinction. An agreement to arbitrate in public would be unusual but would nonetheless be an agreement to arbitrate. Absent any indication of a contrary intention, an agreement to arbitrate will impliedly be understood to mean an agreement to arbitrate in private. To say that in these circumstances the parties have agreed upon a private arbitration as the subject-matter of their agreement, or to say that it is an implied term of their agreement that the arbitration shall be private, might be thought to be a difference in form of words only. The distinction may, however, have influenced Mason C.J.'s approach to the question of confidentiality. About this he said[6]:

> "There is ... a case for saying that, in the course of evolution, the private arbitration has advanced to the stage where confidentiality has become one of its essential attributes so that confidentiality is a characteristic or quality that inheres in arbitration. Despite the view taken in *Dolling-Baker* and subsequently by Colman J. in *Hassneh Insurance*, I do not consider that, in Australia, having regard to the various matters to which I have referred, we are justified in concluding that confidentiality is an essential attribute of a private arbitration imposing an obligation on each party not to disclose the proceedings or documents and information provided in and for the purposes of the arbitration."

He therefore rejected the sellers' case for an implied term, and said that he did not need to consider whether the difficulties in defining the exceptions to any such term would be so great as to preclude its implication.

Mason C.J. accepted that there was an implied obligation to accord to documents disclosed by a party compulsorily, pursuant to an order of the arbitrator, the same confidentiality which would attach to them if the parties were litigating rather than arbitrating. He also said[7]:

---

[6] *Esso Australian Resources Ltd v. Plowman* [1994–1995] 183 C.L.R. 10 at 30.
[7] *ibid.* at 33.

"In argument, reference was made to the principles governing the protection of confidential information generally. No doubt these principles may have some application to information in arbitration proceedings. But these principles do not support the broad claim for confidentiality made by the appellants."

In order for the principles of confidentiality to apply, the information must have the quality of confidence and must be received in circumstances importing an obligation of confidence. Mason C.J. would appear to accept that information disclosed in arbitration proceedings may satisfy both requirements, while rejecting the proposition that this applies to all such information. According to this approach, information disclosed in arbitration proceedings does not innately possess the quality of confidence, but may do so for other reasons.

24–07   Brennan J. and Toohey J. concurred in the result but by different reasoning. Brennan J. agreed with Mason C.J. that any duty of confidentiality would not arise merely from the privacy of the hearing. It must be derived from an implied term of the agreement to arbitrate. Some term could be implied from the fact that documents and information supplied for the purposes of arbitration were given solely for that purpose. But, to the extent that a party would not have agreed at the time of the arbitration agreement to keep documents or information confidential, the implied obligation of confidentiality must be qualified.

Brennan J. gave various examples. If a party was under a statutory or common law duty to communicate the document or information to a third party, no contractual obligation of confidentiality could prohibit performance of that duty. A party might be under a duty, not necessarily legal, to communicate documents or information to a party with a legitimate interest in the outcome of the proceedings (for example, a subsidiary company to its parent) or might wish to reveal them for the protection of its own interests. Nor should an obligation be implied that a party would keep confidential documents or information when he had an obligation, not necessarily legal, to satisfy a public interest—more than mere curiosity—in knowing what was contained in them.

After citing Bankes L.J.'s judgment in *Tournier* Brennan J. concluded[8]:

"I would hold that, in an arbitration agreement under which one party is bound to produce documents or disclose information to the other for the purposes of the arbitration and in which no other provision for confidentiality is made, a term should be implied that the other party will keep the documents produced and the information disclosed confidential except:
  (a) where disclosure of the otherwise confidential material is under compulsion of law;
  (b) where there is a duty, albeit not a legal duty, to the public to disclose;
  (c) where disclosure of the material is fairly required for the protection of the party's legitimate interests; and
  (d) where disclosure is made with the express or implied consent of the party producing the material."

---

[8] *Esso Australian Resources Ltd v. Plowman* [1994–1995] 183 C.L.R. 10 at 36.

These correspond with the qualifications recognised by Bankes L.J. in *Tournier*.[9]

Toohey J. considered that, subject to qualifications where disclosure was **24–08** reasonably necessary to protect the interests of a party to the arbitration or in the public interest, an obligation of confidentiality did attach to the documents and information emanating from an arbitration by reason of an implied term of a commercial arbitration agreement. He said[10]:

> "The term is implied from the entry by the parties into a form of dispute resolution which they choose because of the privacy they expect to result. If this is said to confuse privacy and confidentiality, the answer is that they are not distinct characteristics. As Colman J. said in *Hassneh*:
>> 'The disclosure to a third party of [a note or transcript of the evidence] would be almost equivalent to opening the door of the arbitration room to that third party.'
> Any aspect of disclosure to third parties must infringe the privacy of the arbitration."

Conclusion

Toohey J.'s judgment in *Esso Australian Resources Ltd v. Plowman* accords **24–09** most closely with English law as to the existence and rationale of the duty of confidentiality in arbitration proceedings. The qualifications to such duty are most fully considered in the judgment of Brennan J. In principle English law might reasonably be expected to recognise the same qualifications, although their application and scope would be a matter for determination on the facts of each case.

---

[9] [1924] 1 K.B. 461 at 473.
[10] [1994–1995] 183 C.L.R. 10 at 47–48.

INDEX

265